VICTORIAN BLOOMSBURY

VICTORIAN BLOOMSBURY

ROSEMARY ASHTON

YALE UNIVERSITY PRESS
NEW HAVEN AND LONDON

For information about this and other Yale University Press publications, please contact:
U.S. Office: sales.press@yale.edu   www.yalebooks.com
Europe Office: sales @yaleup.co.uk   www.yalebooks.co.uk

Set in Adobe Caslon Pro by IDSUK (DataConnection) Ltd
Printed in Great Britain by TJ International Ltd, Padstow, Cornwall

Library of Congress Cataloging-in-Publication Data

Ashton, Rosemary, 1947–
  Victorian Bloomsbury / Rosemary Ashton.
    p. cm.
  Includes bibliographical references and index.
  ISBN 978-0-300-15447-4 (cl : alk. paper)
1. Bloomsbury (London, England)—History—19th century. 2. Bloomsbury
(London, England)—Buildings, structures, etc. 3. London (England)—History—19th
century. 4. London (England)—Buildings, structures, etc. 5. Buildings—England—
London. I. Title.
  DA685.B65A84 2012
  2012009771

A catalogue record for this book is available from the British Library.
10 9 8 7 6 5 4 3 2 1

Contents

Illustrations

17 William Smith, The British Museum, printed by Day & Co., 1852. Reproduced by courtesy of the Trustees of the British Museum.
18 Carlo Pellegrini, sketch of Sir Anthony Panizzi, *Vanity Fair*, 1874. Reproduced by courtesy of Look and Learn/Peter Jackson London Collection.
19 Unknown, *Reception of Nineveh Sculptures at the British Museum*, *Illustrated London News*, 8 February 1852. Reproduced by courtesy of Look and Learn/Peter Jackson London Collection.
20 George Shepherd, *St George's, Bloomsbury*, 1811. Reproduced by courtesy of the London Metropolitan Archives.
21 Unknown, *Picturesque Sketches of London.–The Rookery, St. Giles's*, *Illustrated London News*, 22 September 1849. Reproduced by courtesy of Senate House Library, University of London.
22 Henry Meyer after Andrew Robertson, *Edward Irving*, 1823. Reproduced by courtesy of the Regent Square United Reformed Church (Lumen).
23 Unknown, Eleven of the twelve apostles of the Catholic Apostolic Church, in *Gathered Under Apostles: A Study of the Catholic Apostolic Church* by Columba Graham Flegg, 1992. By permission of Oxford University Press.
24 Catholic Apostolic Church, Gordon Square. Reproduced by courtesy of Tom Ue.
25 Catherine Ward, Russell House (left), Bedford House (centre), and Tavistock House (right), 1900. Reproduced by courtesy of the Charles Dickens Museum, London.
26 William Holl, engraving from a photograph by Maull & Co, Henry Crabb Robinson, 1861. Reproduced by courtesy of UCL Library Services, Special Collections.
27 Thomas Donaldson, design for University Hall (now Dr Williams's Library), Gordon Square, 1848. Reproduced by courtesy of the Trustees of Dr Williams's Library.
28 F.M. Simpson, design for the decoration of Flaxman Gallery, University College London, *c.*1922. Reproduced by courtesy of UCL Library Services, Special Collections.
29 Photograph of the Flaxman Gallery, showing John Flaxman's model for his sculpture *St Michael Overcoming Satan*, University College London. Reproduced by courtesy of UCL Library Services, Special Collections.
30 Interior of the Church of Humanity, Chapel Street (now Rugby Street). Reproduced by courtesy of the Library of the London School of Economics and Political Science.
31 Henry Morley, *c.*1847. Reproduced by courtesy of the Charles Dickens Museum, London.
32 Edward Matthew Ward, portrait of Dickens in his study in Tavistock House, 1854. Reproduced by courtesy of the Charles Dickens Museum, London.
33 The Ladies' College, 47 (now 48) Bedford Square. Reproduced by courtesy of Archives, Royal Holloway, University of London.
34 Elisabeth Jesser Reid. Reproduced by courtesy of Archives, Royal Holloway, University of London.
35 Colonnade, off Herbrand Street, London. Reproduced by courtesy of Tom Ue.
36 Nos 42 and 43 Queen Square. Reproduced by courtesy of Tom Ue.
37 Female students at the Slade School of Art, University College London, early twentieth century. Reproduced by courtesy of UCL Library Services, Special Collections.
38 Elizabeth Garrett, *c.*1865. Reproduced by courtesy of the Royal Free Hampstead NHS Trust.
39 Unknown, Aquatint of Queen Square, published in Ackermann's *Repository of Arts*, 1 September 1812. Reproduced by courtesy of the London Metropolitan Archives.
40 Illustrations in Johannes and Bertha Ronge, *A Practical Guide to the English Kinder Garten* 1855. Reproduced by courtesy of the Froebel Archive for Childhood Studies at Archives & Special Collections, University of Roehampton.
41 Photograph of Mary Ward taken by Ethel Ward, 1898. Reproduced by courtesy of Senate House Library, University of London.

Preface and Acknowledgements

THE IDEA for this book came from a sense that the intellectual and cultural history of Bloomsbury has not been fully explored. While there are many studies of the 'Bloomsbury Group' of writers and artists who lived in or near Gordon Square in the first two decades of the twentieth century, there is no equivalent study of the area's rich and developing cultural life in the preceding century. The question about how and when Bloomsbury became the undisputed intellectual quarter of London has not been asked or answered in detail, though there are excellent histories of individual institutions such as the one at the heart of the area, the great repository of the nation's history and culture, the British Museum.

Though much of the discussion will concern the Victorian era, from 1837 to 1901, a longer period will be held in view, from 1800, when the fifth Duke of Bedford began to develop the open fields of his Bloomsbury estate to the north of Great Russell Street, to 1904, when Virginia and Vanessa Stephen (later Woolf and Bell, respectively) left their family home in Kensington to start a new independent life in Bloomsbury. When they moved into the area, it had already acquired its character as London's intellectual quarter, with the British Museum still at its centre, but now surrounded not by fields, but by educational and cultural institutions founded during the nineteenth century, the largest being University College London, where Vanessa Stephen briefly became an art student at its famous Slade School. In the chapters which follow, I hope to reveal in hitherto unattempted detail the extent to which Bloomsbury was the location for educational innovation, from nursery to university, for the middle class and the working class, for men and for women; scientific advance in an age of rapid progress; medical research and teaching in the very large number of hospitals in the region; religious movements outside the Anglican mainstream; experiments in art, crafts, and architecture.

A large number of 'firsts' were achieved in Bloomsbury, including the following at University College London: the first university entrance for non-Anglicans in England; the first teaching of modern languages, geography, architecture, and a number of emerging scientific specialisms; the first use of anaesthetics in surgery in Europe. Bloomsbury was home to the first kindergarten in Britain, the first hospital dedicated to caring for children, the first homoeopathic hospital, the first organisation offering after-school care for the children of working parents, the first school for invalid children, the first vacation school, the first higher education establishment for women, the first medical school for women, the first teacher-training institute, the first female interior design company, the first female landscape gardening firm, the first women's press.

The professionalisation of Britain, through the establishment of organisations dedicated to reforming, regulating, and testing medical practice, teaching, scientific research, and the practice of law, was a notable achievement of the nineteenth century, and one closely associated with Bloomsbury. To be sure, innovations occurred in other areas too. Neighbouring Fitzrovia had its share of progressive activities in the fields of arts and crafts and educational training; towards the end of the nineteenth century South Kensington became known for its museums; Soho had its artists and exotic foreign refugees, and so on. But Bloomsbury was home to the greatest concentration of progressive talent.

The emphasis here is on individuals and groups of men and women intent on reform; they started their new establishments in the face of opposition from conservative forces, whether political, social, or religious. The beginnings of institutions will be to the fore – how and why they were sited in Bloomsbury, the nature of their founding principles, the obstacles encountered by their founders and how these were overcome – and an assessment will be made of their contribution to progress at the national, as well as local, level. Some, such as the British Museum, University College London, the Ladies' College in Bedford Square, the Working Men's College, and the Catholic Apostolic Church in Gordon Square, have had their individual histories recounted by scholars. Others, such as the Society for the Diffusion of Useful Knowledge, University Hall in Gordon Square, the Working Women's College, the kindergarten movement in Britain, and the Passmore Edwards Settlement in Tavistock Place, have had little or no attention paid to them. Through studying the rich archives of these organisations and bringing them together in a narrative shaped by their shared location in Bloomsbury, I hope to add to our knowledge of nineteenth-century culture. The institutions themselves, the large cast of interesting people involved in their foundation and organisation, and the 'Bloomsburiness' of their history are at the heart of my account.

The location is important. How 'central' was Bloomsbury at any moment in the development and enlargement of London as a whole? What was its social status in comparison with other fast-growing regions of the capital, such as Pimlico or Belgravia? To what extent was it planned architecturally? What difference did the placing of three of London's railway termini in mid-century along the northern border of Bloomsbury make to the character of the area? What were the consequences of the decision by parliament to enlarge the British Museum from the 1820s? How did the arrival of so many progressive institutions change or preserve Bloomsbury's character as a place to live or to work in?

It happens that a number of the best-known Victorian novelists lived in Bloomsbury for some part of their lives. Dickens, Thackeray, Trollope, Disraeli, Mary Elizabeth Braddon, and George Gissing not only describe their surroundings in letters and memoirs, but they also send their fictional people walking the streets of London, including Bloomsbury. These writers, along with Wilkie Collins, J.M. Barrie, Robert Louis Stevenson, and other less well known authors, provide astute imaginative and socio-cultural comment, of which I take frequent advantage.

Significant conjunctions of people and place are at the heart of this history. Some of the people are not as well known for their contribution to nineteenth-century culture as they might be: professors at University College, principals of University Hall, men and women involved in dissenting religious movements such as Unitarianism, Catholic Apostolicism, liberal Judaism, or the so-called Religion of Humanity, and pioneering women setting out to acquire equal education with men. Others who are already well known for their contributions to the intellectual or cultural life of the nation – the reforming lawyer and politician Henry Brougham; the radical MPs George Grote and Joseph Hume; Robert Liston, the surgeon who pioneered the use of anaesthetics; William Morris, founder of the famous decorating company known as The Firm; members of the Pre-Raphaelite Brotherhood of artists; the poet Arthur Hugh Clough; Elizabeth Garrett Anderson, the first woman to qualify as a doctor – are seen here specifically in their connection to Bloomsbury. Important people in history are sometimes viewed in isolation from their place of residence, their homes, their families, their colleagues, their workplace, the life chances which made a difference to them and therefore also to their contribution. The aim here is to bear prominently in mind the part played by Bloomsbury in the lives of a number of forward-thinking men and women, and the way in which they in turn acted upon the developing 'character' of the area.

Primary sources, as well as published histories, lie behind this account. I have studied extensively in the archives of a number of Bloomsbury institutions, and am grateful for the assistance of the librarians and archivists who are thanked below. The study of much hitherto unpublished material helps throw light on the life of nineteenth-century Bloomsbury, to make fresh threads of connection between its people and its places, and to show its importance in the history of British culture. The narrative proceeds more or less chronologically, following the natural history of the growth of the area and the progressive founding of establishments within it. There will also be some looping back, as I return from telling the story of one institution to the beginnings of another, or follow the career of a particular individual in his or her connections with more than one institution.

My thanks go to the archivists, librarians, curators, and trustees of manuscripts at the following institutions for permission to quote from unpublished material: the Archives of the Duke of Northumberland at Alnwick Castle; the Bedford Estate, Woburn Abbey; the British Library; the British Library of Political and Economic Science, the London School of Economics; Dr Williams's Library, London; the Museum & Archives Service, Great Ormond Street Hospital for Children NHS Trust; the Institute of Education, University of London; the London Metropolitan Archives; the Mary Ward Centre and Settlement, London; the New Apostolic Church of North Germany, Hamburg; Roehampton University Archives and Special Collections; Royal Holloway, University of London Archives; Senate House Library, University of London; the Swedenborg Society, London; the UCL Records Office; UCL Special Collections.

Individuals who have helped with information and encouragement, and to whom I express my thanks, are: Nicholas Baldwin, Kasia Boddy, Jenny Bourne-Taylor, Joanna Bowring, Kevin Brehony, Lorna Cahill, Ian Campbell, Hilary Canavan, Mark Cardale, Kornelia Cepok, Berry Chevasco, Stephanie Clarke, Roger Cline, Deborah Colville, Elizabeth Crawford, June Day, Richard Dennis, Chris Dillon, Lindsay Duguid, Mark Ford, Alice Ford-Smith, Andrea Fredericksen, Gill Furlong, Tim Grass, Charles Hamaker, Manfred Henke, Shannon Hermes, Vicky Holmes, Christopher Hunwick, Matthew Ingleby, Susan Irvine, Elisabeth Jay, Danny Karlin, Helena Langford, Scott Lewis, Richard Lines, Roger Luckhurst, Fabian Macpherson, Ann Mitchell, Charlotte Mitchell, Dan Mitchell, John Mullan, Pamela Gerrish Nunn, Elaine Penn, Tom Quick, Miranda el-Rayess, Neil Rennie, Beth Shaw, Michael Slater, Laura Speak, Susan Stead, Hugh Stevens, Christopher Stray, John Sutherland, Andrea Tanner, Nicholas Tyacke, Enrica Villari, Barbara Waddington, Lynne

Walker, Anthony Watkinson, Rebecca Webster, Meg Weissmann, Jamie West, Ceri Williams, Sarah Wintle, Christine Wise, Mandy Wise, Peter Woodford, Henry Woudhuysen, John Wyatt, David Wykes.

A collaborative project undertaken in the English Department of University College London between 2007 and 2011, supported by a grant from the Leverhulme Trust and known as the Bloomsbury Project, studied the development of nineteenth-century Bloomsbury in historical and topographical detail. The project contributors included myself as principal investigator; Dr Deborah Colville, the full-time project researcher who carried out the lion's share of the archival research, as well as creating the project website; Matthew Ingleby, a PhD student working under my supervision on a thesis entitled 'Nineteenth-Century Fiction and the Production of Bloomsbury: A Local History of the Novel, 1800–1904'; Dr Juliette Atkinson, a British Academy Postdoctoral Fellow in the UCL English Department; and an advisory board comprising colleagues at UCL and other London institutions.

The Bloomsbury Project website, www.ucl.ac.uk/bloomsbury-project, was launched in April 2011. It identifies and describes the early history of over 300 progressive educational, medical, and cultural institutions which were established in Bloomsbury during its period of physical growth in the course of the nineteenth century. The archives of each institution were sought out and, where they still exist, visited by Dr Colville or myself. The website contains entries on these institutions, their founding principles, their history, and the archival resources relating to them; in addition there are entries on important individuals in the intellectual history of nineteenth-century Bloomsbury, occasional essays on particular topics, papers delivered at the three conferences hosted by the project, maps of the area at different times, and plans of the land-owning estates of Bloomsbury. I am indebted for much of the information which informs this book to the collaborative work of the project. I am grateful to Matthew Ingleby for drawing my attention to a number of little-known Victorian novels which illuminate Bloomsbury. My particular thanks go to Deborah Colville, whose expertise in the literary, legal, and educational history of the nineteenth century, combined with technical expertise in web creation, made her an extraordinarily valuable colleague. To her must go most of the credit for the project website.

I am grateful to the Leverhulme Trust for the grant which made it possible for me to pursue my research for both the Bloomsbury Project and this book. My warmest thanks go to my editor Heather McCallum and my literary agent Victoria Hobbs.

Introduction: Surveying Bloomsbury

For me, for me, these old retreats
Amid the world of London streets!
My eye is pleased with all it meets
In Bloomsbury.

('Bloomsbury', by Anon., 1893)

THE NAME 'Bloomsbury' is thought to derive from the manor house
('bury') of William Blemond, who acquired the land surrounding what
is now Bloomsbury Square in 1201.[1] Mention the word 'Bloomsbury'
today, and many people will think of the 'Bloomsbury Group' of writers and
artists who lived and worked in the leafy squares of London WC1 in the
first two decades of the twentieth century. Virginia Woolf, Vanessa Bell,
Duncan Grant, and their friends could lay strong claim to avant-gardism in
art and literature, but they were not the first to put Bloomsbury on the
cultural map. It was in the nineteenth century that the region of London
known as Bloomsbury acquired its distinctive, important, and above all
progressive role in the life of both London and the nation.

Physically the area evolved and changed remarkably between the last
decades of the eighteenth and the early years of the twentieth century. In
1800 the land to the north and east of the British Museum still consisted
of open fields leading uninterruptedly northwards as far as the villages of
Hampstead and Highgate. When the newly qualified young doctor Peter
Mark Roget, later the author of the celebrated *Thesaurus* which bears his
name, moved into rooms at 46 Great Russell Street in 1800, he described
the air as 'pure' because 'there are no houses at all between the gardens of
the British Museum and Hampstead'.[2] Roget's peace did not last long, for

in that same year Francis Russell, fifth Duke of Bedford, had his London house on the north side of Bloomsbury Square demolished and the area to the north laid out in new streets, culminating in the imposing new Russell Square. From the 1820s to the 1840s the new British Museum was built in neoclassical style by Robert Smirke on the Great Russell Street site of the old one, Montagu House, which was duly pulled down. The new building extended the area covered by the Museum to the west, east, and north, including the gardens enjoyed by Roget in 1800.

London as a whole increased at an unprecedentedly rapid rate in the first twenty years of the nineteenth century. In October 1826 the *Morning Chronicle* carried an article entitled 'Increase of London, from the Rage for Building' which marvelled at the phenomenon, singling out Bloomsbury for particular mention:

> Upon whatever side we turn ourselves towards the suburbs, we find not only houses, but whole streets, squares, villages, and we might almost say towns, raised as if the architects had become possessed of the lamp of Aladdin. Taking the Strand as a centre, and looking north upon that space bounded by the New Road [later Euston Road] and Tottenham and Gray's Inn Roads, we are struck with astonishment to see the ground which, thirty years ago, formed the garden and meadows of Montague [*sic*] House, now covered with spacious and even magnificent houses, and laid out in squares and streets not to be surpassed, if they are equalled by any portion of the metropolis.[3]

Three years later a committee member of the Select Vestry of the united parishes of St Giles-in-the-Fields and St George's Bloomsbury published a history of the area covered by the two parishes, noting with amazement that while in 1739 a total of 954 houses were recorded in the area, the number of new Bloomsbury houses built since 1792 was already 1,198.[4]

Bloomsbury thus increased in size along with the rest of London, but at a notably rapid rate, thanks partly to the long New Road, constructed along its northern border in 1756 to take London's east–west traffic away from the overcrowded Strand.[5] (The stretch of the New Road lying across the northern boundary of Bloomsbury was renamed Euston Road in 1856.) As the *Morning Chronicle* article noted, the first two decades of the century saw a tremendous amount of speculative building, a relatively new arrangement by which builder-architects leased large quantities of land from landowners in order to build houses which were then let to new occupants. This kind of speculation was behind the creation of the many squares and streets of

Bloomsbury. The result was that though there was a certain element of haphazardness in the physical development of early nineteenth-century Bloomsbury, as of most areas of London, it was one of a number of land areas – others are Pimlico, Belgravia, and the Portland Estate near Regent's Park, all being developed at the same time – which were extensively planned. The land was taken over by a few large speculative builders who created whole swathes of streets and squares for new occupation in the building boom of the first half of the nineteenth century. Two such men were closely associated with the building of Bloomsbury: James Burton (1761–1837), and Thomas Cubitt (1788–1855), one of three brothers who constructed large parts of London from the 1820s to the 1860s.

Burton lived for some years in Tavistock House, which he built for himself in the north-east corner of Tavistock Square, part of a large area he developed in the 1790s and 1800s on land owned by the Bedford and Foundling Estates. (A third part of the extended Tavistock House was home to Dickens and his family from 1851 to 1860; the site is now covered by the British Medical Association building.) Burton's name survives in the handsome short streets he built to the east of his house. His handiwork can be admired in Burton Street and Burton Place, and also in the adjacent Cartwright Gardens, originally named Burton Crescent after the architect.[6]

Thomas, William, and Lewis Cubitt owned London's largest building yard, on Gray's Inn Road, where they pioneered the system of directly employing people from all building trades.[7] The youngest brother, Lewis Cubitt, was responsible for King's Cross Station; he had his own architectural practice in Great Russell Street and lived in Bedford Square. William, the middle brother, took main charge of the great building works in Gray's Inn Road in the 1820s, became a member of parliament in 1847, and was elected Lord Mayor of London in 1860. Thomas, the oldest, was the most prolific, building over 160 houses in Bloomsbury from 1824 until his death in 1855 and in the same years developing large parts of Belgravia and Pimlico.[8]

Thomas Cubitt not only completed many of the streets and squares begun by Burton – Tavistock Square, for example – but his first major assignment was the re-roofing in 1812 or so of a Burton building in Great Coram Street. This was the Russell Institution, which Burton had designed a decade earlier as assembly and concert rooms for the use of the tenants of his new houses on the Bedford and Foundling Estates.[9] Perhaps partly because of its location to the east of the grand new Russell Square, it did not thrive as a place of fashionable resort, but was soon turned into a literary institution with a subscription library, a purpose more suited to the lawyers,

doctors, and other middle-class professional men who were the chief inhabitants of the new Bloomsbury, and in that form the Institution survived
with reasonable success for well over half a century.

Bloomsbury's middle-class residents found it convenient to live in comfortable new houses in airy streets and squares. Many worked in City firms or
were lawyers and judges in the Inns of Court just to the south-east. It was
men of this sort, particularly reform-minded lawyers, who were to be instrumental in the making of Bloomsbury into London's intellectual workshop.
Forward-looking women played their part from mid-century, from the
founding of the Ladies' College in Bedford Square in 1849 to the establishment in the later decades of the century of colleges for working women, and
for female teachers, artists, and above all doctors.[10]

By the end of the nineteenth century Bloomsbury was completely
covered by inhabited streets and squares between the boundary roads of
Tottenham Court Road in the west, Euston Road in the north, Gray's Inn
Road in the east, and Holborn and New Oxford Street in the south.[11] By
this time the area, though intended by the landowners and planners of the
turn of the century to offer family residences built to a high standard, had
become in large part institutionalised as a result of the founding of a
number of reforming educational and medical establishments, with the
consequence that single family occupancy of its larger houses declined. This
trend away from residential and towards professional building use was
compounded at the end of the nineteenth century by the falling in of many
99-year building leases.

Multiple occupancy now introduced a hint of shabbiness to the gentility
which had previously characterised the area. Successive Dukes of Bedford,
owners of the largest single parcel of ground in Bloomsbury – the next
largest was the adjacent plot to the east owned by the Foundling Hospital
Estate – had endeavoured to avoid such dilapidation on their land by incor-
porating detailed restrictions in the leases they granted. That the Russell
family were at least relatively successful in their aim is attested today by the
continued elegance of many of the streets and squares built on Bedford
land. In the nineteenth century the Bedford Estate stretched across most of
the area bounded by Great Russell Street, Tottenham Court Road, Euston
Road, and Upper Woburn Place/Southampton Row, together with a small
part of Tavistock Place to the east, where it bordered on the Foundling
Estate.[12]

Restrictions imposed by the Bedford Estate included prohibitions against
carrying on trades in the squares, the streets, and in particular the mews and
alleyways where grooms were employed by respectable families to keep their

horses and carriages; against putting up plaques on doors to advertise services; against any dealing in foodstuffs, alcohol, coal, and a long list of other commodities. In fact the standard Bedford lease forbade trade in anything at all in its buildings, even books and prints, while its prohibition on using Bedford properties as schools, colleges, hospitals, concert halls, places of public worship, or any kind of office caused difficulties for some lessees in the middle and late nineteenth century, who were intent on opening educational and medical institutions.[13]

Fortunately for such pioneering endeavours, other landlords, including the Foundling Estate, were less vigilant. Not so fortunate in social terms were the resultant smaller streets, narrower buildings, pubs, and small shops which were established in some non-Bedford parts of Bloomsbury. Charles Booth's famous 'poverty maps' of 1889, published with selections of the copious notes taken by Booth and his helpers in *Life and Labour of the People in London* (1892–7), classified almost the whole of Bloomsbury as 'yellow' housing, meaning that inhabited by the wealthy middle and upper-middle classes, or 'red' for 'middle-class families who keep one or two servants'. But some troublesome areas on the borders of the Duke of Bedford's land, especially to the south and east, where a certain amount of trading and subletting went on, were coloured purple ('mixed'), light blue (poor), dark blue (very poor, people living hand to mouth), and even in tiny pockets black ('occasional labourers, loafers, and semi-criminals'). Among the poorer streets were Henrietta Street (now Handel Street), Little Coram Street (now part of Herbrand Street), and the narrow cobbled alley Colonnade, where the overcrowded stables and dwellings of old are today occupied by workshops and small craft businesses.[14]

The encroachment of pockets of poverty on an area planned for wealth and respectability demonstrates how vulnerable town planning is to unforeseen or random change.[15] Even the Bedford Estate, though managed with extraordinary care and foresight by a succession of canny agents, could not wholly avoid the dilapidation of certain streets by the 1890s, by which time many respectable families had moved out of Bloomsbury, either to the more fashionable estates to the west and south such as Regent's Park or Belgravia or, after the railways had spread outwards from London, to the newly built suburbs with their large gardens and better air.[16] Already in 1855 *Punch*, demonstrating its eye for the details of contemporary society, carried a cartoon of a snooty butler telling the ladies of the Bloomsbury house where he is employed that he does not object to working for them since the area is – in an echo of Roget's praise of its freshness – 'hairey', and 'the vittles is good'; 'but', he adds, 'the fact is, that all my connections live in Belgravia'.[17]

Thirty-five years later, in December 1890, Alfred Stutfield, agent to
Francis Russell, ninth Duke of Bedford, reported to his employer that,
despite warnings and even court cases, a number of houses in Gower Street
were being used as boarding and lodging houses, in breach of the covenants
agreed with the lessees. 'Some streets are almost entirely occupied by
persons carrying on these businesses,' he wrote despairingly, though in the
case of others, such as Montague Place at the back of the British Museum,
'the evil is of comparatively recent growth and might by the adoption of
stringent measures be checked'.[18] At least it could be said of Bloomsbury's
Bedford Estate that, thanks to the vigilance of Stutfield and his predecessors, it retained the *look* of a residential area even after its houses had ceased
to be predominantly inhabited by the respectable families for whom they
had been built.[19] The boarding houses answered the need, which had
grown along with the development of Bloomsbury itself, to accommodate
increasing numbers of people working and studying in the many educational establishments founded there.

The Bloomsbury which Virginia Woolf, Vanessa Bell, Duncan Grant,
John Maynard Keynes, and other 'Bloomsberries' inhabited early in the
twentieth century was thus part-institutionalised, but it was still home to
some respectable professional people and their families. Vanessa Bell
recalled dining at the house in Bedford Square of Sir George Prothero,
President of the Royal Historical Society, before she and her Stephen
siblings, Virginia, Thoby, and Adrian, found the house at 46 Gordon
Square which was to be their first home in the area. She also remembered
the importance to them of their new beginning in the 'tall, clean' rooms
with their 'white walls, large windows opening on to trees and lawns', and
the freedom associated with having rooms of their own after escaping the
special gloom of the Kensington family home, where their late father's
depression had found perfect expression in its 'pitch-dark' rooms and a
'Virginia creeper which hung down in a thick curtain over the back
drawing-room window'.[20] Bloomsbury represented individual freedom and
a bright new start for the young Stephens. After tramping the area looking
for houses and finding the experience on a cold winter's day at the end of
1903 somewhat dispiriting,[21] Virginia Stephen was also delighted with the
area. She enjoyed exploring Tottenham Court Road with its old furniture
shops, made happy use of the nearby British Museum Reading Room, and
thought Bloomsbury 'altogether a more interesting area than Kensington',
as she noted in her journal in March 1905.[22]

Though the young Stephens were the first of their family to choose
Bloomsbury as their place of residence, the older generation of Stephens

belonged to the new professional class which was most prominently to be found there. As Leslie Stephen's biographer Noel Annan puts it, the family were members of an emerging 'aristocracy of intellect' as the nineteenth century progressed, a group who became influential in public life as civil servants, serious journalists, schoolmasters, museum curators, and scientists, many of them rejecting their Church of England and Oxbridge backgrounds, as did Leslie Stephen, journalist and editor of the great *Dictionary of National Biography*, and his brother, the colonial administrator and judge James Fitzjames Stephen.[23] There is an appropriateness in Leslie Stephen's children moving into the area where much of the widening of professional life had so recently taken place.

Given the prominence of the idea of 'Bloomsbury' as a cultural symbol representing the activities of their circle, there is a further appropriateness in the fact that Virginia and her sister Vanessa both thought of the region they came to call home in imaginative terms from the start. In a short story written in June 1906 and unpublished in her lifetime, Virginia describes the visit of a young woman from the fashionable West End to friends who live in Bloomsbury, a circumstance which fills her with envy:

So Phyllis went separately to the distant and unfashionable quarter of London where the Tristrams lived. That was one of the many enviable parts of their lot. The stucco fronts, the irreproachable rows of Belgravia and South Kensington seemed to Phyllis the type of her lot; of a life trained to grow in an ugly pattern to match the staid ugliness of its fellows. But if one lived here in Bloomsbury, she began to theorise[,] waving with her hand as her cab passed through the great tranquil squares, beneath the pale green of umbrageous trees, one might grow up as one liked.[24]

Much later, while protesting against the catch-all term 'Bloomsbury' to describe the character of a set of friends who had different talents and interests, Vanessa Bell allowed that the very word 'has a pleasant reverberating sound, suggesting old-fashioned gardens and out-of-the-way walks and squares'.[25] Both sisters wrote about Bloomsbury as a release into adulthood and independence after their unhappy life with their oppressive father. They also thought of it as 'distant' from the world of fashion, the distance being understood both spatially and in terms of social class. In thinking like this, they were following a well-documented mental path trodden by plenty of their predecessors in airy, green, respectable, middle-class, intellectual Bloomsbury.

It was during the course of the nineteenth century that Bloomsbury acquired what might be called, with due caution, its distinctive 'character'. Areas continually change culturally and socially, sometimes at an imperceptible rate, at other times more visibly, so to talk of the particular character of a place is to risk monumentalising something fluid and difficult to capture. Yet we do this instinctively, speaking of present-day Chelsea, Hampstead, or Soho as if their identities could be adequately described as 'posh', 'fashionable', or 'bohemian'. What we can say with certainty is that Bloomsbury grew physically with great rapidity between 1800 and 1860, and that in the course of that time it underwent changes of use, from predominantly residential at the beginning of the century to mainly institutional in the last few decades, though in any one part of the area such changes might not have occurred, or might have been reversed. But generally speaking, the status of Bloomsbury altered gradually, as the number of important progressive institutions accumulated, from the founding of London's first university in Gower Street in 1826 to the establishment of the Ladies' College, the Working Men's College, the Working Women's College, and many more during the second half of the century.

These institutions, built in the neighbourhood of the British Museum, the ever-expanding national treasure house established on Great Russell Street in the 1750s, gave Bloomsbury its reputation, still held today, as the intellectual and cultural centre of London. From the late 1850s South Kensington began to rival Bloomsbury in this respect, with the building of the South Kensington Museum (later renamed the Victoria & Albert Museum) to house the treasures of the 1851 Great Exhibition in Hyde Park, the Natural History Museum to take the natural history collections from an overcrowded British Museum, the Science Museum, Imperial College London, and the Royal Albert Hall. By the end of the century, therefore, London could lay claim to two distinct cultural quarters. Of the two, Bloomsbury takes precedence in terms of both chronology and the innovative, progressive motives behind its institutions.

Bloomsbury came to benefit from its relative centrality in the geography of expanding London. It lies midway between Westminster, the long-established heart of national political power, and the City of London, home to the Bank of England and the Inns of Court. During the nineteenth century it was frequently praised, and sometimes slighted, for its 'middling-ness', both geographical and socio-economic. Wilkie Collins catches this midway aspect of the area between London's two centres of power in *Heart and Science* (1883):

The broad district, stretching northward and eastward from the British Museum, is like the quiet quarter of a country town set in the midst of the roaring activities of the largest city in the world ... This haven of rest is alike out of the way of fashion and business; and is yet within easy reach of the one and the other.[26]

This perception of Bloomsbury's convenience for both the West End and the City of London was a relatively late phenomenon, lagging behind the physical development of the area. Bloomsbury not only grew in size during the century, but it 'moved', in part through the coming of the railways and in part as a result of its increasing cluster of educational institutions, from an area considered remote from the centres of power and influence to one recognised as central to London's, and the nation's, public life.

A few joking remarks in parliament and in novels by the Tory satirist Theodore Hook in the mid-1820s about the British Museum and Russell Square being located in some distant wilderness were taken up and repeated for decades to come. Russell Square became a litmus test for observers of London's social and cultural life – was it central or peripheral? Fashionable or merely bourgeois?[27] By 1900 the Museum, Russell Square, and Bloomsbury in general were indisputably 'central'. An article in *The Times* in 1894 expressed the hope that Herbrand Russell, eleventh Duke of Bedford, would agree to sell some properties on Great Russell Street to the British Museum to allow its necessary expansion. This, according to the writer, would prevent the Museum's collections from being 'further dismembered' and moved from their 'central position' in Bloomsbury to 'some *Ultima Thule* in the west', by which was meant the Natural History Museum, which had opened in South Kensington in 1881 when the British Museum became impossibly crowded.[28]

Notions of 'centrality' changed in accordance with the continued physical growth of London, as well as with the shifting point of view (and possibly the place of residence) of the observer. An important factor was the siting of three major railway stations and one of the first underground railway stations on Euston Road, the northern boundary of Bloomsbury. Euston Station opened in 1837, King's Cross in 1852, St Pancras in 1868, and Gower Street, now Euston Square, a station on London's first tube line, in 1863. These developments enhanced the area for some. It became an attractive place of residence for people like the wealthy City grocer Mr Jorrocks in R.S. Surtees's novel *Handley Cross*, who liked to keep horses and a country house in one of the Home Counties, which now became easily accessible from the metropolis. In the second edition published in

1854, Surtees gives a precise sense of Mr Jorrocks's 'arrival' as a respectable Bloomsbury resident despite his humble origins and his continued dropping of 'h's:

> When the gates of the world were opened by railways, our friend's active mind saw that business might be combined with pleasure . . . hunting one day and selling teas another . . . His business place was in St Botolph's Lane, in the City, but his residence was in Great Coram Street. This is rather a curious locality, – city people considering it west, while those in the west consider it east. The fact is, that Great Coram Street is somewhere about the centre of London, near the London University, and not a great way from the Euston station of the Birmingham railway. Jorrocks says it is close to the two best cover hacks in the world, the great Northern and Euston stations. Approaching it from the east . . . [i.e. King's Cross, where the Great Northern Line terminated] you pass the Foundling Hospital on Guilford Street, cross Brunswick Square, and turning short to the left you find yourself in 'Great Coram Street'. Neat unassuming houses form the sides . . . In this region the dazzling glare of civic pomp and courtly state are equally unknown . . . It is a nice quiet street, highly popular with Punch and other public characters.[29]

Surtees probably had Thackeray in mind here. One of the *Punch* writers, he lived in Great Coram Street (now Coram Street) as a young married man in the late 1830s and early 1840s, and shrewdly anatomised Bloomsbury class and culture in his novels and journalism.

Though the arrival of the new railway termini on the edge of the area in mid-century was an advantage to men in the fictional Mr Jorrocks's position, and in due course brought business to the northern parts of Bloomsbury through the building of station and other hotels in the neighbourhood of Euston Road, it contributed, conversely, to the disincentives to well-off families noted by the Bedford Estate's agent Christopher Haedy. These were now looking westward and not filling the fine houses in the last two Bloomsbury squares to be completed, Tavistock and Gordon Squares. The famed airiness of the situation and attractiveness of the (private) square gardens, together with the many gates which had been erected on Bedford land, as on other London estates, to stop through traffic of horses, carts, and omnibuses with their associated noises and smells, were not quite enough to keep the very 'best' families in the area, once it had become known as the residence of choice for the professional and commercial classes. As Haedy wrote as early as May 1840 in his report to Francis Russell, seventh Duke of Bedford:

> The great struggle not infrequently is between men in business and their wives and daughters. Their convenience would keep them here within easy reach of their places of business, but their wives and daughters would give the preference to a more fashionable residence at the west or northwest ends of the town.[30]

Bloomsbury's social position was not without ambiguity, despite the advantage of the west central (WC) code given to it when London was divided into postal districts in the late 1850s.[31] By the end of the century very few aristocrats or people of fashion and leisure lived in its squares and 'better' streets. They were inhabited mainly by members of the increasingly influential professional class: judges, lawyers, doctors, architects, artists, professors, writers, students, and people who worked in various capacities in the great congregation of learned institutions which had found their location in the neighbourhood. Bloomsbury, of all London's regions, was at the heart of the process of 'professionalisation' which happened in the course of the nineteenth century. Reform and regulation were brought to bear on the professions of law, art, architecture, medicine, and teaching, from nursery to higher education. Such modernisation was markedly a Bloomsbury phenomenon, driven by independent groups and individuals, and only later adopted by the authorities, made into law, and put into universal practice.

When the young architect Edwin Lutyens was looking for a home in the months before his marriage in 1897, and for an architect's office too, his wife's uncle recommended Bloomsbury. Lutyens duly took 29 Bloomsbury Square, which he already knew, as it had previously been the headquarters of his professional mentor, 'the great Norman Shaw'. Lutyens was delighted with his house, partly because of the Shaw connection, and partly because of its 'charm' and spaciousness as a home.[32] It was not only professional men who chose to live and work in Bloomsbury; so also, by the end of the century, did the new class of professional women. In 1900 the charity worker Emily Hobhouse published an article based on a statistical survey she and her fellow members of the Women's Industrial Council had carried out. In 'Women Workers: How They Live, How They Wish to Live' her main concern was to highlight the problems independent women encountered in finding somewhere to live in London. According to her findings, 'the boarding-house is condemned as "fussy and frumpish"' and the lodging house as 'in most cases uncomfortable and desperately lonely'. Respondents to her questionnaire desired a 'combination of individual privacy with co-operative advantages', roughly on the model of the innovative Ladies' Residential Chambers, blocks of flats for independent working women recently established in Chelsea and Bloomsbury.

Hobhouse found that what the women wanted most was to have the choice of mixed chambers, since the presence of men would 'elevate the quality of the food' as well as providing interesting company. She concluded that the best place for such a bold venture would be 'a quiet spot in Bloomsbury – for Bloomsbury is the beloved, the chosen of working women'.[33] It was frequently the 'chosen' of men and women in all the professions, including the writing profession, as the struggling young novelist George Gissing noted when he moved into rooms at 15 Gower Place, in August 1881. He told his brother that the neighbourhood, 'a quarter of an hour's walk from the Museum' and close to three railway stations, was 'the only one for a man of my needs'. He had set part of the action of his first novel, *Workers in the Dawn* (1880), in cramped lodgings in the same small street.[34]

An article in *The Times* in 1894, discussing the impending demolition of some of the older properties in Russell Square, consoled its readers with the thought that, despite the inevitability of change, Bloomsbury would probably continue to offer both institutional and residential accommodation as a result of its special status as the intellectual heart of London:

> Bloomsbury is not Mayfair, and the district which lies between Berkeley and Grosvenor squares can hardly be compared to one which lies east of Tottenham-court-road. Bloomsbury is the home of the British Museum, and a more sober-suited architecture would seem to befit a neighbourhood which may still be learned, sedate, and respectable, but can never again be fashionable . . . [It] has already seen its best days as a residential quarter, and perhaps only retains that character at all by virtue of circumstances inseparable from its present condition – its convenience for certain professions and occupations, its moderate rents, and its spacious and commodious houses . . . it is at present a district neither very fashionable, nor very much the reverse, but quiet, respectable, salubrious, and pleasant, not so far removed from the centre of things as to become provincial, nor so much immersed in the bustle of life as to kill tranquillity of study and repose of soul, presenting in its open spaces some far off resemblance to the courts and quadrangles of other seats of learning, and having for its centre and its symbol the great national storehouse of the learning of all ages and the arts of all mankind.[35]

Many a novelist, in addition to Gissing, and many a reader in the British Museum's great Round Reading Room, built in 1857 to the design of Anthony Panizzi, showed a similar fascination with the region in which they lived and worked. A number of the writers who made their homes in Bloomsbury during the nineteenth century had significant connections to the innovators in education who were at the heart of its development as London's intellectual and cultural centre. Dickens, Thackeray, Trollope, the poet Arthur Hugh Clough, William Morris, the Pre-Raphaelite artists and poets, Christina Rossetti, Mary Elizabeth Braddon, and J.M. Barrie – who lived in Bloomsbury lodgings on arriving at St Pancras Station on the overnight train from Scotland in 1885, intent on making his name in London and subsisting at first on 'halfpenny buns from a paper bag' and the spiritual fortification he derived from his favourite book, Roget's *Thesaurus*[36] – interacted in various ways with Bloomsbury's institutions. Others, not Bloomsbury residents, reflected in their writings the phenomenon of fast-growing Bloomsbury, noting its precise social and cultural characteristics at different moments in its history, from Theodore Hook in the 1820s to Wilkie Collins in the 1880s.

One miscellaneous writer who haunted the British Museum Reading Room early in the twentieth century, referring to it as his 'alma mater', was E.V. Lucas.[37] He summed up the area in 1906:

[Bloomsbury] has few shops and many residents, and it is a stronghold of middle class respectability and learning. The British Museum is its heart: its lungs are Bedford Square and Russell Square, Gordon Square and Woburn Square: and its aorta is Gower Street, which goes on for ever. Lawyers and law students live here, to be near the Inns of Court; bookish men live here, to be near the Museum; and Jews live here, to be near the University College School, which is non-sectarian. Bloomsbury is discreet and handy: it is near everything, and although not fashionable, any one, I understand, may live there without losing caste.[38]

From the 1820s on, the emerging area drew in a number of enlightened, energetic, and in some cases eccentric people who made their professional and personal lives there. It was in Bloomsbury, partly by chance and partly by design, that conspicuously large numbers of reforming educational and cultural institutions were established between the 1820s and the 1890s. Inasmuch as an area can be meaningfully characterised as 'radical' or 'progressive', these adjectives applied to Bloomsbury. As political and social reform measures were sought and gained in parliament from the 1820s on, so educational progress was pursued by prominent reforming politicians, men like Henry Brougham, Joseph Hume, and George Grote. The trend they initiated was towards inclusiveness, today described in academic circles as 'widening participation', then known by the much-used phrase, coined in the 1820s, as 'the diffusion of useful knowledge'.[39]

In short, Bloomsbury became transformed from a largely undeveloped area, a scarcely inhabited backwater, at the beginning of the century, into London's main intellectual quarter by its end. Motivated individuals and groups colonised the ever-developing area for their pioneering schemes: higher education for non-Anglicans and for women, education and self-help for working men and women, organised play and learning for poor and disabled children, the kindergarten system of pre-school training, schools of art and design for both men and women, progressive medical schools and specialist hospitals. Several wealthy, influential, non-establishment figures such as Unitarians, Jews, and other religious dissenters played their part. Different interest groups interacted as they worked and lived in Bloomsbury; there was in many cases a significant overlap in the personnel attached to the new institutions. Some innovations turned out to be unsuccessful or transient, while others had a lasting significance for the cultural and educational life of the country.

The earliest and most far-reaching of these progressive institutions was the new University of London, opened in Gower Street in 1828 and known from 1836 to the present day as University College London.[40] Its erection at the north end of Gower Street is a striking example of the mixture of randomness and deliberate choice which characterises the development of the area. The new university was built on its particular piece of wasteland because the land came on to the market just when a group of reformers were meeting to plan their new metropolitan university. Its proximity to the British Museum was a piece of luck which was readily exploited by the university's founders to advertise the merits of their foundation. The two establishments became linked in various ways, from the mutual exchange of books to the sharing of expertise in subjects such as Italian and oriental languages.[41] If the connection between these two seats of learning was thus semi-serendipitous, other links which followed were far from random. University Hall, built in Gordon Square in 1849, and the Ladies' College, opened in a house in Bedford Square in the same year, for example, owed their existence and their locations entirely to their connections with their Gower Street neighbour.[42]

First among the energetic individuals who came together in the interests of political, social, and intellectual progress was the astonishingly active Whig lawyer and politician Henry Brougham, founder with poet and fellow

Scot Thomas Campbell of London's first university. William Wilkins's neoclassical structure of 1826–8 was built on Gower Street to open university education to those who were unable to graduate from Oxford or Cambridge because they were not confessing Anglicans. The new University of London also set out to offer an unprecedentedly wide syllabus; modern languages, geography, and a number of scientific and medical subjects not yet taught elsewhere were on the curriculum either from the start or soon after. The founders could call on a workforce of brilliant men, each at the forefront of his discipline and each unable or unwilling to teach at either of the two established English universities.[43]

Among the most interesting of the institutions that followed was University Hall, built by philanthropic Unitarians in Gordon Square in 1849 to provide students of University College with accommodation on the Oxbridge college model, as its Tudor Gothic architectural building style suggests. One of the most prominent founders and benefactors was Henry Crabb Robinson, the learned long-lived diarist and friend of Wordsworth, Coleridge, Blake, and Goethe. 'Old Crabb' he was called by Walter Bagehot, who, as a brilliant student at University College in the 1840s, attended several of the older man's famous cultural breakfasts at his large home in Russell Square.[44] Crabb Robinson was an early supporter and council member of the University of London, and was also involved in the founding of the first establishment for the higher education of women, the Ladies' College, by his friend the wealthy Unitarian Elisabeth Jesser Reid. Her college was not at first able to admit women to full degree status, but it employed many of the best professors from University College to teach the curriculum. Among those who went to listen to lectures there in its early years was Marian Evans, later to become known as George Eliot.[45]

While University College, University Hall, and the Ladies' College catered for middle-class students from two previously excluded groups – dissenters and women – the Working Men's College was started for another disadvantaged group, working-class men. It was opened in Red Lion Square in 1854 by the unorthodox liberal Anglican theologian and preacher, Frederick Denison Maurice, who had been forced to resign from his post as professor of theology at King's College London (opened in 1831 as a Church-and-State rival to the new university on Gower Street). Ten years later, George Eliot's friend Elizabeth Malleson opened the Working Women's College in Queen Square.[46] Most important of all, perhaps, in terms of social usefulness, was the mission to extend education to all ages and all classes embodied in the acclaimed Arts and Crafts building erected in Tavistock Place in 1897 to house the Passmore Edwards Settlement.

Initially named after its benefactor, John Passmore Edwards, the scarcely educated son of a Cornish carpenter and self-made newspaper magnate who endowed dozens of public libraries and hospitals in the last two decades of the nineteenth century, the building was subsequently renamed Mary Ward House after its equally enterprising co-founder, Mary Ward.

Mary Ward was the granddaughter of Dr Arnold of Rugby School, the niece of Matthew Arnold, and the author, as Mrs Humphry Ward, of the bestselling novel, *Robert Elsmere* (1888), a tale of the travails of an earnest clergyman who loses his faith, gives up his pulpit, and sets off for the East End of London to minister educationally and medically to the local poor. Inspired by the Toynbee Hall settlement built in the East End in 1884–5, and by her own fictional hero's doings, Mary Ward determined to establish a similar settlement in Bloomsbury, where she lived in what Passmore Edwards called 'kid-glovish' Russell Square. (*He* lived in equally respectable Bedford Square.) By persistence, charm, and a strong sense of what it meant to be an Arnold in matters of national education and culture, she succeeded in persuading Herbrand Russell, the eleventh Duke of Bedford, to give land on favourable terms for the project, while Passmore Edwards put up the £14,000 required for the building. Designed by two young Bloomsbury architects, Smith and Brewer, the meticulously detailed structure housed a progressive centre for the education, recreation, and creative play of Bloomsbury's poor children and their parents. The founders embraced the kindergarten system for very young children, a system introduced to Britain by the German political exiles Johannes and Bertha Ronge (in a house a few doors away on Tavistock Place) in the 1850s. The Settlement had a free legal aid centre, coal club, mother-and-toddler group, as well as a chess club, gymnastics classes, lectures on academic and practical subjects, concerts, and music lessons. Gustav Holst was the musical director from 1901 to 1905. In 1899 the Settlement opened the first school for disabled children in the country.[47]

That the 'march of mind', to borrow a phrase much used in the early part of the nineteenth century, sometimes earnestly but as often sarcastically,[48] was progressing predominantly in Bloomsbury is further illustrated by the concentration of innovative doctors and medical lecturers who took up posts at the new university on Gower Street, many of them Scots who had trained in the famous medical school at Edinburgh University. A number of specialist hospitals also settled in Bloomsbury, especially near the area's poor eastern boundary of Gray's Inn Road. These ranged from the pioneering Hospital for Sick Children opened in Great Ormond Street in 1852 to several specialist hospitals in neighbouring Queen Square, such as the Alexandra Hospital for Children with Hip Disease (from 1867), and the Italian Hospital, established in 1884 by Giovanni Battista Ortelli, a successful businessman, to care for his poor compatriots in the adjacent area of Clerkenwell known as 'Little Italy'.[49]

In 1834 the University of London opened its own teaching hospital on the opposite side of Gower Street. Here many an innovative experiment in surgery took place, including the earliest British use of anaesthetics in December 1846, in an operation carried out by the legendary surgeon Robert Liston, who could amputate a limb in twenty-five seconds. Liston announced that the use of ether during the amputation, a 'Yankee dodge' first attempted by a dentist in Massachusetts a couple of months earlier, 'beats mesmerism hollow', thus neatly describing the rapid replacement of one novel method for conquering pain during surgery by another.[50] Mesmerism had been all the rage during the previous few years; its use was most controversial in the lectures and operations of University College's medical professor, John Elliotson, who attracted leading politicians and socialites as well as students to his demonstrations of the power of mesmerism to combat pain. Elliotson went too far even for Gower Street's forward-looking authorities, however, when he allowed one of two sisters whom he used as mesmeric mediums to enter male hospital wards and diagnose diseases while in a mesmeric trance. He was obliged to resign, despite petitions for his reinstatement by his adoring students. Dickens championed him, taking lessons from him and carrying out his own mesmeric practice on his wife and friends.[51]

Meanwhile, other unorthodox medical practices were centred in Bloomsbury. In 1850 the first homoeopathic hospital in London, the Hahnemann, named after the German founder of homoeopathy, was started in Bloomsbury Square. Its rival, the London Homoeopathic Hospital, founded by Frederic Quin in the same year, moved in 1859 to Queen Square, where it still is. Twenty years later, medical training for women was pioneered in Bloomsbury: the London School of Medicine for Women opened in Henrietta Street in 1874. The first woman surgeon, Louisa Aldrich-Blake, studied there in the 1880s. She was taught by Elizabeth Garrett Anderson, the first female doctor to qualify in Britain, who opened her own hospital for women in Marylebone, moving it in 1890 to a specially designed building on the northern fringe of Bloomsbury, the north side of Euston Road.[52]

Henrietta Street was close to the Foundling Hospital, opened by Thomas Coram in 1745 and patronised by Hogarth and Handel in its early years. Coram's foundation had been one of the most innovative ventures of its time. The old British Museum in Montagu House on Great Russell Street and the Foundling Hospital were the only two public institutions in the whole of Bloomsbury in 1800, when the area began to be developed. Both establishments found themselves progressively surrounded by reforming institutions; there is some evidence that they responded to the arrival of new neighbours such as the Hospital for Sick Children, established in Great Ormond Street, just to the south-west of the Foundling Hospital, and the Gower Street institutions, which by 1834 numbered not only the new university, but also its school, its pioneering hospital, and its own museum of zoology, the first of its kind in the country, created by Robert Grant, the university's first professor of zoology.

The British Museum and the Foundling Hospital took steps as the century went on to haul themselves into the modern world in terms of their constitutions, and in the case of the Museum its entrance policy. Rebuilt and expanded by the architect Robert Smirke from the 1820s to the 1840s and pushed onwards by the indefatigable chief librarian Anthony Panizzi, the Museum gradually opened its doors at more convenient hours for the working population.[53] Meanwhile the Foundling Hospital, encouraged by Dickens, an important enthusiast and fund-raiser, began offering a better basic education to its young inmates, who had previously been trained exclusively as apprentices (boys) or domestic servants (girls). By the latter half of the nineteenth century some foundlings were being prepared for entry to teacher-training colleges, themselves a new concept associated primarily with Bloomsbury, where the College of Preceptors was established in 1846 and the Home and Colonial School Society was sited from 1837.[54]

Bloomsbury was also home to a number of experimental or alternative religious foundations. Its two most important established Anglican churches, St George's Bloomsbury and St Giles-in-the-Fields, presented a thought-provoking contrast to one another as the century proceeded, as well as to the dissenting, mystical, and spiritualist foundations which began to arrive in their neighbourhood. St George's, on Hart Street (now Bloomsbury Way), a few steps south of the British Museum, was patronised by the aristocracy and the wealthy middle class and offered its incumbent one of the richest livings in London. The members of its congregation – at least some of them – seemed well matched with the pretensions of the church itself, built to the design of Nicholas Hawksmoor in 1731, with its stepped steeple echoing the mausoleum at Halicarnassus, and topped by a surprising statue of George I in Roman dress.

A short distance to the south-west is the church of St Giles-in-the-Fields, built at the same time as St George's on the site of a twelfth-century leper hospital. In the eighteenth century and until 1847, when in an effort at slum clearance and traffic easing New Oxford Street was cut through, the church sat at the heart of one of London's worst slum areas, a warren of narrow overcrowded alleyways full of poor Irish families known as the Rookery.[55] This miserable quarter was caught on canvas by many an artist, from William Hogarth to George Cruikshank. The latter, born in 1792 in nearby Duke Street (now Coptic Street), knew the area as the 'Holy Land' or 'little Dublin'.[56] Hogarth had set his famous print *Gin Lane* (1751) in this area straddling the southern border of Bloomsbury, though – provocatively – it is the spire of smarter St George's, not that of St Giles, which is to be seen rising just behind the slums, as if to show how close the rich parishioners attending Sunday service at St George's could find themselves physically to the squalid living conditions of the urban lumpenproletariat in the St Giles rookeries. An enduring paradox, much commented on in the press, was the close proximity of the British Museum, that great repository of Britain's cultural collections and therefore index of the country's wealth and global power, to one of the worst slums in the capital.[57]

Into this interesting joint parish of St George and St Giles came in the nineteenth century the Swedenborg Society, based in nearby Charlotte Street. Among those attracted to its mystical unorthodoxy was James John Garth Wilkinson, an influential and successful homoeopathic doctor who lived in Store Street in the early 1840s. In the parish of St Pancras to the north-east, in unfashionable Regent Square, rose the Scottish Church, a large neo-Gothic building erected in the 1820s for the charismatic Edward Irving and his large following. Irving, a schoolfriend of Thomas Carlyle, had become London's most fashionable preacher, attracting large crowds, including aristocrats and parliamentarians, to his Sunday services at the small Caledonian Chapel in Hatton Garden. By the time the new building in Regent Square was ready for him in 1827, he had displeased the church authorities with his unorthodox sermons prophesying the imminent fulfil-ment of the Books of Daniel and Revelation in preparation for the end of the world. He was expelled; he and his breakaway congregation increasingly became the subject of scandal and gossip in their imposing new church in Regent Square on the eastern fringes of Bloomsbury, where the coroneted carriages which had thronged the streets round Hatton Garden did not penetrate. Irving, having begun with the intention of reforming and renewing Christian faith in the face of growing materialism and religious doubt, allowed outbreaks of prophesying and speaking in tongues by members of his congregation, distressing old friends like Carlyle, who tried to warn him of his folly.[58]

By 1834, when Irving died of consumption at the age of forty-two, a number of 'Irvingites' were gathering around the wealthy banker Henry Drummond, the prime mover of the millenarian group known as the Catholic Apostolic Church, which built its great cathedral-like church on the west side of Gordon Square in 1850–4, having for its adjoining neighbour to the north the Unitarian-inspired University Hall. Here, next door to one another, were establishments representing religious 'progressiveness' in starkly contrasting forms; one was set up to support the non-denominational University College on plain Unitarian principles, free from the Church-and-State patronage and the influence of Oxford and Cambridge, while the other represented the most demonstrative form of millenarianism to emerge in the nineteenth century. Both sets of worshippers considered themselves 'dissenters' from Protestant and Catholic orthodoxy alike, the Unitarians by rejection of the idea of Christ as part of the Godhead, their dislike of formal creeds, and their desire for simple worship, and the Catholic Apostolics by cutting across all existing sects, claiming converts from all the established churches, adopting lavish rituals, and cleaving to the prophetic books of the Bible in the belief in the imminence of the Second Coming of Christ and the Day of Judgment.[59]

These unlikely neighbours were enabled to build their respective establishments on Bedford land in mid-century only because, during the slump that followed the great building boom of the early 1820s, Thomas Cubitt had been unable to sell some of the houses he had already constructed; parts of the east and west sides of Gordon Square were still not built on at all by the later 1840s. Christopher Haedy, the astute Bedford Estate manager, urged his employer, the seventh Duke, to permit the erection of both University Hall and the Catholic Apostolic Church, despite this being a breach of the custom that allowed only residential uses for Bedford Estate buildings. His reasoning was that the demand for middle-class housing in the area was unlikely to pick up, that it was depressing for residents to live beside empty houses or spaces, and that the danger of the properties being devalued would be greater if Cubitt were forced to sell the land on to other builders, who might erect inferior houses, than if two carefully regulated, respectable establishments were given permission to build.[60]

Haedy and the Duke were undoubtedly influenced by the grand designs of the two buildings. The Tudor Gothic University Hall was the work of Thomas Donaldson, professor of architecture at University College, the Hall's neighbour to the west. And Haedy was certainly impressed by the huge Gothic church by Brandon and Ritchie going up next door; he wrote in his 1852 annual report for the Duke of Bedford:

The Church erecting by the Irvingites on the west side of Gordon Square and on the north side of Torrington Square is in a state of great forwardness. It will be a magnificent Structure and in extent, will probably be equal to any Eccleciastical Edifice in London except Westminster Abbey and St Paul's Cathedral.[61]

The construction of these two large institutional buildings in Gordon Square in mid-century marked the shift in the Duke of Bedford's Bloomsbury from mainly residential to greater institutional occupancy.

Bloomsbury was the main London location for the activities collectively known as 'the march of mind' or 'the march of intellect'. The phrases were used regularly in the 1820s to describe the efforts of leading progressives, many of whom were associated both with the agitation for parliamentary and electoral reform which culminated in the first great Reform Act of 1832 and with the education movement. The latter took the form at the highest level of founding a university in London to right the obvious wrong that the greatest metropolis in the world possessed no university, unlike Paris, Berlin, Florence, and many other cities. The avowedly secular university, known variously in journals such as the Tory organ *John Bull* as the 'godless' institution of Gower Street, the 'radical infidel college', and 'the Cockney College', was viewed with suspicion by orthodox churchmen as well as by anti-reform politicians and journalists. For such people Bloomsbury was a 'dangerous' area, one where radical, subversive, destabilising, and – in the view of some commentators – immoral ideas were put into practice.[62]

Hosts of cartoons, caricatures, and comic poems picked up the idea of knowledge on the march in Gower Street and its environs. Some suggested that the new university intended to teach tradesmen the classics and, worse, foment revolution among the working class, who – newly literate and inquiring – would press for an even wider extension of the franchise than that currently being canvassed in parliament. Winthrop Mackworth Praed caught the mood in his clever poem 'The London University; A Discourse delivered by a College Tutor at a Supper-Party', published in the *Morning Chronicle* in July 1825. Praed predicts the furore likely to be created among establishment politicians and churchmen, especially dons at Oxbridge, by the projected university:

Ye Dons and ye doctors, ye Provosts and Proctors,
    Who are paid to monopolize knowledge,

Come make opposition by voice and petition
  To the radical infidel College . . .

Deliberately ludicrous though such attacks were, they expressed a real
fear among cautious and reactionary observers, who saw that a small
number of influential individuals were the driving force behind parliamentary and electoral reform, the new university, *and* the movement for mass
education. The comic novelist Thomas Love Peacock reflected these anxieties and suspicions in *Crotchet Castle*, published in 1831, a book full of
witty allusions to the troubling signs of the times. In chapter 2, entitled
'The March of Mind', a reactionary clergyman turns on a thief with the cry:
'You are a schoolmaster abroad, are you? You are marching with a detach-
ment of the march of mind, are you? You are a member of the Steam
Intellect Society, are you? You swear by the learned friend, do you?'
Contemporary readers would immediately recognise 'the learned friend'
as Henry Brougham, recently appointed Lord Chancellor in Lord Grey's
reforming Whig government, prime mover of the new university and its
first council chairman, and principal actor, with George Birkbeck, in the
recent founding of the Infant School Society and the London Mechanics'
Institution. Brougham had made a famous speech in parliament in 1828,
attacking the Duke of Wellington and using the much-quoted phrase 'the
schoolmaster is abroad' to suggest that mass education was the way forward.
He had also founded, in 1826, the Society for the Diffusion of Useful
Knowledge (SDUK), to which Peacock here alludes under the title the
'Steam Intellect Society'. Peacock cleverly merges the idea of industrial and
educational progress at a time when railways were just beginning to revolu-
tionise the country's transport connections and simultaneously serious
attempts were being made to educate the masses.[63]
With Brougham at the wheel, supported by radicals and Whigs, including
James Mill (father of John Stuart Mill), Birkbeck, Zachary Macaulay, father
of the historian Thomas Babington Macaulay, and the enterprising publisher
Charles Knight, the Society for the Diffusion of Useful Knowledge was an
extremely successful organisation during its twenty years of existence.
Founded in the same year as the new University of London and by the same
people, the Society was run from the offices of its secretary, a Bloomsbury
lawyer interested in reform. Thomas Coates operated first from his chambers in Gray's Inn, and later from 42 Bedford Square. Other lawyers
prominent in the early years of both the University of London and the
SDUK were William Tooke, who practised in Bedford Row and lived at 12
Russell Square, and James Loch of Bloomsbury Square. By 1846 the Society

had done its work and could dissolve itself as no longer necessary. Its main contribution to education was through its sixpenny treatises, published as the Library of Useful Knowledge from 1827 with the intention of bringing knowledge to 'uneducated persons, or persons imperfectly educated'. By employing the latest techniques of stereotyping, the Society was able to make such knowledge available at prices even the poorest could afford; moreover, it was soon possible to use the expanding train network to transport these cheap publications quickly to all parts of the country. The 'Steam Intellect Society' treatises were written by established experts in their fields – David Brewster wrote the one on optics, for example – or by up-and-coming young academics, many of them appointees to the first chairs at the University of London. These included Augustus De Morgan, who wrote several scientific and mathematical works for the Society, and the self-educated professor of botany John Lindley (after whom the Royal Horticultural Society's Lindley Library is named).

The most famous of the treatises was George Lillie Craik's *Pursuit of Knowledge under Difficulties* (1830–1), an account of the successful overcoming of educational disadvantages or disabilities by a number of working-class people. Reprinted several times over the next few decades, it was a direct predecessor of Samuel Smiles's phenomenally successful *Self-Help* (1859). Craik's title quickly became a catch phrase; it crops up again and again in the memoirs of autodidacts who grew up in the years before the Education Act of 1870 prescribed schooling for all. It is the title of a chapter in the brief autobiography of John Passmore Edwards, *A Few Footprints* (1905). Edwards describes growing up with very little formal schooling in an industrial district of Cornwall in the 1820s. He recalls how his father subscribed to the SDUK's *Penny Magazine*, 'the only London periodical that came into the village', how he read at the age of twelve an article in it about John Hunter the famous anatomist, using a dictionary to explain difficult words, and felt 'boyish flutterings of ambition to become known and useful in some way myself'.[64] This he eventually did by making his fortune in the newspaper business and giving away huge chunks of it for philanthropic purposes. Finally, he financed Mary Ward's project, named after him in gratitude for his generous donation. He watched from his home in Bedford Square as the Passmore Edwards Settlement building rose on nearby Tavistock Place in 1896–7.

The making of Bloomsbury into the prime location for progressive educational ventures begins with the activities of the group of reforming lawyers and politicians whose aim in the early decades of the nineteenth century was the extension of civil freedoms, the diffusion of knowledge, the secularisation of education, and in particular the establishment of a university for the great city of London. For this purpose a site was found in 1825. From then on the area's continued development through Cubitt's streets and squares was accompanied by new institutions and the people who came to inhabit them.

Though we often use the word 'Bloomsbury' as shorthand for the group of artists, writers, and thinkers who lived there in the early twentieth century, the word already carried a rich cultural resonance which it owed to the multifarious activities of the Bloomsbury Group's predecessors in the area. Of the many men and women who had a vision of an improved society, progressives and pioneers who put their ideas into practice, the first were those who established a university for London on new principles, planting it on Gower Street. It is to them that we turn first.

CHAPTER ONE

Godlessness on Gower Street

O n Monday 6 June 1825 an article entitled 'The London College' was printed in *The Times*. It gave an account of a meeting at the Crown and Anchor Tavern in the Strand the previous Saturday of 'about 120 of the gentlemen who have taken a principal interest in the formation of the London College, or University'.[1] In the chair was Henry Brougham. Among the 'public characters' supporting him were several prominent Whig and reforming members of parliament, including Lord John Russell, third son of the sixth Duke of Bedford, and Joseph Hume, famous for his dogged attacks on royal and aristocratic profligacy and the scandalous expense to the public purse of the navy and other national services.[2] Also there was Dr George Birkbeck, founder of the London Mechanics' Institution in 1823. At the foot of the table sat the poet Thomas Campbell, whom Brougham graciously described as having been 'most active' in the many private meetings which had recently taken place in Brougham's legal chambers in Lincoln's Inn to plan the new institution.

All those present were agreed, *The Times* reported, on 'the necessity of establishing for the great population of this metropolis a college, which would comprehend all the leading advantages of the two great universities', while allowing the students to remain at home with their parents, thus both catering for their 'domestic supervision' and offering an education much cheaper than that at the ancient residential universities of Oxford and Cambridge. In his grandiose way, Brougham announced at the meeting that he had sounded out the Chancellor of the Exchequer and William Huskisson, the President of the Board of Trade, about the possibility of applying for a royal charter to establish the new university, but had been discouraged. He was now in the process of putting a private bill to the House of Commons, explaining to his fellow MPs that there was no intention at present of 'founding fellowships, or conferring degrees, or giving a theological education'. Despite not being able to take degrees at the new institution – a concession to the vested interests of Oxford and Cambridge which Brougham saw as an unfortunate necessity for the time being – the young men of London would be offered a full higher educational syllabus. The founders' most radical and contentious step was to exclude theological teaching. The syllabus would be much expanded to include, in addition to the traditional subjects of mathematics and the classics, 'science, literature, and the arts'.

There would be no sinecures or residences for the professors. Nor would there be any religious tests such as those operating at Oxford and Cambridge, where students were obliged to sign the Thirty-Nine Articles of the Church of England in order to take their degrees and where all teaching fellows had to do likewise. At the new university there was to be 'no barrier to the education of any sect among His Majesty's subjects'. Medical studies were envisaged, and London students would have the advantage over their peers at Oxbridge (though this was diplomatically left by Brougham to be inferred) of combining the academic study of anatomy and physiology with attending practical medical classes at one of the London hospitals.

Treading thus warily to avoid stepping on the toes of the two ancient universities, which would be unlikely to welcome a London rival, Brougham described how the money would be raised for the new institution. 'The capital intended for the undertaking was estimated at £200,000, and the mode of raising it by transferable shares of £100 each', The Times reported. At the meeting a committee was appointed to take the plan further, and letters of support were read out from the Dukes of Bedford and Norfolk, the former a leading Whig and the latter a Roman Catholic who would naturally take a close interest in the founding of an institution which would not discriminate against his fellow religionists.[3]

The editor of The Times, Thomas Barnes, a friend of Brougham, continued to report the doings of the fledgling institution in some detail, and usually in an encouraging spirit, from its conception in 1825 to the opening of its new building on Gower Street to welcome the first intake of students in October 1828. The newspaper had been the chosen vehicle for the very first public suggestion of a university for London four months earlier, in February 1825, when it carried a long, diffuse open letter from Thomas Campbell to Henry Brougham entitled 'Proposal of a Metropolitan University'.

Though Campbell did not put the case as succinctly as his colleagues would have wished, it is apparent from his letter that the aim of the planned university was fourfold: to offer higher education in the politically and financially most important city in the world, and thus remove the ignominy of London having no university; to educate the sons of the expanding middle class; to welcome non-Anglicans of every kind by avoiding the religious tests for entry (Oxford) or graduation (Cambridge) which had excluded them from English universities for so long; and to enlarge the curriculum beyond the traditional classical, mathematical, and theological education offered by Oxford and Cambridge. The radicalism of the proposal did not go as far as to propose higher education for women, though when women were finally permitted to take degrees in 1878, it was at University College London that the innovation was introduced.[4]

One attraction for parents stressed by Campbell was the relative cheapness of keeping their sons at home instead of sending them away to live in a college: 'Say a man has £1,000 a year, he can hardly send one son to an English University. To send three sons, would cost him at the least £750.'[5] Each son kept at home in London would cost about £25–£30 for his education, with perhaps clothing and pocket money amounting to another £25. Not wishing to alienate the two ancient universities too much, Campbell does not state explicitly the further advantage to parents of being able to keep a close eye on their offspring, and so to thwart the well-known propensity for young men at university to run up wine and tailoring bills, not to mention such costly and tempting pursuits as gambling and visiting prostitutes.

In the end, once the new university had been launched and the dust settled on the controversy it aroused, the two aims which were to prove truly important and influential for the education and culture of the whole country were the opening of higher education – and from 1836 of full degree status – to people of all faiths and none, and the expansion of the curriculum. The University of London was the first to include a range of subjects not taught before, including several branches of science and medicine, geography, architecture, modern history, English language and literature, and other modern languages and literatures including French, German, Italian, Spanish, and Hebrew.

These progressive aims of the proposed institution were vigorously opposed from the start by newspapers supporting the Tory government and defending the special position of the Church of England. None entered the lists more combatively than *John Bull*, the newspaper founded in 1820 to support the unpopular George IV in his efforts to keep his estranged wife Caroline from attending his coronation as queen. (Brougham was Caroline's legal adviser.) *John Bull* immediately seized on Campbell's letter in *The*

Times to 'his friend Brougham' and began a campaign, taken up by other newspapers, to ridicule the new university. It reminded readers of its founders' recent involvement in establishing Mechanics' Institutions,[6] and suggested that the new university was intended for the same clientele. It also carried broad, exaggerated warnings about the potential threat to 'Church and State' of a non-Anglican university. For good measure it hinted, despite Campbell's remarks designed to forestall such objections, that London was a place of moral danger to young men. A short article on 14 February 1825 begins the onslaught. Campbell, Brougham (whose name, pronounced 'broom', was a gift eagerly accepted by all satirists), and Birkbeck are placed firmly in the paper's sights:

> It is understood that this magnificent national establishment will speedily be undertaken, under the immediate surveillance of a learned and liberal committee. Its objects are evidently of first-rate importance, and its end will be most salutary – for instance, it is proposed to instruct butchers in geometry, and tallow-chandlers in Hebrew – tailors are to be perfected in Oriental literature, and shoemakers finished up in mathematics – servants out of livery are to be made good Grecians, while lacqueys are only to learn Latin. Campbell Fellowships (so called after the great founder) are to be created for the benefit of dustmen and chimney-sweepers; and a Brougham exhibition appropriated annually to erudite house-maids.
>
> To Dr Birkbeck the nation is already indebted for a great work of enlightenment – journeyman carpenters, and tailors, and bricklayers, and plaisterers [*sic*], now dignified into operative artisans, listen with wonder and advantage to the lecturing of popular professors.[7]

The article finishes with a 'prospectus' invented by *John Bull*, asserting that the new university will be built in Tothill Fields, a notorious slum near Westminster Abbey, and that pub owners and prostitutes will make a killing:

> The morality of London, its quietude and salubrity, appear to combine to render the Capital the most convenient place for the education of youth . . . .
>
> It is therefore intended to erect a spacious College, with proper residences and offices, for the reception of the metropolitan and suburban youth, in Tothill-fields; and in order to meet any objections

which heads of families may make to the perilous exposure of their sons
to the casualties arising from crowded streets, a large body of plain
respectable females, of the middle age, will be engaged to attend students
to and from the College in the mornings and evenings of each day.

Attacks and squibs like this became commonplace as the new university
slowly became a reality. Traditionalists feared the changes which reform
agitation inside and outside parliament sought: the removal of Catholic
disabilities, which passed into law in 1829 and which many bishops and
others viewed as putting the Church of England 'in danger', and the
enfranchisement of a proportion of working men, which came about
through the Reform Act of 1832. The fear of a working-class revolution on
the French model was also prevalent. A new university intended to open
opportunities to hitherto marginalised groups might encourage social
unrest.

Campbell and his colleagues were aware of the prejudices which would
greet their project; hence the cautious statement of their aims in the letter
to *The Times*. Campbell was a man of some fame as a writer, and though
his reputation was in decline, he was a well-known and well-connected
London literary figure when he proposed the idea for the university. He was
editor of the *New Monthly Magazine* and still residually celebrated for his
youthful poem, *The Pleasures of Hope*, published in 1799, in which he had
expressed, in trite and flowery rhyming couplets, his sympathy with political reform and in particular the anti-slavery movement. Just at the time
when Wordsworth and Coleridge were inaugurating a new Romantic
poetry with their *Lyrical Ballads* (1798), in which they experimented in both
form and subject matter, Campbell's much-reprinted poem harked back to
the pallid Miltonising of much eighteenth-century poetry, even as it exhibited impeccable reforming political views:

Primeval Hope, the Aonian Muses say,
When Man and Nature mourned their first decay;
When every form of death, and every woe,
Shot from malignant stars to earth below;
When Murder bared his arm, and rampant War
Yoked the red dragons of her iron car;
When Peace and Mercy, banished from the plain,
Sprung on the viewless winds to heaven again;
All, all forsook the friendless guilty mind,
But Hope, the charmer, lingered still behind.[8]

Much more useful to the cause of reform than this versifying was Campbell's experience as a Scot who had graduated from the University of Glasgow and saw a partial model in the Scottish system. Four long-established universities (Edinburgh, Glasgow, St Andrews, and Aberdeen) flourished; they had a proud tradition of lecturing to young men who usually lived at home, as distinct from the college tutorial system that prevailed in England. In Scottish universities there was no religious requirement in order to graduate. Several of the founders of the new metro-politan university had studied at a Scottish university, either because they were Scots or because they were Englishmen who did not subscribe to Anglicanism; Brougham was born and educated in Edinburgh, for example, while Birkbeck, the son of a Quaker merchant from Yorkshire, studied medicine at Edinburgh.

Campbell also brought to the new venture a knowledge of the German educational system, having visited Bonn in 1820 (where he was fêted as an admired poet) and been struck by the tolerance of all religions at the recently established university there. In September 1825, with the new London university plan going ahead, Campbell went on a fact-finding visit to Berlin, where he attended lectures and spoke with professors, coming away impressed by the 'encouragement given to universities' in Prussia, a country where the roads were still mainly 'sandy tracks', the carriages 'bone-shaking', and the streets of Berlin as yet unpaved, but where the universities were havens of philosophical scholarship.[9] Campbell's father had had trade connections with America and his brother was living in Richmond, Virginia; these contacts meant that he could also bring forward the example of the new University of Virginia, founded by Thomas Jefferson in 1819 with the intention of educating American youth not only in all the tradi-tional subjects, but also in medicine, modern languages, law, politics, and economics.[10]

Until the Crown and Anchor meeting of 4 June 1825, when Brougham took over as the public face of the university, Campbell was its prime mover. He was also responsible for ensuring that the institution did not become a university exclusively for Protestant dissenters and that – in the interests of openness – it did not teach theology of any kind. As the plan took shape in the spring of 1825, a number of interest groups came together to discuss how they might co-operate. Brougham, like Campbell, Birkbeck, and Joseph Hume, was an agnostic and against the teaching of religion, but he was aware of the need to secure the support, not least financially, of the often wealthy set of Presbyterians and Unitarians who were also keen to found a non-Anglican establishment. At a meeting with dissenters led by the charismatic Scottish preacher Edward Irving, Brougham and one or two others gave ground, to Campbell's disgust.

According to Campbell's account in a letter of 30 April 1825, Brougham had decided they would have to 'have a *theological* college' for dissenters, whereupon Campbell had gone to some liberal Church of England supporters of the scheme and told them this, getting a reply from them that 'either the Church of England must predominate, or else there must be no church influence'. This threat brought Brougham and others back to the original idea of avoiding religion altogether. Irving and his group withdrew their support at this juncture, while other dissenters conceded that the only way forward was to have a university 'without religious rivalship'. Campbell (somewhat prematurely, as it turned out) basked in the success of his ruse: 'You cannot conceive what anxiety I have undergone, whilst I imagined that the whole beautiful project was likely to be reduced to a mere Dissenters' University! ... *I regard this as an eventful day in my life*' [Campbell's italics].[11]

Having set things in motion in this way, Campbell soon faded from the scene. His domestic circumstances were difficult; he had a mentally unstable son and a sick wife, who died in May 1828. His election to the rectorship of Glasgow University in 1826 meant that his energies and interests were divided, and he missed the ceremony and dinner at the laying of the foundation stone of London University in Gower Street on 30 April 1827 because he was fulfilling his duties in Glasgow. The newspaper reports of the London occasion highlighted the contributions by the great orator and master of ceremonies Brougham, and when he read these Campbell felt understandably slighted.[12] Though he was a member of the first council of the university, he resigned on grounds of ill health as early as January 1828, several months before the doors were opened to students: 'I feel it a duty to my Electors to give up a situation the duties of which I can no longer perform.'[13] With that Campbell's contribution ended; in due course his name faded from the record, while his first collaborator, the phenomenon that was Henry Brougham, became the chief figure, adept alike at self-promotion and promotion of the interests of the university of which he was the first president from 1827 until his death, aged eighty-nine, in 1868.

During his long life, Henry Brougham was one of the most talked about, written about, and caricatured people of his age. In the politically fraught 1820s only George IV and the Duke of Wellington were more often the subjects of caricature and cartoon.[14] When the satirical magazine *Punch* was launched in 1841, most of Brougham's achievements were already in the past, but he was still a major if controversial public figure, a fact reflected in his appearance in almost every number of the magazine during the 1840s and 1850s. His accomplishments as a lawyer, journalist, and Whig politician were astonishing. In parliament he agitated while in opposition in the 1820s for reform of the law and the voting system, argued in favour of extending education, against slavery, for Catholic rights, and helped his own Whig government bring in the great Reform Act of 1832 after a decade's debating.

On 7 February 1828 Brougham, then still in opposition, made the longest speech ever heard in parliament, on the state of the law. The *Standard* reported that Brougham had talked for almost seven hours, during which time he 'detailed the usages and practice of all the courts of the land, high and low, alleging numerous objections to each, and suggesting remedies'.[15] In November 1830 the incoming Whig Prime Minister, Lord Grey, appointed Brougham Lord Chancellor in the parliament that brought in the Reform Act. Alongside these legal and parliamentary activities, Brougham helped Birkbeck found the London Mechanics' Institution and the Infant School Society, was the chief founder of, and writer of pamphlets for, the Society for the Diffusion of Useful Knowledge,[16] and became the prime mover of the new university. All this time, too, he was writing copious long articles for the *Edinburgh Review* and *The Times*, not to mention dealing with sexual blackmail from the notorious courtesan Harriette Wilson, to whom he gave legal advice when she was taken to court for libel after publishing her *Memoirs* (1825). She blackmailed several prominent men, including the Duke of Wellington, who is famously supposed to have replied to her threats with 'Publish and be damned'. Brougham helped her, but by having an affair with her himself he fell victim to her threats to tell his wife and the world of his 'faults of adultery and other follies'.[17] Though he spent much of his time during his long life in the committee rooms of Bloomsbury, Brougham had his residence in fashionable Mayfair.

In 'The History of University College', a speech given in 1897 by the professor of medical jurisprudence George Vivian Poore, the early days of the institution were surveyed and Brougham's contribution described:

His mind was like a dry sponge; it soaked up everything in the shape of knowledge it came across, and before he was thirteen he had learned everything they could teach him at the High School at Edinburgh. He learned languages, science, philosophy, and everything else without the least trouble ... Lord Brougham was a man of enormous industry, and was connected with the foundation of the *Edinburgh Review*, and to show you what his mind was, it may be stated that he wrote nearly the whole of one number of the *Edinburgh Review*, and that his articles ranged over a great variety of subjects, from Chinese music to the operation of Lithotomy. His versatility was astounding and it is recorded that [Samuel] Rogers, the poet, when he saw Lord Brougham driving off from Panshanger [Lord Cowper's country house] said, 'There goes Solomon, Lycurgus, Demosthenes, Archimedes, Sir Isaac Newton, Lord Chesterfield, and a great many other persons, in one post-chaise!'[18]

While Campbell brought the German and American higher education models to the university project, and made sure Isaac Lyon Goldsmid, the financier and campaigner for Jewish rights, was a founding member, Brougham brought Birkbeck and various influential dissenters, including the Revd Francis Cox, a Baptist minister of independent means, who acted as unpaid librarian to the new university in its early years, Benjamin Shaw, and the fire-breathing Presbyterian minister Edward Irving.[19] After the tussle over whether theology should be taught, some of these left. Irving in particular was bitter about his brief encounter with the project, telling his friend Thomas Carlyle in October 1825 that he had been, in Carlyle's words, 'a party in some of the conferences which the Utilitarians had carried on with the Religionists', but had 'left the concern "because religion was not cared for"'.[20] As one of the university's founders, the evangelical Zachary Macaulay, reported to a friend in January 1829, Irving and his supporters believed that the others were preparing 'to promote the reign of infidelity on the earth'.[21]

The Utilitarians on the committee, followers of Jeremy Bentham's philosophy of social usefulness and his arguments for widening education, included Bentham's closest friend and disciple James Mill, the radical politician and historian of Greece George Grote, and the Bloomsbury lawyer William Tooke, who gave his services free to the new university, acting as its solicitor from his chambers in Bedford Row.[22] Bentham himself played no direct part; he was by this time nearly eighty, and left all the active work to his younger friends. His close association with the university was consolidated after his death in 1832, when about 4,000 of his books were bequeathed to the institution, and later in 1849 when John Bowring, another disciple, donated Bentham's voluminous collection of papers. In 1850 Thomas Southwood Smith, who had presided over the dissection and preservation of Bentham's body in June 1832, passed on the skeleton, the

famous 'auto-icon' which Bentham had instructed be made of his body in
the interests of science, to University College, where it still sits, dressed in
Bentham's clothes, in a glass-fronted box.[23]

Brougham presided from the first over this heterogeneous and often ideo-
logically split group, and he did it, in the main, brilliantly. Most of the
meetings were held in his chambers in Lincoln's Inn; he regularly fed reports
of them to the press, particularly *The Times*. He also published long articles
in praise of the new university in the *Edinburgh Review* between 1825 and
1828, as did the *Review*'s rising star, Thomas Babington Macaulay, who
predicted in February 1826 that the 'infant Institution' was 'destined to a
long, a glorious, and a beneficent existence', and that it would be 'the model
of many future establishments'.[24]

Though his fame as a lawyer and party politician meant that Brougham
was much attacked in the conservative and religious press and gleefully
satirised in cartoons, such exposure did not have an entirely negative effect
on the new institution, which was thus kept constantly in the public eye.
Brougham was a skilful diplomat in a way, keeping the Jewish, Catholic,
free-thinking, and dissenting members of the body more or less together
and taking a full share in the fund-raising that had to be done to get the
university built and opened, but he was also divisive. Francis Place, a
veteran radical reformer since the 1790s and a friend of Bentham, had
offered his services in drawing up the plan to raise money for the university
by selling shares. Brougham had accepted the offer, but, according to Place,
'objected that my name if mixed up with the College might be injurious on
account of the Infidel opinions I was (he said) known to entertain'. Place
was indignant, noting that 'the council itself contained men of various
religious opinions, and some notorious free thinkers'. He concluded in a
blunt diary entry of July 1826:

> The conduct of Brougham is as usual that of a shuffling lawyer, he is
> much better known as an Infidel than I am and he is known too as
> I am not known and cannot be known to be a shuffler in Politics. I will
> challenge him to go round with me to sell shares and I dare say he will
> do it.[25]

Whether Place went round selling shares is not known, but Brougham
was famously drawn doing so as early as July 1825 by Robert Cruikshank,
brother of the more famous caricaturist George Cruikshank. The cartoon,
called 'The Political Toy-Man', shows Brougham in his lawyer's wig and
gown walking round Lincoln's Inn with a model of the 'London College'

on his head, a book at his waist entitled 'List of Share Holders' and a money bag over his arm inscribed 'Subscriptions'.[26]

The group had now turned in earnest to the matter of raising money. The plan was to amass at least £150,000, and the hope was that they would find enough 'good men and true', in Brougham's words, to take shares which would 'pay four per cent on a nominal hundred'. By October 1826 it was clear that 200 extra shares needed to be taken to reach the required amount. At this point Goldsmid and the banker John Smith took fifty supplementary shares each, and by February 1827 enough money had been acquired to start building the university.[27]

Goldsmid and Smith, together with Benjamin Shaw, were directly responsible for the new university finding its location in Bloomsbury. In November 1824 a banker named Bevan bought a site of nearly eight acres of wasteland on the Mortimer Estate at the top end of Gower Street, an undeveloped piece of what was known as the Long Fields leading north from Great Russell Street. Maps of the time show a projected square, Carmarthen Square, on the site, but this was never built, as the three wealthy founders bought the land from Bevan for £30,000 in September 1825 and held it until enough money was raised to start building.[28] When William Wilkins's neoclassical design was chosen, the die was cast for a building and a purpose which was to help define the character of the area from that moment until the present day. Bloomsbury would from now on be associated with education and culture, while visually it was represented by elegant, classical, and – some said, thinking of the 'godless college' in Gower Street – pagan architecture.

The building committee set up in 1826 consisted of Brougham, Hume, Tooke, and Lord Auckland, a Whig politician and one of a handful of reform-minded aristocrats who lent their support to the new university. The choice of Wilkins's design was an interesting one. Wilkins was a Cambridge-educated man (he had graduated as sixth wrangler – sixth best mathematical student – in 1800), who had toured the ancient Greek empire after graduation, published an account of what he saw there, and was the designer of the Greek revival building for Downing College, Cambridge, and of buildings for three other Cambridge colleges.[29] He was reconstructing East India House in London when he won the competition to design the new university on Gower Street, and was later to design the National Gallery, opened in 1838 on the north side of the new Trafalgar Square. His neoclassical buildings were much admired, though they went out of fashion – as did Georgian Bloomsbury as a whole – when the Gothic style became the rage in the 1840s and 1850s, as epitomised by Charles

Barry and Augustus Pugin's new Houses of Parliament built to replace the old ones destroyed by fire in 1834.

It was Wilkins who read the Latin oration at the foundation ceremony for his new university building on 30 April 1827.[30] As *The Times* reported, the event was a splendid one, with upwards of 2,000 people attending. There were speeches by several of the founders, and the Duke of Sussex, the only one of George III's many sons to take an interest in cultural matters, laid the first stone. At the dinner which followed in Freemasons' Hall, over 400 people heard speeches from the Duke of Sussex, the Duke of Norfolk, and finally Brougham. All went out of their way to stress that their university was not intended as an act of aggression towards Oxford and Cambridge, but rather, as the Duke of Sussex said, to 'supply a deficiency which was notoriously felt, and had been created by changes in circumstances and time since the foundation of those two great seminaries of learning', namely the lack of opportunity for dissenters and other non-Anglicans to attend an English university.[31]

Brougham's speech was the longest and most elaborate. When he stood up he was apparently greeted by 'the most vehement expressions of approbation'. According to the report in *The Times*:

> He rose, he said, in acquiescence to the command imposed upon him by the council, to return thanks to the Royal Chairman, for the kind and cordial manner in which he had been pleased to express himself towards the new University ... The task had been imposed upon him, God knew, not from any supposed peculiar fitness on his part to execute it, but from a well-grounded recollection that he was amongst the earliest and most zealous promoters of the good work they were met to celebrate.

This was Brougham's usual style of oratory: rhetorically pseudo-humble but at the same time nakedly self-advertising. No wonder Campbell, away in Glasgow, felt unfairly eclipsed when he heard about the event. Campbell's friend and biographer Cyrus Redding remembered that at one of the early meetings in the London Tavern, Brougham, 'as usual, a lion at such meetings', had come in late. 'There is a policy in this sort of conduct', wrote Redding; 'it raises and fixes expectation. He began by an allusion, often had recourse to in his own case, to his having been unexpectedly detained in another place by most important business'.[32] Brougham's contemporaries were frequently moved to express their astonishment at his attainments and simultaneously their dislike of his stratagems. One seasoned Brougham-watcher, his erstwhile friend and political ally Thomas Creevey, had been struck when they stood together for parliamentary seats in Liverpool in October 1812 by 'the endless mine of his intellectual resources' and by his popularity as a public speaker. 'I have been perfectly amazed during this campaign', he wrote, 'at the marvellous talent of Brougham in his addresses to the people'. His 'volley of declamation shook the very square and all the houses in it from the applause it met with'. Yet Creevey could not like his colleague, suspecting that there was 'always some game or underplot out of sight'.[33] For all Brougham's game-playing, the effects of his dazzling eloquence were more positive than negative when his contribution to the verbal 'selling' of the new university is weighed. Just as in parliament and courtroom, in the university meetings he carried all before him.

Wilkins was assisted in the task of raising an edifice worthy of Brougham's ambitions for it by the architect whose plans came second to his in the competition, John Gandy. The chosen builder was Henry Lee, who made the lowest tender for the work, £107,767. The plan was for a long building facing Gower Street with a ten-column Corinthian portico in the middle, topped by a dome, and for two side wings, with smaller domes in the angles between the long building and the wings.[34] When submitting his design, Wilkins stressed its grandeur and unusualness, features which were no doubt attractive to the founders: 'There is no example in England of a portico with ten columns in front. It is for this reason that I have chosen as my prototype the magnificent Portico of the Olympeum at Athens, the proportions of which I have closely followed.'[35]

The Times reported in August 1828 that the building was nearing completion, with scaffolding due to come down before the opening of the establishment in two months' time, when 'the public will have an uninter-rupted view of a handsome and commodious structure, – no gaudy affecta-tion of ornament, or incongruous embellishment, defects which disfigure so many of the public buildings of the metropolis, but a chaste and truly classic specimen of Grecian architecture'.[36]

In the event, there was not enough money to complete Wilkins's elegant plan, and the two wings were not built until the 1870s. This gave the building a slightly disproportionate look, as commentators noted. James Fergusson in his *History of the Modern Styles of Architecture* (1862) praised the portico as Wilkins's masterpiece and the best such feature in the whole of British architecture, but regretted that the lack of wings meant the porch was 'too large for the building to which it is attached'.[37] When a building fund to add the wings was started by a £1,000 donation from Samuel Sharpe, a wealthy Unitarian who joined the council of University College in 1866, the designer, the professor of architecture Hayter Lewis, was careful to complete the building in the proportions set down by Wilkins.[38]

Even in its unfinished state the new building was imposing, but the fact that it was on wasteland where rubbish was dumped and dirty puddles abounded was too delightful a gift for opponents to ignore. *John Bull* repeatedly represented the new university as a disreputable business. The paper was edited and written by Theodore Hook, a Bloomsbury-born prankster and man-about-town (in July 1825 he had only recently left debtors' prison after 'losing' £12,000 of government money while occupying the post of accountant and treasurer in Mauritius[39]). On 4 July 1825 there appeared an article entitled 'Joint Stock Cockney Learning Company, Capital £300,000'. Hook pretended to be horrified at the supposed political and religious subversiveness of the new institution, and cleverly coupled this with the mania at the time for the floating of companies dealing in insurance, gas, mining, canals, and the new steam technology.[40] The implication was that there was something dodgy about selling shares in the university, and that the risk of collapse was great.

Even more of a gift was the foul-smelling site. In December 1825 a comic poem called 'Stinkomalee' was printed in *John Bull*. To be sung to the tune of 'Derry Down', it began:

> 'The *fiat* is issued', says REASON to FAME,
> 'My College in Gower-street at length has a name.
> Go trumpet it forth both by land and by sea,
> My College is christen'd, Ma'am, Stinkomalee!'

Hook subsequently has Joseph Hume congratulating his fellow founder Brougham:

> 'The choice of its site', says HUME, 'properly falls,
> To cultivate strong common sense in its halls,
> For whoever will come, will find, my dear B,
> Very STRONG COMMON SCENTS in your STINKOMALEE!'[41]

On went *John Bull* relentlessly; another poem, 'Stinkomalee Triumphans', greeted the soon-to-be-opened university in April 1828, followed in May by an article describing Brougham and his colleagues as 'shareholders in the joint-stock dirt and learning company of STINKOMALEE', and so on.[42] Others took up the cry. The *Age*, an even more scandal-mongering Tory newspaper than *John Bull*, indulged in some unsubtle anti-Jewish and anti-

Scottish jibes, reporting in May 1828 that the radical proprietors of 'TOM CAMPBELL's University of Stinkomalee' were 'dipping their pincers-shaped fingers into a money-bag' with the result that 'some of the contents very naturally disappear, in a fashion that would do credit to BILL SOAMES, or IKEY SOLOMONS' (the latter a Jewish fence on whom Dickens was to model Fagin in *Oliver Twist*). In a swipe at the Utilitarian philosophers, among them the Scots Joseph Hume and James Mill, the article continues: 'money, money, money, is the perpetual cry of the "feelosophers"'.[43]

The nickname 'Stinkomalee' stuck for a time, as did others started by *John Bull*, such as Cockney College or Cockney University, which also appeared in the titles of cartoons such as William Heath's engraving published in February 1826, showing Brougham hammering on an anvil inscribed 'Public Support' with a red-hot iron bar named 'Philosophy'.[44] The most imaginative poem attacking the university was that by Winthrop Mackworth Praed, a young Tory and old Etonian, born in 1802 in Bedford Row, the elegant wide Bloomsbury street which was then, as now, filled with lawyers' chambers. His 'Discourse Delivered by a College Tutor at a Supper Party, July 1, 1825' imagines the response by an Oxbridge don to the news of a new rival. Having urged his colleagues to 'make opposition' to the 'radical infidel College', the don continues with an awful warning of social revolution:

Tis a terrible crisis for CAM and for ISIS;
Fat butchers are learning dissection;
And looking-glass makers become sabbath-breakers
To study the rules of reflection.[45]

A future political star, the young Bloomsbury resident Benjamin Disraeli, also had fun with the planned university in his first novel, *Vivian Grey*, the first part of which was published in April 1826. Disraeli had been born in 1804 in King's Road, just off Bedford Row; his father, the antiquarian scholar Isaac D'Israeli, moved the family to Bloomsbury Square in 1817 to be even nearer the British Museum for his studies, and, being a non-observant Jew with ambitions for his son, attended church at St George's Bloomsbury, where Benjamin was baptised in the same year. Disraeli did not go to university; he was a solicitor's clerk from 1821 to 1824, and entered Lincoln's Inn, but refused a legal career, preferring to travel about Europe before attempting to gain a foothold as a journalist and writer. Though a Tory, Disraeli aimed his satire in the anonymously published

Vivian Grey at both real-life radicals and dyed-in-the-wool Tories. One of
the latter, given the name Sir Christopher Mowbray in the novel, is a
county member of parliament in his seventy-ninth year but still able to
'follow a fox', though he has 'no idea of "liberal principles", or anything else
of that school'. Disraeli mocks his horror at the idea of a modern university
in London:

> The only thing which he does not exactly comprehend, is the London
> University. This affair really puzzles the worthy gentleman, who could
> as easily fancy a county member not being a freeholder, as an University
> not being at Oxford or Cambridge. Indeed, to this hour the old
> gentleman believes that the whole business is 'a damnational hoax'; and
> if you tell him, that . . . there is little apprehension, that in the course of
> a century, the wooden poles which are now stuck about the ground, will
> not be as fair, and flourishing, as the most leafy bowers of New College
> gardens, the old gentleman looks up to heaven, as if determined not to
> be taken in, and leaning back in his chair, sends forth a sceptical and
> smiling 'No! no! no! that won't do.'[46]

Against virulent opposition from the real Sir Christopher Mowbrays,
compounded by lack of funds and some poor decision-making in its early
days, the new university did emphatically 'do'. Though it took several
decades of dogged determination on the part of its supporters and employees,
the university eventually fulfilled Macaulay's apparently outlandish prophecy
that it would set the standard for the universities of the future.

A council of twenty-four was elected in December 1825 to undertake the
great educational project; committees were chosen to deal with finance,
building, and education, and they reported back to council. It was hoped
that, with London now a city of nearly two million souls, at least a thousand
students would present themselves, but this proved wildly optimistic.
According to the institution's first annual report in February 1829, a total
of 557 students were following courses, 269 in 'general education', 123 in
law, and 165 in medicine. In February 1832 it was noted that numbers had
dropped to 400 – about the same number as attended the University of
Cambridge and a quarter of those studying at Edinburgh[47] – and the
university faced the possibility that it might have to close as a heroic failure.
Its saviour was the opening of a junior school in 1830, which attracted
healthy numbers and so rescued the parent institution, but the university
did not reach the desired 1,000 until the turn of the twentieth century, by

which time it had admitted women, who accounted for 397 of the 1,098 registered in 1900–1.[48]

There were several reasons for the difficulties the new university encountered in attracting students, chief among them the inability until 1836 to confer degrees. There was also suspicion, fuelled by the press, of the institution's political and religious radicalism, and, crucially, some of the very groups for which the university was intended proved unresponsive. In a rare moment of public pessimism, Brougham was reported to have said at a dinner celebrating the Orphan Working Asylum in May 1835 that

> no plan in which he had ever been engaged *had caused him so much mortification as the failure (he might call it) of the University of London.* There were several most eminent professors in every department of literature and science employed in the University; but the truth was, that the people of London were so aristocratically inclined, that they would rather starve themselves to pay £250 to send their sons to Oxford or Cambridge, where they might associate with the sons of Lords and Bishops, than pay £10 per annum to the University of London, where they might receive an education quite as complete and extensive.[49]

Such temporary bitterness may be explained in part by the fact that Brougham was at this time in a depressed state because of his removal as Lord Chancellor in 1834 and ostracism by his own party for his inconsistency and recklessness in parliament,[50] but the disappointing numbers do suggest that some such reluctance out of snobbishness and suspicion was operating among London's middle class. Brougham also expressed disappointment in the religious dissenters who could have done more to support the institution both by taking more subscriptions at the beginning and by sending their sons to study there during its first years.[51]

The financial troubles of the university were exacerbated by some poor early decisions by the council under Brougham's chairmanship. Professors, without the offer of richly endowed chairs, would be paid from student fees, and any surplus would go to the university. As it was realised that at first there might not be enough students to make this possible, especially in new subjects, the plan was to guarantee a salary of £250 or £300 a year for the first two years.[52] This hardly sufficed for many of the first appointees; only those with an outside income, such as medical or law professors with a lucrative private practice, or bachelors without families, could manage on such a small salary. Things got worse for a while. The Annual Report of

February 1831 showed that the arrears due from shareholders amounted to £6,570. And student numbers after the first two years did not bring enough money in fees to pay the professors, who actually took a pay cut in the university's most difficult years, 1830–32.[53] Matters soon came to a head between the first cohort of professors and the man brought in to head the establishment, Leonard Horner, who was appointed Warden in May 1827 on a staggering salary of £1,000 a year plus a rent allowance of £200 for the house at 12 Upper Gower Street which the council acquired for him in June 1827.[54] (No. 12 Upper Gower Street was to be Charles Darwin's first married home from January 1839 to September 1842. He knew Horner from Edinburgh, where he had also met, and been taught by, Robert Grant, Gower Street's first professor of comparative anatomy and zoology. But Darwin, though living side by side with the new university, appears not to have mingled with his fellow scientists in Gower Street. He disliked London, living a life 'of extreme quietness', as he told a friend, having 'given up all parties' soon after his marriage. Within three years he had moved to Down House in Kent, where he pursued his researches away from the competitive scientific world of London.[55])

Horner, born and educated in Edinburgh, was an old friend and colleague of Brougham, Mill, Birkbeck, and other Edinburgh-educated men associated with the new college. He had some experience of starting an educational establishment, having founded the Edinburgh School of Arts in 1821 and promoted the new Edinburgh Academy in 1823–24, but his appointment as Warden was a disaster. He took his job seriously enough, but expected to have more power than the council allowed him; he was really a kind of glorified message-boy between the hard-worked, underpaid, and soon disgruntled professoriat and the aloof, dictatorial council. His way of dealing with the professors was high-handed. As far as they were concerned, Horner was 'merely the medium of communication between them and the Council',[56] while he thought he stood in authority over them.

One professor, the brilliant young mathematician Augustus De Morgan, complained in 1831 to his friend and later father-in-law William Frend that to the council and proprietors of the University of London a professor 'is on the same footing with regard to them as a domestic servant to his master, with, however, the disadvantage of the former not being able to demand a month's wages or a month's warning'.[57] And those wages were a sore point. The annual receipts for the university for the year 1829–30 illustrate the absurd mismatch between the relative salaries paid to Horner and to the professors. The guaranteed salaries to the professors – about twenty of them – amounted to a total of £2,949 19s. 8d. for the year, just under three times the amount being earned by Horner.[58] After a series of disputes Horner left in July 1831, to the relief of both the professors and the council, who did not replace him, thus saving £1,200 a year which they had been ill able to afford.

The business had begun with high hopes. When the university advertised the first chairs in twenty-four subjects at the end of 1826, with a closing date of May 1827, there were plenty of applications from distinguished scholars, and many more from very young men who would soon become distinguished in their fields. In February 1827 some good people applied, including Roget for physiology, John Conolly for the nature and treatment of diseases, Hyman Hurwitz for Hebrew, the distinguished, if elderly, orientalist John Borthwick Gilchrist for Hindustani, Antonio Panizzi for Roman law, and Anthony Todd Thomson for materia medica, the branch of medicine concerned with remedies and prescriptions.[59] This first batch of applicants illustrates the unusual range of expertise, nationality, politics, and religion available to the new institution, making it truly distinct from Oxford and Cambridge.

Two of them, Gilchrist and Thomson, were among the large number of Scots associated with the new university. Both, along with Conolly and Roget, had graduated in medicine at Edinburgh, Gilchrist in 1774, and Thomson, a contemporary of Brougham, in 1797. Gilchrist had been an assistant surgeon with the Royal Navy in India, staying on to learn Hindustani and to write a grammar and dictionary of the language, before returning to Edinburgh, where he became an enthusiastic supporter of Bentham's educational and political views. In 1816 he left for London to give private language tuition to young men destined for careers in India. He supported Birkbeck's Mechanics' Institution, and in 1827 he wrote to the council of the new university 'offering his gratuitous services in forming classes of Oriental Literature'.[60] He did not stay long, being already nearly seventy and in poor health; he was reported to be absent through sickness only three weeks into the first teaching term, and soon resigned, to be replaced by a young German polymath, Friedrich Rosen.[61] Anthony Todd Thomson had moved to London soon after graduating at Edinburgh. He was a member of various learned societies and a successful practitioner, retiring in 1826 when his practice was worth £3,000 a year; he was also a prolific author on medical subjects for the *Lancet* and other medical journals. His book on materia medica, published in 1832, was highly regarded, but his lectures at the university were pompous, according to his students.[62]

Another medical colleague, John Conolly, had started a general practice in Stratford-upon-Avon in the early 1820s, where he took a special interest in insanity and became an inspector of the lunatic asylums of Warwickshire.

Through his friendship with Brougham and Birkbeck, and his co-operation with them in writing educational treatises for the Society for the Diffusion of Useful Knowledge, he was encouraged to apply for a medical post at the new university. The outline of Conolly's course in the nature and treatment of diseases, written for the university to publish in advance of its opening, shows his inclination to progressiveness. He promises to use drawings, models, and even 'preparations of morbid parts' to illustrate his lectures; the students will have access to 'instructive examples' in the university's dispensary, and he will subject common assumptions and diagnoses to sceptical questioning. The 'supposed effects of some medicines, which are customarily and implicitly prescribed', will be 'freely questioned'.[63]

Things started well, but Conolly resented the interference of the apothecary at the university's dispensary, and he found that so much of his time was being taken up by the institution, which paid him very little, that he could not supplement his income sufficiently by carrying on his private practice. He therefore left at the end of session 1830–1, moving back to Warwickshire before taking on the post of Superintendent of the Hanwell asylum in Middlesex, where he pioneered the humane treatment of patients, removing chains and straitjackets and substituting kindness and persuasion. Conolly kept up his connection with University College, writing to the secretary from Hanwell in 1847 to agree to the request that some of the students be allowed to visit the asylum to observe his methods. 'It would of course gratify me', he wrote, 'to show in any way the particular interest I take in any thing relating to the Medical School of University College.'[64]

One applicant who mysteriously withdrew before his application could be considered was Roget. In 1827 he was a well-known figure in London's medical and scientific circles; a fellow of the Royal Society since 1815, he became its secretary in November 1827. The son of Jean Roget, a Swiss clergyman and pastor of the French Protestant church in Threadneedle Street until his early death in 1783, Roget had studied medicine at Edinburgh University, graduating in 1798. His education was paid for by his mother's brother, the great law reformer and radical MP Sir Samuel Romilly, through whom Roget met Bentham in 1800, working with him on inventing a 'frigidarium' to preserve food.

Roget lived in Bloomsbury all his adult life, first lodging briefly in airy Great Russell Street, then from 1809 in Bernard Street, recently built to link the newly constructed Russell Square with Brunswick Square to the east and named after Sir Thomas Bernard, a philanthropic lawyer and treasurer of the Foundling Hospital. Finally, from 1843 Roget lived in Upper Bedford Place (now Bedford Way), a wide street leading north from

Russell Square to Tavistock Square. He was a leading figure in the tragedy which befell Romilly in the latter's house in Russell Square. Romilly's wife had died of cancer after a long illness on 29 October 1818; Romilly was known to be suicidal, and Roget was his chief medical attendant. Having sat up with his uncle all night on 1 November, Roget was replaced by Romilly's teenage daughter Sophie.[65] Romilly persuaded her to leave the room, and in her absence he slit his throat. Roget was so distraught that he was unable to attend the inquest, which was held on 3 November at the Colonnade pub in Roget's own street, Bernard Street. *The Times* reported the proceedings in full.[66]

When he applied for the post of professor of physiology at London University early in 1827, Roget was a member of a great many scientific societies, including the Royal Medical and Chirurgical Society (founded in 1805), the Geological Society of London (1807), the Royal Astronomical Society (1820), and the Zoological Society (1826). Having known Brougham, Birkbeck, and Horner since his student days in Edinburgh, he was naturally an early recruit to the Society for the Diffusion of Useful Knowledge in 1826, and he was a regular lecturer on scientific subjects at the Royal Institution, the London Institution, and, close to his home, the Russell Institution on Great Coram Street.[67] In 1824 he had made a discovery predictive of the later innovation of moving pictures when observing the traffic through a venetian blind in his basement kitchen in Bernard Street. He described, in a paper read to the Royal Society in December 1824, 'Explanation of an Optical Deception in the Appearance of the Spokes of a Wheel Seen through Vertical Apertures', how the slats of the blind acted like frames, breaking up the motion of the wheels of a carriage passing his window. His observations were taken up by Michael Faraday and others, who created disc mechanisms to give the illusion of motion. All this time Roget was also working as the senior physician to the Northern Dispensary to the north of the New Road (now Euston Road), giving his services free.[68]

As a leading innovator in his field, Roget was an ideal candidate for a chair at the new university. The council, however, having noted his early candidature in February 1827, recorded in July that he had withdrawn his application; no reason was reported.[69] He did later become a member of the Senate of the University of London as newly constituted and chartered in 1836 when the original university took the name University College London, and examined in comparative anatomy and physiology from 1839 to 1842.[70]

Another of the earliest candidates, Hyman Hurwitz, was appointed to the chair of Hebrew. His application was accompanied by a reference from his illustrious Highgate neighbour, Samuel Taylor Coleridge, who knew of his academy for Jewish boys there. Coleridge's testimonial was noted by council on 17 February, but Hurwitz's appointment was not made until January 1828.[71] The council minutes are silent about the delay, but a letter from Campbell to his fellow council member Lord Auckland expresses a fear that Hurwitz might try to proselytise for Judaism. He was the author in 1820 of a work, written in answer to a fellow scholar, called *Vindiciae Hebraicae: or, a Defence of the Hebrew Scriptures, as a Vehicle of Revealed Religion*, and Campbell was understandably anxious, though he knew that Isaac Goldsmid, the most generous of the new university's backers, was keen to have Hurwitz appointed. He told Auckland:

> I regret that this matter has some relation & a delicate one to our excellent friend Goldsmith [*sic*] to whom the scheme is so deeply indebted – I am glad that he – of Jewish faith [–] is of our Council – & I should be very glad to waive my recommendation of my own Hebrew Master in Germany for the mere sake of obliging Mr Goldsmid as I believe Hurwitz to be as good a teacher as we need – But [I] query what will the world say to a Jew expounding the scriptures – Woe betide that poor Jew if he makes one remark that [a] Christian bigot can pick a quarrel with & it is a desperate trammel on a teacher of Hebrew when he cannot give free opinions about the history of the Hebrew language & its books.[72]

Hurwitz was eventually appointed, but he was not even paid the guaranteed mimimum salary of £250; none of the first language professors were, as they were expected to make up their salaries by teaching private pupils.[73] Poor Hurwitz, who had hardly any students the whole time he was a professor, from 1828 until his death in 1844, wrote to the council in January 1829 asking for financial aid to get him through the year. Council grudgingly voted him £100.[74]

The last of the initial batch of applicants was Antonio Panizzi, who applied to teach Roman law. He was appointed to a professorship, though not until February 1828 and not in Roman law but in Italian language and literature. A forceful figure, he had arrived in London a penniless political exile in May 1823 while a court case was carried on against him in his home duchy of Modena for the capital crime of belonging to a secret society. Many of his comrades in the struggle for Italy's liberty and unification were murdered or executed, and in October 1823, in his absence, he too was condemned to death. Sentence was pronounced on 'the contumacious doctor of law,

Antonio Panizzi, to the penalty of death, to be duly carried out in effigy, to the confiscation of all his goods, and to bear the cost of his trial and execution'.[75] By this time Panizzi was giving Italian lessons in Liverpool, from where he wrote a few months later to 'the Inspector of Finances and Tax-gatherer of the Province of Reggio', who had billed him for the court expenses, including the fees of the hangman. For the purposes of Panizzi's letter, Liverpool became the 'Realm of Death, Elysian Fields'; he signed himself 'the soul of A. Panizzi', after cordially wishing his correspondent 'a death such as mine'.[76]

When Panizzi had first arrived in London, he was welcomed by a group of Italian exiles, including the poet Ugo Foscolo, who lived in a cottage in Regent's Park, where he gave temporary refuge to new arrivals and introduced them to the many British friends of Italy with whom he consorted, including Thomas Campbell.[77] Several of them lived precariously, taking pupils where they could; there being no room for yet another language tutor in London, Panizzi went to Liverpool with a letter of recommendation from Campbell to William Roscoe, a Liverpool banker and literary scholar. Campbell wrote on 5 July 1823:

> My dear Roscoe, Will you permit me to request you to interest yourself, if you can without inconvenience, in the gentleman who will deliver this to you. He is a Mr Panizzi, an exile (on account of his patriotism) from Modena. From your attachment to the cause of liberty I thought I might reckon on you … Mr Panizzi was a barrister in Modena and left his country in consequence of the persecutions that spring out of the Piedmontese insurrection. He has written a spirited treatise on the conduct of the Duke of Modena. He proposes to teach Italian in Liverpool – if he can find any pupils – a most requisite condition no doubt.[78]

With the help of Roscoe and others, Panizzi managed to get some teaching in and around Liverpool. By a piece of luck, he came to Brougham's attention in 1827 when he accompanied the latter to a celebrated trial at Lancaster, where Brougham was one of the prosecuting team. Panizzi was connected to the affair by being the tutor of the teenage Ellen Turner, daughter of a millionaire, who was abducted in March 1826 by Edward Gibbon Wakefield (future coloniser of New Zealand) and taken to Gretna Green, where she was tricked into marrying him.[79]

Both Brougham and Campbell encouraged Panizzi to apply for the chair of Italian at the new university; he was appointed in preference to a number of other Italian exiles who were also friends of Campbell – Foscolo himself (though he was ill and withdrew), Giuseppe Pecchio, and Gabriele Rossetti, father of Christina, William Michael, and Dante Gabriel Rossetti.[80] The chair of Roman law, for which Panizzi had initially applied, was not offered him; a fellow exile, Gaetano De Marchi, was asked by Horner if Panizzi's spoken English was good enough for that post, and replied diplomatically that he had not seen Panizzi for two years and so could not be certain.[81] The council delayed over the Italian appointment, as it did on all the modern language chairs, for which applications were flowing in, from Frenchmen and Germans in particular. The problem was partly money – how much could and should the council pay such men? – and partly an uncertainty about what they would be expected to teach other than the languages themselves, and whether it was appropriate to give a professorship to any of the legions of mere language tutors who applied.[82]

Panizzi himself was clear that he wanted to profess his subject to a standard well beyond mere linguistic competence. He visited Horner in London in February 1828 to find out what was expected; in his forthright way he told Horner that he did not want to teach elementary Italian himself but should have an assistant for that part of the job, and with the supreme confidence he was to show when he later made his way through the ranks at the British Museum to the top position of librarian, he set out for Horner his views on how modern languages and their literatures should be taught.[83] He was told firmly but politely that he would have to teach the language himself, and was formally appointed by council on 16 February.[84]

Even Panizzi, with all his flamboyance and force of personality and with the promising fact that there was a lively interest in Italian patriots among the London literati, failed to make enough from his post at the university, the number of his students in the first few years peaking at eight.[85] In April 1831 he was appointed as an assistant librarian at the British Museum, thanks largely to Brougham's influence – as Lord Chancellor at the time Brougham was *ex officio* one of the three principal trustees of the Museum.[86] Panizzi continued in both posts, though nearly all his time was spent in Great Russell Street rather than Gower Street. On his promotion in 1837 to Keeper of the Printed Books at the Museum, he resigned his professorship. He had used his librarianship experience to draw up a scheme for a catalogue of the university's embryonic library at the request of its library committee in October 1833. He also wrote two books for the use of students, one an elementary grammar, the other consisting of extracts from Italian prose writers, which were brought out in 1828 by the university's publisher, John Taylor of 30 Upper Gower Street.[87]

These early achievements notwithstanding, Panizzi's considerable contribution to British cultural life was to come mainly during his long stint at
the British Museum.[88] He was from now on a formidable figure about the
streets of Bloomsbury, where he lived until his death in 1879, first in rooms
at 2 Upper Gower Street, then from 1837 in a staff flat inside the British
Museum, and on his retirement from October 1865 in a house 'in a very
unfashionable quarter, though very respectable, near here, being 31,
Bloomsbury Square', as he wrote to a friend at the time.[89] Panizzi attracted
controversy throughout his long life. In his early days at the university, he
wrote an adverse criticism in the *Foreign Review* of an edition of Dante by
one of his rivals for the chair, Gabriele Rossetti (who was appointed to the
chair of Italian at the new King's College London when it opened in
October 1831). Rossetti responded in an unpublished poem in which he
satirised 'il gran Panizzi' as superior to the 'great Malagigi', the magician of
Ariosto's *Orlando Furioso* and other Italian romances.[90] Rossetti soon had
to watch as Panizzi became a great man in his adopted country, performing
feats of reform among the reluctant bureaucrats of the British Museum.

Another remarkable foreigner who took up a language chair at the
university and was simultaneously employed by the British Museum was
Friedrich Rosen, who, like Panizzi, soon anglicised his Christian name.
Much more would have been heard of Frederick Rosen if he had not died
a few days after his thirty-second birthday in September 1837. A precocious
philological scholar and student of Sanskrit who attended lectures in
Leipzig and Berlin before going to Paris to study Semitic languages, he was
invited in February 1828 to come to London for an interview at the university, and was appointed to the chair of Sanskrit (soon renamed oriental
literature).[91] Like all the language professors, he was paid less than £250 a
year; he suffered financial hardship, especially after the council's mean-
minded decision in November 1829 to give the language professors no
guaranteed salary after the current session.[92] So concerned was Joseph
Hume at this treatment that he wrote to his fellow proprietor and council
member James Loch urging him to use his influence to ensure that Rosen,
'the most celebrated man on the Continent' for 'the joint knowledge of
Sanscrit, Arabic & Persian', but with too few students in Gower Street to
support him financially, would be offered a salary by the East India
Company in return for teaching its students.[93]

In the event, council agreed that Rosen be given a salary of £150 for the
session in addition to his proportion of 'the fees he may receive from his
pupils'.[94] Rosen, still only in his early twenties, seems to have been the most
generous and upright of men, as well as being a linguistic genius. At the

request of the education committee in November 1828 he had learned Hindustani in order to replace the ailing and absent Gilchrist in teaching it; a few months earlier he had offered to teach Latin after the sudden resignation before the beginning of the opening term of the Latin professor, the Revd John Williams, and in October 1830 he stepped in to replace his friend and fellow German, Ludwig von Mühlenfels, who asked for temporary leave of absence from his German post.[95]

Rosen stuck to his task on his meagre salary until the summer of 1831, when he resigned, along with some other professors, in protest at the dismissal for incompetence of the professor of anatomy, Granville Sharp Pattison. Rosen survived, just, writing for the publications of the Society for the Diffusion of Useful Knowledge and taking a few pupils, then accepted the invitation to return to the chair of oriental languages in 1834. In the same year he was appointed to the British Museum to help revise the Museum's catalogue of Syrian manuscripts at a salary of one pound 'for one day's service in each week'. In April 1835 the trustees asked him to increase his time to three days a week.[96] When the catalogue was finally completed in 1839, nearly two years after his untimely death, thought by his biographers to have resulted from overwork and a subsistence diet,[97] the Museum sent a complimentary copy to Rosen's father, and soon after that the sculptor Richard Westmacott the Younger was engaged to make a marble bust of Rosen for display in the British Museum, where it remains.[98]

Of the other language professors, Antonio Alcalá Galiano and von Mühlenfels were both political refugees like Panizzi; neither stayed in Britain for very long, but both were interesting. Galiano was appointed to the chair of Spanish in February 1828, having been encouraged to do so by a young Bloomsbury woman, Jane Griffin, who would gain fame as the widow of the Arctic explorer Sir John Franklin when she organised several voyages in search of her lost husband after his departure to find the Northwest Passage in 1845. Jane married Franklin in 1828, after an unsatisfactory on–off flirtation with Roget a decade earlier.[99] Jane's father had invited Galiano to his home in Bedford Place to give Jane Spanish lessons in 1827; the following year he recommended Galiano, who lived in Marchmont Street, off Tavistock Place, for admission as a reader to the British Museum Reading Room.[100] Jane described him in her diary:

> He is little, dark, mysterious looking, very heavy or swol[le]n eyelids & dreadfully near-sighted – speaks & writes English well – he was in England 13 y[ea]rs ago – & was a member of the late Cortes – he has now been twice condemned to death.[101]

Encouraged by the outbreak of revolution in Paris in 1830, and with few students to keep him in London, Galiano resigned from the university in July of that year.[102] He was not replaced. By 1865 he was Minister of the Interior in Madrid, where Jane, now Franklin's widow, met him again days before he died suddenly of a seizure.[103]

Von Mühlenfels, too, was a political exile. The chair of German was offered him in May 1828, when he came to London from Sweden, having escaped there in 1821 after twenty-three months in prison in Germany for alleged revolutionary activities. He had been a student leader in Heidelberg, and retained his liberal sympathies after being appointed to an official legal post in Cologne in 1817. In Sweden he lived quietly, by his own account, teaching and attempting to gain permission to return to his homeland and resume his position. Meanwhile he took the chair in London, gave lectures on German literature, and wrote articles for the *Foreign Review*, all the time hoping to return, pardoned, to Germany.[104] His reason for asking the university authorities for leave of absence in the autumn of 1830, when Rosen did his teaching for him, was that he needed to go to Germany to negotiate his official pardon. He finally succeeded in being reinstated in 1831; Rosen told council on his behalf in July 1831 that he was resigning the chair of German.[105] Unlike the Spanish professorship, the German post was filled, but for several years only by language tutors. The French chair, too, was held as a purely language post for many years by P.F. Merlet, who also taught at the university's school.[106]

Though some of the foreign appointees to chairs stayed only a short time in Gower Street, teaching pitifully small numbers of students, their very presence on the staff of an English university was an indication of the boldness of the founders. The picturesque heterogeneity of the men who staffed the cockney college in its earliest years could not have been more different from the exclusively Anglican and largely clerical personnel of the ancient universities, even allowing for the individual eccentricities to be found in any body of professors.

When it came to appointing professors, the council had to face once more the problem of what to do about religion. It had been agreed after some divided opinion that theology would not be taught, but what about the propriety of appointing a clergyman to any of the chairs? After all, the pool of applicants was bound to include a number of men who had taken orders; some might be practising clergymen with a scholarly interest, while others would be schoolmasters or fellows of Oxbridge colleges. Many of those who did apply for posts were Anglican clergymen; others were Baptist, Presbyterian, or Unitarian ministers.

The university was facing the classic dilemma of a liberal institution: would it demonstrate more religious tolerance if it ruled out clergymen of whatever sect, thus demonstrating a negative egalitarianism, or if it judged solely on intellectual grounds, turning a blind eye to the title 'Reverend', whether Anglican or otherwise? An area of particular sensitivity was philosophy, which contained within it questions not only of morality but also of belief. Could a clergyman take an impartial view when teaching this subject? It was over the chair of philosophy that the university experienced its first protests and resignations.

At an education committee meeting on 22 May 1827, attended by Brougham, Mill, Grote, and Birkbeck, applications were noted for the two philosophical chairs it was proposed to fill, logic and philosophy of mind, and moral and political philosophy. The Revd John Hoppus had applied for the first and the medical doctor and sanitary reformer Thomas Southwood Smith for the second. Hoppus was a dissenting minister who had studied at Edinburgh and Glasgow and had resigned from his chapel in London over doctrinal differences with his congregation. In 1827 he wrote an account of Francis Bacon's philosophy for the Society for the Diffusion of Useful Knowledge; to make ends meet he took private pupils in the classics. Grote opposed his candidacy for the chair on the grounds that no minister of religion should be appointed. Meanwhile Southwood Smith's appointment, backed by the Benthamites, was blocked by Zachary Macaulay, who as an evangelical Christian was appalled by Smith's known heterodoxy. Smith had been a Unitarian preacher in Edinburgh, where he took a medical degree in 1816, was physician to the London Fever Hospital at Battle Bridge (later the site of King's Cross Station), and was to be a prominent campaigner for sanitary reform, as well as presiding over the dissection of his mentor Bentham's body in 1832. The upshot was that neither philosophy post was filled before the university opened its doors in October 1828.[107]

In November 1829 the education committee recommended to council that Hoppus be given the chair of logic and the philosophy of mind. He was duly appointed, but Grote, feeling betrayed by his allies Brougham and Mill, resigned his seat on council on 2 February 1830.[108] This was the university's first loss on a matter of principle. Grote resumed his position on council in 1849 and was to become the university's second president in 1868 on the death of Brougham. In 1866 he ensured that another independent clergyman, the country's foremost Unitarian preacher James Martineau, did not succeed Hoppus in the philosophical chair.[109]

As luck would have it, Hoppus held on to the chair from 1830 to 1866, attracting few students and not impressing those few. Edward Fry, judge and father of the artist and Bloomsbury Group member Roger Fry, had studied law at University College London from 1848; he remembered taking philosophy classes with Hoppus, who had 'considerable learning and sound sense rather than great brilliance'.[110] Another former student, J.B. Benson, was even more damning. According to him, Hoppus used to walk into the lecture hall with lecture notes in his hand and a newspaper under his arm. 'After his first or second lecture he seldom had a pupil; because, burying his face in his manuscript, he mumbled so that only an acute ear could catch much of what he said.' Hoppus was more often to be found reading his newspaper in a completely empty room than lecturing, though he was conscientious and 'always sat out his hour'.[111]

The philosophy chair was not the only example of dissension caused by religious differences. Council, in a bid for openness, had appointed to its early chairs not only an Independent minister, Hoppus, but also no fewer than three Church of England clergymen. The three caused the university a great deal of trouble, starting with a plan which they managed to pass through a council keen to avoid bad relations with Oxbridge and the Church of England, reeling from the volume of vocal opposition in anti-reform newspapers, and fearful that bad publicity would mean too few fee-paying students. The professors' idea was to offer theological lectures on a voluntary basis to students whose parents felt anxious about the lack of such teaching, and to open an Anglican place of worship for any students who might wish to take advantage of the opportunity. An uneasy council permitted them to go ahead on the understanding that any advertisements they placed would make it clear that these activities, though sanctioned by the university, had nothing to do with its formal structure or syllabus, and also that a place of worship must be found outside the buildings and grounds owned by the university.[112]

The three professors were the Reverends Dionysius Lardner, appointed to the chair of natural philosophy and astronomy in July 1827, John Williams, appointed professor of Roman language and literature in November 1827, and Thomas Dale, appointed to the chair of English language and literature (the first of its kind in Britain) in January 1828.[113] Lardner hailed from Trinity College Dublin; though eagerly wooed by Brougham and one of the very earliest appointees, he was to be a thorn in the side of the university until they wrestled his resignation from him in 1831. The Oxford-educated Williams was headmaster of Edinburgh Academy, the school Horner had been involved in founding a few years earlier. Dale was an evangelical Anglican educated at

Cambridge; having been ordained in 1823, he was assistant preacher at St Bride's, Fleet Street, and was tutor to a number of private pupils when he applied to the university.

On 10 May 1828 a letter was read out to council from Dale and Lardner 'stating their intention of providing a place of public worship & a regular course of religious instruction in a place contiguous to the University for such of the pupils as belong to the Established Church', and 'requesting the sanction of the Council so far as is consistent with the principles on which the University is established'. Council discussed the matter at its next meeting; its reply reflected the dilemma of a liberal institution when faced with an unwelcome request to which a refusal would appear illiberal:

> The Council have considered the establishment of an institution for religious instruction in the neighbourhood of the University as a natural & desirable consequence of the plan of general education there to be pursued; & they confidently rely that whatever arrangements Dr Lardner & Mr Dale may be induced to make will not in any way interfere with their duties as professors.[114]

Lardner and Dale, with Williams, lost no time in announcing their plan. *The Times* of 27 May carried an advertisement headed 'UNIVERSITY OF LONDON. RELIGIOUS INSTRUCTION':

> We, the undersigned Professors in the University of London, who are Clergymen of the Established Church, having from the period of our appointment entertained the intention of providing RELIGIOUS INSTRUCTION for those students who are members of our Church, do hereby give notice, that final arrangements have at length been made, with the full approbation of the Council, for that purpose. An Episcopal Chapel has been purchased contiguous to the University, to be called 'The University Chapel', where accommodation will be afforded to the Students for a due attendance on divine service, and where a course of DIVINITY LECTURES will be regularly delivered during the Academical Session.

The wording of this advertisement, with its suggestion for the chapel's title and its provocative use of capital letters (probably the work of the combative Lardner), cannot have been to the liking of the majority of council members. Certainly at its meeting of 14 August 1828 it delivered a rebuke to Lardner for a further advertisement he had submitted to them for approval in which he wanted to suggest that council itself would provide opportunities for attending public worship.[115] The council was now coping with a backlash from dissenting ministers. The Revd Dr Cox, one of the university's founders and its first librarian, wrote asking permission to give non-Anglican divinity lectures in the immediate neighbourhood of the university with his colleague and fellow dissenting minister Joseph Fletcher. On 3 July council replied in the same terms it had used with the Anglican trio, and soon enough – on 8 July – these men were advertising their own plans in the *Morning Chronicle*.[116]

None of this projected activity took hold. The Anglicans had problems with the lease of their chapel, though they did take temporary premises at 62 Gower Street and a fund was started for a divinity lectureship, to which Dale was appointed.[117] However, events overtook this private project for theology by the back door. On 28 June 1828, only three months before the Gower Street institution was due to open its doors, *The Times* described a meeting the previous week at Freemasons' Hall of a group under the chairmanship of the Duke of Wellington, at which it was announced that a new metropolitan college, under the king's patronage and to be called King's College London, was to be founded. It would follow the Gower Street model in not seeking to confer degrees (in deference to Oxford and Cambridge) and also – interestingly – in offering 'a liberal and enlarged course of education', including modern languages and the other subjects about to be taught at the University of London. It would, however, 'be an essential part of the system to imbue the minds of youth with a knowledge of the doctrines and duties of Christianity, as inculcated by the United Church of England and Ireland'.[118] Shares would be distributed, as in the case of its Bloomsbury rival (the new college was given land next to Somerset House on the Strand), but by contrast it could already boast several large subscriptions, including £1,000 from the Archbishop of Canterbury and the same from the Bishop of London. Its council was to have several establishment figures on it *ex officio*, including the Archbishops of Canterbury and York, the Bishop of London, the Lord Chancellor (who in 1831, when King's College opened, was none other than Brougham), the Lord Chief Justice, the Home Secretary, the Speaker of the House of Commons, the Dean of Westminster, and the Dean of St Paul's.[119]

Back in Gower Street, Williams in particular reacted rather strongly to this announcement. On 10 July Horner read out a letter from his friend to the council, dated 1 July, resigning his chair and using the extended metaphor of a losing battle to do so:

You will be as much surprised at receiving as I am grieved at writing this letter; but the truth is I have not courage to have the hostility of my own order & to array myself in battle against the lawn sleeves & mitred fronts of my ecclesiastical superiors. Had only the Duke of Wellington, supported by all the ministerial squadrons, taken the field, I would not have cared a straw but I honestly confess that such are my feelings that I must feel wretched if I find myself in direct opposition to the Rulers of the Church.[120]

This was the point at which Rosen offered to step in if the university could not find a replacement for the chair of Roman language and literature at such short notice; in the event, the young Thomas Hewitt Key, a Cambridge graduate who had been headhunted by the University of Virginia, was appointed. Key was to be an important figure in the future of the university and of its school.

Lardner and Dale did begin teaching the academic subjects for which they were appointed, dropping the chapel idea. Dale resigned the chair of English in August 1830, partly on financial grounds, for though his classes attracted better numbers than some of his colleagues (twelve in the first session, rising to thirty in the second), they brought less money to keep his growing family than he already earned from the large number of private pupils he taught. He was also alienated by the opposition of some professors to his friend Horner, by the 'unhappy state' of the university in 1830–1, when student numbers and university morale were low, and finally by a public statement by Key to the effect that students should study Latin and Greek and did not need to study English.[121] Lardner, of whom Brougham had had extremely high hopes, and whose lectures on natural philosophy and astronomy were successful, was a complicated man leading a complicated life who had expected to earn a great deal more than he did and who tried the patience of council to its limits until he was manoeuvred into resigning in November 1831, though this was not to be the end of his connection to the Gower Street concern.[122]

And so the new university opened to students in October 1828 against a background of struggle. The early years were hard, as were those of the school and the hospital it created.[123] But as the century progressed, the extraordinary people who were connected with the institution forced it into the forefront of national educational debate about medical ethics, the use of anaesthetics in surgery, the appropriateness of widening the syllabus at both school and university level, and the use of corporal punishment in schools. A new type of university teacher and a new type of university student emerged thanks to the University of London, which was the first and for many years the only possible place of resort in England for a certain kind of person.

An example of the new professor is John Lindley, appointed to the chair of botany in May 1828. The son of a Norwich nurseryman, he did not attend any university. A collector of seeds since his schooldays, he had been taken on as an assistant by the great naturalist and President of the Royal Society, Sir Joseph Banks. The celebrated geologist Charles Lyell gave him £100 to buy a microscope, and Lindley began a herbarium which had extended to huge proportions by his death in 1865. During his time at the university, from 1829 until his retirement in 1860, he wrote over 200 books and pamphlets. He helped revive the Horticultural Society in 1830, was the principal botanical writer for the Society for the Diffusion of Useful Knowledge, and left his rich collection of botanical works to the Royal Horticultural Society.

A type of the new student is Edwin Lankester, father of the more famous Sir (Edwin) Ray Lankester, professor of zoology at University College London in the 1870s and 1880s. The elder Lankester was the son of a Suffolk builder who died when his son was four; Edwin's formal schooling ended when he was twelve and he was articled to a local surgeon. In 1834 friends lent the twenty-year-old £300 to support him through a medical course at the University of London, where he was taught by Lindley and won the Lindley silver medal for botany. He proceeded to make a career from writing, mainly in favour of medical and social reform, giving popular lectures and working at dispensaries; in 1854 he supported John Snow's much-disputed theory of the spread of cholera through contaminated water, and soon after that he was appointed first medical officer of health for Westminster. Alongside the doughty medical campaigner, editor of the *Lancet* and resident of Bedford Square, Thomas Wakley, Lankester fought for the passing of the Medical Reform Act of 1858; he succeeded Wakley on the latter's death in 1862 as coroner for central Middlesex. As with Lindley, this active and progressive man was able to set out on his useful career because the University of London gave him a start. Brougham's remarks about the relative cost of an education at Oxbridge and in London proved true in Lankester's case. His friends would have needed to advance him a great deal more than £300 to see him through Oxford or Cambridge.

CHAPTER TWO

Steam Intellect: Diffusing Useful Knowledge

A S WILKINS'S grand new building with its promise of higher education for London was going up on Gower Street in 1827, another modernising educational venture was being unveiled with the publication of the first of many sixpenny treatises under the auspices of the Society for the Diffusion of Useful Knowledge (SDUK). The Society had no permanent headquarters, but it was in essence a Bloomsbury organisation, closely related to the developing university not only by sharing temporary offices in Percy Street, just west of Tottenham Court Road, until the Gower Street building opened, but also by having a number of personnel in common, including the first secretary and the first chairman of both enterprises, Thomas Coates and Henry Brougham, respectively. The Society was founded in 1826 with the widely advertised intention of bringing instruction to a new mass readership by making use of up-to-date printing technologies to supply the population with cheap educational pamphlets and periodicals. Within a couple of years, it was also taking early advantage of the wonders of rail travel to ensure prompt distribution of its publications to all parts of the country.

The SDUK was proposed at a meeting convened by Brougham in Furnivall's Inn in November 1826. Among the reform-minded lawyers, educators, and politicians supporting Brougham were several of his collaborators on the new university – George Birkbeck, James Mill, Zachary Macaulay, Lord John Russell, William Tooke, and James Loch. Many of them were also supporters of the London Mechanics' Institution, which Birkbeck had founded in Holborn in December 1823 on the model of the very first Mechanics' Institution, which he had started in Glasgow over twenty years earlier to give technical and academic classes to working men.[1]

In the mid-1820s, as part of the discussion about political reform which led to the 1832 Reform Act, the topic of education was debated in parliament, in newspapers like *The Times*, in the influential *Edinburgh Review*, and in speeches and pamphlets. In 1825 Brougham published a thirty-three-page pamphlet, *Practical Observations upon the Education of the People, addressed to the Working Classes and their Employers*, which went through at least thirteen editions in that year. In it Brougham told the story of the classes for mechanics which Birkbeck had begun in Glasgow, the success of which had convinced him that working men could take advantage of an education as yet denied them by the state. The pamphlet finished with an appeal to employers to recognise that there was now no going back from educational progress and an encouragement to working people to find time in their overworked lives to reap the benefit of new opportunities:

> To the Upper Classes of society, then, I would say, that the question no longer is whether or not the people shall be instructed – for that has been determined long ago, and the decision is irreversible – but whether they shall be well or ill taught . . .
>
> To the Working Classes I would say, that this is the time when by a great effort they may secure for ever the inestimable blessing of knowledge.[2]

The SDUK came into being to ensure the extension of education to all groups in society. Its motto was the Benthamite phrase, taken from Francis Bacon, 'Knowledge is Power'. The aim of the Society was to publish cheap, informative works to 'supply the appetite which had been created by elementary instruction' and 'direct the ability to read to useful ends'.[3] At the Society's inaugural meeting in November 1826, it was agreed that its publications would steer clear of party politics and religion. In this way they would appeal to the widest audience and would avoid controversy among the Society's own members, who represented a broad spread of religious affiliation, from non-believers to liberal Anglicans and dissenters of various kinds.

The precaution was sensible, though it did not stop the Society from being perceived by traditionalists as radical and secularist, a close cousin of the new University of London in particular. The cousinship was obvious: Brougham was the chairman of both the SDUK and the university's first council; Birkbeck, Macaulay, Mill, Lord John Russell, Joseph Hume, George Grote, and Isaac Lyon Goldsmid served on the committees of both institutions. Tories and churchmen seized on the connections, attacking the SDUK, the Mechanics' Institutions, and the university as a composite entity. While Praed nicknamed the university 'the radical infidel college' and Hook called it 'the Cockney College' and worse, satirists and cartoonists mocked the 'march of intellect' in general, affecting to believe that illiterate and possibly rebellious workers, encouraged by reading SDUK pamphlets, would form the student body in Gower Street.[4]

The suggestion of such objectors was that together these institutions presented a danger to society by encouraging the masses to aspire above their station, perhaps even to the point of starting a revolution. They feared the implementation of changes which could not be reversed – precisely the outcome envisaged with enthusiasm by Brougham in his pamphlet *Practical Observations upon the Education of the People*. In the *Communist Manifesto* twenty years later, Marx took delight in frightening his 'bourgeois' readers by telling them that the working class was about to do to them what they – the respectable middle class – had done to the aristocracy, namely gain power at the expense of the previous order, in the case of the bourgeoisie through the technological invention and manufacturing progress of the Industrial Revolution. Marx's analogy for the inexorable march of social and political change was Goethe's story of the sorcerer's apprentice, who called up a spell when he did not know the words to stop it and nearly drowned in the water his brooms were endlessly collecting in buckets from the Rhine at his rash command.[5]

William Thomas Moncrieff's poem, 'The March of Intellect; or, Mechanical Academics', is typical of the critical response to the new broom being taken to society by the happily named Brougham and his friends. Moncrieff adopts the reformers' rallying cry for the title of his poem and pretends to think that workmen will down tools to read improving books, write poetry, and even become students and professors at the new university:

Oh, Time! how Strange thy changes –
Learning's now become mechanical;
Scientific men and scholars,
Are seized with a sudden panic all.
The lower *classes* in the *classic* art,
Are *penny*-trating low;
And *operative learning* has
So *work'd* its way, it's all the *go*!
Tol lol lol, &c.[6]

The word *'penny*-trating' alludes pretty clearly to the weekly newspaper the *Penny Magazine*, which the SDUK started publishing at the end of March 1832.

The SDUK's first publications were the sixpenny treatises brought out from early 1827 in the series called the Library of Useful Knowledge, which aimed to 'give the people books which might convey knowledge to uneducated persons, or persons imperfectly educated' and to 'reduce the price of scientific and other useful works to the community generally'.[7] The early treatises, mostly of thirty-two pages, gave up-to-date accounts of their subjects; many were by rising stars at the new University of London, men like John Lindley and Dionysius Lardner. Augustus De Morgan wrote most of the mathematical articles for the SDUK, and served on its committee for several years, before taking on the post of secretary in 1845 with the task of winding down the Society's activities.[8] The emphasis was on science, particularly its newest branches. Among the sixty or so subjects covered by the Library of Useful Knowledge were hydrostatics, hydraulics, pneumatics, mechanics, electricity, physical geometry, and galvanism. The treatises were published at fortnightly intervals and sold between 20,000 and 25,000 copies each.[9]

The Society was fortunate in attracting an enterprising publisher for its works. Charles Knight had recently attempted to start a 'national library' of cheap abridgements of important works of information, only to be defeated by the financial panic of 1826 which caused the collapse of many publishing firms. He was an indefatigable writer and editor as well as publisher.[10] The chief printer was William Clowes of the Strand, a friend of Knight, who embraced the new technologies and employed the largest number of compositors of any printing firm in the world.[11] Knight published the SDUK's two 'Library' series, the Library of Useful Knowledge and its companion the Library of Entertaining Knowledge, introduced in 1828 following criticisms from some representatives of Mechanics' Institutions that the Useful Knowledge treatises assumed too much of their readers in the way of a basic understanding of subjects like arithmetic.[12] Knight willingly took financial risks on some of the SDUK's loss-making ventures, such as the *Penny Cyclopædia*, which he published in twenty-nine volumes from 1833 to 1846; he also acted as co-editor and contributor for the early volumes.

The Society's first series, the Library of Useful Knowledge, got off to a flying start with Brougham's introductory treatise, published in March 1827 and achieving sales of 42,000 by 1833.[13] Entitled *A Discourse of the Objects, Advantages, and Pleasures of Science*, it offers a clever, breezy survey of the field of science, from mathematics to natural philosophy, the solar system, electricity, and – topically – the workings of the steam engine. After a breathtaking run through the whole of science, Brougham ends on a Panglossian note, extolling the 'solid benefits' of science in making our everyday lives both 'more agreeable' and morally better.[14]

Brougham's pamphlet drew an immediate response. The friendly *Times* welcomed the 'little tract, which touches with admirable adroitness, and in natural order, on all the arts by which man is aided in his daily operation, or by the study of which his mind is enlarged'.[15] But Brougham's enemies were quick to ridicule it, and a number of mathematicians found fault with his calculations. The most detailed attack came from 'Paul Pry', the pseudonym of the caricaturist William Heath, most famous for his version of the 'march of intellect', a drawing done in 1829 depicting fantastic flying machines, a vacuum tube offering transport 'direct to Bengal', and a comical 'Steam Horse' on wheels.[16]

The Blunders of a Big-Wig; or Paul Pry's Peeps into the Sixpenny Sciences, published in 1827 at 1s. 6d. for fifty-two pages – Brougham's *Discourse* cost sixpence for forty-eight pages – took issue with the details of Brougham's pamphlet, and with the second work issued by the SDUK, the treatise on hydrostatics, also by Brougham. How could both these treatises be by Brougham? asks Pry. 'Why, his time must be wholly engrossed at the Bar or in the Senate.' Of Brougham's account of the speed of objects falling to earth, Pry comments that as Newton apparently received a letter from the Chinese emperor addressed 'Newton, Europe', so Brougham will surely now get letters from all over the world addressed to 'Brougham, The Earth', 'the gravity of the earth being the subject-matter of his most sublime discoveries!' The pamphlet concludes with the claim that 'every voice has bawled itself hoarse in plaudits of all these schemes of Reform and Philanthropy, as well as in wonderment at the tomes already sent forth to the world, as part and parcel of this Library of Useful Knowledge', which Paul Pry prefers to call 'Useless Knowledge' in his warning to the 'dupes' of the SDUK.[17]

The most lasting satire on the doings of Brougham and the SDUK is the witty but not vicious reference in Peacock's *Crotchet Castle*, one of a series of works set in country houses and notable less for their plot or story, which is always minimal, than for their good-humoured swipes at the fashions and foibles of the time. Peacock is happy to ridicule people and ideas of all parties, but Brougham attracts his fascinated attention. Chapter 2 opens with the Revd Doctor Folliott 'bursting, one fine May morning, into the breakfast-room' and crying out:

I am out of all patience with this march of mind. Here has my house been nearly burned down, my cook taking it into her head to study hydrostatics, in a sixpenny tract, published by the Steam Intellect Society, and written by a learned friend who is for doing all the world's business as well as his own, and is equally well qualified to handle every branch of human knowledge. I have a great abomination of this learned friend; as author, lawyer, and politician, he is *triformis*, like Hecate: and in every one of his three forms he is *bifrons*, like Janus; the true Mr Facing-both-ways of Vanity Fair. My cook must read his rubbish in bed; and as might naturally be expected, she dropped suddenly fast asleep, overturned the candle, and set the curtains in a blaze.[18]

Here Peacock seizes on the interest in technological progress expressed in the Society's treatises, while at the same time alluding to the anxiety in conservative circles about the social effects of the newfangled steam railway. Like so many of his contemporaries, Peacock expresses mingled admiration for Brougham's multifarious talents and exasperation at his untrustworthiness. When the novel was published, Brougham had recently been ennobled on his appointment as Lord Chancellor by the incoming ministry of Lord Grey, and it was an open secret that Grey gave him the job to put an end to his power to destroy Whig unity in the House of Commons. An especially hostile comment appears in the diary of Charles Greville, Clerk to the Privy Council, on 20 November 1830:

Great was the surprise, greater still the joy at a charm having been found potent enough to lay the unquiet spirit, a bait rich enough to tempt his restless ambition . . . As it is the joy is great and universal; all men feel that he is emasculated and drops on the Woolsack as on his political deathbed; once in the H. of Lords, there is an end of him, and he may rant, storm and thunder without hurting anybody.[19]

Brougham certainly wielded plenty of power in the five years before his elevation in November 1830, in his leading roles with the SDUK and the University of London, and in his speeches in the House of Commons, where he frequently astonished with his eloquence and ability. As well as giving his great speech on legal matters in February 1828, he had delivered, only a week earlier, the even more famous speech, a diatribe against Wellington, in which he coined the phrase 'the schoolmaster is abroad'. This lengthy speech from the opposition benches was a culmination of his many efforts to plead for the widening of opportunities in education, which

he saw as a necessity for the progress of both the individual citizen and the
nation. In a rhetorical manoeuvre much used by him – and strongly
resented by those who were its objects – he began by elaborately praising
the military achievements of the Duke of Wellington, who had just given
up his post as commander in chief of the army to become Prime Minister
in a Tory ministry opposed to Catholic emancipation and electoral reform.
After some silky praise of Wellington the great commander comes the
attack on what Brougham sees as Wellington the politician's desire to
undermine the constitution by digging in against reform. The next day's
Times reported the speech:

> There had been periods when the country heard with dismay that 'the
> soldier was abroad'. That was not the case now. Let the soldier be
> abroad, in the present age he could do nothing. There was another
> person abroad, – a less important person, – in the eyes of some an insig-
> nificant person, – whose labours had tended to produce this state of
> things. The schoolmaster was abroad (*cheers and laughter*)! And he
> trusted more to him, armed with his primer, than he did to the soldier
> in full military array, for upholding and extending the liberties of his
> country (*Hear.*).[20]

The floodgates opened, and from now on 'the schoolmaster is abroad'
became a favourite catch phrase of writers and cartoonists. Peacock picked
it up in *Crotchet Castle*, and the print shops of Haymarket and the Strand
were soon full of pictures of Brougham, now represented not as a broom
himself, but as a schoolmaster holding a birch broom for chastising
wayward pupils. After he became Lord Chancellor in November 1830,
many combined the visual images associated with that office – wig
(a pun also on Whig), gown, and Great Seal – with the already familiar
broom, now supposedly sweeping away legal injustices and cleaning out
the political Augean stable, and additionally the figure of the schoolmaster,
his broom ready for hitting miscreants.[21] Throughout the 1840s and
beyond, *Punch* employed variations on the phrase in sundry articles and
cartoons.[22]

Though Brougham was not the originator of the phrases 'march of intellect' and 'march of mind', for obvious reasons these were soon being
combined with the idea of the schoolmaster abroad. Only four weeks after
the schoolmaster speech, the *Morning Post* of 28 February 1828 carried a
brief article entitled 'The March of Intellect'. It began with the salient
extract from Brougham's speech on 29 January, then went on to profile

Brougham himself as a moderniser managing every progressive enterprise of the day:

> He carries not in his satchel the tomes of antiquated philosophy, nor the venerable volumes of Revelation; they are to him as dust thrown into the eyes of reason, and as cobwebs that entangle the poor insect in its flight after truth. He is the *Solomon* of science – the master of mechanical systems – the chemist of nature refining human virtues from the dregs of corruption . . .
>   Would that the time were come that his army was in the field; but he is abroad now, beating for results. He has founded his University – he has established his Institutes – he is heard in the Senate, and at meetings for mutual instruction . . . The day is at hand when he shall stand forth the Great Captain of the Age, and at the head of his legions begin the march of intellect.[23]

As well as writing the first two publications of the Library of Useful Knowledge, Brougham seems also to have read and corrected most of the manuscripts sent in by other contributors. Indeed, the committee of the Society, like the council of the new university, was sometimes too busy-bodyish for the organisation's good. Dionysius Lardner offered several subjects for the Library of Useful Knowledge, only some of which got through the rigorous review process. He was a quick, clever writer, with scholarly knowledge combined with the knack of writing in a simple, popular style, but just three treatises of his, on mechanics, pneumatics, and Newton's *Optics*, saw the light under the banner of the SDUK. Many more were to be published in the *Cabinet Cyclopædia* Lardner himself edited for Longmans. In 1829, when Lardner was already planning this encyclopædia, he wrote in frustration to the SDUK secretary, Thomas Coates, about the treatment his manuscript on Newton was receiving. 'I suppose the MS has by this time been honoured by the perusal of all the peers and commoners on the Committee,' he commented in March 1829. The SDUK records show that his work was indeed being pored over by no fewer than seven readers, from the reforming politician and committee member Lord Nugent to Henry Coddington, a fellow of Trinity College, Cambridge, senior wrangler in 1820 and one of several Cambridge mathematicians who were asked for their opinions by the Society.[24]

These Cambridge mathematicians also recommended the young Augustus De Morgan to the SDUK committee, at the same time as they were sending glowing testimonials to support his candidature for the chair of mathematics at the new university. (At twenty-one, De Morgan was the youngest candidate for the post.) In the mathematical works he wrote for the Library, De Morgan combined a pleasing wit with a formidable grasp of his subject. He was a striking character in the story of educational reform. A resident of Bloomsbury for many years, he lived with his mother at 90 Guilford Street from 1828 to 1832, then at 5 Upper Gower Street until his marriage in 1837 to Sophia Frend, with whom he lived at 69 Gower Street until 1844, when they moved to Camden to accommodate their growing family. He combined brilliance and a love of his subject with an uncompromising uprightness. The history of his association with the University of London is one of years of excellent service punctuated by two resignations on matters of principle, the first in protest at the dismissal of the anatomist Pattison in 1831, the second in 1866 when he felt James Martineau had been unfairly denied the chair of philosophy, for which he was the best qualified candidate, simply because he was a dissenting minister. On that occasion he wrote to Martineau to say that he had come to the university at its foundation on the 'understanding that a man may have any theology provided he sticks to his own subject in his class'.[25]

Though De Morgan could be a hard taskmaster with his students – he locked the doors of his lecture room five minutes after the start of his classes and would not let latecomers in[26] – he was also much loved in Gower Street. Edward Fry remembered De Morgan's 'domed forehead', 'decided and handsome features', and engaging wit.[27] His private letters and papers demonstrate his lighter side, with a joke genealogy, a made-up coat of arms, and little self-caricatures including a 'Sketch of Professor De Morgan in the Pillory, without hope of escape'.[28] While he passed on his mathematical genius to his son George, co-founder of the London Mathematical Society while a student at University College London in 1864, his artistic talent was inherited by another son, the famous designer and potter William De Morgan, whose doodles and sketches closely resemble those of his father.[29]

Though many of the writers of the SDUK's treatises were Gower Street academics, the Society deliberately recruited a number of contributors who were early examples of the very kind of self-taught men and women at whom the Library was aimed. One treatise was written by a Bloomsbury resident of this sort. David Booth, an uneducated Scot in his sixties, had managed a brewery in Fife before coming to London to make a precarious living from occasional writing, and his treatise on the science of brewing got him and the Society into trouble. It denigrated the methods of the famous breweries of Burton on Trent, whose owners sued the Society for defamation early in 1830. Luckily the SDUK committee was full of lawyers, who averted disaster by agreeing to insert a note apologising on the author's behalf. Booth turned to the Society from time to time when he got into debt. He was an idiosyncratic figure and a determined sceptic in religion. According to a visitor to his home at 25 Charlotte Street (now Bloomsbury Street, the southern continuation of Gower Street), Booth was less than five feet in height, with a 'very dark visage, eyes very red and watery, and presenting altogether an impish and fiendish look'.[30] In one begging letter to the SDUK in 1831 he pulled no punches about his view of the law and of Brougham's recent elevation to its highest office:

> I have again got into the clutches of one of the harpies of the Law; and six pounds, which is all that he has a right to, will become eight tomorrow, and probably a dozen within a week after. To oppose this I have not a shilling.
>
> Should you see Lord Brougham, you may tell him that his law Reforms are all worthless, as long as a pettyfogging Attorney can make the debt of a poor man rise from five to ten pounds in the twinkling of an eye.[31]

Contributors to the Library of Useful Knowledge earned between twenty and forty guineas for their short treatises, with the distinguished David Brewster, editor of the *Edinburgh Encyclopædia* and inventor of the kaleidoscope, being paid the latter amount, while most contributors received £25–£35. With the introduction of the Library of Entertaining Knowledge in 1829, the works became longer and the payment correspondingly more. These books, less technical and more generalist in approach, dealt with topics such as birds, trees, insects, criminal trials, and travel. Knight was made general editor of the series, and brought some new writers to the Society, the most notable being George Lillie Craik, a Scot educated at the University of St Andrews, who wrote by far the most famous of the works published in the Library of Entertaining Knowledge.[32]

The Pursuit of Knowledge under Difficulties; Illustrated by Anecdotes was published in two volumes in 1830–1, and continued to be reprinted until 1906. Offering actual examples of difficult lives made better and happier by the acquisition of knowledge, Craik's book complemented Brougham's 1825 pamphlet addressed to employers and workers. Dickens alluded with amusement to Craik's book in chapter 33 of *Pickwick Papers* (1837), in which Sam Weller's father, on seeing his son struggling to compose a valentine, says, 'But wot's that you're a doin' of? Pursuit of knowledge under difficulties, Sammy?' Nonetheless, Dickens took the book and its subject seriously. In September 1843 he asked his publishers Chapman and Hall to send him 'those Volumes of The Library of Entertaining Knowledge, which contain "The Pursuit of Knowledge under difficulties"' when he was preparing to give a speech in Manchester on 5 October for which he wanted examples of self-taught men.[33]

Here was another instant catch phrase for the press. It was used widely in newspapers for the next thirty years, sometimes seriously, when the writer wanted to bring forward a new example of a person who had overcome disadvantages, and often jokingly: several numbers of *Punch* played with the original phrase in cartoons such as 'The Pursuit of Matrimony under Difficulties', drawn in 1842 by 'Alfred Crowquill' (pseudonym of brothers Alfred Henry and Charles Robert Forrester) in a series called 'Social Miseries', 'The British Lion under Difficulties' during the canvassing for a general election in 1847, and 'The Pursuit of Journalism under Difficulties' in 1850.[34]

The SDUK employed self-taught men and women as contributors to two ambitious new ventures, the *Penny Magazine* from 1832, and the *Penny Cyclopædia*, begun in January 1833. One such figure perfectly embodied the idea of the pursuit of knowledge under difficulties: John Kitto, the son of a Plymouth stonemason, who became completely deaf after falling off a ladder at the age of thirteen. Knight later told the story of his introduction to Kitto:

> On the 18th of July, 1833, a short stout man, of about thirty years of age, presented himself to me ... He tendered me a note from Mr Coates, at the same time uttering some strange sounds, which could scarcely be called articulate. The few lines of introduction said that the bearer, Mr Kitto, laboured under the misfortune of nearly absolute deafness, and that I must therefore communicate with him in writing.

Coates informed Knight in his letter of introduction that Kitto had been employed as a printer in Malta by 'a religious society' (the Church Missionary Society), and had subsequently lived for some years in Baghdad, which he had reached after travelling through Russia. He was willing to write articles on his travels for the SDUK's publications. Knight immediately engaged him to write a series of articles for the *Penny Magazine* entitled 'The Deaf Traveller', which began appearing in August 1833.[35]

The *Penny Magazine*, a weekly paper of miscellaneous information begun on 31 March 1832, was remarkable for the eclecticism of its articles and for its innovative use of woodcut illustrations of high quality for such a cheap publication. The opening article of each number was an account of a historic building – Somerset House, St Paul's Cathedral, the Grande Chartreuse – accompanied by lavish drawings and plans. There were features on animals, on trades and manufacture (sugar, coffee, tea), some short poems, and the occasional review of a recent useful publication. The first number sold 50,000 copies within a few days of publication. In his memoirs, written in the 1860s, Knight acknowledged that a rival weekly had started six weeks earlier than the *Penny Magazine*, in February 1832. This was *Chambers's Edinburgh Journal*, brought out by the self-educated publishing brothers William and Robert Chambers. Knight wrote that the Chamberses 'were making readers'; they 'were raising up a new class' to be 'the purchasers of books'.[36] Though the Edinburgh pair beat the London group to the starting line, they in turn conceded that their inspiration came from the books and treatises already published by the SDUK. Their journal, costing a penny-halfpenny, sold widely, though initially less so than their penny rival, probably because their paper was not illustrated.[37]

Knight was justly proud of the innovations he had introduced and of the worldwide influence of the *Magazine*:

In 1836, the 'Penny Magazine' was producing a revolution in popular Art throughout the world. Stereotype casts of its best cuts were supplied by me for the illustration of publications of a similar character, which appeared in eleven different languages and countries ... Germany – France – Holland – Livonia (in Russian and German) – Bohemia (Sclavonic) [*sic*] – Italy – Ionian Islands (modern Greek) – Sweden – Norway – Spanish America – the Brazils. The entire work was also reprinted in the United States from plates sent from this country.[38]

He praised the contribution to the *Magazine*'s success of the printing engineer and inventor Edward Cowper, whose new steam-powered printing press delivered sheets at the rate of 4,000 an hour.[39]

One sign of the success of the magazine was the number of imitations and spoofs it engendered. First came the *Saturday Magazine*, published on the same day of the week, from the long-established Society for the Promotion of Christian Knowledge (SPCK, founded in 1698). The SPCK was intent on offering religion to the new reading public. According to De Morgan's wife, some orthodox Christians thought the SDUK was intended as a parody of their older society. She wrote that the *Saturday Magazine* was hurriedly started to counteract the feared subversion of 'all law and religion' by the *Penny Magazine* and other SDUK publications.[40] The orthodox party followed up in 1846 with the *Churchman's Penny Magazine* and in 1848 with the *Sunday School Penny Magazine*. Others, secular like the SDUK's, were the *Irish Penny Magazine* from 1833, the *Malta Penny Magazine* (1839), the *Juvenile Penny Magazine* (1853), and many more. One-off parodies appeared in 1832 in the shape of the *Penny Comic Magazine of an Amorous, Clamorous . . . and Glorious Society for the Diffusion of Broad Grins*, the *True Half-Penny Magazine of a Society for the Diffusion of Useful Knowledge*, and the burlesque *Frontispiece for the Penny Magazine of the Society for the Diffusion of Useful Knowledge. Vol. 1. The March of Intellect*, which consisted of a series of illustrations with captions.[41]

As secretary of the SDUK, Coates received enough letters from readers of the *Penny Magazine* to confirm that it was reaching the kind of readers it wanted. 'A Baker and one of the People' wrote appreciatively in 1833, and a Mr Wickes sent in wax impressions of a silver coin he had found in a field near Dover, asking for information about it and writing that 'the benefit of coin study was first impressed on me by an article in the Penny Magazine'.[42] The newspaper magnate and Bloomsbury benefactor John Passmore Edwards paid tribute to the boost given him by reading the *Penny Magazine* in its early years when he was an unschooled boy in distant Cornwall.[43] And Christopher Thomson recalled, in *Autobiography of an Artisan* (1847), living as a young house painter in a small village in Nottinghamshire:

> Squatting down here, penniless, without a table, or three-legged stool, to furnish a cottage with, it may easily be imagined that I had tough work of it. My great want was books; I was too poor to purchase expensive ones, and the 'cheap literature' was not then, as now, to be found in every out-o'-the-way nooking. However, Knight had unfurled his paper banners of free trade in letters. The 'Penny Magazine' was published – I borrowed the first volume . . . Since that period, I have expended large sums in books, some of them very costly ones, but I never had one so truly valuable . . . The 'Penny Magazine' was the first intellectual milepost put down upon the way-side, wherefrom coming ages may measure their progress towards a commonwealth of books.[44]

Knight's preface to the first annual volume of the *Magazine*, published in December 1832, claims a total sale of 200,000 of the weekly and monthly issues during the nine months of the paper's existence, attributing its success to its cheapness, the quality of its woodcuts, and the fact that it eschews 'party politics'. Knight also draws attention to the recent arrival of steam travel:

> The steam-boat upon the seas – the canal – the railway – the quick van – these as well as the stage-coach and the mail – place the 'Penny Magazine' within everyone's reach in the farthest part of the kingdom, as certainly as if he lived in London, and without any additional cost. This is a striking illustration of the civilization of our country; and when unthinking people therefore ask, what is the benefit of steam-engines, and canals, and fine roads to the poor man, they may be answered by this example alone.[45]

Here Knight, like Brougham in his speeches and pamphlets, enthusiastically embraces modern technology and harnesses it to the work of making educational progress. In September 1832 the *Magazine* had welcomed the fourth edition of Lardner's *Lectures on the Steam Engine*, brought out by the University of London's publisher, John Taylor, as 'decidedly the best popular account which we have of the Steam-Engine'.[46] If members of the SDUK were familiar with Peacock's nickname the 'Steam Intellect Society', they undoubtedly took it as a compliment rather than an insult.

As with everything connected with the Society, with Knight, and with Brougham, the *Penny Magazine* attracted complaints, on this occasion not only from conservative and religious observers and diehard opponents of all the reform measures going forward at the time, but also from publishers of other cheap papers, both radical reforming ones and scurrilous or comic publications. There was jealousy of the influential personnel involved in the production of the *Penny Magazine*. Brougham had used his position as Lord Chancellor to help the Society receive a charter in May 1832, with the treasurer William Tooke handling negotiations.[47] This gave the SDUK an advantage, as did the frequent exposure of Brougham's doings in the national press. A number of small radical papers appeared at the height of Reform Bill excitement; many lasted only a few weeks or months, and their editors resented what they called the 'monopoly' over cheap literature exercised by the Society, as well as opposing the moderate Whig politics behind a Reform Act which fell far short of their ideal of universal suffrage.

The radical publisher Henry Hetherington was one such enemy. He had set up his own printing business in Holborn in 1815, was active in the Mechanics' Institution, supported the social reformer Robert Owen, and agitated for universal suffrage. He boldly flouted the law which required fourpence in stamp duty to be paid on any paper carrying news by publishing a series of unstamped and therefore illegal newspapers. Hetherington was prosecuted several times, spending many months in prison. The most famous of his papers was the provocatively titled *Poor Man's Guardian; a Weekly Newspaper for the People. Established, contrary to 'Law', to try the Power of 'Might' against 'Right'*, which ran from July 1831 to December 1835. Hetherington was hostile to the new Whig government and to the SDUK, which he saw as entering into competition with him and scorned for its deliberate avoidance of politics in its publications. On the front page of his paper on 14 April 1832, just two weeks after the launch of the *Penny Magazine*, he writes that the 'hypocritical society for the Diffusion of *Useful* Knowledge has commenced a Penny Magazine, abounding with what the false-hearted and plundering Whigs call *Useful Knowledge*'. He goes on to exhort his readers to choose between his own penny paper, which offers knowledge 'calculated to *make you free*', and the 'namby-pamby stuff published expressly to stultify the minds of the working people, and make them the spiritless and unresisting victims of a system of plunder and oppression'.[48]

One of the points made by Hetherington and others stifled by the tax on newspapers was that the *Penny Magazine*'s proprietors were given preferential treatment by being exempted from stamp duty. Knight and his colleagues had successfully persuaded the Solicitor of Stamps that the *Magazine* did not carry 'news',[49] and the cry of monopoly went up. The caricaturists took up the subject, often including their favourite figure, easily recognisable by his long, upturned nose even when not being shown with wig or broom. Brougham features in a print by C.J. Grant in September 1832. Called 'The Penny Trumpeter!', the cartoon shows Brougham in his Chancellor's wig, running along with several copies of the *Penny Magazine* and with a sack on his back labelled 'Materials for the Penny Cyclopædia to commence in 1833 & to end the Devil knows when'. He carries a trumpet, which blasts out 'Entertaining Knowledge here – Trump Trump Trumpery Trump – Just printed and published the Penny Magazine, All works not issued by the Society for the Diffusion of Useful Knowledge are illegal.'[50]

It was a case of ultra-radical newspapers attacking their liberal Whig counterparts as not radical enough at a time when the Whigs were in the ascendant in parliament, finally getting into government at the end of 1830 to become the 'establishment' in their turn after three decades of almost uninterrupted Tory rule. The *Penny Magazine* did not, in fact, carry news, nor did it promote radical politics. The radicals' complaint of monopoly was therefore unfair; on the other hand, the *Magazine*'s harmlessness politically irked them at least as much as its consequent exemption from stamp duty.

Another print was by Robert Seymour, who had executed one of the many 'march of intellect' drawings (and who in 1836 commited suicide after finding that his etchings of the activities of a sporting club were to be subordinate to the text for which the publishers, Chapman and Hall, had engaged the young journalist Charles Dickens, a text which became *Pickwick Papers*).[51] Seymour's 'Patent Penny Knowledge Mill', published in McLean's *Monthly Sheet of Caricatures* in October 1832, shows a mill being cranked by a skinny Brougham and a distinctly artisanal figure, who was, in fact, Viscount Althorp, soon to be third Earl Spencer, a stalwart member of the council of the University of London and the committee of the SDUK. The monopoly idea is suggested by a legal paper sticking out of Brougham's pocket with the words 'Ready made Injunction against any new Penny Mag' and a notice saying 'No one else need attempt to print or publish any thing; as we intend to do all and every thing cheaper and better than it ever was or will (by other means) be done'.

Various other people associated with the SDUK – and many also with the University of London – appear in the print. Thomas Denman, who had assisted Brougham at the trial of Queen Caroline, is shown in his lawyer's wig stirring the mashing vat and saying 'Send out the Police, and see no other unstamp'd things are selling'. Lord John Russell, standing on a ladder (he was very small), and a large fat bishop are pouring liquids labelled 'frothy' into a huge receptacle, while 'twaddle' streams out of a pipe. The Bishop is Edward Maltby, the only senior churchman to have supported the founding of the University of London (he had said the blessing at the foundation ceremony) and to sit on the committee of the SDUK. He was also the only bishop in the House of Lords who voted for successive Reform Bills, having been elevated to the Lords as Bishop of Durham in Lord Grey's incoming Whig administration.[52]

While the *Penny Magazine* made a profit for the Society until it was wound up in 1845, when all SDUK activities were coming to an end, the *Penny Cyclopædia* lost the Society and Knight personally a lot of money. Though Knight could call on his large stable of expert writers, an encyclopaedia was a much more ambitious project than a weekly magazine. He was hampered by the cumbersome committee structure which meant that, as with the offerings for the Libraries of Useful and Entertaining Knowledge, too many people were considering each entry. Time was lost and arguments were frequent, not least on the ever thorny subject of religion.

An encyclopædia had to include articles on religion, and the Society thought it had found a neat solution to the problem of partisanship in the decision to ask a member of each sect to write the entry on that sect. Nicholas Wiseman, later Cardinal Wiseman, contributed the essay on Catholicism, for example, and the leading British Swedenborgian, James John Garth Wilkinson, wrote on Swedenborg. But the policy came unstuck in 1842 when an article on 'Socinians, Socinus, and Unitarians' was commissioned. Against the rule, a Trinitarian, Thomas Ormerod, was invited to write this one; it offended Unitarians and caused an agonised discussion about whether a new article should be substituted.[53] The thankless task of editing the *Cyclopædia* fell to George Long, who had been appointed first professor of Greek at the University of London, and had resigned along with De Morgan and Rosen on the controversial dismissal of the anatomy professor in 1831.

The *Cyclopædia* had De Morgan for its mathematical articles; geography was covered by William Wittich, teacher of German and geography at the University of London and praised by Long as the father of descriptive geography in Britain; Lindley and his former star pupil Edwin Lankester wrote on botany, the latter helped by his wife Phebe. Southwood Smith did anatomy, medicine, and physiology; the German scholar Leonhard Schmitz and the writer of classical dictionaries William Smith, a graduate of the University of London and teacher of classics at the university's recently founded school, shared the task of writing on classical subjects. According to Knight, Frederick Rosen of the university and the British Museum 'wrote all the articles on Oriental literature from "Abbasides" to "Ethiopian Language"'. Knight paid tribute to him:

> His labours were terminated by his sudden death in 1837, at the age of thirty-two. This distinguished native of Hanover acquired in England a host of friends, whose admiration he had won by his high intellectual attainments, and whose love was commanded by his gentle manners and kind heart.[54]

The venture was hugely ambitious. Unlike the many other encyclopaedias already in circulation or beginning about the same time, the SDUK's was to be no scissors and paste affair, no 'hash from German and French sources', as Knight put it, but a compendium of original writing.[55] The plan was to issue the *Cyclopædia*, following an alphabetical system, in weekly parts costing one penny each, but at that rate, as *The Times* pointed out after the dissolution of the SDUK, 'it would have taken exactly 37 years to complete the business'.[56] The Society, realising this, began to issue two sheets a week, at twopence, then after three years four sheets at fourpence.

This 'destroyed its commercial value', according to Knight, who added somewhat bitterly: 'Had it been a careful compilation, instead of an original work furnished by nearly two hundred contributors, it would have been to me a fortune.' The sale, having started encouragingly at 75,000 per weekly number, fell to almost half that when four sheets a week began to be issued, and by 1843 stood at 20,000. The combination of a large original outlay through payment to contributors and illustrators (about £40,000, according to Coates's recollection), the cost of paper and printing, the long period of publication (eleven years), and the dramatic drop in sales, meant that a loss was inevitable. Knight bore the brunt of it.[57]

The SDUK's committee, having undertaken several publications and series for a wide readership and in the interests of promoting the education of the masses, decided in 1830 that it could usefully produce a periodical directed at teachers and those who were concerned to establish proper universal state education. The *Quarterly Journal of Education* was launched in 1831, published by Knight, with Long as editor. Knight later remembered the excitement of the first meeting to arrange for this new venture. The SDUK's offices were at that time in Gray's Inn Square, in the south-eastern corner of Bloomsbury. Grey's new Whig ministry had just been appointed, in November 1830, and at the first monthly meeting of the Society after the Christmas vacation, 'our table presented a scene which lives in my mind as one of national importance'. The office was too small to accommodate all those who attended:

> We met, therefore, at the Gray's Inn Coffee House. I well remember talking to Mr Lubbock [John Lubbock, banker and astronomer] about the extraordinary spectacle of so many men of political importance – cabinet ministers, great officers of state and of the law – assembled in frank fellowship with physicians, professors of education, elders of science, astronomers and mathematicians just rising into note in the world of wider limits than Cambridge, and barristers not yet aspiring to silk gowns. It was really very striking to observe how, as it were, by one simultaneous movement, nearly all the committee had come together to hail the triumph of liberal opinions.[58]

The *Quarterly Journal* proved, however, to be a difficult thing to sell. It lasted for four years, during which time ten volumes were published, but after its initial number it never sold enough to break even. At five shillings an issue, it was relatively expensive, and its initial print run of 2,000 was soon reduced to 1,500 and then to 1,250. By August 1835 the journal was nearly £1,000 in debt, and the decision was reluctantly taken to cease publication at the end of that year.[59] It was the periodical's misfortune to be ahead of its time, since the backward state of education meant that there was no ready-made readership of educators.

The material offered by the *Journal* was novel. There were essays and factual reports on education for all ages and in all types of schools, including the great English public schools, dissenting academies, schools for the deaf and dumb, and universities in Britain and abroad. Many of the Society's chief writers were employed to write for the journal, including Long himself, who contributed pieces on Greek dictionaries, Greek language, and geography; Knight, who tackled almanacs and pauperism; Thomas Hewitt Key, professor of Latin in Gower Street, who wrote on Latin grammar and prosody; and Rosen, who did comparative grammar and etymology.[60] De Morgan contributed over thirty articles, on various branches of mathematics, on the Ecole Polytechnique in Paris, on the Royal Naval School, on gravitation, and on many more subjects.[61] The Edinburgh-educated John Ramsay McCulloch, the best-known political economist of the time, wrote an article on elementary education in Scotland and another putting forward 'reasons for establishing a public system of elementary instruction in England'.[62] McCulloch also wrote a couple of treatises for the Library of Useful Knowledge at this time, one on wages, and one on commerce. But he expected better wages himself than the Society could afford, and soon curtailed his activities on its behalf.[63]

Like so many of the SDUK writers, McCulloch was also connected with the University of London, having been appointed to the chair of political economy in 1828. As with some of his professorial colleagues, the council's over-optimism about student numbers and its financial meanness made him regret the connection. Despite his reputation, he was unable to attract many students to his classes. He was outraged by the system of paying professors a small guaranteed salary for the first two or three years, and subsequently according to the fees brought in by students. After a copious correspondence with the university's council about his pay and conditions, in January 1835 McCulloch refused to give any more lectures unless his salary was guaranteed, leading the council to declare his chair vacant two years later.[64]

Though the Libraries of Useful and Entertaining Knowledge, the *Penny Magazine*, and other SDUK publications such as maps and almanacs proved profitable, the *Quarterly Journal of Education* and the inevitably long-term *Penny Cyclopædia* lost the Society money, and one final crazily ambitious project hastened its end. This was the *Biographical Dictionary*, embarked upon in 1841 against the instincts of many on the committee. It was the brainchild of Althorp, who was by this time Lord Spencer, and he was able to push it through mainly because he was prepared to finance it in large part himself. The scope was immense; it was to be a universal biographical dictionary, on the model of the French *Biographie universelle*, which, as Spencer noted, already ran to sixty volumes and was likely to reach a hundred.[65]

When, forty years later, Leslie Stephen took on the job of editing the great *Dictionary of National Biography*, which included only British subjects, not international ones, he had ten years of exhausting work ahead of him before he resigned the editorship because of ill health; his deputy, Sidney Lee, was obliged to carry on for another ten years with a group of helpers before the *DNB* was completed in sixty volumes (not counting supplements). It is hardly surprising, therefore, to find George Long, having accepted the editorship of the SDUK's universal *Biographical Dictionary*, writing despairingly to Coates two years into the task and still on the letter A: 'I think the B[iographical] D[ictionary] will be more than a match for me ... We are now in a mess with these Arnalds, Arnolds, Arnaldi, Arneldi, Arneuf, Arnoul, etc. all names occasionally for the same persons.'[66]

The strains on the editor were enormous, as Long's annotations on his correspondents' letters show. One contributor, Leonhard Schmitz, sent in a number of articles on Germans with names beginning with A. He wrote to Long's assistant in November 1842 that he had been astonished to discover that the 'great theologian' Christoph Friedrich von Ammon was still alive. Long annotated this with a humorous 'We can well omit the living men. We have plenty of dead ones.'[67] Schmitz, who later became rector of the Royal High School in Edinburgh, sent over fifty letters complaining of delays in receiving proofs and payment. In July 1843 he returned proofs of his piece on Apollonius, telling his editors that he was off to the Continent for two weeks, having asked a certain Dr Plate to write four more German 'A' entries. Long's scratched note on this letter reads 'not to be done by Dr P. unless he is a German. I don't know who he is.'[68]

William Plate was a German scholar living in Bloomsbury. On 12 June 1850 he would be the recommender of 'Dr Charles [Karl] Marx' of Dean Street, Soho, in the register of admissions to the reading room of the British Museum, Plate himself having been recommended for a reader's ticket by Frederick Rosen in December 1836. He was, like Rosen, an orientalist, and after his abrupt introduction to Long for the *Biographical*

Dictionary, he was engaged by the SDUK in 1845 to write the long entry on Arabia in the *Supplement to the Penny Cyclopædia*. In 1847 he was living just behind the British Museum in Montague Place. He published a map of Asia Minor with Charles Knight in about 1850, and died at his home in Charlotte Street, Bloomsbury, in August 1853, the death certificate recording 'Suicide with Oil of Bitter Almonds. State of Mind Unknown'.[69]

Knight was not the publisher of the *Dictionary*, being already burdened by the *Cyclopædia*. Longmans undertook the task, but the cost of production exceeded the publisher's estimate, and the sale of the first half-volumes to appear averaged only 1,000 copies. Brougham, Goldsmid, and the Bishop of Durham helped to sustain the venture by contributing about £50 each; by October 1842 Spencer had raised his own annual contribution from £200 to £500 and Brougham followed suit by offering £500 a year for the next three years. Still it was not enough. Only Spencer's persistence kept the *Dictionary* going through 1843 and 1844, and when he died suddenly in October 1845, that was the end of it.[70] Long had resigned the editorship three months earlier, exhausted and in any case now engaged elsewhere, having succeeded his friend Key as professor of Latin at University College in 1842.

At the time of its demise, only seven half-volumes had struggled into print, covering the letter A. Requests had gone out from Long for articles on people with names beginning with B. The sixty-eight-year-old Henry Crabb Robinson of Russell Square, having offered to write on Anna Amalia, Duchess of Saxe-Weimar, had sent back a revised proof in April 1843 with the gloomy but accurate forecast that 'the As will monopolise the Alphabet nearly', adding, 'I talked of living to G – I shall be lucky if I live to C: or rather the Dictionary itself will be lucky if it reach half a dozen letters.'[71]

The writing had been on the wall for the Society itself since the mid-1830s. At the beginning of 1835 there was just £6 left in the bank, and a fund-raising effort was made. By April, £1,750 had been donated, mainly by the same men who had stepped up to found the University of London a decade earlier, chief among them Brougham, Spencer, and Goldsmid. Annual subscribers reached 515 in 1829, but by 1842 the number had dwindled to forty-nine.[72] The SDUK's affairs were wound up in 1846, twenty years after its energetic start. The best and most important work had been done, as its adherents saw, in its early years, when it had contributed to the larger movements for parliamentary and educational reform.[73]

The Steam Intellect Society had run out of steam, yet despite the sneers of those opposed to reform and the susceptibility of the Society to parody, it played a significant part in nineteenth-century education and culture. Sales figures indicate that its treatises and magazines were widely read. The influence of its publications can be judged by its imitators. The Society for the Diffusion of Useful Knowledge led the way at the beginning of a new era in educational publishing. If Knight was among the first to make use of new methods of stereotyping and mass printing, others soon followed. As he recalled in his autobiography, 'nearly all the leading publishers appear to have engaged', in the years between 1830 and the 1860s, in producing series of cheap reprints of books, as well as new journals and reference works. Constable, Bentley, Longmans, Blackwood, and John Murray followed the lead given by the SDUK and the Chambers brothers; by the 1850s most of them had begun phenomenally successful 'Railway Libraries', consisting of cheap editions of their bestselling novels for sale at railway stations.[74] David Brewster edited the *Edinburgh Encyclopædia* for Blackwood in eighteen volumes in 1830, Longmans commissioned Lardner to edit the *Cabinet Cyclopædia*, often known as *Lardner's Cabinet Cyclopædia*, in no fewer than 133 volumes from 1830 to 1849, and in 1860 the Chamberses added an encyclopaedia to their journal and various educational book series.

When Thomas Carlyle wanted to send the latest news about British literature and culture to Goethe's secretary Johann Peter Eckermann in March 1830, he singled out 'the universal effort to render all sorts of knowledge *popular*' and accessible to 'the largest possible number of readers':

> Our zeal for *popularizing* . . . is to be seen on every side of us. To say nothing of our *Societies for the Diffusion of useful Knowledge*, with their sixpenny treatises, really very meritorious, we have now I know not how many *Miscellanies, Family Libraries, Cabinet Cyclopedias* and so forth.[75]

Inevitably, when the stamp duty on newspapers was reduced in 1836 from fourpence to a penny, the majority of the cheap publications which ensued did not share the educational zeal of the SDUK's penny publications. In March 1838 Thackeray, not yet a famous novelist but a busy young journalist and illustrator recently married and living in Great Coram Street, noticed the phenomenon in the conservative *Fraser's Magazine*. He took a dim view of the many scurrilous publications now appearing, and though he nowhere blamed the SDUK, he could not resist alluding to the uses to which Brougham's phrase about the schoolmaster being abroad were now being put. His essay, 'Half-a-Crown's Worth of Cheap Knowledge', discusses the most radical and the most scurrilous of the newspapers now taking advantage of a new mass readership tutored by the SDUK. The article is headed by a list of fifteen publications including the *Poor Man's Friend*, Henry Hetherington's follow-up to the *Poor Man's Guardian; The Penny Story-Teller, The Penny Age,* and *The Penny Satirist;* and some sporting papers costing twopence. There is also '*Oliver Twiss*, by Bos', a penny serialisation cashing in on Dickens's recent rise to fame, and finally a number of scandal sheets such as *The Town* and *The Star of Venus; or, Shew-up Chronicle.*

Thackeray considers these rubbishy publications an unwelcome effect of the 'march of mind' movement of the previous decade:

> A walk into Paternoster Row, and the judicious expenditure of half-a-crown, put us in possession of the strange collection of periodical works of which we have given the catalogue. We know not how many more there may be of the same sort; but, at least, these fifteen samples will afford us very fair opportunity for judging of this whole class of literature. It is the result of the remission of the stamp laws – has sprung up in the last few months, or years – and may be considered the offspring of the 'March of Intellect', which we have heard so much about: the proof of the 'intelligence of the working classes', and the consequence of the meritorious efforts of 'the schoolmaster abroad'.
>
> These are the three cant terms of the Radical spouters: any one of these, tagged to the end of any sentence, however lame, never fails to elicit a shout of approbation at White Conduit House or the Crown and Anchor [well-known venues for radical meetings].[76]

The language associated with the SDUK, that of diffusion, useful knowledge, the march of mind, and the pursuit of knowledge under difficulties, though misused by some and derided by others, permeated serious political speeches and journalistic essays too in the decades following the foundation of the Society. Dickens, quick to make fun of bombast, wary – like others – of Brougham, and reluctant to associate himself with any political faction, nonetheless made use of SDUK-style language in some of his socially concerned journalism. In an early pamphlet written in 1836 under the pseudonym Timothy Sparks, *Sunday under Three Heads*, he attacked a bill going before parliament to enforce 'the Better Observance of Sunday'. He first sketches Sunday 'As It Is' for 'mechanics and poor people', with few shops open and few leisure activities available to them, while the 'pampered aristocrat' can ride in a carriage through the elegant parks and eat and drink food brought to him by servants. Next comes Sunday 'As Sabbath Bills Would Make It', with no shops and facilities at all for the poor, while the rich carry on as before. Finally Dickens comes to the third picture, his vision of Sunday 'As It Might Be Made'. Sports might be practised, and the British Museum and National Gallery could be opened on Sundays for the amusement and instruction of all classes:

How different a picture would the streets and public places then present! The museums, and repositories of scientific and useful inventions, would be crowded with ingenious mechanics and industrious artisans, all anxious for information, and all unable to procure it at any other time. The spacious salons would be swarming with practical men: humble in appearance, but destined, perhaps, to become the greatest inventors and philosophers of their age.[77]

Brougham himself could not have painted a more optimistic picture of what might be possible if the working class had access to useful and entertaining pursuits. Meanwhile, he and his colleagues were steering the University of London through difficult times, facing down debt and scandal, and hatching a plan to solve the financial problems and extend the educational reach of the institution by opening a school in Gower Street.

CHAPTER THREE

Gower Street Again: Scandals and Schools

A NY NEW institution with a radical or progressive agenda is liable to attract both ground-breaking pioneers who make a difference to national as well as local culture and society – the founders of the University of London taken as a group, and a number of the early professors, come into this category – and inevitably also some mavericks, quacks, and chancers. The exotically named Dionysius Lardner, Church of England clergyman, editor of an encyclopaedia, and populariser of steam engine technology, belongs in part to the latter group, and history has forgotten him, though he made a contribution to the rapid advance of science in the early Victorian period through his lectures, books, and journalism, particularly in connection with the science of steam travel. Lardner's career offers an extreme but illustrative example of the ups and downs of the brave new world of professional science which emerged in the 1820s. He was a divisive figure, admired and ridiculed in the press, and he caused the Gower Street pioneers more trouble than any other professor in the difficult early years of the university. He also enjoyed a scandalous private life, though his employers appear to have been unaware of this during his tenure as an academic. Exposure came, mercifully, long after he had left.

Science was not widely taught until the University of London was established with its chairs in various subdivisions of the subject, among them astronomy, chemistry, botany, zoology, geology, and mineralogy. Up to this time, most of those who took up a scientific career did not do so within an institution of higher education, and science itself was in a relatively unadvanced state. As Thomas Henry Huxley pointed out as late as 1858, the 'branches of human knowledge' pursued in universities until then had come under the headings of 'Arts, Theology, Law, and Medicine':

No evil could result from this arrangement, to the undeveloped Science of a century ago, when Electricity, Heat, Magnetism, Organic Chemistry, Histology, Development, Morphology, Geology, Palaeontology, branches of knowledge which constitute the very essence of Science as distinguished from Arts and Medicine, were non-existent.[1]

The main scientific forum in the early part of the nineteenth century was the Royal Society, founded in 1660; in the 1820s it was riven with rivalries and run by people with entrenched views, so much so that Charles Babbage (inventor of the the first computer, or calculating machine, the so-called Difference Engine, which Lardner welcomed in an article in the *Edinburgh Review* in 1834),[2] David Brewster, and others set up the tellingly named British Association for the Advancement of Science in 1831 in direct opposition to the backward-looking tendencies of the Society.[3]

The advancement of science was one of the aims of the new University of London. Things got off to a good start when the university opened in October 1828, with Lardner as one of its star performers. He was a strong proselytiser for his subject, and his first two lectures as professor of natural philosophy and astronomy in Gower Street attracted welcome attention from the press. The *Morning Chronicle* reported that 'the theatre was uncommonly well attended' and the applause warm at his opening lecture on 27 October. The following day his second lecture was even more successful, according to the friendly *Examiner* newspaper:

Dr Lardner delivered on Tuesday his second lecture on natural philosophy. Long before three o'clock every seat in the lecture room was occupied, and the *tout ensemble* presented a most gratifying scene, not only to the well wisher of the University in particular, but to all persons who are favourable to the dissemination of the arts and sciences. At the hour appointed the council and professors entered and took their places around the lecturer's table, and Dr Birkbeck and other gentlemen most distinguished among them, and best known to the public, were received with marked applause. Dr Lardner followed, and was received in the most distinguished manner by the audience, who, in their plaudits, gave ample testimony of the high estimation to which his lecture of the preceding day had raised him. When he had proceeded about ten minutes, Mr Brougham entered the room at the council door; he was immediately recognised, and received with thunders of applause; the audience were not content with giving him one peal – a second followed still louder than the first. There were upwards of 700 in the room.[4]

Seven hundred exceeded by far the total number of students newly enrolled at the university for all subjects, so if the *Examiner* is not exaggerating wildly, the university contingent in the audience must have been joined by a great many members of London's lecture-going public. That this was a large body is shown by the accounts of the crowds attending McCulloch's public lectures on political economy, or of the carriages of 'women of distinction' which blocked Albemarle Street when Coleridge was lecturing on literature at the Royal Institution.[5] How Lardner felt on being upstaged in the familiar manner by Brougham is not recorded. It was Brougham who had recruited him, and both men had high hopes of Lardner's success.

Lardner was the first professor in the country to lecture on the steam engine. On taking up his post in July 1827, more than a year before the start of the first session, he was given a salary of £300 for the pre-teaching year, space in the house in Percy Street taken for the university's offices until the Gower Street building was completed, and a grant to cover construction of the equipment he would need to accompany his lectures.[6] During the four-and-a-half years of his connection with the university, Lardner corresponded constantly with the council, sending requests, demands, suggestions, and complaints about equipment, the hiring of an assistant, the state of the lecture rooms, the needs of the professors (he became a kind of shop steward for that mishandled body), the demands of the timetable, ways of attracting students, and above all his professorial salary, which he deemed completely inadequate to his needs.[7]

Brougham was partly to blame for this, as he had personally pursued Lardner, first making extravagant promises about what he might earn, then removing himself from the scene when the reality turned out to be different. At Brougham's suggestion Lardner had visited London from his home in Dublin in the spring of 1827 to discuss the splendid plans for the new university. Back in Dublin in May, Lardner attempted to raise his value to London by informing Brougham that his prospects in Dublin were 'better than I had expected them to be'. Up to now he had been a popular public lecturer and holder of a teaching position at Trinity College Dublin, of which he was a graduate. He tells Brougham that he has now been 'given to understand' that he might gain two Dublin professorships simultaneously, the value of which 'cannot be estimated at a less sum than £1000'. He can earn this by giving about thirty lectures a year:

> Under these circumstances I should wish, if possible, to have more definite information as to the prospective advantages of the professorship of

Mechanical Philosophy in the London Univ[ersit]y. In your last letter you requested to know what emoluments I expected. With your permission I shall in a general way lay before you my views of the duties of that chair and, as I understand them, the probable emoluments.

There follows a plan to give three courses of lectures, one to be delivered 'in a popular manner' to junior students, one teaching 'the elements of mechanical science' with 'experimental illustration', and the last for more senior students 'on the sublimer mechanics aided by the exclusive and powerful resources of the modern analysis'. He would prepare the apparatus needed to demonstrate his lectures and would publish 'three elementary works as text books for the junior mathematical students and which indeed are much wanted for general purposes'.[8]

Brougham's reply outlined the council's plan to guarantee £300 for the first two years until enough students were enrolled to make it profitable to the professors to be paid entirely out of their fees. With grandiose visionariness he told Lardner that he could expect much more than £300 even in the first year: 'The class you will teach cannot be of less value than £1200 a year. Our plan prevents us from securing a larger salary than £300 – but there will be pupils to pay 5 or 6 guineas each – say 6 for two classes of 6 & 3 months and I look to 300 pupils as the least number which may be expected.' Brougham even thought Lardner might have 500 students and so earn £2,000 a year.[9] (When the session started in October 1828, he actually had sixty-seven students in his junior class, many more than most of the professors, while only two had enrolled for his senior class.[10])

Two weeks later, in June 1827, Lardner was back in London, from where he wrote in wonderfully optimistic spirit to a Dublin acquaintance, the writer Maria Edgeworth:

My present visit to London has been occasioned by an invitation sent over to me from the Council of the University now being established here, soliciting me to take the chair of Natural Philosophy and Astronomy. In every point of view the chair must be considered the most important in the University and I have little doubt that it will soon be the most important in Europe. The emoluments are considered as likely to exceed £2000 p. ann . . . I need scarcely say that I have, under such circumstances, accepted the invitation which I have been honored with so that I shall be immediately removing from Dublin to this place.[11]

Lardner's energy and talent were not in doubt. He superintended the building of two models of the famous Boulton and Watt steam engine, a 'large condensing Model' and a 'high pressure Model'. He wrote a very long, elaborate statement of the courses he intended to teach for the university's *Second Statement explanatory of the Plan of Instruction*, printed in November 1828. De Morgan's description of his maths courses took up four pages of this document; Lardner's statement, which followed it, went on for eighteen pages.[12] At the same time he was negotiating with Longmans to edit the *Cabinet Cyclopædia* and gathering contributors, and he was also going into London society and persuading fashionable people to come to Gower Street to see his model engines. His compatriot, the poet and man about town Tom Moore, described a visit to the university in June 1829, 'in consequence of an invitation from Dr Lardner, to meet Lord and Lady Stafford &c. &c., to whom he was to display his Sections of Machinery'. A few days later Moore called on Lardner to arrange about 'showing the samples of his machinery at the University to Lady Lansdowne'.[13]

Some of Lardner's activities, however, annoyed the council. Not only was he the leader of the threesome who asked permission to introduce Anglican worship and religious lectures, but he put himself at the head of the professors when it came to making suggestions to the council, which, it seemed, had no intention of asking their advice about anything. It was Lardner who sent council a long letter, or 'memorial', on behalf of his colleagues in August 1828 recommending a robust advertising campaign ahead of the autumn opening of the establishment. No doubt he was motivated partly by the desire to drum up students for his own lectures, but he had a point when he observed that the recently advertised plans to found King's College London were receiving much attention and threatened to overshadow the start of the university on Gower Street. His language is colourful and deliberately alarming, but the substance of his remarks is perfectly true, and the council, consisting as he says of busy public men with other things on their minds, did indeed miss a trick by being reluctant to respond to the spoiling tactics of the Church-and-State faction:

It is known that an institution in most respects similar to ours has lately been projected. The most unsparing exertions are made for the advancement of this scheme ... Innumerable circulars are scattered over the Kingdom. Every engine of excitement is at work. The fire of party spirit is kindled. Religious animosity is awakened. The most influential members of several of the medical schools of the metropolis have coalesced with the promoters of this project. Students are scared from our walls by the stigma of infidelity which calumny has fixed upon them.[14]

A cartoon which appeared at this time, 'King's College versus London University, or Which is the Weightiest', depicts a seesaw with the protagonists of the university, including Birkbeck, Brougham brandishing a broomstick, and a banner saying 'Sense and Science', heavily outweighed by three very fat bishops (one of them the Archbishop of Canterbury with mitre and crosier) and a clergyman, their end of the seesaw weighed down further with a money bag inscribed 'Money and Interest'.[15] Lardner was right to worry about the effect of the announcement of the founding of King's College on the very eve of the opening of the Gower Street establishment, which had battled its way into existence with hard-earned money and without the blessing and influence of Church or government.

The letter to the council points out that not enough publicity for the university has been arranged. The professors suggest that an advertisement drafted by them (or by Lardner on their behalf) and enclosed with the memorial should be placed in six daily papers and two Sunday papers every week for three months. The same should happen in at least one local paper 'in every principal town in England', and the advertisement should be placed in the monthly and quarterly periodicals and the SDUK's Library of Useful Knowledge. Finally – what would the council make of this? – a copy of the advertisement should be *delivered at every respectable house in London and its environs* [Lardner's italics]. Anticipating the objection that this would cost too much, Lardner finishes by saying that if only ten students were attracted to the university by this means, the cost would be more than recouped. The council responded to this with suspicion at its meeting on 14 August. Horner was deputed to ask Lardner why the memorial was signed only by him when it purported to come from all the professors; Lardner was to be told that much had already been done in the way of advertising the opening session. Though some of the other professors subsequently wrote to the council to express their support for Lardner, he does seem to have exceeded his brief, and to have made himself an irritant to his employers.[16]

Lardner, disappointed with the number of students who turned up for his classes, especially the senior ones, and with Brougham's promises of riches still fresh in his mind, sent letter after letter to the council during 1829 and 1830 demanding more than the guaranteed £300 salary and half threatening resignation if his demands were not met. A motion to remove him was narrowly defeated at a meeting in May 1830, but he was finally manoeuvred into resigning in November 1831 'in consequence of the inadequate remuneration which the class affords'.[17]

Lardner was not the only professor to complain or resign on the grounds of financial hardship at this time. Hyman Hurwitz earned practically nothing from attempting to teach Hebrew; Robert Grant, pioneering teacher of anatomy, had to teach long hours in other institutions to make enough to live even a modest bachelor's life in his small house near Euston Station; Benjamin Heath Malkin, briefly professor of history, resigned in May 1830 because of 'pecuniary difficulties'; and although McCulloch the political economist did not leave for another few years, he had a request for an advance of £175 humiliatingly turned down in December 1830.[18]

Lardner encapsulated the very idea of the diffusion of knowledge in the late 1820s and early 1830s. His contributions to the SDUK's Library of Useful Knowlege, his massive *Cabinet Cyclopædia*, his lectures on the steam engine, not only in the university but in public theatres in London, and his books on the subject represent the mood of optimism and energy of those nineteenth-century thinkers who embraced progress in science and technology.[19] During the 1830s he was consulted by railway companies and gave evidence to parliamentary commissions on the railway. In 1834 he lectured to large audiences once more at the Royal Institution; the university, which owned the steam engine models built to Lardner's specifications in 1827, lent them for Lardner's lectures at the request of Michael Faraday, the chief scientist at the Royal Institution.[20] In May 1840 *The Times* announced that the Regent Street Polytechnic Institution had bought 'Dr Lardner's beautiful Models of the Steam Engine (including his sectional model of Watt's Condensing Engine, 9 feet in length)' for the use of its lecturer, Mr Maugham.[21] These famous models were among the first to be used to illustrate the teaching of modern technology in a university.

However, even as Lardner was making these contributions to scientific progress, he was turning into a figure of suspicion and mockery among his contemporaries. Though he was able to persuade a number of well-known people to contribute to his *Cabinet Cyclopædia* – Walter Scott on Scottish history, Moore on Ireland, Brewster on optics – he was distrusted by some of them. Robert Southey, who wrote an article on naval history, disliked Lardner's liberal politics. Southey had been a radical in his youth in the 1790s, but was now politically conservative, horrified at the progress of electoral reform, and uneasy about Lardner's connection with the godless institution on Gower Street. In October 1828 he told a friend that 'the Revd. Dionysius Lardner', 'a knave who is Professor at the London

University', had asked him to contribute. He was inclined to refuse, but could not turn down the generous payment offered by the publisher, and in March 1830 he informed another friend that he was 'engaged for a volume of "Naval Biography" to Dionysius, Tyrant and Pedagogue, of Stinkomalee, and Cabinet-maker to Messrs. Longman, Rees, Orme, Brown and Green'.[22]

Lardner's first name opened him to ridicule, as did his tendency to boast about his attainments. The University of London's publisher John Taylor announced in July 1828 that a new edition of Lardner's book on Euclid's *Elements*, designed for his students, was due to be brought out in time for the opening of the institution. His name appears in the advertisement as 'the Rev. Dionysius Lardner, LL.D., Professor of Natural Philosophy and Astronomy in the University of London; F.R.S.E.; Hon. F.S.P. Camb.; F. Ast. S.L.; Hon. F.S.A. Scot.; M.R.I.A.'[23] Thackeray, with his sharp eye and ear for pretension of any kind, seems to have come across Lardner a few years after this. In 'The Yellowplush Correspondence', one of his satirical sketches (verbal and visual) in *Fraser's Magazine* in 1838, he skewers Lardner and his *Cabinet Cyclopædia*. When Yellowplush the butler announces the arrival of 'Docthor Dioclesian Larner' at a literary dinner party, Thackeray describes him as short and pale, wearing spectacles, a wig, and a white neckcloth, and talking in an outlandish Irish accent about his encyclopaedia:

'It's the littherary wontherr of the wurrld', says he; 'and sure your lord-ship must have seen it, the latther numbers ispicially – cheap as durrt, bound in gleezed calico, six shillings a vollum. The illusthrious neems of Walther Scott, Thomas Moore, Doctor Southey, Sir James Mackintosh, Docther Donovan, and meself, are to be found in the list of conthribu-tors. It's the Phaynix of Cyclopajies.'[24]

Lardner divided opinion. He was clearly talented, and was much in demand as a scientific writer. He continued, for several years after resigning from the university at the end of 1831, to be a popular lecturer on the new technology in the lecture rooms of London. Faraday's Royal Institution welcomed him, and he was a frequent speaker at the London Institution, at Birkbeck's London Mechanics' Institution, and in scientific societies up and down the country. He served on the committee of the British Association for the Advancement of Science.[25] He not only edited the *Cabinet Cyclopædia* for Longmans, but wrote on scientific matters in the *Edinburgh Review*, as well as publishing several updated reprints of his book on the steam engine from the 1830s to the 1850s. He testified to two parliamentary committees on steam communication, in 1834 and 1837.

His writings were aimed both at a metropolitan middle-class audience of professional people – who he believed ought to know about science – and at mechanics and men whose job it was to apply technology. He shared the principles of Brougham and the Society for the Diffusion of Useful Knowledge, and was generally optimistic about the economic, intellectual, and moral benefits that steam travel, by land and sea, would bring, especially to isolated communities. Being combative and attracted to controversy, however, he became embroiled in arguments with railway companies about their practices, criticised the great engineers Isambard Kingdom Brunel and Robert Stephenson, and was widely ridiculed for a lecture he gave at the British Association meeting in Bristol in 1836. There he expressed caution about the practicality of steam travel across the Atlantic, warning that in order to carry enough coal for such a voyage a ship would have to cut the load of passengers or freight to levels which would make such journeys uneconomical. His view was distorted by his opponents and in the popular press, which accused him of saying such journeys were impossible at the very time when the first steam crossing was being successfully undertaken. He himself travelled by steamship to America in October 1840, as *The Times* pointedly recorded.[26]

The reason for this journey to America was to escape from the scandal that filled the newspapers in March and April 1840, when Lardner, then living in Brighton, eloped with the young wife of a Captain Heaviside (cue punning from the press – the *Era* quoted a remark that Lardner had made the scientific discovery of Mrs Heaviside's '*light* side').[27] The couple escaped to Paris, where they were pursued to their hotel apartment by Captain Heaviside and Mrs Heaviside's father. The former beat Lardner with his cane; according to *The Times*, which reported the story for several weeks in April 1840, Lardner crept under a piano to escape the blows, while his wig was thrown into the fire by the irate husband. Later that year, Lardner and his mistress sailed for America, where Lardner resumed his scientific lecturing with some success; meanwhile a court in Sussex heard the husband's case in August 1840 and declared Lardner liable for damages of £8,000.[28]

In September 1843 the actor-manager William Charles Macready, on an acting tour in New York, was surprised to receive a note from Lardner. Macready had been among Lardner's admirers in the days of the latter's successful lecturing in London. He noted in 1833 that after dinner one evening Lardner's conversation was 'very interesting, whether on politics, religion or science, in all of which one gains new or clearer views of a subject by its discussion with him'. Macready saw Lardner often, lapping up his knowledge of astronomy, attending one of his lectures – on Halley's comet – at the Royal Institution in May 1835, at which Faraday was also present, and accompanying him to be shown the workings of a steam engine. For his part, Lardner often visited Macready in his room at the theatre. Macready's many journal entries about seeing Lardner in company at that time are admiring, though one, in June 1835, suggests that the strait-laced family man Macready wondered what Lardner was getting up to with actresses:

> Went on the box of Shiel's carriage to Dr Lardner's, where I saw and was introduced to the Guiccoli [Byron's mistress] – saw Mrs Norton, Mrs L. Stanhope, etc. Was surprised to see Mr Cooper, Miss Betts, and Miss———enter the room. Oh, Dr Lardner! Is this society for a philosopher?[29]

When the scandal of Lardner's elopement with Mrs Heaviside broke in 1840, Macready was 'truly sorry for this wretched act of folly and crime'; he deplored Lardner's actions, but pitied his situation: 'He has shown real interest in me, he has sat often at my table – I had a sincere regard for him, and I cannot see him sink thus into hopeless misery and infamy without compassion.'[30] The kindly Macready accepted a visit from Lardner, now aged fifty, in New York on 1 October 1843; he was under the impression that Lardner had married Mrs Heaviside, though it seems likely that the marriage did not take place until 1846, in France.[31] In New York Lardner talked to Macready 'about Mrs Lardner and his young child'. A week later Macready called on them:

> Alas! alas! I saw the *ci-devant* Mrs Heaviside, now Mrs Lardner, a very fine and handsome woman; and Lardner not now a *ci-devant jeune homme*, no longer dandy in his dress and appointments, but old and almost slovenly. There was a child there, the fruit of their indiscretion – that, poor thing! And poverty and neglect, the sad result of their blind, absurd infatuation![32]

This child was not the first born to Lardner outside marriage. Astonishingly, when he came to London from Dublin in 1827 he brought with him not his wife but a married woman, Anne Boursiquot, her children, two of his own legitimate children, Henry and George, and Dion,

Anne's youngest son, fathered by Lardner. The arrangements were complicated, since his wife Cecilia was also engaged in an extramarital affair back
home in Dublin. Lardner spent ten years, from 1829 to 1839, seeking a
divorce from Cecilia. Before the passing of the Matrimonial Causes Act of
1857, divorce was attainable only by the slow and expensive method of
acquiring a private act of parliament, and this was the course taken by
Lardner.[33] (No wonder he made constant requests for a better salary at the
university.)

His case finally came before the House of Lords in April 1839 in
proceedings chaired by none other than Lardner's old university champion
Brougham. Mrs Lardner did not contest her husband's charge against her
of adultery with a Mr Murphy of Dublin. Lardner's brother, sister, and
mother testified that he had married his wife Cecilia in Dublin in December
1815, and that while he had invariably been kind to her, she had shown a
'violent and uncontrollable temper' towards him from the beginning of the
marriage. These witnesses told how Cecilia had entered into a relationship
with Mr Murphy, by whom she had a child.[34] Nothing was said of Lardner's
own relationship with Anne Boursiquot, his fathering of Dion in 1820, and
his living in London with Anne and their various children.[35] The House of
Commons gave Lardner his freedom: 'Lardner's Divorce Bill was read a
third time and passed,' reported *The Times* on 5 June 1839. It was only a
few months after this that Lardner appeared in the headlines once more,
after his sensational elopement with Mrs Heaviside.

Lardner seems to have managed to keep his earlier domestic arrangements secret at the time when he was lecturing at the university and
agitating, with his fellow divines Dale and Williams, to introduce Anglican
worship to Gower Street's students. It was only in the 1840s that Lardner's
paternity became common knowledge. By then Dion Boursiquot, or
Boucicault, as he chose to spell his name, had become famous as a comic
playwright after the startling success of his first play *London Assurance*,
produced at Covent Garden theatre in 1841 when Boucicault was twenty
years old.[36] There is a bizarre *Times* report of one of Boucicault's many
bankruptcy cases in 1848 in which 'the insolvent, described as a literary and
dramatic author', said his name was Dion de Bourcicault [*sic*], 'but he had
borne the title of Vicomte, to which he was entitled in France, until lately'.
He also said that 'he had never gone under the name of Lardner, nor stated
himself to be the son of Dr Lardner, but that gentleman had christened
him, and he had thereupon received the name of *Dion*'.[37] By this time,
Lardner's escapade with Mrs Heaviside had sealed his reputation as a
blackguard. It was just as well for the University of London that Lardner

left Gower Street when he did; if his private life had been exposed at that time, it would have been a gift to the institution's many ill-wishers. Lardner died in Naples in 1859, his personal reputation ruined but his books on the steam engine still selling well.

While Lardner was doing his bit to bring students to Gower Street – though he was also trying the patience of the council members with his demands – the university as a whole was in a precarious position. From 1830 to 1835 student numbers at the new university fell even from the original disappointing figure of 557.[38] In 1831 professors and council members resigned on matters of principle; internal dissension reigned, particularly in the medical school; Horner, the absurdly overpaid Warden, resigned; and news of the troubles leaked out to a national press greedy for bad news to tell about the godless college. To make the situation worse, down on the Strand the university's Anglican rival King's College London opened its doors to students for the first time in October 1831, supported by members of the establishment. Through it all Brougham, now Lord Chancellor but as busy as ever in promoting the university's interests, talked up the institution in an effort to boost flagging spirits. Charles Greville, a practised Brougham-watcher, reported in June 1831, at the height of professorial revolt, that Brougham had told a large company at a dinner party that 'Sir Isaac Newton was nothing compared to some of the present professors'.[39]

   An answer to the acute problems facing the new university in the years 1830–1 was found. The council sanctioned a plan by some of its members and other proprietors of the institution to start a school which would bring in much-needed fees and also, in due course, provide a cohort of pupils properly prepared to go on to attend the university itself. Horner had already put the suggestion in a letter to his old Edinburgh friend and member of the council, James Loch, in October 1828, just as the new university was opening to its first students. He invoked his experience of having helped to establish the Edinburgh Academy a few years earlier:

Have I yet told you of my scheme for a great Classical School (a Day School) to be attached to the University? I rather think not. It is shortly this – To apply the ground floor & Basement of the *South* Wing [not yet built, and not to be built for another forty years] to the purposes of a School, with the ground behind for the play ground which is ample for the purpose, & with a separate entrance from Gower St . . . I would have the School very much upon the Model of the Edin[burgh] Academy, & introduce the system of teaching large numbers by the Master . . . We may have a School of 500 boys educated for £10 or £12 a year – a capital nursery for the University.[40]

Some months earlier, in December 1827, Lardner, zealous for the success of the institution he was joining, had written to Horner with the same idea, declaring that 'immense advantage would be reaped from the establishment of a great preparatory school in immediate connection' with the university, to be superintended by the council and professors.[41] The idea was finally taken up in 1830, when the university's finances looked dire and opening a school seemed a promising way to attract students and make an income. Another supporter of the university, Henry Sass, had also suggested opening a school in an impassioned letter to the council in June 1827, asking that the university itself take on boys younger than the minimum age of fifteen which had been proposed. (Fifteen was younger than the age at which most students matriculated at Oxford and Cambridge, though the precocious Jeremy Bentham had gone to Oxford at the age of twelve; Scottish students often started university at fifteen.[42])

Sass was the celebrated, if unstable, art teacher who ran London's most famous school of drawing outside the Royal Academy Schools, for which he prepared promising pupils. He had started his school at 50 Great Russell Street, opposite the British Museum, in 1818, hoping to capitalise on the proximity of the Museum's recently acquired Elgin Marbles. In 1820 he had moved to larger premises nearby at 6 Charlotte Street (now Bloomsbury Street). Dante Gabriel Rossetti was a pupil here in 1841, and John Millais, who lived only a few yards to the north in Gower Street with his parents, attended briefly until 1840, when, at the age of eleven, he became the youngest pupil ever to be admitted to the Royal Academy Schools.

The popular artist W.P. Frith was also a pupil of Sass's, from 1835, when he was sixteen, to 1837. He recalled that the Charlotte Street house had a large gallery filled with casts, with a bust of Minerva over one of the doors. Sass was irascible but kind-hearted and hospitable; he introduced his pupils to famous painters such as John Constable, David Wilkie, and Charles Eastlake at dinners and *conversazioni* in the house. According to another of his former pupils, John Callcott Horsley, Sass was 'eaten up with vanity', sending self-portrait after self-portrait to the Royal Academy for consideration, always calling these unsuccessful paintings 'Portrait of a Gentleman'. Horsley remembered a large room with a vaulted roof, which Sass told visitors was a scale model of the Pantheon at Rome. Sass ended his life in 1844 in an asylum.[43] He was immortalised by Thackeray in *The Newcomes* (1853–5) as Mr Gandish, who runs a fine school of art, despite being a pretentious and vulgar cockney. Gandish draws a picture of his son as 'an infant 'Ercules', and invites visitors into 'the Hatrium', where they can view 'my great pictures from English 'ist'ry'.[44]

In 1827, as one of the original proprietors of the new university, Sass was keen to help, offering to give lectures on fine art and hoping to get his sons enrolled. The problem was that they were not old enough, so in his long letter to the council of 21 June he requested that the starting age for the university be reduced from fifteen to ten. He presented his reasoning as more than self-interested, demonstrating his awareness of the kind of clientele for whom the establishment was intended, namely 'what is usually termed the middling class, including the Professions & the higher pursuits of Commerce'. As he understood it, the plan was as follows:

> To give the children of this class a useful, solid, and well grounded education suitable to the purposes of active life; as well as to afford opportunites to those who might be desirous of pursuing the various branches of education on the more extended scale, but in a more economical manner than has been usual. To secure the morals from contamination by being educated as it were under the eyes of the parents & having the shelter of the paternal roof; thereby superceding [*sic*] the necessity of sending our Sons to those public schools where is notoriously practised every vice which can disgrace humanity, from which they bring no useful knowledge; & where their minds become too often vitiated, that numbers when they mix in the world, show themselves to be, at least, very questionable characters. These are well grounded & acknowledged facts.[45]

Concentrating on the needs of this new mercantile class, Sass declares that under the present plan 'injustice must be done to many Proprietors embarked in Commerce, who might be anxious that their Sons should commence the active duties of life at the age proposed for admitting them to study'. Then he turns to his own case, declaring that he 'cannot calculate upon living more than ten years longer' (he was forty), and that it would be twelve years before one of his sons could 'have any advantage from the establishment'. He confesses frankly that £200 is 'too much for me to subscribe without my children benefitting, which was unquestionably the more immediate object of my becoming a proprietor'.[46]

Of course the university could not turn itself into a grammar school just to suit Sass's needs; fortunately he lived until 1844 and was able to enrol three sons in the University of London School between 1831 and 1839.[47] By January 1830 Horner was describing the plan for a school to be formed along the same lines as the university itself: a day school teaching both the classics and modern subjects such as languages and the sciences, in order to accommodate 'persons of moderate fortune' living in London who would like their sons to have as good an education as that at the great public schools but at less expense and without boarding. The university's council would appoint a head at a salary of about £800 per annum; the head would be responsible for appointing the masters, and he would pay their salaries out of the fees as a 'private concern'. Council would oversee the arrangement but keep clear of management. Until there was enough money to build a school in the Gower Street grounds a house big enough to take 150 boys aged between ten and fifteen would be rented in the vicinity.[48]

In March 1830 the council cautiously and with some reluctance took Horner's advice, appointing a committee to consider 'the practicability of establishing a Day School in connexion with the University; and whether it can be done without calling upon the funds of the University'. Lord Auckland chaired the committee, which also had James Loch and James Mill as members.[49] Auckland and some of the proprietors raised a subscription to start the school, since a number of council members, troubled by the poor finances of the university and exhausted by having to referee disagreements between Horner and the professors, were nervous about attempting a new venture. Horner was ahead of the committee, already seeking a suitable headmaster in February 1830, when his friend the Revd Edward Maltby recommended a young man he knew. This was the Revd Henry Browne, aged twenty-six, a graduate of Cambridge who was assisting his father at a school in Norfolk.[50]

Horner sent Browne the prospectus for the Edinburgh Academy, and Browne in turn recommended that Latin and Greek be taught on the system used in Bavarian schools. On his appointment in June 1830, he was authorised to visit Munich to inspect its schools, and he came back ready to teach the classics according to the methods he found there; he also advertised that the school, to be called the London University School, would teach modern languages including German, one of several innovations introduced into the British public school system by the new establishment.[51] The committee which recommended his appointment, led by Lord Auckland, was aware that there was 'a great disinclination on the part of some members of the Council to embark on any thing new which involves expense'; consequently the committee had agreed as a group of individuals 'to advance the necessary funds, and to take upon themselves the whole risk of loss attendant upon the establishment of this School. If it succeeds they will hand it over with all its advantages to the University, so soon as they are repaid their advances.'[52]

The new school would differ substantially from existing schools by being, like its parent institution, open to boys of all faiths and none; its curriculum, like that of the university, offered many more subjects – French and German, geography, and history, with fencing, gymnastics, and dancing as extras – and, importantly, there would be no flogging of younger boys by their elders, in fact no corporal punishment of any kind, whether inflicted by pupil or teacher. However, its first headmaster was not only an Anglican clergyman, like all headmasters at traditional schools, but he tried, as Lardner, Williams, and Dale had done before him at the university, to introduce Anglican prayers and scripture-reading to the school curriculum. Though Browne was made to add to his draft prospectus the sentence 'a pupil will be allowed to absent himself from these acts of worship if his parent or guardian shall, in writing, claim exemption for him from the Head Master', several of the university's founder members objected, and Brougham hurriedly arranged for a new prospectus to be published, removing the act of worship altogether.[53]

After this brief uprearing of the familiar problem of religion, the school opened on 1 November 1830 with fifty-eight pupils. Horner had taken a nearby house, 16 Gower Street, in June, leasing it for five years at an annual rent of £105. The house, unlike the university site, was on land owned by the Duke of Bedford, and was therefore subject to various restrictions. Horner was confident, on reading the lease, that there was 'no objectionable clause in it, nothing which prevents us using the House as a school, save that we are not to put out a Sign Board, which I apprehend will be quite unnecessary, and indeed *infra dig*'.[54] In fact the school was to have repeated trouble with the solicitors of the leaseholder, since a brass plate was put up at the door of No. 16, in contravention of Bedford Estate restrictions, and Horner received regular letters demanding that the plate be taken down. The school also got into trouble with the Estate over the 'nuisance' to neighbouring tenants on Gower Street of a building erected in the garden at No. 16.[55]

On all hands it was agreed that the school should move as soon as possible into the university's premises, both to be free of Bedford Estate restrictions and to capitalise on its immediate success in attracting pupils of the required ages, between eight and fifteen. By February 1831 numbers had doubled to 116, the house in Gower Street was too small to hold them, and plans were being laid to move. The school promised to be the saviour of the university, which was so hard up in December 1830 that Horner offered to take £200 less of his £1,000 salary that year and until matters improved.[56] But so unhappy was the mood in Gower Street, with the professoriate angry about Horner's salary and interference, and about their own poverty and insecurity, that the Revd Henry Browne decided in the summer of 1831, after less than a year in post, that he had had enough. He felt uncomfortable as an Anglican clergyman in an institution where some were openly hostile to Anglicanism, and he may have been worried by what he regarded as the hounding of Horner, who gave notice in March that he would leave that summer.[57] Browne soon became a vicar in Sussex and from 1841 was principal of the theological college attached to Chichester Cathedral.[58]

The tension in the university and the efforts to revive its fortunes by opening a school were not missed by the sharp-eyed Theodore Hook, who had taken to calling Gower Street 'Gore Street' in the aftermath of the Burke and Hare body-snatching scandal in Edinburgh, and who kept up with all the university news, probably primed by an insider. *John Bull* noted in April 1831:

> MR HORNER, the something – we forget what the thing is called – but the head of the Cockney College in Gore-street, has resigned; some of the Governors or Council, or whatever they are, cut him off two hundred a year, and he has bolted. This seems silly – a thousand a year is a good salary for being at the top of a thing that is at the bottom of everything else.
>
> It will hardly be believed – yet, after there being University chop-houses, and University taps, and University oyster-shops, and all the rest of it, there is nothing likely to surprise one – but at number 16, in Upper *Gore-street, or* Gower-street – we do not exactly remember how the name of the region is spelt – there is, on a brass plate fixed on a little two-roomed Cockney-hole of a house, these words in large letters – '*London University School*'. – An University School! – Number sixteen, Gore-street! . . . and then, farther on, is that most absurd of all things, the College of Cockayne itself, with a portico contrived on purpose with a variety of steps *outside the building* to keep the poor devils who are obliged to go up them, in the wet and fog of a suburban climate, and the stinking vapours arising from stagnant pools, half filled up with the refuse of the dust-carts.[59]

On and on goes Hook, recalling the wasteland on which the university was built, reviving the nickname Stinkomalee, ridiculing both the grandiosity of the Palladian front of the university and the meanness of the small house taken for its school, and suggesting that the whole enterprise is driving neighbouring residents from their homes as a result of the 'nuisance' created by the institution. Their 'once quiet village' (here Hook apparently forgets that he has just described the area as a stinking stagnant rubbish dump) has been ruined by the comings and goings, including the opening of various eating establishments in the area claiming to cater for the influx of students.

In the summer of 1831 both the university and its school were on the brink of disaster. Browne's resignation threw the council into turmoil. They needed the school and they had a duty to the boys who were already being educated there, many of them sons of the very professors who were so unsettled. They rushed into appointing, on Browne's recommendation, one of the assistant masters whom Browne had taken on, John Walker, who lived with his family at 32 Alfred Place, near Bedford Square.[60] His short reign was a fiasco. Council found it had brought trouble on itself by the hands-off arrangement it had made with the school's headmasters. Browne and after him Walker were required to take the lease on the house in Gower Street, which was to be vacated in January 1832, when space would be made available in the university itself; they were also given full charge of the school's finances, paying the masters out of the fees. Walker, a graduate of Trinity College Dublin, brought in his own assistant masters, including two Maturin brothers, one a clergyman, and the new session began apparently smoothly in October 1831 under his rule.

Scarcely a month after the beginning of term, council made the unwelcome discovery that Walker had been declared bankrupt in 1825, when he was a schoolmaster and bookseller in Kennington, south of London.[61] In a paper drawn up in December 1831 on the feasibility of removing Walker from his post, the university's secretary and treasurer of the school, Thomas Coates, recited the facts:

In August 1826 [Walker] had obtained his certificate [of bankruptcy]; in Feb. 1828 took the benefit of the Insolvent Act his deficit being £1700; . . . he was at the time of his appointment (and is still) carrying on the trade of School Agent in partnership with a Mr Pike – . . . his two Sureties were this Pike (his Partner) and Pike's son who with a brother or son is a discount Agent in the City – and notorious as the Watford Banker, they having failed at Watford & paid 8d. in the pound

. . . Mr Walker had given no notice of these facts to the Subscribers or their Treasurer.[62]

The university thought it could get rid of Walker immediately by announcing that the school, without Walker, would move into university premises in January 1832. But Walker would not give up without a fight. He held the lease on 16 Gower Street until Lady Day (25 March) 1832, and he refused to surrender it. On 26 December 1831 he sent out a printed notice to the parents of his pupils, claiming misrepresentation on the part of the council and injustice in its intention not to (re)appoint him once the school removed within the walls of the university. This amounted, he declared, to dismissal without notice. He admitted to 'pecuniary embarrassments in which I was *formerly* involved', but disagreed that these rendered him ineligible for the position of headmaster. Finally he requested the parents directly to 'entrust the further education of your son to my care', claiming that 'every Master of the School has most kindly offered me the command of those talents and exertions, which had hitherto enabled me to pursue that effective Instruction . . . which appears to have afforded general satisfaction' to parents.[63]

Confusion now arose, as the university scrambled to start its own school within its walls. The professors of Greek and Latin, Henry Malden and Thomas Key, respectively, offered to be joint headmasters in addition to keeping their professorial appointments, and to take the financial risk on themselves. But parents were unsure of the arrangements. Dionysius Lardner, himself on the way out, having resigned his chair on 30 November 1831 while expressing his willingness to continue lecturing until a successor could be found, inquired of Coates on 27 December if he could enrol his two (legitimate) sons, Henry, aged fifteen, and George, aged thirteen, at the school. Coates sent him a prospectus, to which Lardner replied on 2 January 1832 that he had meant the school 'successively conducted by Mr Brown[e] and Mr Walker'. The only change he had heard of was the move from 16 Gower Street into the university building; he subsequently received Walker's printed letter about the continuation of the school at 16 Gower Street and was unsure what to do. He now wrote to Coates that he had heard the charges 'circulated to the prejudice of Mr Walker' and believed them to be groundless. He was therefore going to send his sons to Walker's school, and asked Coates to remove their names from the list for the new school to be run by Malden and Key. By September 1832, however, Lardner was sending Coates his banker's order for the quarterly fees for Henry and George at the new university school.[64]

The University of London School, under Key and Malden, was advertised to begin on 23 January 1832.[65] Meanwhile, Walker repeatedly advertised *his* school, calling it 'University School, 16, Gower Street, Bedford
Square', from January 1832 until 12 March, less than two weeks before his
hold on the lease on 16 Gower Street expired, when the advertisement in
The Times read as follows:

UNIVERSITY SCHOOL, 16, Gower-street, Bedford-square.

Head Master – JOHN WALKER, A.B. of Trinity College Dublin.

Vice-Master – Rev. CHARLES MATURIN, A.M., Fellow of King's
College, Cambridge.

TAVISTOCK HOUSE and GROUNDS, Tavistock-square, having
been taken for this Institution, the pupils and present establishment of
masters will be transferred thither on Monday, the 19th of March, from
which date it will be designated the London High School ... The
extent of the premises admitting of the appropriation of distinct school
rooms, and also of a separate play ground for junior boys, a Preparatory
School for those under 8 years of age will be opened in connexion with
the High School. A prospectus may be obtained at the present school-
house, 16, Gower-street, where an interview with the Head Master may
be had daily from 12 to 1 o'clock.[66]

The mischievous Walker continued for a few years to run his London
High School in Tavistock House, which would later become the family
home of Charles Dickens. Dickens knew a thing or two about such schools;
his mother had attempted, and failed, to start one – complete with brass
plate on the door saying 'Mrs Dickens's Establishment' – in Bloomsbury.
She had opened her short-lived and pupil-less school in December 1823 in
a recently built house on land opposite the site which was soon to be taken
for the university. Number 4 Gower Street North was rented in the forlorn
hope of saving the family from the event which followed the failure of this
enterprise, namely the removal of her husband to debtors' prison. Dickens
later recalled that he was sent round with circulars for the school, but that
nobody came. His mother and siblings soon left the house in Gower Street
North (later renumbered 147 Gower Street, and demolished about 1898)
to join John Dickens in the Marshalsea prison, while Charles was sent, aged
twelve, into lodgings in Camden Town, from where he walked daily to
work in the hated blacking factory near Hungerford Bridge, nursing a

resentment against his parents for removing him from school and abandoning him to this fate.[67]

Anyone could set up a school in those unregulated days, but it was a risky business. Walker advertised the London High School until January 1835, by which time the Revd Charles Maturin was named as the headmaster and Walker as the assistant master, probably because Walker was once more gazetted as a debtor in May 1834.[68] In 1833 the school had been puffed in the *Morning Chronicle* as having become, 'we understand, the most flourishing seminary in the environs of the Metropolis'. 'Its system of education', the notice continued, 'embraces all that is taught either at the London University or at King's College.'[69] By November 1835 the London High School, still in Tavistock House, was being run by Dr J.W. Niblock, and no more was heard of John Walker.[70]

Meanwhile, back in the real University of London school, Key and Malden set about making a success of their enterprise. Malden, who had graduated from Cambridge in 1822, had only recently been appointed to the chair of Greek at the university, after the resignation of George Long in August 1831.[71] Malden was known as a gentle, benevolent teacher, at both the school and the university.[72] Key was a more fiery spirit, engaging in controversy with the short-lived Thomas Dale over the place of English in the university syllabus and angrily refuting an accusation made by Horner, after the latter had left Gower Street in some bitterness, that he, Key, had plotted with others, including De Morgan and Isaac Lyon Goldsmid, to remove Browne from the headmastership of the school.[73]

Between them, Malden and Key made a success of the university school, teaching the classics themselves and hiring Emanuel Hausmann and P.F. Merlet, already language tutors at the university, but with few students, to teach German and French respectively. Science was taught, and the boys had the use of the university's laboratories, a facility unavailable to pupils at other schools until nearly the end of the nineteenth century.[74] By February 1835 the number attending the school had reached 303; that the university recorded only 489 students at the same audit indicates how vital the school was to the survival of its parent institution, with 20 per cent of the school fees going to the university.[75] When the university changed its name to University College London in 1836, the school's name changed too, first to the Junior School of University College, then in 1838 to University College School.

A number of professors and proprietors sent their sons there, including Lardner, the professor of English law Andrew Amos, George Birkbeck, Isaac Lyon Goldsmid and his brothers, William Wilkins, Thomas

Donaldson the architect (and later the first professor of architecture at University College), Henry Sass, and the famous German-born artist and recorder of the changing face of London, George Johann Scharf. Many of these men lived in Bloomsbury, including Scharf, whose home was in Francis Street (now Torrington Place). His two sons, George – later to become the first secretary of the National Portrait Gallery – and Henry, were among the first pupils at the school. Their father executed a fine print in 1833 of the boys playing in the Gower Street playground to the south of the university building, dedicating it to the pupils themselves.[76] Later pupils included Augustus De Morgan's son William; Roget's son John; Thomas Henry Huxley's brilliant son Leonard; John (later Viscount) Morley; Joseph Chamberlain, the son of a Unitarian manufacturer; and Ford Hermann Hueffer, later known as the novelist Ford Madox Ford. The school remained in Gower Street until 1907, when it moved to Hampstead, following the exodus from central London of several large schools – Charterhouse, Christ's Hospital, King's College School – in search of space.

One pupil who would go on to become highly successful as an actor, playwright, and producer, and be quite as notorious for his sexual adventures as his father, was Lardner's illegitimate son Dion Boucicault. The two legitimate sons, Henry and George, had attended for three terms, from October 1832 until August 1833, when Henry went on to the university.[77] In 1834–5 Dion Boucicault attended for five terms, boarding with the school's assistant writing master Mr Haselwood in Upper Gower Street.[78] Though Dion was not acknowledged as the son of Lardner, the latter paid his fees at the school and subsequently at a school in Dublin which Dion attended when his mother returned there in 1836 after separating from Lardner. Boucicault's later life experiences included bankruptcies, extramarital affairs, and bigamy.[79]

The opening of the (second and official) school in January 1832 heralded a steady improvement in the fortunes of the university itself. From modest beginnings, the school, like its parent, became a model for others. There was no caning, no licensed bullying of younger boys by their elders (fagging), as in other private schools, and, of course, no religious requirement or practice. It was a day school, so cold and near-starvation such as that suffered by boarders at the great schools of Eton, Winchester, and Westminster did not exist. The syllabus, widened to include modern languages, geography, and non-academic subjects such as gymnastics, from seeming outlandish at first, became the norm by the end of the century, as did the use of a laboratory for science classes.[80] The school saved the university financially by coming into existence at the same time that ambitious plans for the university to have its own teaching hospital – another first – were being laid. During the next few decades Gower Street was to become as famous for medical progress as it was for radicalism and godlessness, and Bloomsbury in general consolidated a reputation first gained in the eighteenth century for its association with hospitals, dispensaries, doctors, and medical reform.

CHAPTER FOUR

Bloomsbury Medicine: Letting in the Light

IT HAD been part of the plan for the new university from the beginning that it would have an up-to-date medical faculty and also its own hospital to serve the double function of caring for the local community and teaching students the practice of medicine to complement the theory being taught in the classrooms of Gower Street. Lack of money and the council's preoccupation with setting the university itself on a firm basis meant that there was a delay before a new hospital could be built on the opposite side of the road. When the building opened in 1834, it led the way in medical research while catering for the enlarged population living in the recently developed streets of north-west Bloomsbury. Like the university itself, the hospital experienced problems of finance and of quarrelling personnel in its early years, but by mid-century it had become recognised as one of the most advanced hospitals in the country.

Bloomsbury was already rich in medical facilities. The area to the south and east of Gower Street had long been associated with doctors, hospitals, and pioneering activities, though neither of London's ancient hospitals and their medical schools – St Thomas's and St Bartholomew's (twelfth century) – nor Guy's (early eighteenth century), was located in Bloomsbury. The nearest well-established hospital was the Middlesex, founded in the mid-eighteenth century on Charles Street (now Mortimer Street), west of Tottenham Court Road, with which the new university attempted, unsuccessfully, to make reciprocal arrangements for the medical students of the one and the apprentice doctors of the other.[1]

From the eighteenth century onwards Bloomsbury was central to medical progress. London had lagged behind other capital cities like Paris in not having a 'hospital' (in the loosest sense) to take in abandoned and illegitimate babies and children. Captain Thomas Coram put that right when he persuaded aristocrats and royalty to contribute to his humanitarian plan to take abandoned infants off the streets of London, the result being the establishment of the Foundling Hospital in 1739. A committee of governors was formed, with John Russell, fourth Duke of Bedford, as its president, and a building was sought for the hospital. The Earl of Halifax offered Montagu House on Great Russell Street, but Coram thought it unsuitable and twenty years later it became the first British Museum instead.[2]

Land in eastern Bloomsbury was bought, and the architect Theodore Jacobsen was commissioned to build the hospital, which opened in 1745. Fifty years later James Burton was hired by the Foundling Estate to develop the surrounding land, in order to bring in much-needed revenue from rents. Brunswick and Mecklenburgh Squares were created on the grand scale, with houses built to a high standard in order to keep the immediate neighbourhood of the hospital respectable. This was felt to be necessary both because of the nature of the mothers coming to deliver their babies – many of them poor abandoned girls, some of them prostitutes – and because of the poorer housing which was being built to the east of Gray's Inn Road as London expanded in the last years of the eighteenth and the first decades of the nineteenth century.[3]

While the Foundling Hospital was really a children's home with medical attendants on hand, houses in the nearby streets and squares were occupied by a number of doctors. Richard Mead, physician to George II and a promoter of the Foundling Hospital – and of its art gallery, to which Hogarth, Gainsborough and others contributed – lived in Great Ormond Street in the very house which was to be taken a century later for the Hospital for Sick Children. Nearby Queen Square was full of doctors, including one who attended George III. By the 1860s almost every second house in the square was a specialist hospital or charitable home for disadvantaged people: the list includes the Ladies' Charity School at No. 22 from 1859, the National Hospital for Nervous Diseases at No. 24 from 1860, Louisa Twining's St Luke's Home for epileptic and incurable women at No. 20 from 1866, two Catholic charities at No. 31 in the 1860s, the Alexandra Hospital for Children with Hip Disease at No. 19 from 1867, and the Alexandra Home for the Blind at No. 6 from 1869.[4] Robert Louis Stevenson described the square in the early 1870s, noting that 'every second door-plate' seemed to offer 'help to the afflicted'.[5]

Many more hospitals were added in the later years of the nineteenth century, and Queen Square today houses the National Hospital for Neurology and Neurosurgery and the UCL Institute of Neurology. The Hospital for Sick Children opened in 1852 just round the corner in Great

Ormond Street, and the London Homoeopathic Hospital moved in 1859 into three houses nearly next door, one of them previously the residence of Zachary Macaulay and his family. Both these hospitals survive, though in more recent buildings; the London Homoeopathic Hospital is now part of UCL and has been renamed the Royal London Hospital for Integrated Medicine.

By the end of the nineteenth century the trend for wealthy and fashionable residents to move westward to Regent's Park and Marylebone, where successful doctors colonised Harley Street and Wimpole Street for their private practices, or south-west to Belgravia and St James's, meant that fewer well-off families or doctors practising from home now lived in Bloomsbury's elegant squares. Queen Square, Bloomsbury Square, and Red Lion Square in particular were increasingly populated by institutions: hospitals, nursing homes, children's homes, and offices of charities such as the Mendicity Society in Red Lion Square. As the historian of London Edward Walford noted in 1878, this area of Bloomsbury could be described as 'once-fashionable', many of its squares, especially Red Lion Square, being now largely 'devoted to public and charitable purposes'.[6]

On its opening in 1834 the University of London's hospital, at first called the North London Hospital, was, like the university itself and its school, an innovative institution which had to battle prejudice and even scandal in its early years, before establishing a reputation for research, teaching, and practical excellence. As James Fernandez Clarke, one of the first medical students at the university, recalled in 1874, 'medical education in this country was in a most unsatisfactory, anomalous, and imperfect state' when the University of London was first established.[7] By 'this country' he meant England, where Oxford and Cambridge had no medical school or university hospital attached, unlike universities in many European cities and in Scotland, where Edinburgh University had established its own medical school in 1736. Between 1750 and 1800 the Scottish universities produced nine-tenths of all medical graduates in Britain.[8] In London anatomy was taught in a number of private schools, where a few celebrated surgeons and physicians associated with Guy's, St Thomas's, and St Bartholomew's had a monopoly of the lucrative business of teaching medicine. Since nepotism was rife, young men without family influence or money could not easily get into the profession. The new university intended to offer a universally accessible alternative to these monopolies, and it began by appointing a 'formidable phalanx' of professors, mainly recruited from the University of Edinburgh.[9]

As with the founding of the university itself, so with the establishment of its medical school, opposition came from vested interests and existing institutions, in this case the London hospitals and their schools as well as the lecture halls of Oxford and Cambridge. Successive attempts by the new metropolitan university to be granted degree-awarding powers were fiercely opposed. In 1834 no fewer than ninety-nine physicians and surgeons from the older London schools petitioned William IV not to grant the privileges of a university to 'the medical school in Gower Street', the main reason being 'that the London University resembles in no respect the ancient universities of England; that it is a joint-stock association, founded and supported by money subscribed in shares, which may be bought and sold in the market, like those of canals, gas-works and other speculative undertakings'.[10]

It was a variation on the old snobbish accusation which had been levelled in 1825–6 by Tory wits such as Hook, Disraeli, and Praed. Buying and selling in the realm of education was vulgar; the value of the education acquired in such newfangled institutions might well be suspect in this 'marketing' environment. Hook's *John Bull* soon took up the conservative hue and cry against medical reform. During the first session of the new university, 1828–9, one of *John Bull*'s targets was the medical faculty and in particular the known views of Bentham and his supporters on the importance of allowing dissection of bodies as part of a medical education. At the time it was illegal to dissect the body of anyone who was not an executed murderer, but with recent progress being made in medical science, surgeons and anatomists were desperate for corpses. In December 1828 the notorious Edinburgh pair Burke and Hare were brought to trial for murdering tramps in order to supply Professor Robert Knox of Edinburgh University with cadavers to dissect. Hare turned king's evidence and was eventually released, while Burke was hanged in January 1829. The case brought round those such as the Archbishop of Canterbury who had blocked previous legislative attempts, and a reforming Anatomy Act, allowing for bodies to be dissected under strict regulations, was finally passed in the summer of 1832, just weeks after the public dissection of Bentham's own body in accordance with the terms of his will.

The sensational nature of the Burke and Hare story ensured its lasting fame. Knox maintained that he had had no knowledge of the manner in which the people whose corpses he bought from Burke and Hare had died, but a skipping song soon became common in Edinburgh:

Up the close and down the stair,
But and ben with Burke and Hare.
Burke's the butcher, Hare the thief,
Knox the boy who buys the beef.[11]

Always up to date in its references, *John Bull*, in the person of Hook, started accusing the University of London of dark practices as early as September 1828, a few weeks before its doors opened to medical students: 'The Council of Stinkomalee have expended vast sums in building, in pulling down, or rather rooting up, and re-building again, dissecting-rooms, lecture-rooms, catacombs for corpses, and contrivances for getting exhumated bodies out of the neighbouring burial-grounds . . .'[12]

In January 1829, with Burke soon to be hanged, the paper went even further, connecting the 'Cockney College in Gower-street' directly to the Edinburgh scandal and returning with black humour to its previous hints about the moral danger to students of London's prostitutes. Hook completes his dire warnings, just for good measure, with another scornful reference to the march of intellect:

> We have no doubt that the scheme of inveigling unhappy individuals into secret places and depriving them of life for the purposes of dissection, is in progress of execution here as well as in Scotland – why not? – the facilities are much more evident – the number of unhappy victims of prostitution . . . is a hundred-fold greater than that in Edinburgh . . . The defection of the females of that class from the neighbourhood of Stinkomalee has been generally attributed to the activity of the Council in weeding the environs of the University; we differ, and we think they are quite right to go; for if we harbour amongst us any of these murderous traffickers in human flesh, the vaunted facilities for receiving subjects into the College might prove a terrible incentive to the monsters, and the convenient proximity of the poor girls render[s] them easy victims to the cause of science and the march of intellect.[13]

Augustus De Morgan composed a light-hearted response to this in a witty verse of his own, slyly set to the rhythm of the Scottish song 'Comin' through the Rye', with its innocent use of the word 'body' ('Gin a body meet a body/Comin' thro' the rye,/Gin a body kiss a body,/Need a body cry?'). De Morgan's version reads:

Should a body want a body
   Anatomy to teach,
Should a body snatch a body,
   Need a body peach?[14]

Council set up a hospital committee early in 1828, several months before the university itself was due to open. Lord Auckland was on the committee, as was the MP Henry Warburton, who advocated medical reform in parliament, where he chaired a committee investigating the teaching of anatomy in the wake of the Burke and Hare case. He brought successive anatomy bills until the Anatomy Act was finally passed by the House of Lords in 1832.[15] Also on the hospital committee were James Loch, Isaac Lyon Goldsmid, whose family would be generous benefactors to the hospital throughout the nineteenth century, and Leonard Horner. The committee met on 8 March 1828 to examine plots of land in the neighbourhood. Thomas Cubitt was to be consulted. But nothing more appears to have happened until January 1829, when William Wilkins attended a meeting in order to submit plans for four different sites, three of them across the New Road to the north. In the end, none of Wilkins's plans was accepted, and the architect Alfred Ainger of Doughty Street got the commission to build directly across the road from the university. Construction did not start until 1833, by which time £3,000 in subscriptions had been raised.[16]

The delay was caused by the dire financial position of the university. With money tight, it made do for the first six years with a dispensary on George Street, across the New Road, where the medical professors were expected to put in a few hours each week for no extra pay, and where students could watch them diagnose diseases and dispense medicines. It seemed sensible at this time for the university to join forces with the Middlesex Hospital, with students going in both directions, until the dream of opening the university's own hospital could be realised.[17] Tensions arose, however, with anxieties in the Middlesex about the bad press the university was attracting for its 'godlessness', and snobbishness towards the 'joint-stock university' among some of the hospital's leading doctors. On the other side, too, there was a reluctance on the part of some of the new professors to send students to the Middlesex for practical lessons.

The first medical professor to be appointed, and the one who was asked to give the opening lecture at the university, Charles Bell, already famous as the discoverer of Bell's palsy and a successful surgeon at the Middlesex, complained that his professorial colleagues were not inclined to co-operate with the Middlesex people.[18] An Edinburgh-educated friend of Horner, Bell argued endlessly with his colleagues and resigned from the university in September 1830 when his suggestions for restructuring the medical faculty were rejected.[19] He commented in February 1831 that the university was 'going fast to the dogs' through 'misrule and mismanagement'. A month later he noted that his friend Horner had offered his resignation, 'worn out by vexation and injustice'.[20] Bell himself returned to Edinburgh in 1836 to take up the chair of surgery there.

The university was entering the arena at a time of rapid development in medical science and reactionary responses on the part of existing medical bodies. It is therefore not surprising that the council made some mistakes in its appointments and arrangements. A set of determined, if brilliant, individuals arrived in Gower Street without being clear how the subject would be divided between them. This uncertainty, combined with the combativeness of many of the professors, and disagreements about medical methods, brought about the prolonged and damaging Pattison affair.

Granville Sharp Pattison was one of several Scots appointed to the first London chairs; like some of his compatriots, especially in medicine, he brought controversy and rivalries with him, though in his case not directly from Scotland, but from America. He had been dismissed from his post in anatomy at Glasgow University after accusations of incompetence and involvement in the clandestine acquiring of corpses for dissection. He left Glasgow after being named in 1819 as co-respondent in the divorce of a colleague. In Philadelphia and then Baltimore he fought duels with opponents who accused him of claiming their discoveries and causing disruption in their institutions. His appointment in London, given his known history, was a risk, though he was admired in some medical circles for his anatomical skills. The university soon found that he was no less able to stir up trouble in London than he had been in Scotland and America.[21]

The querulous Pattison, the imperious and authoritative Bell, and a third appointee, J.R. Bennett, argued amongst themselves about the division of labour in anatomy, surgery, and physiology. They plagued Horner with their rows. Meanwhile a number of students began to complain during the second session, 1829–30, that Pattison was a poor lecturer with little knowledge of the subject, that he neglected his class, and that he lectured – when he did lecture – 'in a desultory manner', sometimes wearing a pink coat and riding boots.[22] The charge of incompetence related to Pattison's clinging to traditional descriptive anatomy, when some of his colleagues, such as Bennett, were expounding new ideas, brought both from Edinburgh and from Parisian medical circles, where researchers such as Bichat were correlating post-mortem findings with symptoms in living patients in order to understand the causes and conditions of disease.[23] Pattison counter-complained to council – and to Horner, whom he accused of bias against him – that some of his colleagues were in league with the students. In a long reply to a document signed by eighty-nine students alleging his incompetence, Pattison charged Horner with writing it for them after holding meetings with them in a nearby tavern.[24] Horner and the council dallied until the whole business became fodder for the press. The reforming medical paper, the *Lancet*, edited by the crusading Thomas Wakley, published in 1830 some of the complaints against Pattison and drew attention to a pamphlet by a Philadelphia opponent in 1820, in which it was alleged that Pattison was 'an adventurer with a tainted reputation'.[25]

After nearly two years of trouble, council finally achieved Pattison's dismissal, but at the cost of having to hold a publicised special meeting of proprietors on 8 October 1831 in order to vote Pattison a grant of £200 in compensation. A number of proprietors wrote to *The Times*, endorsing the council's proceedings but declaring that Pattison's 'general character' and 'professional skill' had not been impeached by the unfortunate circumstances of his leaving.[26] Worse still, some of the best professors resigned their chairs in protest at the removal of Pattison, not because they supported the details of his case – most of them were non-medical and not involved in the dispute – but because they felt council had handled it poorly, especially by appearing to allow students to hold sway over the appointment or dismissal of a professor. Their anger really arose from dislike of Horner and resentment at their status as employees without a voice in the management of the university. During the long summer of 1831 the university lost Horner, demoralised by the criticisms of his management and salary, Browne as headmaster of the newly established school, and the excellent professors De Morgan (until he was persuaded to return in 1836), Long, who took up the editorship of the Society for the Diffusion of Useful Knowledge's large publications, and Rosen. Conolly, professor of the nature and treatment of diseases, and Lardner were lost in 1831 too, in their case because of the lack of sufficient remuneration for their teaching. One good thing to result from the Pattison affair was that the council learned a lesson: it dispensed with the post of Warden and created a Senatus committee which would include professors in the decision-making of the university from now on.

The new and evolving divisions in science were reflected in the titles of the chairs being established in the University of London, some of them cumbersome, like Lardner's, and others liable to change as the professors argued among themselves about their place in the new era of specialisation. The medical chairs offered the most extreme example of disagreement and dispute in Gower Street, partly on personal and partly on intellectual grounds. Bell and Pattison did not agree about how to conduct their subject, and they did not get on personally. Both had left by 1831; as the third early medical appointee, James Bennett, died at this time, a whole new set of medical professors had to be appointed.[27] Of these the most significant were John Elliotson and Robert Liston. If the university authorities now hoped for smooth progress and concord, they were to be disappointed, for their new professors proved to be thoroughly controversial.

Both were showmen, demonstrating their medical skills to audiences which turned up in large numbers, as they did for Lardner's lectures on the steam engine, from well outside the university precincts. In this they were adapting to the university lecture hall a tradition of exhibiting scientific experiments to lay audiences which had begun with the formation by the Royal Society of the Royal Institution in Albemarle Street in 1799. Here Humphry Davy, discoverer of nitrous oxide (laughing gas) and inventor of the safety lamp for miners named after him, had demonstrated his chemical experiments in the early days. Davy's erstwhile apprentice Faraday was now the leading light at the Royal Institution, working on electro-magnetism, while guest speakers such as Lardner were invited to lecture on new topics.[28]

In May 1831 John Elliotson was appointed to Conolly's vacant chair, the name of which was soon changed to the theory and practice of medicine and later to the principles and practice of medicine. The son of a London chemist, Elliotson had studied medicine at both Edinburgh and Cambridge, was a physician at St Thomas's Hospital, and had been elected a fellow of the Royal Society in 1829. He was an innovator, one of the first doctors in England to use the stethoscope, developed in Paris in 1816 by René Laennec, and the first to discover the uses of iodine in relieving swollen thyroid glands and to prove 'by direct experiment the value of quinine as an anti-periodic remedy, of prussic acid in vomiting &c'.[29] Now aged forty, he had a hugely successful practice at his home in Conduit Street in London's smart West End, but as a young doctor he had struggled against the class snobbery, nepotism, and absolute power of the great surgeon at St Thomas's, Sir Astley Cooper.[30] In 1829 he began sending accounts of the clinical cases he dealt with to the *Lancet*, whose editor Wakley supported him in his efforts to improve clinical practice and expose injustice and incompetence in the established medical schools.

Both Elliotson and Wakley were pugnacious in their drive to reform the medical profession and medical education. Wakley, the son of a prosperous farmer, had been a pupil at St Thomas's and ran a successful medical practice near Oxford Street until an incident in 1820 when he was beaten unconscious by intruders and his home was set on fire. He turned to journalism, founding the *Lancet* in October 1823, having chosen the title to indicate both the sharpness of the surgical instrument for cutting out bad material and the letting in of light through a window – 'lancet' meaning a narrow window. Wakley set about opening up the world of medicine, publishing extracts from medical lectures without permission, exposing mistakes made by eminent surgeons, and campaigning relentlessly against the secretiveness and traditionalism of some of the country's leading surgeons and physicians.

Wakley was often sued for his pains; on one occasion in 1825 he was defended in a libel case by Brougham.[31] He delighted in being rude about the medical establishment, inventing unflattering nicknames such as 'the BATS' for those in charge of the medical colleges, because of their refusal to emerge into the light of modern medical methodologies, 'Rhubarb Hall' for the Society of Apothecaries, and 'the Warehouse for surgical diplomas' for the Royal College of Surgeons in Lincoln's Inn Fields. Wakley explained these nicknames in a sustained attack on the existing medical establishment in a *Lancet* article in October 1831, excoriating the restrictive practices of the colleges of physicians, surgeons, and apothecaries, and pointing out the uselessness of medical education at Oxbridge. The article bore the provocative title 'Preface, Advertisement, Address, and a Rare Whack at the Voracious Bats. Not forgetting a few useful hints to our beloved but cruelly-plundered friends, the British students in medicine'. In it Wakley declared: 'To become Fellows of the College of Physicians, it is necessary that the candidates should be graduates of the Universities of Oxford and Cambridge, where it would be a calumny on the science of medicine to say that there exists a medical school.'[32]

This attack was written at a time when Wakley knew that the University of London, just up the road from his home at 35 Bedford Square, was intending to open a teaching hospital when funds allowed. He took the opportunity to praise the Gower Street medical professors as constituting 'by far the most powerful medical school in the metropolis'.[33] The societies he was condemning were among the forces which regularly blocked moves to allow the new metropolitan university to confer degrees. In criticising them, Wakley was working towards the same ends as the university, which he supported in many of his *Lancet* articles. In 1835 Wakley became a radical MP for the newly created borough of Finsbury, which included part of Bloomsbury. In 1839 he was elected coroner for West Middlesex, the first medical man rather than lawyer to occupy the post. One of his early post-mortems was carried out at University College Hospital in August 1841.[34]

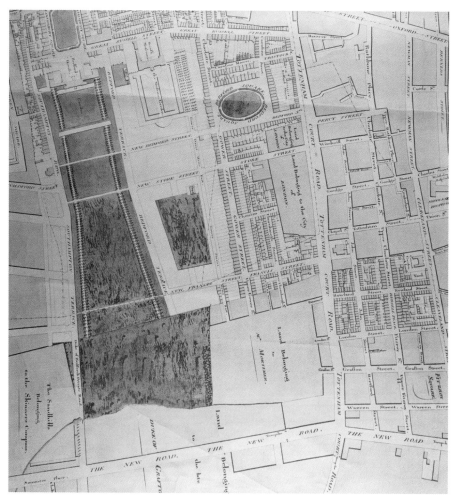

1 *Map of London comprising the Bloomsbury estates of the Duke of Bedford*, 1795. Until 1776 only the southern part of Bloomsbury, along Great Russell Street, was developed. From 1776 the area of fields and dairy farms to the north was developed, first with Bedford Square and then with Gower Street leading north.

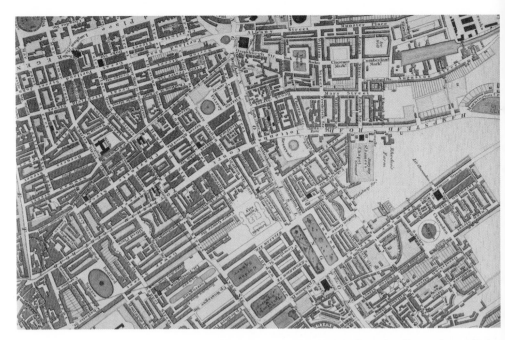

2 *Map of London from an Actual Survey made in the Years 1824, 1825 and 1826* by Christopher and John Greenwood, 1827. This section shows how the northern part of Bloomsbury was now covered in new streets and houses, mainly developed by the architect-builders James Burton and, from 1824, Thomas Cubitt. The map includes the ground plan for William Wilkins's building for the new University of London on Gower Street.

3 Portrait by Spiridione Gambardella of Henry Brougham, the brilliant Scottish lawyer and reforming Whig politician who was the most energetic of the founders of the new University of London on Gower Street and its first president from 1827 until his death, aged eighty-nine, in 1868.

4 Clothed skeleton of Jeremy Bentham in its box in University College London. Bentham, the great Utilitarian philosopher and legal and educational reformer, was not directly involved in the founding of the University of London; his friends and followers, including James Mill and Joseph Hume, were among those who founded the university on Benthamite principles. On his death in 1832 his body was embalmed, according to the instructions in his will, in an 'Auto-Icon' which was presented to University College by one of his executors in 1850.

5 Robert Cruikshank cartoon of Brougham selling shares in the University of London, July 1825. Brougham, dressed in his wig and gown, is seen parading about Lincoln's Inn hawking shares, an activity more often associated with trade than with educational institutions.

6 William Wilkins's University of London as it appeared when opened to students in October 1828. The north and south wings which were part of Wilkins's design were not built until the 1870s, as finances in 1828 were insufficient to complete the design.

7 No. 12 Upper Gower Street, the house rented by the University of London for its Warden Leonard Horner and later the first married home of Charles Darwin from January 1839 to September 1842. The house, later renumbered 110 Gower Street, was damaged by a bomb in 1941 and was subsequently demolished.

8 'The Valentine', illustration to Chapter 33 of Dickens's *Pickwick Papers* (1836–7) by Hablot Knight Browne ('Phiz'), in which Mr Pickwick's faithful servant Sam Weller struggles to write and is asked by his father if he is engaged in the 'pursuit of knowledge under difficulties' in an echo of the title of the most popular educational treatise published by the Society for the Diffusion of Useful Knowledge.

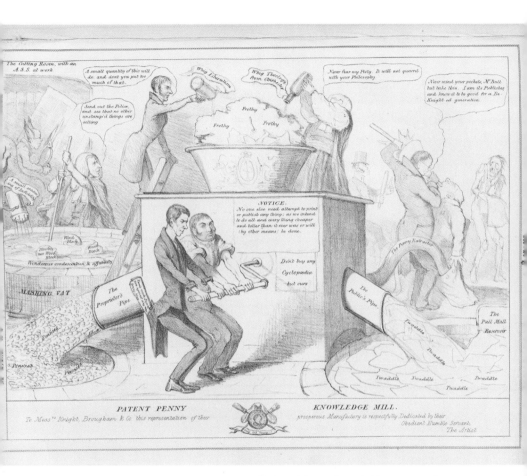

9 Robert Seymour cartoon, *The Patent Penny Knowledge Mill*, October 1832, a satire on the *Penny Magazine* and other cheap publications of the Society for the Diffusion of Useful Knowledge.

10 Posthumous portrait of the University of London's first professor of natural philosophy, *Dionysius Lardner*, by Edith Fortunée Tita De Lisle, given to the National Portrait Gallery by Lardner's son George in 1896.

11 Robert Seymour cartoon, *King's College versus London University, or Which is the Weightiest*, 1828.
A few months before the opening of the avowedly secular University of London in Gower Street, the
founding of a rival Church-and-State university, to be called King's College, was announced. The
cartoon shows fat bishops with plenty of money weighing down the seesaw, while the famously lean
Henry Brougham, complete with broom, and his Benthamite colleagues have only books, 'sense', and
'science' on their side.

12 George Scharf engraving of the University of London School playground, 1833. The school was opened in a house on Gower Street in 1830 to provide students for the university; Scharf's two sons, George (later the first secretary of the National Portrait Gallery) and Henry, were among its first pupils.

A FULL DISCOVERY

OF THE

STRANGE PRACTICES

OF

Dr. ELLIOTSON

On the bodies of his

FEMALE PATIENTS!

AT HIS HOUSE, IN CONDUIT STREET, HANOVER SQ·

WITH ALL THE SECRET

EXPERIMENTS HE MAKES UPON THEM,

AND THE

Curious Postures they are put into while sitting or standing, when awake or asleep!

A female Patient being blindfolded, to undergo an operation.

THE WHOLE AS SEEN

BY AN EYE-WITNESS,

AND NOW FULLY DIVULGED!

&c. &c. &c.

13 Pamphlet, 'A Full Discovery of the Strange Practices of Dr. Elliotson', 1842. Elliotson had been the popular professor of the theory and practice of medicine at University College London until his forced resignation in December 1838 after he controversially used mesmerism in the wards of University College Hospital.

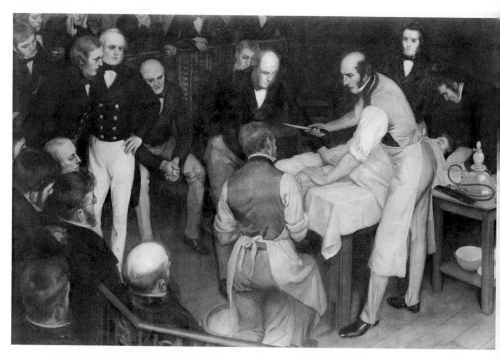

14 Posthumous painting by Ernest Board, *c.*1912, of Robert Liston operating with ether at University College Hospital in December 1846, the first surgical operation under anaesthetic in Britain.

15 Design of a custom-built block for the Hospital for Sick Children, Great Ormond Street, by Edward Middleton Barry, *c.*1871. This building replaced the original house taken for the hospital by its founder in 1852, Charles West.

16 Engraving of the original British Museum building, Montagu House in Great Russell Street, 1829–31. Montagu House was home to the Museum from its opening in 1759 until the completion of Robert Smirke's neoclassical building in 1846.

17 Print by William Simpson of Robert Smirke's new British Museum building, 1852, after twenty years of constructing the replacement for the original Montagu House.

18 Carlo Pellegrini sketch of Sir Anthony Panizzi, *Vanity Fair*, 1874. Panizzi had arrived in Britain in the early 1820s as a political exile from Italy; he was appointed the first professor of Italian at the University of London and became the energetic and reforming principal librarian of the British Museum.

19 *Reception of Nineveh Sculptures at the British Museum, Illustrated London News,* 8 February 1852. The huge sculptures of human-headed winged lions and bulls were brought to England by the archaeologist Austen Henry Layard. This one is a 'colossal Lion, the weight of which is upwards of ten tons', according to the *Illustrated London News.*

20 *St George's, Bloomsbury,* watercolour by George Shepherd, 1811. The church, located to the south of the British Museum, was designed by Nicholas Hawksmoor and opened in 1731 with the unusual and often-derided feature of a statue of George I on top of the steeple.

21 Rookery, St Giles's, *Illustrated London News*, 22 September 1849. The notorious crowded slum area in the neighbourhood of the church of St Giles-in-the-Fields was known as the 'Holy Land' because of its predominantly Irish population.

By the end of the 1830s Wakley and Elliotson had become enemies, Elliotson's activities at University College London and in the University College Hospital across the road being the cause. Elliotson's career in Gower Street had begun well. His lectures were popular; students admired him.[35] In May 1834, as an energetic dean of the medical faculty, he described the state of the medical school in his annual report to council. 'I am proud to announce', he wrote, 'that it is in the highest degree prosperous', with medical student numbers having grown from 248 in 1832 to 351 in 1834. Elliotson expressed the hope that he would see 'our hospital open & our students enjoying full means of clinical instruction without being compelled to resort any longer to other institutions'. He next urged council to speed up its efforts at raising enough money to open the hospital in October 1834, which it did.[36]

Elliotson was soon agitating for the title of the North London Hospital to be changed. Writing at the beginning of 1837, he set out the reasons for renaming it University College Hospital. Claiming to speak on behalf of his colleagues, he declared:

At the foundation of the hospital all of us upon whom the labors & support of the Institution were to fall, were anxious that it should be called University Hospital: but we were overruled by others, not destined to labor for it, on the ground that such a name would prevent tories, hostile to the University, from giving it their support. This reason appeared to us perfectly invalid, because concessions to tories had always failed; & they have failed on this occasion. The tories are equally cold & hostile to the hospital, under the name of North London, as it was feared they would be to it under the name of University Hospital. They do not subscribe to it, & indeed, the Institution is supported not by the subscriptions of any sect or party of men, but by the students, whose fees we pay into the Hospital chest.

No better time could be chosen for changing the name, because the University has just changed its own . . .

The reason of the preference to the name of University Hospital or University College Hospital is . . . that it would set forth the real character of the hospital – would show that it is in connection with, nay a very part of, the School of University College.[37]

Elliotson concluded this robust request by saying that King's College was 'expected soon to possess the Charing Cross Hospital', which it would rename King's College Hospital. His barely concealed contempt for the pusillanimity of the council in the naming of their hospital was accompanied by a strong sense of injustice that it had taken until November 1836 for the university to be granted a charter. Not only had Brougham's attempts to gain degree-awarding powers by putting bills before parliament in 1825 and 1828 been thwarted in both the Commons and the Lords, while King's College and St David's, Lampeter, were awarded charters in 1828–9, but even in 1831, when Brougham was Lord Chancellor in a Whig government and a petition was put forward once more, the bid failed when the University of Cambridge entered a counter-petition against the godless college. In 1832 the new University of Durham – like King's and St David's, Lampeter, an Anglican foundation – was granted a charter. Not until 1836 was it accepted that the Gower Street institution should be granted equal rights with these successors, but the price that had to be paid for a charter was for the university to change its name to University College London, while a second charter was given to a new body, confusingly called the University of London, which would be a purely examining body set up to examine students of both University and King's Colleges.[38] The revised arrangement came into law in 1837.

The newly named University College Hospital, in Ainger's 'handsome but plain building', as Charles Knight described it,[39] carried on successfully with its healthy student numbers and excellent professorial staff, led by Elliotson, until in 1838 he himself brought the hospital and University College into disrepute by his adoption of mesmerism as a method of healing patients. Elliotson was already a convinced follower of phrenology, the science of reading character by analysing the contours of the head; he had founded the London Phrenological Society in 1823.[40] Now he became interested in the phenomenon of animal magnetism, or mesmerism, according to which one person could affect the mind or body of another by making 'magnetic' passes of the hand over the subject. The forerunner of hypnotism, this practice, begun in the late eighteenth century by the German Franz Anton Mesmer, was tried out in lecture rooms and private drawing rooms across Europe. Its potential as a medical method was soon seized on.

In 1837 a French practitioner, 'Baron' Dupotet, arrived in London to demonstrate his mesmeric skills. Both Herbert Mayo, professor of physiology and anatomy at King's College and surgeon at the Middlesex Hospital, and Elliotson at University College Hospital invited Dupotet to experiment in their hospital theatres. Mayo was discouraged by the disapproval of his colleagues, but Elliotson became convinced of the potential of mesmerism in curing patients. In May 1838 Elliotson gave a demonstration of magnetism to a large audience in the theatre of University College Hospital, announcing that a committee had been formed by the Royal Society to consider its claims to scientific validity. The committee was composed of a number of luminaries, including Charles Wheatstone, professor of experimental physics at King's College London and co-inventor in 1837 of the electric telegraph. Some familiar Bloomsbury figures also sat on the committee. From University College there were the comparative anatomist Robert Grant and James Joseph Sylvester, a brilliant former mathematical student of De Morgan's and now professor of natural history, and, from among Bloomsbury's many practising doctors connected with University College, Roget and his neighbour and friend John Bostock.[41]

Elliotson's hospital case notes, articles in newspapers, and accounts in the journals and letters of people who came to see him perform mesmeric practices on patients at the hospital give a sense of the widespread fame of his activities at this time. Among those who attended and were at least partly persuaded were George Cruikshank, Macready, Faraday, Wheatstone, Roget, some academics from Oxford and Cambridge, and also Lardner, who joined Elliotson in a series of experiments during the spring and summer of 1838, writing up his notes of the experiments for the *Monthly Chronicle*.[42] Harriet Martineau, the influential writer on political economy and social matters, came to believe that she had been cured of a tumour by mesmerism, as she announced in her celebrated 'Letters on Mesmerism', published in the *Athenaeum* in December 1844.[43] In 1849 Prince Albert's birthday celebrations included a mesmeric event, at which the prince was put into a trance during which he was immobilised and unable to get up from his chair even when a pistol was discharged in his face.[44]

One of the most enthusiastic of Elliotson's spectators was Dickens, who was then living in Doughty Street. He included a topical reference to a mesmeric experience (though not one induced by another person) in a late chapter of *Oliver Twist*, published in volume form in November 1838. Oliver, while asleep, seems to see the activities of Fagin and his accomplices taking place in another location. Dickens writes of a kind of sleep which 'holds the body prisoner' but in which 'we have a consciousness of all that is going on about us'. Moreover:

> It is an undoubted fact, that although our senses of touch and sight be for the time dead, yet our sleeping thoughts, and the visionary scenes that pass before us, will be influenced, and materially influenced, by the *mere silent presence* [Dickens's italics] of some external object; which may

not have been near us when we closed our eyes: and of whose vicinity we have had no waking consciousness.[45]

George Cruikshank, also a willing spectator of Elliotson's demonstrations, illustrated this scene, showing Oliver in a trance-like state similar to those adopted by mesmeric subjects.[46]

On 23 May 1838 Elliotson requested permission to give, in University College itself, a 'clinical lecture upon the important philosophical & medicinal facts of the ill appreciated and stigmatised agency commonly known by the name of animal magnetism'. Writing in the third person, as he usually did in his communications with council, he continued:

> His reason for making this request is that the phenomena which he has had the happiness to effect in the Hospital have gradually attracted the earnest attention & wonder of the highest scientific characters of Oxford and Cambridge, of the Royal Society, King's College &c & of the great body of medical men engaged in private practice & in the public schools.[47]

He went on to say that he had received so many requests to attend from peers and members of the House of Commons that the hospital theatre would not be large enough to accommodate them all; he therefore needed a theatre in the College itself. At the meeting of council to consider the request, William Tooke, seconded by Henry Crabb Robinson, moved that Elliotson be allowed to give one such lecture. Five members voted for the motion, and eight against.[48] He gave the lecture in the hospital, not the College.

The unease felt about Elliotson in Gower Street grew in the following months, as he took his experiments further and became the subject of sustained attack in the *Lancet* by his erstwhile champion Wakley. Elliotson used the magnetic treatment from early 1837 until December 1838, especially on people with epilepsy, which he considered responsive to Mesmer's system. Two long-term patients, the young servants Elizabeth and Jane O'Key, aged sixteen and fifteen, were diagnosed by Elliotson as having hysteria and epilepsy. He kept them on the wards of University College Hospital for several months. Elizabeth exhibited extreme changes of behaviour while entranced; audiences were gripped by the displays.[49] Not content with mesmerising the two girls when they were seized with fits, however, Elliotson began to use them as experimental subjects for his demonstrations to students and the public, inducing mesmeric trances at will. He came to believe that in magnetising them he was passing on his mesmeric influence, so that they became a sort of 'medium' through which he could cure others.

Until the summer of 1838 Wakley had reported Elliotson's experiments in the *Lancet* in a neutral way, but some other medical journals were hostile from the start, suspecting fraud on the part of the O'Keys, while Elliotson's colleagues at University College were divided. Robert Liston, another charismatic medical professor who welcomed audiences to his own displays of rapid surgery, disliked both Elliotson's fame and the 'quackery' of his demonstrations. Others agreed, and in May 1838 Anthony Todd Thomson joined Liston in suggesting to council that Elliotson's exhibitions were 'detrimental to the character and the interests of the College and the Hospital'. Council requested the pugnacious Elliotson to stop, which he refused to do.[50] By August Wakley at last began to suspect fraud. He publicly invited Elliotson to perform magnetic experiments in his own house at 35 Bedford Square in front of a 'jury' of men, some chosen by Wakley and some by Elliotson.

A long article in the *Lancet* on 1 September 1838 described these experiments, which were carried out on the O'Key sisters on 16 August. They consisted of Elliotson testing the magnetic qualities of nickel and lead as aids to mesmerism. Nickel was thought to have the right qualities, lead not. Wakley arranged for his deputy on the *Lancet*, James Fernandez Clarke, to substitute lead for nickel without Elliotson or Elizabeth O'Key knowing. When she held the lead, thinking it was nickel, she produced the dramatic symptoms – a kind of fit – which were supposed to come only through nickel. Elliotson was exposed, Wakley concluded, as either a fraud or the dupe of a fraudulent girl. His final word, as reported in the *Lancet* by Clarke, was that 'the effects which were said to arise from what had been denominated "animal magnetism", constituted one of the completest delusions that the human mind ever entertained'.[51]

Clarke also recalled the episode in his autobiography, published in 1874, in which he took a more lenient view than Wakley, thinking Elliotson sincere but partially deluded, while the O'Keys, he believed, faked only some, not all, of their reactions to magnetism. Clarke accepted that they genuinely felt no pain under mesmerism, and that their altered speech when magnetised was not feigned. But, like the authorities at University College, he believed Elliotson went too far when he began in the autumn of 1838 to take the mesmerised sisters into the male wards of the hospital to help diagnose patients.[52] He saw that University College had no alternative but to remove Elliotson, but he nevertheless retained his admiration for his old teacher. Clarke had been a medical student under Elliotson, and remembered him as 'the greatest clinical teacher of his time', far ahead of the age in encouraging the students to use the stethoscope when examining patients and to offer their opinion on the cases he brought, before giving his own views and his reasons for reaching them.[53]

Of course Elliotson had to go. Council, aware of his excellence as a teacher, his popularity with students, and his role in bringing success to the medical school, did not dismiss him; instead its members dismissed the O'Keys from the hospital. At this Elliotson submitted his letter of resignation to council on 27 December 1838. He wrote:

> I have just received information that the Council, *without any interview or communication with me* [Elliotson's italics], have ordered my patient Okey to be instantly discharged & forbidden me to cure my patients with mesmerism . . .
>
> As a gentleman in the first place, & as a physician in the next, I feel myself compelled at once to resign my offices of Professor of the Principles & Practice of Medicine & of Clinical Medicine in the College, & of Physician to the Hospital – and I hereby resign them all, & shall never again enter either building.[54]

He added proudly that he had raised the numbers attending his class from ninety to 197 during his time at the College; he also expressed the wish that the session's fees be refunded 'to the young gentlemen, who are perfectly welcome to the lectures which I have already delivered'.

On 5 January 1839 council considered this, as well as a memorandum from the medical students regretting the resignation and another from one of Elliotson's patients, claiming to have got great benefit from his treatment. The students wrote that they had held a meeting and they now 'earnestly and strenuously' requested the council to try to get back 'our esteemed professor'. This resolution had been supported by 124 students, while 113 had signed an amendment regretting the resignation and thanking Elliotson for his 'valuable services as a teacher', but stopping short of asking him to withdraw his resignation. At the council meeting Goldsmid (one of the most dedicated benefactors of the hospital and its first treasurer), Brougham, and Tooke were among a minority to move for a delay in accepting the resignation until they had met Elliotson to discuss it. They were outvoted by nine members, and the resignation was accepted.[55]

Though fiercely indignant and resentful of council, Elliotson showed magnanimity in offering to take no fee for the lectures he had already delivered, and he readily acquiesced in April 1839, when Goldsmid visited him to ask if he would attest to the attendance of his pupils during the autumn term before his resignation, 'without reference to any difference that might have existed between him & any of them, or between him & any one of the professors'.[56] Wakley may have thought that he and University College had between them done for both Elliotson and mesmerism as a medical instrument, but his triumphalism was premature. Mesmerism, and from 1843 hypnotism, described as a nervous sleep induced not by animal magnetism but by visual fixation on a bright object, and introduced by James Braid, a Scottish surgeon who had settled in Manchester, continued to be the subject of enthusiasm in amateur and professional circles even after the arrival in the late 1840s of ether and chloroform as anaesthetics in surgery.[57]

As for Elliotson, he returned to his lucrative private practice, supported by friends and famous patients including Dickens, who learned from him how to mesmerise, using his skill on his wife and friends to relieve headaches. Dickens and Cruikshank dined with Elliotson on the day after his resignation; Elliotson was often invited to Dickens's house, and was called in on several occasions to diagnose and cure members of the Dickens family. 'Blue Beard', as Dickens nicknamed him on account of his thick black beard, was invited in February 1841 to be a godfather to his son Walter Dickens.[58] In accepting, Elliotson joked in words which, if made public, would have confirmed what many of his detractors suspected, namely that he was a materialist who had abandoned his religious faith:

I shall be delighted to become father in God to your little bopeep: you still retaining your title of his father in the flesh, with all the rights, privileges, perquisites & duties thereto annexed, from the moment you determined to construct him to the end of life. I should, however, have been compelled to forego this delight had you not absolved me from religious duties & every thing vulgar – For nothing could I consent to teach him in the vulgar tongue – nor would I have spoiled him for arithmetic by teaching him that three are one & one is three, or defaced his views of the majesty of God by assuring him that the maker of the Universe once came down & got a little jewess in the family way.[59]

Thackeray, too, was an admirer and willing patient, declaring that Elliotson saved his life – though not by mesmerism – when he suffered a serious case of cholera in September 1849 while writing *The History of Pendennis* (1850). The novel carried a grateful dedication to his preserver on its title page:

My Dear Doctor,

Thirteen months ago, when it seemed likely that this story had come to a close, a kind friend brought you to my bedside, whence, in all probability I never should have risen but for your constant watchfulness and skill . . . as you would take no other fee but thanks, let me record them here in behalf of me and mine, and subscribe myself

Yours most sincerely and gratefully,
W.M. Thackeray.[60]

In 1843 Elliotson founded and wrote a periodical called the *Zoist*, dedicated to phrenology and mesmerism. Mesmeric hospitals were established around the country and abroad.[61] In 1846 Elliotson himself was involved in founding the Mesmeric Infirmary, which opened in March 1850 a short distance from his previous place of employment. The house taken for the infirmary, 9 Bedford Street, was also just round the corner from the Bedford Square home of mesmerism's arch-enemy, Thomas Wakley. A number of members of parliament were involved, including Richard Monckton Milnes, later Lord Houghton, with Elliotson himself as treasurer. Old colleagues from University College were also represented on the committee; Isaac, now Sir Isaac, Lyon Goldsmid, was one of the first vice-presidents and in 1853 Augustus De Morgan was a member of the committee.

Henry Crabb Robinson, who had voted to allow Elliotson to perform in the College, continued to take an interest in both Elliotson and mesmerism. In March 1842 he went to the doctor's house to observe him put a girl into a magnetic sleep. Elliotson 'assured the company that he had cured her of epilepsy'. Crabb Robinson noted:

The girl was set asleep by his pressing down her eye-balls. He was 10 minutes doing it. There was no appearance of collusion whatever & that suspicion being removed there were remarkable phenomena such as convulsive twitchings following the motion of his hands, inclinations of the body, rigidity of the muscles . . .[62]

Two years later Robinson recorded visiting Sir Isaac Goldsmid's house, where he was told about a former governess in the Goldsmid family who had been sent by Elliotson to Paris for treatment, and who had subsequently spent five months in the Goldsmids' house 'following the prescriptions of the mesmerising doctor', after which she 'left the family entirely cured!!' Robinson remained somewhat sceptical. After meeting

Elliotson at a dinner party in April 1847 he noted in his diary that 'he told anecdotes of mesmerism which made me stare and feel uneasy, because I could not for a moment doubt his veracity, & yet could not trust his statement'.[63]

By May 1854 the Mesmeric Infirmary had moved to 36 Weymouth Street, Portland Place, after a brief unhappy spell in Fitzroy Square, where neighbouring residents had objected. Monckton Milnes was clearly one of those who thought Bloomsbury and the neighbouring area around Fitzroy Square unfashionable and out of the way, for he described the move westward as one from 'an obscure part of town' at the annual meeting of the infirmary in June 1854. The institution continued to advertise at Weymouth Street until 1869, the year after Elliotson's death, but by this time it was hard up and soliciting funds. It seems to have folded soon after this.[64]

Elliotson had been a mixed blessing for University College and Bloomsbury. He helped to put the College and its new hospital on a firm footing in the 1830s, but the attention he attracted through his mesmeric experiments elicited mainly negative responses. That University College Hospital did not immediately shake off its unwanted notoriety is indicated by an article in *Punch* in 1842. It lists London's hospitals, describing the so-called 'attributes' of 'gentlemen walking the wards' in each. According to the article, the doctors at Guy's and St Thomas's are known for 'half-and-half, anatomical *fracas*, and billiards', those at St George's for 'doings at Tattersall's' (the famous horse auctioneers at nearby Hyde Park Corner), while the Gower Street medical men are characterised by 'conjuring, juggling, and mesmerism'.[65]

Robert Liston, who arrived in London in 1834, was a conjurer of another kind, his 'tricks' destined to usher in long-term benefits to surgery. Like Elliotson he was a controversial figure in the contentious field of nineteenth-century medicine. Another Scot – meetings of the university's medical faculty must have sounded more like a gathering in Edinburgh than one in London – Liston had been both successful and notorious in his various posts at the University of Edinburgh. As a twenty-four-year-old surgeon in 1818 he joined the practice, already widespread in the Edinburgh medical community, of disinterring bodies for dissection. Henry Lonsdale, who acted as assistant to the great Robert Knox, receiver of bodies from Burke and Hare a decade later, recounted one Liston exploit in colourful terms. According to Lonsdale, the six-foot two-inch Liston was bold, dexterous, aye ready, and in the van of danger, and single-handed equal to any three of the regular staff of workmen. Thus one night, when a party of medicals headed by this surgeon saw they were discovered in a city churchyard, the chief actor laid hold of two large 'adults' that moment disinterred, and, carrying one under each arm, escaped by a door which led into the garden of a private Institution. Perhaps no man in Edinburgh could have done such a feat of strength, or made so good a retreat, whilst under 'the cover' of blunderbusses.[66]

Liston's legendary physical strength and speed with the surgical saw made him a renowned surgeon in the days before anaesthetics, but his quarrelsome temper saw him passed over for the chair of clinical surgery at Edinburgh. In October 1834 he was appointed surgeon to the newly opened North London Hospital in Gower Street, and soon after that became professor of clinical surgery in the university as well.[67] Here he got into arguments with Elliotson, whom he sneeringly referred to as 'Cantab'.[68] On one occasion in 1835 he wrote rudely to yet another pioneering Scottish medical colleague at the university. Robert Carswell was professor of pathological anatomy – the first such post in the country – and had worked with Laennec in Paris, where he spent some years studying and drawing diseased organs for the collection he brought to the university as a teaching aid, a series of over 2,000 water-colour drawings.[69] In October 1835 Liston wrote to Carswell refusing his request for some gallstones Liston had removed from patients at the hospital and referring to 'a smartish observation' made by Carswell 'as to my performance of the duties of an Hospital Surgeon'.[70]

Though Liston is best known for performing the first surgical operation in Britain, indeed in Europe, using an anaesthetic, he already had a reputation for the speed with which he could amputate a limb before anaesthesia became possible. James Fernandez Clarke remembered seeing him remove a toe in 1834 with great dexterity; Clarke was also present at the operation under ether on 21 December 1846 which made history. Liston had invited a large audience for the mid-thigh amputation; reports of the occasion agreed that Liston asked his audience to time the operation, which took twenty-five seconds according to one account, and twenty-eight seconds according to another.[71]

Two days before this momentous feat, a dentist of 7 Gower Street, James Robinson, and his neighbour the American physician Francis Boott, used ether to extract a tooth, having heard that the American dentist William Morton had successfully done so a couple of months earlier. Boott, a member of University College Senate, alerted Liston, who lost no time in arranging for his own operation. Robinson's success led to Liston's triumphant remark about the 'Yankee dodge' beating mesmerism hollow, and in sending the news to an Edinburgh friend, James Miller, he revealed his lasting rivalry with Elliotson and his system:

> HURRAH! Rejoice! Mesmerism, and its professors, have met with a 'heavy blow, and great discouragement'. An American dentist has used ether (inhalation of it) to destroy sensation in his operations, and the plan has succeeded in the hands of Warren, Hayward, and others in Boston.[72]

Though Liston acted quickly after hearing about the dental operation further down Gower Street, he was afraid that the O'Key debacle at the hospital a few years earlier would predispose observers to be suspicious of another untried attempt at pain relief. According to William Squire, the chemist who administered the ether for him, Liston spent the two days between Robinson's operation and his own studying Robinson's apparatus and trying out an improvised inhaler on Squire and another chemist before deciding to go ahead with the leg amputation in front of a hastily invited audience.[73] Over the next few years notable surgeons, including James Young Simpson and John Snow, quickly followed Liston's lead with ether, and soon after that with chloroform, as a pain reliever in surgery and childbirth. Liston himself did not live long enough to achieve further results in the field of experimental surgery; he died in December 1847, aged fifty-three, despite his active life of riding, boxing, fencing, and yachting, as well as performing his pioneering operations in Gower Street.

After the excitements and controversies of the first twenty years, University College and its hospital made steady progress, acquiring a reputation for clinical and research excellence. Among its celebrated alumni was Joseph Lister, pioneer of antiseptic surgery, who studied at University College from 1844 to 1847 and was a member of the audience at Liston's groundbreaking operation. Another was the progressive medical psychologist Henry Maudsley; he graduated from University College in 1856, became professor of medical jurisprudence there in 1869, and was married to the daughter of John Conolly, whose humane methods of treatment of the insane Maudsley admired and followed. Almost from its earliest days, University College Hospital became a rival to Edinburgh and the leading European universities in its excellence in medical training. William Jenner, the son of an innkeeper in Rochester, proved Wakley's point about

University College offering medical opportunities to young men without connections. He was one of the earliest medical students in Gower Street, becoming professor of pathological anatomy at University College in 1849 and the first physician to the Hospital for Sick Children when it opened in 1852. His observations there led to his important work on rickets and diphtheria; he was made a baronet for his achievements in 1868.[74] Henry Crabb Robinson offered testimony to the excellence of the medical education when he recorded in 1851 that Edward, later Sir Edward, Sieveking, the London-born son of a Hamburg merchant, having attended medical classes at Berlin, Bonn, Edinburgh, and University College, 'gave his decided opinion that the medical school of our University College was the best in Europe'.[75]

At a dinner given on 12 April 1864 to celebrate the thirtieth anniversary of the hospital, the guest speaker was Dickens. Without divulging that he had briefly lived in Gower Street North at the age of twelve in a house extremely close to the site of the hospital while his mother attempted school-keeping, he reminisced about playing at that age on 'a certain spot in north-western London', 'a very uninviting piece of wet waste ground, and a miserable pool of water' overrun with nettles, known as the 'Field of the Forty Footsteps'. This was the bit of open ground between the back of the old Montagu House and the New Road, of which a story was told of two brothers fighting a duel at forty paces in the early eighteenth century, after which no grass grew where their footsteps had been. A novel by Jane Porter, *The Field of the Forty Footsteps*, had been published in 1828 and adapted for the stage.[76]

Dickens turned adroitly from this introduction to the hospital, thought by some to be on or near the site of the legend. It had become, he announced, 'the field of 440,000 odd footsteps', that being the number of sick people who had been looked after in the thirty years since the hospital opened. Complimenting both the hospital and the University College School of Medicine on their 'immense service to the cause of medical education all over England', Dickens moved on to praise the 'liberality of opinion' at the institution. 'It excludes no one – patient, student, doctor, surgeon, nurse – because of religious creed.' Indeed, the example set by University College had proved a 'wholesome influence' even on 'the rubbed eyes and quickened steps of those famous old universities', a pointed reference to a bill which was going before parliament even as Dickens spoke to abolish religious tests at Oxford.[77] (The bill passed its second reading on 16 April 1864, only to lose by two votes on the third reading; it was 1871 before the tests were finally abolished.)

Dickens's services as an after-dinner speaker were much in demand, and he was generous in agreeing to support a wide range of charities and medical institutions. One to which he gave much of his time was the Hospital for Sick Children, established by Charles West in Great Ormond Street in 1852. West had studied medicine at St Bartholomew's Hospital and also in Bonn and Paris, where he walked the wards of L'Hôpital des Enfants Malades; being the son of a Baptist minister, he could not study at Oxford or Cambridge, and he took his degree at the University of Berlin in 1837.[78] He struggled against medical opposition to have children treated separately from adults, but by 1852 he had persuaded a number of influential physicians and patrons, and the house at 49 Great Ormond Street was taken for the new children's hospital. Progress was slow, however, and Dickens's support was vital in ensuring the hospital's survival and eventual flourishing.[79]

In April 1852 Dickens welcomed the newly opened hospital in the weekly newspaper he edited, *Household Words*. In 'Drooping Buds', an article written jointly with his colleague Henry Morley, he described the lack of facilities in London for sick children until No. 49 Great Ormond Street was taken to put things right. The eighteenth-century street itself and adjacent Queen Square are characterised as 'cut off, now, from the life of the town', 'a suburb left between the New Road and High Holborn', not far from the 'rattle' of these streets but 'quiet (very quiet), airy, and central', the ideal place, in fact, for the work to be carried out there. The old-fashioned mansion, its grand staircase, large rooms, richly ornamented ceilings, and plentiful toys are described approvingly.[80]

A few years on, the Hospital for Sick Children was badly in need of more funds. At the fourth annual meeting of its governors in February 1856 it was noted that expenditure had slightly exceeded income, and that India bonds had been sold to repay the balance due on the previous year's accounts.[81] The hospital still had only thirty-one beds, and a decision was taken in October 1857 to hold a fund-raising dinner the following spring.[82] Dickens, who was once more living in Bloomsbury, in Tavistock House, agreed to take the chair at the dinner, which was held in Freemasons' Hall in February 1858. In his speech he told of the grim statistics of child deaths in London, asking his audience to show compassion and talking of the 'courtly old house' in Great Ormond Street 'where once, no doubt, blooming children were born' and in which now 'little patients' are tended to by kind doctors and nurses in 'airy wards' with cheerful pictures on the walls. The speech contributed to the raising of over £3,000; a new building fund was started; Dickens was made an honorary governor and agreed to give a public reading of *A Christmas Carol* at Easter in St Martin's Hall to bring in more money.[83]

He continued to take an interest and to praise the hospital on every possible occasion. In *Our Mutual Friend* (1864–5) he describes a child, little Johnny, surrounded by toys and friends, being looked after in the 'fresh airy room' at Great Ormond Street by nurses with fresh pleasant faces.[84] At a celebratory dinner for the hospital in 1867 Dickens was credited by the grateful West with having 'first fairly set her on her legs and helped her to run alone'. 'In a few eloquent words which none who have heard can ever forget, like the good fairy in the tale,' West continued, 'he gave her the gift that she should win love and favour everywhere; and so she grew and prospered.'[85]

Other medical innovations interested Dickens too. While he was convinced, thanks to Elliotson's tutoring and his own amateur efforts, of the efficacy of mesmerism in relieving ailments among his family and friends, he was also attracted to another of Elliotson's enthusiasms, homoeopathy, the system according to which 'like cures like' by the administration of very small doses of a drug which produces symptoms close to those of the disease being treated. Dickens was on friendly terms with Frederic Quin, the leading English proponent of the method, which had preceded mesmerism and was to outlast it in popularity. Quin, having studied the system, established by the German Samuel Hahnemann in the last years of the eighteenth century, founded the British Homoeopathic Society in 1844. He was denounced as a quack in the medical journals, but had a following among London's aristocracy and literati at his successful practice near fashionable St James's Square. He was a regular guest of Dickens – often invited with Elliotson – and attended a dinner at Dickens's Doughty Street home to celebrate the christening at St Pancras New Church in January 1839 of Mary (known as Mamie) Dickens.[86]

At much the same time Thackeray was writing to his mother from his first married home in Great Coram Street, five minutes' walk west of Doughty Street, suggesting that Quin be called in to see the child of a friend.[87] Thackeray was more sceptical than Dickens. In a letter of October 1841, he described his stepfather's willingness to try every sort of treatment, including the increasingly popular water treatment, as well as various pills advertised as cure-alls, especially James Morison's Universal Vegetable Pills, and finally homoeopathy:

The Governor though by Heaven's blessing perfectly well, nevertheless for the love of science gets up every morning at four, sweats for 4 hours, douches, forswears wine at dinner, douches again, and concludes the day's amusements by sitting for nearly an hour in a tub of icy-cold water. In the last twenty years he has been successively a convert to Abernethy's blue pills, of wh he swallowed pounds – to Morison[']s ditto – wh he flung in by spoonfuls [–] to St John Long[88] to whom he paid 100 guineas for rubbing an immense sore on & then off his back, to Homeopathy wh put the nose of all other systems of medicine out of joint.[89]

James Morison was highly successful with his universal pills, dispensed from the British College of Health he established in 1828 on the south side of the New Road and advertised in his *Hygeian Journal*.[90] Though quackery was by no means confined to Bloomsbury, it seems to have flourished in the area, so notable for its respectable doctors and their families. (The Census for 1851 shows almost every second house in Bedford Square to have been occupied by a medical family.) One member of the Royal College of Surgeons drew attention to the nuisance in Bloomsbury in 1865. Dr F.B. Courtenay complained that he had 'constantly had to deplore the ignorance and credulity displayed by a class of patients with whom I have come into contact'. These patients had consulted universal pill dispensers in Bedford Place, Mecklenburgh Square, Charlotte Street, and Bernard Street, among other Bloomsbury addresses.[91]

Homoeopathy flourished, despite Wakley's attacks and the occasional court case after the death of a patient. Until the passing of the Medical Act of 1858, medical practice was unregulated and the boundaries between 'orthodox' and unorthodox systems were blurred.[92] The use of anaesthetics was thought to be a dangerous and irregular intervention in some medical circles in its early days. Though Robert Liston is now venerated as a pioneer of a method which has since become the orthodoxy, his ground-breaking operation in Gower Street in 1846 was attended by considerable risk, as he well knew. Like many pioneers, he experimented with unknown methods and substances on himself and on willing human guinea pigs among his associates. It is reported that he tried out belladonna as a possible cure for erysipelas, consulting the homoeopath Quin on the matter, all the while ridiculing Elliotson, who was himself busy experimenting with nitrate of silver for the same complaint.[93]

In several quarters homoeopathy was taken seriously, although, like every other fashion, it attracted ridicule too. *Punch*, noting that 'two distinct homoeopathic dinners' were held in London in April 1850 to celebrate the late Hahnemann's birthday, played with the idea that the turtle soup might have been served 'by teaspoonfuls' and a single whitebait served to the whole company, but added that the subscriptions pledged at the dinners were anything but infinitesimal, one raising £1,000, and the other £800 towards the opening of London's first homoeopathic hospital.[94] Two rival hospitals were opened in 1850, one at 39 Bloomsbury Square, called the Hahnemann Hospital, and the other, the London Homoeopathic Hospital, at 32 Golden Square in Soho. The chief medical man at the former was Dr John Epps of 89 Great Russell Street, a medical graduate from Edinburgh; Epps quarrelled with Quin and joined the English Homoeopathic Association in opposition to Quin's British Homoeopathic Society. Both groups had the support of aristocrats, members of parliament, and experimental doctors, but of the two new establishments it was Quin's hospital in Golden Square which survived. It moved to Bloomsbury in 1859, to the corner of Queen Square and Great Ormond Street, where it survives in a building dating from 1895 under its new name, the Royal London Hospital for Integrated Medicine.[95]

With its next-door neighbour, the Hospital for Sick Children, the new homoeopathic hospital was soon surrounded by the headquarters of many more medical specialisms in houses around Queen Square. In 1884 Giovanni Ortelli, a successful Italian businessman living in Russell Square, opened the Italian Hospital on the south side of Queen Square with the motto 'Charity knows no restriction of country'. The hospital was intended in the first place for the poor Italian immigrants crowded in Clerkenwell just to the east of this south-east corner of Bloomsbury, but patients of all nationalities were welcomed.[96] In the 1870s the first school of medicine for women was opened in nearby Henrietta Street, off Brunswick Square, and in 1890 Elizabeth Garrett Anderson's New Hospital for Women moved from Marylebone to purpose-built quarters on the north side of Euston Road. The story of women's medicine will be told as part of the larger history of women's education in the second half of the nineteenth century.

From Gower Street to Queen Square Bloomsbury was notable throughout the century for pioneering efforts in the cure of bodies. Bloomsbury was also the home of much cure, or care, of the soul, both artistically and spiritually speaking. Our attention turns next to these fields of activity, and first to cultural progress as represented by the reforming of the British Museum and illustrated by the oddly persistent question, repeatedly asked in the press, about the whereabouts of Russell Square.

CHAPTER FIVE

The British Museum, Panizzi, and the Whereabouts of Russell Square

I N HIS article on penny literature in *Fraser's Magazine* in March 1838, 'Half-a-Crown's Worth of Cheap Knowledge', Thackeray mentioned in passing 'Mr Croker's old joke, who new not, positively, where about was Russell Square'.[1] The reference was to a remark made by John Wilson Croker in parliament in 1825; thirteen years on, Thackeray did not feel the need to explain what the joke was about, so well known was it to his readers. His own relation to Russell Square was a close one geographically; he moved in the same month that the *Fraser's* article was published to nearby Great Coram Street as a recently married man with little money, a young wife, a baby, and a second child expected in the summer. Though much of his time was spent in Paris as a newspaper correspondent during the next few years, the Great Coram Street house was his London home until 1843, by which time Thackeray's family life had been ruined by his wife Isabella's attempted suicide in 1840 and her confinement in an asylum.[2]

In *Vanity Fair*, written in 1847–8, but set in the 1810s and 1820s, Thackeray placed his upwardly mobile – or rather recently arrived – businessmen and their families, the Osbornes and the Sedleys, in large, comfortable houses in Russell Square. The location was carefully chosen; the families live in solid, middle-class comfort amongst the fictional lawyers and judges of the square. Thackeray was nothing if not an astute observer and historian of social hierarchies and the significance of location in signalling them. His fictional inhabitants mirror the first non-fictional occupants of the houses built by James Burton from 1800 to 1804 around a large private garden intended for their sole use. Thackeray's Russell Square is a simulacrum of the real place, with its respectable, professional, middle-class inhabitants. His families are constantly 'placed' socially by being explicitly contrasted with the upper-class residents of squares further west. He undoubtedly knew that, as far as Bloomsbury was concerned, Russell Square was not only the largest, but also the 'top' square in the early years of the century. A pocket companion to London published in 1811, with a map, describes the 'principal squares' of the area, declaring Russell Square 'remarkable for the elegance of its houses' and its 'ornamental area'.[3] In 1835 *Cruchley's Picture of London* explains that Russell Square is 'the largest and most uniform square in London' and praises both the 'great taste and variety' of its interior layout and the airiness of its situation.[4]

No doubt with feelings of private pleasure and amusement, Thackeray puts Mr Todd, one of the Osborne firm's clerks who has been promoted to junior partner, in a modest house in Great Coram Street, a street which, he writes, 'trembled and looked up to Russell Square' as the *ne plus ultra* of wealth. But in its turn Russell Square cannot compete with Hanover Square or Berkeley Square, where 'the nobs of the West End' live, a set of people for whom Russell Square is located in a social wilderness. The Croker joke is half invoked in the novel, when Thackeray describes the rise of an artist, Mr Smee, 'very celebrated since as a portrait-painter and R.A. [member of the Royal Academy], but who once was glad enough to give drawing lessons' to Mr Osborne's daughter. 'Mr Smee has forgotten where Russell Square is now, but he was glad enough to visit it in the year 1818, when Miss Osborne had instruction from him.'[5]

Thackeray was neither the first nor the last commentator to pick up and revive the Croker joke. As late as 1878 Edward Walford alludes to it in his chapter 'Bloomsbury – General Remarks' in *Old and New London*. Describing the area, and in particular Bedford and Russell Squares, as associated with 'gentlemen of the long robe' (i.e. lawyers), he notes that as the area began to be deserted quite early in the nineteenth century by the wealthiest classes, so the 'very absence of knowledge of its locality' came to be associated with high breeding, 'and this notion was once forcibly illustrated by Mr Croker's inquiry in the House of Commons, "But where *is* Russell Square?"'[6]

The question was indeed asked, in jest, by John Wilson Croker, Tory MP, Secretary to the Admiralty in the Tory government during the 1820s, and waspish writer in the *Quarterly Review*, famous in the annals of literary history for his devastating criticism of Keats's poetry. The context for his remark, made in March 1825 during a parliamentary debate about the future of the British Museum, is complicated. Croker was certainly the originator of the query about Russell Square, but he was preceded in his implied scorn for the square and its immediate neighbourhood by his young friend and protégé Theodore Hook. As well as writing the whole of *John*

Bull from his berth in debtors' prison in 1824, Hook dashed off a set of fictions describing the lives of fashionable folk for the publisher Henry Colburn. The first series of his *Sayings and Doings* was published early in 1824; it was successful enough for Hook to be encouraged to write a second series, as well as several other frothy tales of the high life over the next few years.[7]

In one story in *Sayings and Doings*, 'Merton', Hook follows the ups and downs of the life of a young man of fashion who, to his exaggerated horror, finds himself invited to dinner at the house of an 'eminent banker' in Russell Square. He negotiates his way to 'the recesses of Bloomsbury', past the British Museum to 'the remote scene of gaiety' at 'an undisguisable distance' from 'all the civilized part of the world', a scene inhabited by 'a different race of people' from the Mayfair and St James's set in which young Henry Merton normally moves. The dinner is described by the amused and snobbish narrator as a failed copy of a fashionable dinner. The narrator notes that the dress sense of the women present is gaudy, and that one of the guests, now a Lord Mayor, was once 'a shoe-maker, or a linen-draper, or something of that sort'.[8] With these remarks Hook, the middle-class, Bloomsbury-born son of a far from wealthy composer, sitting in confinement for alleged embezzlement, started a positive craze for calling Russell Square and Bloomsbury remote, geographically and socially, from London's centres of power and influence. The idea gained traction from the debates in parliament at this time about the future of the largest institution in the neighbourhood of Russell Square, the British Museum.

The Museum had been founded in 1753 on the death of the collector Sir Hans Sloane, who kept a private museum of his botanical, geological, and anatomical specimens in his house in Great Russell Street. Sloane, who died in the manor house in Chelsea to which he had retired, left instructions in his will that his great collection of specimens and books should be offered for sale to the king to buy for the nation, stipulating that it should be 'kept and preserved together whole and intire [*sic*]'. It should be 'visited and seen by all persons desirous of seeing and viewing the same', and 'rendered as useful as possible, as well towards satisfying the desire of the curious, as for the improvement, knowledge and information of all persons'.[9]

In the event, parliament decided to raise the money to buy the collection for the nation by means of a lottery. The 1753 Act to incorporate the British Museum stated that 'one general repository shall be erected' for 'public use to all posterity' with 'free access' to 'all studious and curious Persons'. The Museum was the first public national museum in Britain; it was governed by a board of trustees, most of them appointed on account of their offices of state. The three principal trustees were the Archbishop of Canterbury, the Lord Chancellor, and the Speaker of the House of Commons. A further fifteen were official appointments, including the Bishop of London, the Prime Minister, the Attorney General, and the Presidents of the Royal Society and the College of Physicians. Two members were nominated by the Sloane family and two each by the Harley and Cotton families, since parliament had added to the Sloane material by acquiring the manuscript collections of the Earls of Oxford (Harleys) and those left to the nation in 1700 by Sir Robert Cotton. Fifteen further trustees were elected by the official members; at first these were usually aristocrats in public positions, but as the nineteenth century progressed, and the British Museum came under increasing scrutiny in press and parliament, trustees began to be elected because of their contributions to literature and science.

Sloane's house in Chelsea was considered too far from central London to be suitable for the collection; Buckingham House (later Buckingham Palace) was offered, but was too expensive. Montagu House on Great Russell Street, owned by the Earl of Halifax, was bought for just over £10,000 and adapted for use as a museum.[10] The British Museum opened in January 1759. Under the terms of Sloane's will and the Act of Parliament, access to the Museum was to be free and open to all, but although it was more accessible than any other European museum at the time, in practice there were several restrictions. The Museum was not open at weekends or outside working hours during the week, thus denying access to ordinary working people. Visitors had to apply for an entry ticket, a process which could take weeks; when they did get in, they were rushed through the galleries by guides. In 1810 the rules were changed: guided tours were stopped and people could walk round at their own pace and stay as long as they liked, but not until 1879 was the Museum opened from Monday to Saturday, and Sunday opening was delayed until 1896; it was granted only after much opposition from Museum employees and trustees and from Sunday observance societies.

Unlike most European institutions, the British Museum combined a national collection of books and manuscripts with collections of antiquities, prints and drawings, medals and coins, maps, and natural history specimens. As a consequence it was called variously a 'noble cabinet', in the first published guide to the collections (1761); a 'mishmash' and jumble, by several visitors from abroad during the 1810s and 1820s; and an 'old curiosity shop', by the Museum's scourge in parliament in the mid-1830s, the radical MP William Cobbett, who attacked it as a place of lazy sinecurists and upper-class 'loungers', rather than the institution open to all classes that it was intended to be.[11] As collections were added, the Museum soon became chronically short of space. It also had to battle for annual grants from an often parsimonious parliament in order to fund the building plans and the extra employees required to cope with new accessions.

By the early 1820s it was clear that old Montagu House was inadequate to hold the increasing numbers of books and objects, and the decision was taken to commission Robert Smirke to build a new museum on the site covered by the house, its gardens, and as many houses to the west, east, and north as parliament agreed to fund and the Bedford Estate agreed to release for demolition. Negotiations to buy up land and old houses along Great Russell Street between Smirke on behalf of the Museum trustees and the Bedford Estate manager Christopher Haedy acting for John Russell, sixth Duke of Bedford, were protracted and sometimes combative during the 1820s and 1830s. The Museum's solicitors, Bray, Warren, and Harding of Great Russell Street, were kept busy by petitions from the Duke of Bedford's tenants occupying houses on the south side of Montague Place, whose gardens were to be overlooked by Smirke's new buildings in the back garden of the old Montagu House.[12]

Rebuilding started in 1823, when Smirke began to construct an east wing to house the King's Library, the magnificent book collection of George III offered to the Museum by George IV. The new building finally emerged in the late 1840s, by which time Smirke had retired from ill health and had passed on the completion of the work to his younger brother Sydney. At every turn, the Museum was obliged to seek grants from parliament, which held lively debates about its management, the terms and conditions of its employees, its opening hours, and the constitution of its board. Government grants for the rebuilding totalled £606,500 19s. 5d. from Michaelmas 1823 to Christmas 1846; the estimated cost of completing the building during 1847 and 1848 was a further £106,911 0s. 7d.[13]

The pressure for reform at the Museum came at the same time as, and was not unconnected with, the reform movement generally in the 1820s, including the drive by Birkbeck, Brougham, and others to extend the provision of education. Members of parliament aired their views about the unsatisfactoriness of the British Museum when they were asked to vote on its annual grant in the early years of Smirke's rebuilding. In a debate on 1 July 1823, for example, MPs complained that the Museum was 'a piece of patchwork' (the radical Whig John Cam Hobhouse), and 'a most jumbling and incongruous arrangement' of 'antiquities, books, natural history, and marbles' (Alexander Baring).[14] The following year Grey Bennet quoted an article in the *Edinburgh Review* which attacked the neglect of Sir Hans Sloane's huge collection of birds, beasts, and insects, and of his great herbarium, many of its volumes now 'covered with dust and penetrated by worms'. Bennet blamed the trustees for mismanagement. As *Hansard* reported:

> He objected to making trustees ex officio – trustees of straw – trustees merely for the sake of their names. The lord chancellor was a trustee, and had never been in the museum, he understood, but once; and then only because some matter of form compelled him to go. Now such trustees were useless. Men of activity were wanted.[15]

Writers to *The Times* were indignant at the short and inconvenient opening hours for the galleries and reading rooms and the difficulty of acquiring a ticket if you did not know a trustee to recommend you; one letter published on 10 October 1823 complained that the rooms 'of this great establishment are hermetically sealed against the majority of those who would wish to frequent them for scientific purposes'.[16]

To this debate about the uses of the Museum and the exact plans for its enlargement was added another problem in the years 1823–5, namely whether the British Museum was the right place to receive not only George III's library, but also two large and valuable collections of paintings which had become available, or whether a new national art gallery should be built for them, and if so, where. This is when the location of Russell Square became a hot topic.

The two collections of old masters belonged to John Julius Angerstein, who died in January 1823, and Sir George Beaumont, who campaigned for a new national gallery, offering the best of his own collection to the government on condition that the Angerstein collection was purchased, both collections together to form the foundation of the new gallery. In the end, this was achieved, and William Wilkins's National Gallery was built in the early 1830s on the newly planned Trafalgar Square. But arguments in parliament raged from 1823 about whether the collections should go to the British Museum, to Somerset House, or to a new building. Objections were made to Somerset House on the grounds of its location by the river and its state of incompleteness at the time; the British Museum was said to be already bursting at the seams, unable to look after its valuable natural history collection, and ill-managed generally.[17] It was the debate of 25 March 1825 which brought forth Croker's famous remark, the context being an argument about whether the British Museum was a central enough location to house a national gallery of paintings.

Robert Peel started the attack, making the point – repeated by others for decades afterwards – that the location of the British Museum so close to the notorious slums of St Giles's was unfortunate and told against it. Twenty years later the driving through of New Oxford Street, removing some of the narrow streets and alleys, allowed the Museum partially to overcome this disadvantage, though the area to the immediate south was still densely crowded, and despite occasional plans for a grand avenue leading up to the Museum at the front to show off Smirke's neoclassical building, it remained, and remains, hemmed in and without an impressive approach. In 1825 John Nash planned an avenue leading from Charing Cross to the Museum as part of the Trafalgar Square development; in 1872 there were hopes of a 'noble street' stretching between Somerset House and the Museum which would show both buildings to advantage.[18] Neither scheme succeeded.

At the time of the March 1825 parliamentary debate, even New Oxford Street had not yet been thought of, and the Museum seemed to some to be geographically beyond the pale. Peel said that 'if the national gallery were banished to the neighbourhood of St Giles's and Russell-square it would much lessen the value of the collection'. 'It ought to be established where, to use an expression of Dr Johnson, "the great tide of human existence flowed"; and he knew of no more fit situation than the neighbourhood of Pall-mall or Charing-cross.'

Croker then entered the debate, complicating it with a reference to the Dulwich Picture Gallery, established in 1811 in the village of Dulwich to the south-east of London to house the picture collection of Sir Francis Bourgeois. Croker said that the Dulwich collection was 'at least as fine as that of Sir George Beaumont; and was quite as distant as Russell-square; though he did not profess to know exactly where Russell-square was [a laugh]!' He went on to say he thought the collection should not be deposited in the British Museum, where it 'would only be visited by a few cognoscenti, virtuosi, and picture-dealers'; it should go to Charing Cross, as Peel and others had suggested. His remark about Russell Square being 'distant' was meant in irony; his joke relied on people knowing that Dulwich was much further from the centre of London than the unfortunate square. Indeed, Sir Charles Long, a trustee of the British Museum, pointed out during the debate that 'in the last year, upwards of 100,000 persons' had visited the maligned institution, which was clearly not too out of the way, since such large numbers found their way there.[19] But the die was cast by

Croker's joke. It was quoted and embellished by a host of commentators and writers until it became one of the phrases of the century.

First into the field was Henry Brougham's legal colleague Thomas Denman, himself living the life of a wealthy lawyer at 50 Russell Square. Denman made a point during a parliamentary debate about judges' salaries in May 1825; judges, he said, were

> at the head of people of middling fortune, which was better than being at the foot of the higher order; and, though some aristocratical gentlemen in that House had treated their usual residence with so much contempt as to profess they did not know where Russell-square was, he thought they were much more respected in that quarter than they would be were they to intrude themselves amongst the wealthy inhabitants of Grosvenor-square.[20]

Next came the *London Magazine* in June 1825, with pretended 'Extracts from Mr Croker's Journal, kept during a late attempt to discover the topographical position of Russell-Square'. The extracts are delivered as if by an explorer recording a naval expedition into unknown waters, starting from Croker's office at the Admiralty; the style mimics the *faux naïf* tone of Swift's Gulliver among the Yahoos:

> On the 8th of May, 1825, two carriages bearing stores for the journey, left the Admiralty about eleven A.M. and, shortly after, dropped down to Charing Cross. Our company was divided as to the direction we should now take ... we steered our course up the Haymarket ... Pursuing our way due north, we arrived at Dyot-street ... The savages inhabiting this part of the world, which is laid down in the charts as Saint Giles's (and is so named from the reputed piety of the natives), speak a jargon very nearly resembling Irish ... Mr Barrow [John Barrow, explorer and Admiralty colleague of Croker] was convinced that the distant buildings which we observed formed the square for which we were so anxiously searching; several savages were seen on our way, quite different in their attire and manner from those we had left; being much fairer in their complexions; and dressed with more regard to decency.

The author, no doubt aware of the close relationship between Croker and Hook, declares that the women encountered in the neighbourhood of Russell Square were handsome, 'but in their dress and manner, in

Mr Hook's opinion, were what he wittily styled *Bloomsburyish*. This, the writer continues, 'was a word [Hook] had caught from one of the creatures of this distant region; we could not discover its meaning, but it was often repeated by these savages, and seemed to be the name of some remote territory'.[21]

In its article on the 'building rage' in London, the *Morning Chronicle* of 25 October 1826 incorporates Croker's remark into its survey of the growth of Bloomsbury. After noting how in the space of thirty years the garden and meadows of Montagu House have become 'covered with spacious and even magnificent houses, and laid out in squares and streets not to be surpassed, if they are equalled by any portion of the metropolis', the author adds, 'Russell-square, known to every one, except that *knowing* personage, Mr Croker, has for several years stood pre-eminent in size and rank.'[22] The quick-witted Disraeli helped the joke to survive by embellishing it in *Vivian Grey*; here the eponymous hero and a friend discuss an invitation to 'an assembly, or something of the kind, at a *locale*, somewhere, as Theodore Hook, or John Wilson Croker, would say, "between Mesopotamia and Russell Square"'.[23]

Hook's fictional dinner, Croker's joke, and Disraeli's contribution in *Vivian Grey* gave William Hazlitt the opportunity to attack both Toryism and the snobberies of the fashionable novel in an article entitled 'The Dandy School', in which he coined the term 'silver-fork' for this rash of novels which flourished for a few years in the 1820s and early 1830s. Writing in the radical *Examiner* in November 1827, Hazlitt criticises the new novelists for turning 'the great business of life' into 'a kind of masquerade or melo-drama got up for effect and by particular desire of the Great'. Hook's *Sayings and Doings* and the anonymous *Vivian Grey* are singled out, and Hazlitt demonstrates rhetorical wit as he pretends to believe that the hostile Tory descriptions of Bloomsbury by Croker and his friends are bringing the area down, causing a drastic decline in actual occupancy:

> So Mr Croker (in his place in the House of Commons) does not know where [Russell Square] is; thus affecting to level all the houses in the metropolis that are not at the court-end, and leaving them tenantless by a paltry sneer, as if a plague had visited them. It is no wonder that his *protégés* and understrappers out of doors should echo this official impertinence – . . . arrest a stray sentiment at the corner of a street, relegate elegance to a fashionable square – . . . reduce the bulk of mankind to a cypher, and make all but a few pampered favourites

of fortune dissatisfied with themselves and contemptible to one another.[24]

Theodore Hook reminds you, says Hazlitt, that 'a few select persons eat fish with silver forks', while insinuating that 'something is wanting' when 'people in the neighbourhood of Russell-square give dinners'. In another review, this time of Disraeli's second novel, *The Young Duke*, in 1831, Hazlitt gives the genealogy of the work, wrongly putting Croker before Hook, but unerringly describing the phenomenon for which they were jointly responsible:

> *Croker* begat *Hook*, and *Hook* begat *Vivian Grey*, and *Vivian Grey* begat *The Young Duke*. The spawn of all the fashionable novels was dropped one night by Mr Croker, in the House of Commons. Mr Croker flirted out a boast of ignorance of the site of Russell-square. The idea was seized by Mr Hook, who commenced a series of pungent satires on Bloomsbury; *Vivian Grey*, following another prong of the silver-fork school, took up the exaltation of the West End squares, and soared to the conception of aristocratic dinners, visions of great tables, instead of quizzing cold mutton and pickles at little ones.[25]

The 'silver fork' novel, typically written by middle-class authors who titillated their middle-class readers with scenes of the high life in Mayfair, while allowing themselves the latitude to mock both the extravagances of the aristocracy and the anxious imitation of that class by the upwardly striving bourgeoisie, seemed to settle most often on Bloomsbury for its middle-class examples. Catherine Gore, in a story in her collection *The Fair of Mayfair* (1832), joins the fun, exposing the snobbery of one character who declares of the London arrangements of her country neighbours, 'Fortunately they live in some place at the other extremity of the globe – Russell Square, I believe – so that we never have the misfortune of meeting them' when in London.[26]

By 1833 the joke was being thrown back at Croker in the House of Commons itself. William Cobbett, radical MP for Oldham, in a sustained attack on the expense and mismanagement of the British Museum which led to a committee of inquiry, adapted Croker's remark to his own purpose. Opposing the motion to vote £16,000 to the Museum for the ensuing year, Cobbett was reported in *Hansard*'s parliamentary record as follows:

> He would ask of what use, in the wide world, was this British Museum, and to whom, to what class of persons, it was useful? . . . The ploughmen

and the weavers – the shopkeepers and the farmers – never went near it; they paid for it though, whilst the idle loungers enjoyed it, and scarcely paid anything. Let those who lounged in it, and made it a place of amusement, contribute to its support. Why should tradesmen and farmers be called upon to pay for the support of a place which was intended only for the amusement of the curious and the rich, and not for the benefit or for the instruction of the poor? If the aristocracy wanted the Museum as a lounging place, let them pay for it. *For his own part he did not know where this British Museum was* [my italics] . . .[27]

A week later, on 1 April 1833, Cobbett was supported by the merchant and art collector James Morrison, a proprietor of the University of London and a member of its council from 1828 to 1831, who argued for longer opening hours at the Museum. The two men pointed out that it was open only during the winter months, and for just three days a week between the hours of ten and four, when working people of all classes were unable to visit. Their radical Benthamite colleague John Roebuck added that he hoped something would be done about opening the Museum during the summer months and on 'those days when the working-classes were able only to attend it, such as Christmas-day, Good Friday, and even on Sundays', to which the choral response of the assembled MPs was 'No, no'.[28]

More than sixty years were to pass before Roebuck's wish for Sunday opening was granted. But reforms of various kinds did slowly begin as a result of continued complaints in parliament and the press. Bowing to pressure, the House of Commons appointed a select committee in 1835 to investigate the organisation of the Museum. The composition of the board of trustees came under scrutiny. The committee interviewed the leading figures at the Museum, including the amiable but complacent Sir Henry Ellis, Principal Librarian since 1827, who defended the tradition of electing trustees from the ranks of the aristocracy rather than from among scientists and men of letters. 'I look to the benefit of the Museum, not to the general benefit of science', he said; 'it never entered into the contemplation of the trustees to select poets and historians.' As for having longer opening hours, to the reasonable reply that the staff was not large enough to manage and there would therefore be an extra expense if the hours were extended, Ellis added that it would not be a good thing since 'the more vulgar class would crowd into the Museum'.[29]

A further committee sat in 1836, and its report recommended certain changes. Officers in the Museum should be better paid but should not hold second jobs outside the Museum; opening hours should be extended to 7 p.m. during the summer months; trustees who seldom or never attended meetings should be encouraged to resign, and men of distinction should be elected in their place. On being interviewed by the committee, Robert Grant of University College objected to the aristocratic constitution of the Museum's board, advocating that men of science be elected.[30]

Reform of this kind was slow in coming, but a start was made. The first man of learning to be elected a trustee was the historian Henry Hallam in 1837; like the man who was elected in his place on his death in 1859, the historian of Greece George Grote, Hallam was a reformer who had supported the foundation of the University of London in 1826 and sat on its council. Another historian, Bloomsbury-born Thomas Babington Macaulay, was elected a trustee in 1847, and in 1888 the scientist and champion of Darwin, Thomas Henry Huxley, joined the board. This represented progress, though the Museum board was still heavily weighted towards the aristocracy and serving politicians and ministers throughout the nineteenth century.[31]

Pressure to open at hours convenient to the majority of the population continued throughout the 1840s and 1850s. *Punch*, established in 1841, had the Museum in its sights straight away; in 'Punch's Strangers' Guide to the Metropolis' published early in 1842, the reader was directed to go to the British Museum, 'which, when you get there, you will of course find closed; but the inspection of the sentry-boxes will repay the curious visitor, and you can read the synopsis of the Museum in a neighbouring public house, which, assisted by a prolific imagination, will answer all the purposes, without the fatigue'.[32]

When in March 1855 Sir Joshua Walmsley proposed Sunday opening for the British Museum and National Gallery in order to 'promote the moral and intellectual improvement of the Working Classes of this Metropolis', he was defeated in the House of Commons by 235 votes to forty-eight.[33] Dickens, long an advocate of Sunday opening of shops and museums and a supporter of Walmsley's motion, describes a gloomy Sunday evening in London in chapter three of *Little Dorrit* (1855–7), with 'no relief to an overworked people', no plants, animals, or pictures available for them to visit. *Punch* also returns to the theme at the time of Walmsley's attempt, mockingly congratulating the working people of Britain by comparison with their French brethren: 'How much happier you are than the French! They have no kind Peers and Members of the House of Commons to restrain them from committing spiritual suicide by walking over the Louvre on a Sunday.'[34] After becoming a trustee of the Museum in 1859, George Grote moved at several meetings in 1861 that the Museum be opened on Sunday afternoons, but was defeated on each occasion.[35] It was not until March 1896 that a motion was passed in the House of Commons to allow the galleries and museums to open on Sundays after 2 p.m.[36]

The chief reforming figure inside the Museum was Antonio Panizzi, who took British citizenship, anglicising his name to Anthony in 1832. While still nominally professor of Italian at the University of London, Panizzi was appointed to the post of extra assistant librarian at the British Museum in 1831; he was promoted to Keeper of Printed Books in 1837, and so it fell to him to implement the changes urged by the select committee. His testimony to the committee had pointed in the opposite direction from that of Ellis. Perhaps remembering his own position as a penniless exile on his first arrival in London, he declared:

> I want a poor student to have the same means of indulging his learned curiosity, of following his rational pursuits, of consulting the same authorities, of fathoming the most intricate inquiry as the richest man in the kingdom, as far as books go, and I contend that the Government is bound to give him the most liberal and unlimited assistance in this respect.[37]

Panizzi was not slow to make the required changes, adding a number of reforms of his own. In 1856 he was rewarded for his extraordinary energy on behalf of the Museum Library by being appointed Principal Librarian on the retirement of the inactive Henry Ellis, who moved out of his Museum flat to a house in Bedford Square.

Distrusted as a foreigner and political refugee, resented for his forthrightness, sometimes even rudeness, when responding to complaining readers, uncomprehending trustees, and jealous colleagues, Panizzi was a whirlwind of energy and ideas. In his thirty-five years of employment at the Museum he oversaw the great task of compiling an adequate catalogue of printed books, a task for which he drew up his famous ninety-one rules; introduced the system of having readers request books on printed forms rather than haphazard bits of paper; enforced the 1842 Copyright Act, taking publishers to court when they continued to flout the rule about giving a copy of every book they published to the Museum Library; lobbied the trustees for fairer wages and conditions for the low-grade officers; and enlarged every part of the Department of Printed Books.[38]

In July 1837, on his first promotion, to Keeper of Printed Books, Panizzi began to wield influence and power in the institution in the face of obstinate and sometimes hysterical opposition from his colleagues. As one of the senior officers of the British Museum, Panizzi now moved from his Gower Street North lodgings into an apartment inside the Museum. He was already showing his combative nature by arguing his case for a better apartment than his equal, the newly appointed Keeper of Manuscripts, Sir Frederic Madden, on the grounds that, though Sir Frederic had been an employee for longer, Panizzi's new appointment had preceded Madden's by three days.[39] Panizzi lost this petty battle, but was to win most of the many skirmishes between the two men over the next twenty years, culminating in his appointment as Principal Librarian in 1856, the post coveted by Madden. Madden's diary exhibits his obsessive hatred of the 'vagabond Italian' (13 January 1847) and shows him boiling with rage on learning that he has been passed over for the principal librarianship by 'this cursed fellow' who 'came to England with a rope around his neck' (1 March 1856).[40]

Panizzi did not care whom he offended – colleagues, trustees, press, politicians – in his drive to make the British Museum Library the best in the world. He even took on the most famous and respected writer of the day, Thomas Carlyle, historian of the French Revolution (1837) and leading commentator on the social ills of contemporary Britain with his influential pamphlet on Chartism (1839) and his vivid description of urban poverty and despair in *Past and Present* (1843). Carlyle had used the Museum's reading room in preparing his great history of the French Revolution, but he made sarcastic mention of the chaotic state of the materials and the lack of a proper catalogue, alluding to Panizzi's less than accommodating response to his requests for help. In an essay in the *London and Westminster Review* in 1837 surveying the literature on the French Revolution, Carlyle tells of the huge collection of revolutionary books, newspapers, pamphlets, handbills, and prints in repositories in Paris, and adds a cutting footnote:

> It is generally known that a similar collection, perhaps still larger and more curious, lies buried in the British Museum here, – inaccessible for want of a proper catalogue. Some eighteen months ago, the respectable sub-librarian [Panizzi before his promotion] seemed to be working on such a thing: by respectful application to him, you could gain access to his room, and have the satisfaction of mounting on ladders, and reading the outside titles of his books, which was a great help. Otherwise you

could not in many weeks ascertain so much as the table of contents of this repository; and after days of weary waiting, dusty rummaging, and sickness of hope deferred, gave up the enterprise as a 'game not worth the candle'.[41]

In 1838 Carlyle asked Frederick Denison Maurice to investigate the possibility that he might be allowed to read in a private room – 'some kind of inhabitable closet to oneself' – at the Museum, rather than in the public reading room.[42] His request was denied. So dissatisfied was Carlyle with the facilities at the Museum that he became the prime mover in the formation of the London Library. At the meeting to found the library in June 1840, Carlyle spoke about the impossibility of using the British Museum Reading Room because of its inconvenient opening hours, adding that 'no man could read a book well with the bustle of three or four hundred people about him'. A library where you could read in comfort, and at useful hours, and from which you could borrow books to read at home, was required.[43] (Though Carlyle gave the impetus to the new library, he soon took a back seat; it was Lord Clarendon who chaired the meetings, and, since the project was supported by many politicians and noblemen, the library found its location in an area convenient for them, namely London's clubland. They first took rooms at the Travellers' Club in Pall Mall, where Prince Albert paid a visit in May 1844, then leased more spacious premises in May 1845 in nearby St James's Square, where the London Library still is.[44])

Some years later, while researching his monumental history of Frederick the Great of Prussia, Carlyle needed to use the resources of the British Museum once more; he wrote politely to Panizzi to ask for 'a quiet place to study in, now and then, in your Establishment'.[45] He finished the letter of 11 April 1853 by saying, 'At any rate, if you are obliged to refuse me, I shall know it was with regret', a remark which drew forth from Panizzi a savage reply. Carlyle had made an enemy of him not only by setting up the London Library as a kind of rebuke, but by giving forthright evidence to a commission of inquiry into the British Museum in February 1849. There he had complained about the slow progress of the catalogue, compared the library's facilities unfavourably with those of the Advocates' Library in Edinburgh and the Bibliothèque Royale in Paris, and spoken of the crowdedness of the reading room and its stuffiness, which induced in him 'what I call the Museum headache'. Finally he had stated that 'there are several persons in a state of imbecility who come to read in the British Museum, sent there by their friends to pass away their time'.[46]

Panizzi's reply to Carlyle's request in April 1853 was, as expected, a refusal, but it was not expressed 'with regret'. On the contrary, he responded with evident relish:

> Dear Sir, I have had the honor of receiving your letter of yesterday & beg to say in answer that I do not recollect ever having stated that either you or any one else could have a private room to study in at this institution. I did on the contrary say that everything ought to be done that could possibly be done to make the reading rooms comfortable for the use of the public, but that all readers should be – and were in point of fact – treated alike at the British Museum ... Our reading-rooms of course are not as quiet and as snug as a *private* study; ours is a *public* place; no public convenience can equal a private carriage: even in a first class carriage you must occasionally put up with squalling babies and be deprived of the pleasure of smoking your cigar when most inclined to enjoy it; even the luxury of fresh air is sometimes denied a passenger who is obliged to share a carriage with six or seven more travellers.[47]

Panizzi added that if Carlyle wished to apply to the trustees and they were disposed to make an exception in his case, he would of course 'obey their directions'. At their meeting on 7 May 1853, the trustees, who included on this occasion Carlyle's fellow (and rival) historians Macaulay and Hallam, approved of Panizzi's dusty answer to the quick-tempered Sage of Chelsea.[48]

Though Panizzi would hardly say so in his rebuff to Carlyle, he was acutely aware of the limitations of the reading room, not least because he had himself greatly increased the number of books coming to the library by forcing publishers to give copies of their books or face prosecution. Indeed he had already sketched, in April 1852, an idea for a new, larger reading room. The fine Round Reading Room which resulted was perhaps his greatest achievement of all. Though others had already suggested ways of making use of the redundant inner courtyard of the new Museum building, Panizzi's idea was enthusiastically taken up by the architect Sydney Smirke, and in January 1854 the Treasury approved his detailed plans and allotted £86,000 for the Reading Room's construction.[49]

The room was built in three years, opening on 2 May 1857. As well as making innovative use of cast iron and installing a modern system of heating and ventilation, Smirke and the builders reduced noise by covering the floor with a mixture of rubber, cork, and other materials, and space for the ever-increasing number of books was maximised by building bookstacks of perforated iron. The structure was massive and grand, the diameter of its dome being only sixty centimetres less than that of the Pantheon in Rome; the ceiling was painted in cream and azure to suggest the sky, and elegant gilding added to the beauty of the room. Most observers were delighted and awed by the sight of this 'circular temple of marvellous dimensions, rich in blue, and white, and gold', though Panizzi's enemy Madden predictably hated it. A 'gilded dome', he wrote in his diary two weeks before the opening, 'utterly unfitted for the real purposes of study', and 'a monstrous example of the abuse of [Panizzi's] influence'.[50] Madden stayed away from the opening, which was attended by many of the official trustees.

Henry Ellis wrote generously from his retirement in Bedford Square, telling Panizzi that he was the true 'contriver and real architect throughout' and expressing his delight at the 'kind reception' Panizzi had received at the opening of the new Reading Room.[51] Ellis had already acknowledged Panizzi's talents the previous year, when he resigned as Principal Librarian and Panizzi was anxiously waiting to hear if he would be chosen as Ellis's successor:

Yours is, unquestionably, the portion of the Museum which is not only the largest, but the most useful and extensive for public instruction; the time of life, the toil, and the power of mind which you have brought to bear upon it and upon its improvement convince me that no stranger, especially without the knowledge which the experience of a quarter of a century has given you in the view of general management of the place, ought to be allowed to compete with you on this occasion.[52]

In spite of this support, Panizzi's many successes were achieved against the background of constant sniping from his nearest colleague and rival for promotion, Madden, and he also faced the antagonism of some newspaper writers and politicians who disapproved of a foreigner taking charge of a great national British institution. Richard Monckton Milnes was noticeably aggressive in the debate in the House of Commons to vote the Museum's annual grant in April 1856, just after Panizzi's appointment as Principal Librarian. An anti-Catholic bias is perhaps evident in his remark that 'he was always desirous that men in such a position [i.e. political refugees] should be received in this country as those Protestants who took refuge here after the revocation of the edict of Nantes were received'; but he believed that 'the chief position in the great library and museum of the country' should have been bestowed on an Englishman, not a foreigner.[53] Others, however, recognised Panizzi's qualities, including, perhaps surprisingly, the majority of the Museum's official trustees, who voted for his promotion.

When Panizzi retired through ill health in 1865, the trustees resolved to 'record their deep sense of the ability, zeal, and unwearied assiduity with which he has discharged the many arduous and responsible duties which from time to time have been committed to him'. They voted, unprecedentedly, to recommend to the Treasury that he should receive as his pension the full amount of his salary, £1,400.[54] In October 1865 Panizzi moved out of the Museum and into a house at 31 Bloomsbury Square, to live a quiet bachelor life until his death in 1879, aged eighty-one, in that 'very unfashionable quarter, though very respectable'.[55] He had turned down the offer of a knighthood in 1861, but accepted a KCB in 1869.

Panizzi had been a force of nature, bringing his enormous energy to the task of making the British Museum's library one of the best in the world. All the Museum's departments were growing, however, and the lack of space became chronic, despite the fairly regular purchase of neighbouring houses and land from the Bedford Estate to make more space for the collections. The Museum's history in the nineteenth century was one of constant debate about expansion and expense, and increasingly about whether to split up the collections and move the natural history collection out of Bloomsbury, which finally happened, after nearly thirty years of negotiation, in the early 1880s, when the new Natural History Museum opened in South Kensington.

As early as 1856 the man in charge of the natural history departments, the forceful Richard Owen, had suggested moving them, but was defeated by the lobbying of the scientific community, which wanted to keep the collections close to the library and to their places of work, University College and, a little further away, King's College in the Strand. After many meetings and changes of mind, the trustees decided early in 1862 to move natural history out and build a new home for it on the South Kensington site which had been acquired with the proceeds from the Great Exhibition of 1851 in nearby Hyde Park. Delays continued into the 1870s, and it took several more years before Alfred Waterhouse's building was ready for occupation.

In 1861, when the move was being debated, *Punch* praised Panizzi for his work both in building the Round Reading Room and in keeping natural history objects out of it, noting that he 'boldly and nobly seized the Quadrangle, reversed the problem, Circled the Square, and fortified the Quadrilateral against all attempts to take it for mummies, dried fish, moonstones, south-sea island clubs, coal-lumps, crocodiles, tertiary strata, and other instructive matters.'[56] The magazine also commented in verse on the plan for natural history to leave Bloomsbury:

Mother Nature, beat retreat,
Out, M'm, from Great Russell Street!
Here, in future, folks shall scan
Nothing but the works of Man.[57]

Owen, who made as many enemies by his extreme sensitivity and quarrelsomeness as Panizzi did by his insensitivity and rudeness, had to fight hard. Opposition to moving the natural history collection out of the Museum was based not only on its convenience for London's scientific professors, but also on its popularity with visitors; a survey conducted over fifteen days in June–July 1860 showed that in that time there were 3,378 visitors to the Natural History galleries, 2,557 to Antiquities, and 1,056 to the King's Library and reading rooms. The House of Commons select committee which ordered the survey also reported that 'removal of these most popular collections from their present central position to one less generally accessible would excite much dissatisfaction', especially among those who lived outside London, 'to whom the proximity of the British Museum to most of the railway termini' (Euston, St Pancras, and King's Cross) was 'of great practical importance'.[58] Great Russell Street had, in the thirty-five years since Croker's provocative remark, shifted, as it were, from remoteness to centrality, partly with the advent of rail travel and partly by the consolidation of the surrounding area as London's intellectual and cultural quarter.

Every department of the Museum went on expanding during the nineteenth century, as new collections, bequests, and discoveries were added. Departments proliferated, as did sub-departments. There were Books and Manuscripts; Antiquities, including Coins and Medals and Oriental, Greek and Roman Antiquities, to which were added Egyptian and Assyrian Antiquities in the later decades of the century; Prints and Drawings; and the three branches of the natural history collection – botanical, mineralogical and geological, and zoological – which eventually moved to South Kensington.[59] After the famous addition of the Elgin Marbles in 1815, the next most eagerly welcomed arrivals were the Assyrian sculptures excavated by the young archaeologist Austen Henry Layard in the late 1840s. The most popular items among the treasures he dug up from the lost palace of Sennacherib in the biblical city of Nineveh were several pairs of human-headed winged creatures, including the 'Great Bull of Nineveh' with 'a man's head and dragon's wings, weighing twelve tons', objects which caused a sensation when they were brought to the British Museum in 1850.[60]

When in 1852 the King of Prussia requested casts of some of Layard's Assyrian sculptures to display in the Neues Museum, which was under construction in Berlin, the proximity of University College with its academic experts proved useful, for Thomas Donaldson, the professor of architecture, acted as a go-between. He wrote to the trustees of the British Museum in September 1853 to chivvy them along. 'I trust that I may not appear importunate', he wrote, 'but His Majesty the King of Prussia, who is so munificent a promoter of all researches into Antiquity and a generous contributor to the British Museum Library, takes especial interest in the completion of the Berlin Museum.'[61]

Donaldson's intervention was one of several examples of the professional connections which developed between individuals or departments at the Museum and their counterparts at University College, beginning with the early appointments to both institutions of Panizzi and Rosen. Augustus De Morgan was consulted in May 1859 over the 'scientific value' of a Galileo manuscript which the Museum was considering purchasing.[62] University College also provided some of the early lecturers under the terms of Dr George Swiney's bequest in 1846 to the Museum trustees to fund public lectures in geology for a period of five years. Swiney's will stipulated that the lecturer 'must be a Doctor of Medicine of the University of Edinburgh'.[63] William Benjamin Carpenter, a former Gower Street student who took his MD at Edinburgh, and who became professor of medical jurisprudence at University College in 1849, was the first Swiney Lecturer from 1847 to 1851. He was followed by his colleague Robert Grant, University College's leading zoologist and comparative anatomist, an expert on the structure of sponges, and creator of an incomparable museum of anatomical specimens for use in teaching which he bequeathed to University College on his death in 1874.[64]

Grant was among those academics who opposed the removal of the natural history collections from Bloomsbury to South Kensington. In the end, however, the move became inevitable. Panizzi was keen to be rid of the collections in order to make more space for the library; Richard Owen thought that to be seen to advantage his collections needed a separate new building; and problems of space only increased as the century went on, while the cost of buying up houses in the immediate area of the Museum was often more than parliament would sanction. From 1836 onwards the Museum had negotiated with the Bedford Estate for houses to the east and west of the Museum, but such negotiations were often protracted, as they involved not only the Duke of Bedford and his agents but also the lease-holders and tenants of the houses, who were sometimes reluctant to leave.[65]

Even after the opening of the completed Natural History Museum in South Kensington in 1881 – its Gothic magnificence in stark contrast to the neo-Grecian style of Smirke's building in Georgian Bloomsbury – the parent institution in Great Russell Street continued to grow. It had to accommodate new materials, new readers in the library, and an increase in visitors as the opening hours became progressively longer: from 1879 the public were allowed in six days a week. In 1895 the Museum finally acquired another sixty-nine Bedford Estate houses in the surrounding streets, paying Herbrand Russell, the eleventh Duke of Bedford, over £200,000 for them. John James Burnet was commissioned to build on the newly acquired land, and the Edward VII Galleries he built along Montague Place were finally opened in May 1914. But his plans to offer a vista at the back of the Museum at the same time were destined to be as unsuccessful as Nash's project for an avenue leading south from the front on Great Russell Street. Burnet's 'British Museum Avenue', sketched in 1905, would have led north from the new building on Montague Place to be continued by Torrington Square and lead on into Gordon Square. As so often before, however, there was not enough money to carry out this scheme to set the British Museum in an open space appropriate to its proportions and purpose.[66]

In the seventy years since Croker and Hook had mocked Russell Square, the British Museum, and Bloomsbury in general as being out of the way both literally and metaphorically, the area had come to be seen as central. The constant enlargement of the Museum, along with the arrival of University College London and other educational establishments in the neighbourhood, and the continued residence of some lawyers, doctors, and architects and their families, confirmed the area as London's intellectual quarter. Its relative centrality geographically (if we take Oxford Circus or Piccadilly Circus or Trafalgar Square as the 'centre') was enhanced during the same period, as was noticed by the House of Commons Select Committee in 1860, by the construction of the three major railway stations along Euston Road. The British Museum welcomed more and more visitors from outside London who might travel to the capital for a day's outing in the later decades of the century, as opening hours improved, thanks to years of petitioning from *Punch*, Dickens, George Grote, and an assortment of MPs who raised the matter every time parliament was asked to vote on its grant to the Museum.

In March 1894 *The Times* urged the Museum to make a statement as the country's leading repository of treasures by seizing the opportunity to

acquire the expiring leases on the sixty-nine neighbouring houses on the
Bedford Estate:

> The museum, in fact, lies in the centre of the square plot of land which
> is bounded on the south by Great Russell-street, on the east by
> Montague-street and a corner of Russell-square, on the north
> by Montague-place, and on the west by part of Bedford-square and by
> Charlotte-street; and north, west, and east the plot is bordered by the
> lines of houses and gardens which form parts of those streets and squares
> and effectually enclose the great building in their midst. It needs only a
> glance at the map of the district to see that the natural frontiers of the
> British Museum should embrace the entire block of land and buildings,
> the possession of which would at once satisfy the two principal require-
> ments which must always be present in the minds of the Trustees of the
> great national Museum − isolation from surrounding buildings and
> room for future expansion.[67]

Smirke's great neoclassical building was extended at the back over the
next decade, so that its outer shell grew to become a visibly appropriate
enclosure for the great expanding collections inside. It was able to bear
comparison with the legion of neoclassical museum buildings which went
up in many major cities of Europe during the nineteenth century, all
designed on a scale deemed apposite to the wealth and power of countries
which could acquire objects important enough to be housed in such grandeur. Examples were the Glyptothek in Munich (1816–30), the Altes
Museum in Berlin (1825–8), the Neues Museum in the same city, for which
Donaldson requested the Assyrian casts (1843–55), and the twin museums
in Vienna, the Kunsthistorisches Museum and the Naturhistorisches
Museum (1872–91). Despite its relative lack of space, as compared to its
European counterparts, the enlarged Museum building ably reflected
Britain's pre-eminent position in the world of trade, exploration, geopoli-
tics, and expanding empire.

As for Russell Square in its role as representative of Bloomsbury at large,
it had never been the remote area of Hook's and Croker's mischievous
imaginings. In the years immediately following their jokes, both the physical development of Bloomsbury and its colonising by cultural institutions
gained it national significance in matters of education and culture. Right at
the end of the century the area acquired a bit of a bohemian reputation too,
though it never rivalled Soho or Covent Garden in that respect. Unlike
those regions, Bloomsbury was not rich in theatres, music halls, or pubs

(especially in the Bedford parts), but a small cult of eccentricity did haunt the British Museum itself. Just across the road on Great Russell Street was the Museum Tavern, an inn established in the eighteenth century, before the Bedford Estate forbade the siting of public houses on its land. In 1855, at the height of the agitation for longer opening hours at the Museum, a public meeting was held in the pub's upper room to support the cause.[68] By the 1880s, according to the memoirs of the actor-playwright George Arliss, the son of a local newspaper proprietor who lived round the corner from the tavern in Duke Street, 'the Museum Tavern was a regular meeting place' for 'a lot of useless hangers-on of the British Museum, a certain literary group of that great and wonderful Reading Room'. These people constituted 'a picturesque and fascinating literary fringe – men who got a hand-to-mouth existence with their pen and lived Heaven knows where'.[69]

Arliss mentions no names, but two young men who fit the description are George Gissing, living in mean lodgings near University College with his drunken ex-prostitute wife, trying to get a foothold in London's literary world, and punishing that unwelcoming world in *New Grub Street* (1891), his gloomy novel detailing the failure through poverty of an aspiring writer who haunts the Reading Room; and H.G. Wells, who scraped a living as a student in the 1880s by copying drawings at the Museum for a biology tutor, and who lodged a little later for four shillings a week in nearby Theobald's Road. His living quarters were 'not really a whole room', according to Wells, 'but a partitioned-off part of an attic'.[70]

This touch of bohemianism in Bloomsbury was not restricted to the pub opposite the British Museum and the dingy lodgings of literary people in the meaner streets nearby. In the 1890s a remarkable family lived inside the building itself, in one of the residences reserved for senior employees of the Museum. In June 1890 Richard Garnett junior, on becoming Keeper of Printed Books (his father, also Richard, had been Assistant Keeper until his death in 1850), moved his family into staff quarters in the east wing, facing Montague Street. This was the apartment which his great predecessor Panizzi had inhabited, and here Garnett's daughter Olive kept a diary of her activities.[71] Olive, born in 1871, shared the revolutionary beliefs of her teenage acquaintances, the children of William Michael Rossetti, who edited their anarchist newspaper *The Torch* from the basement of their house near Regent's Park. She also consorted with the Rossettis' more conservative-minded cousin Ford Hermann Hueffer. The Rossetti and Ford children were grandchildren of the painter Ford Madox Brown, friend and encourager of the Pre-Raphaelite Brotherhood in mid-century.

The young Olive Garnett moved in circles which included British Museum personnel, Christina Rossetti, whom Olive's mother visited regularly during the poet's last illness in her Torrington Square house, which on her death in January 1895 Olive reported as 'tumbling to pieces' with 'no paint left' and threadbare carpets,[72] William Morris, whose socialist meetings Olive attended, and – most strikingly – a set of Russian exiles intent on creating revolution or anarchy in their homeland. She visited Prince Kropotkin, Felix Volkhovsky, and Sergei Stepniak in their various homes about London, and even invited them to her house in the Museum. 'Went out to buy cake, lemons etc. for tea,' reads her diary entry for 24 February 1892, when the nihilist Volkhovsky was expected. A couple of months earlier she had attended a meeting of the Friends of Russian Freedom at which William Morris 'sprang up & dashed into English Socialism'.[73] On 13 January 1894 Olive and her sister Lucy put on their Russian blouses and set off for a Russian New Year party in a room over a baker's shop in Gower Place, the small street behind University College where Gissing had lodged a decade earlier.[74]

The Garnett sons invited W.B. Yeats to lunch, and the daughters were permitted to travel across London to political meetings by underground train, to attend theatres in Soho and the Strand, where they saw plays by Ibsen and other 'dubious' modern writers, even to walk across Tottenham Court Road to Fitzroy Square, where a colony of French anarchists lived, political meetings took place in the streets, and 'a good many loafers' and 'shabby looking foreigners' were to be seen lounging about.[75] Bloomsbury was not quite so excitingly disreputable, of course, and after all, Olive lived in a respectable, middle-class, professional family home situated at the heart of cultural London, under the very roof of the great national museum and beside the erstwhile 'distant' Russell Square.

CHAPTER SIX

Towards the Millennium

I F A little bohemianism touched the Bloomsbury of the British Museum late in the nineteenth century – from 1871 University College had its share too, in the form of art students attending its Slade School of Art – a very different set of people made their mark in Bloomsbury somewhat earlier. These were men and women who belonged to a variety of dissenting religious groups, some of them rather exotic and colourful in their own way, and all of them intent on reforms of their own. Their desire was to counter both the perceived complacency of the established Church and the threat to spiritual life they saw in the very measures for progress, including secular educational reform, of which the imposing 'pagan' building of the godless college on Gower Street was a visible symbol. Spiritual, not material or social, reform was their watchword, and they set about trying to take religion in a new, revitalised direction. The phenomenon was not confined to Bloomsbury, but the area featured prominently, not least in the erection of imposing new church buildings to embody some of the reforming ideas which were developing in British religious life.

By the beginning of the nineteenth century a number of Nonconformist faiths, including Methodism, Baptism, and Congregationalism, had begun to challenge Anglicanism in many communities, particularly the fast-growing industrial cities of the north of England. The Church of England was itself divided into 'High' and 'Low' Church movements, the former privileging ritual and sharing some forms of worship with Catholicism, the latter favouring simple worship and a reliance on the Bible rather than ecclesiastical tradition. In the 1830s, in an effort to reclaim authority for the Church of England, the so-called Broad Church movement arose as a liberal branch of Anglicanism dedicated to tolerance of multiple interpretations of worship, from Anglo-Catholicism to strict evangelicalism, and to reform of the Church from within. Coleridge's late works, *Aids to Reflection* (1825) and *On the Constitution of Church and State* (1830), were influential, as were the sermons and writings of Dr Thomas Arnold of Rugby School, who came to represent the tolerance of Broad Churchism.[1]

A different response from within the Church of England in the 1830s was that of the 'Oxford Movement,' which wished for a return to older rituals and emphasised the shared heritage of the Church of England and Roman Catholicism. Its members maintained that many of the Thirty-Nine Articles of the Church of England, drawn up in 1563 under Elizabeth I to consolidate the Church as a reformed church, were closer to Catholic belief than had been generally admitted. The most famous figure among the Oxford clerics and dons of the movement was John Henry Newman, who, along with some followers, eventually went over to Rome.[2]

Numbers of young men who might have become Anglican clergymen, or been happy to sign the Thirty-Nine Articles in order to become fellows of Oxbridge colleges, were unsettled in the middle years of the century by Newman's turn away from the Church of England, and equally by works of history, philosophy, and science which undermined their traditional beliefs. Increasing pressure was being put on literal belief in the Bible by philosophers and historians, especially in Germany where the so-called 'higher criticism' of the Bible flourished, with its suggestions of a mythological basis for Old Testament prophecies and New Testament accounts of the miracles of Jesus.[3] At the same time the movement for social and political reform leading to the Reform Act of 1832 naturally included among its targets the established Church with its entrenched privileges, often complacent and inactive clergy (the practice of clergymen employing curates to perform their parish duties for a small stipend was institutionalised), and close association with political as well as ecclesiastical conservatism.

Since the parish was the chief administrative unit of local government and often constituted an electoral district, the relation between Church and State and between clergy and congregation, as well as each church authority's attitude to the social conditions of its parishioners, became the subject of widespread contemporary discussion. Anglican parishes came under scrutiny in Bloomsbury as elsewhere, none more so than those represented by the neighbouring churches of St George's Bloomsbury and St Giles-in-the-Fields. Hawksmoor's extravagant St George's building seemed to some observers emblematic of the wealth and social class of its congregation. In 1827 Theodore Hook quoted a verse on the pretensions of the 'absurd spire' topped by its statue of George I:

When Harry the Eighth left the Pope in the lurch,
The King by the law was made Head of the Church;
But the sagacious Bloomsbury people,
Instead of the Church, made him Head of the Steeple.[4]

When the Revd Henry Montagu Villiers, brother of the Earl of Clarendon, was appointed to the living of St George's Bloomsbury in 1841, the parish, most of it on Bedford land, was one of the largest and wealthiest in London, containing 17,000 parishioners.[5] Dickens captured its social character in an early piece in the *Monthly Magazine* in April 1834, 'The Bloomsbury Christening', in which the Kitterbells, an upwardly striving young couple living in Great Russell Street, take pride in having their child christened in St George's.[6] In 1848 Dickens noted how the building stood 'very prominent and handsome', coldly surveying the recent cutting of New Oxford Street through the surrounding slums while itself remaining 'passive in the picture'.[7] The church building is here made to stand for its clerical personnel, apparently cruelly impervious to the plight of large numbers of their nearest neighbours to the south, while catering for the wealthier folk of Bedford Square and its environs.

As Hook, Dickens, and others never tired of remarking, the adjoining parish of St Giles contained by contrast some of Bloomsbury's – and London's – poorest inhabitants. There had been a leper hospital and church on its site from the twelfth century, and the current church was built under the same Act of Parliament in 1711 which provided for the building of St George's, an act ordering fifty new churches to be built, in part to replace those lost in the Great Fire of London forty-five years earlier. St Giles was a byword for insanitary overcrowding and petty crime by the mid-eighteenth century, when Hogarth drew his famous *Gin Lane*.[8] The 'Rookery' stretched south and west from Great Russell Street to High Street, Bloomsbury, taking in warrens of narrow alleys inhabited, it was estimated in 1815, by about 6,000 poor Irish people.[9] Though parishioners in the sense of inhabiting the parish of St Giles, these people were not worshippers there (or indeed anywhere).

This 'Holy Land', as the area was known in caricature and satirical journalism from Hogarth to Cruikshank and Hook, was often referred to in jest for the 'piety' of its (Irish Catholic) population.[10] More seriously, an article in the *European Magazine* in 1824 described this part of south Bloomsbury as 'one of the greatest receptacles in the metropolis for wicked characters'.[11] In 1816 the surgeon of the Bloomsbury Dispensary, located at 62 Great Russell Street, had reported on the filthy state of the Irish quarter, with hogs, asses, and dogs all mixed up with human beings in the crowded dwellings.[12] Even after New Oxford Street was driven through in 1847, St Giles's social problem remained acute, as a commentator in the *Illustrated London News* noted; 'like a nest of ants' the inhabitants had been turned loose, simply to settle in the nearest alleyways left untouched by the new street.[13] The Revd Thomas Beames, in the second edition of his *Rookeries of London*, published in 1852, declared: 'The Rookery is no more! a spacious street is in its stead; but will you tell us that any poor man has gained by the change?' He went on to quote figures from the council of the Statistical Society, to show that the total number of inhabitants in twelve houses in one of the worst streets, Church Lane, actually increased from 277 to 461 between 1841 and 1847. 'The conclusion is obvious: if Rookeries are pulled down, you must build habitable dwellings for the population you have displaced.'[14]

Bodies such as the Statistical Society and the Metropolitan Board of Works, set up by a parliamentary act of 1855, ensured that reports were made by medical officers, whose accounts of hard facts reinforced the rhetoric of observers such as Beames and resulted in efforts to manage social problems. One of the first model lodging houses, built for poor families by the Society for Improving the Condition of the Labouring Classes, was placed in this part of Bloomsbury in 1850 – a block of flats which still stands on the corner of Streatham Street and Dyott Street, to the south-west of Great Russell Street, the seventh Duke of Bedford having given the site at a nominal ground rent of 1½d. per foot.[15] Its location gives an excellent idea of the physical juxtaposition of extreme wealth and high social status with its polar opposite in this bottom corner of Bloomsbury, a mere stroll from the British Museum.

The worst excesses of misery were alleviated in the latter decades of the century. In 1906 E.V. Lucas in *A Wanderer in London* pronounced that, though still not savoury, the area could no longer be described, as it habitually was by social observers, as the antipode of St James's in the West End.[16] This opposition of the two London parishes had been in the minds of the parliamentarians debating whether or not the nation's art collection should be placed in the British Museum. Not only was it then pretended that Russell Square was distant from the 'centre'; the paradox of the great repository of the nation's culture being in such close proximity to a great slum was constantly invoked. In 1842, when *Punch* attacked the Museum for always being closed to visitors, it pointed out the further hazard awaiting the disappointed tourist in the form of pickpocketing in the immediate area. After turning away from the gates of the Museum, you pass 'the frontier which separates the Rookery from Oxford-street, [when] an examination of personal baggage frequently takes place by expert persons brought up to the business from infancy ... At this point of your peregrinations you may possibly discover that you have lost your pocket-handkerchief.'[17]

If the wealthier congregation of St George's attended church regularly, their poorer brethren in the parish of St Giles were a great deal less likely to do so, and not just because a large number of them were Irish Catholics. According to the 1881 Census, as many as 45,382 souls lived in the united parishes of St George's Bloomsbury and St Giles's,[18] but the statistics on churchgoing told a vastly different story. Under the authority of Lord John Russell, then Prime Minister, the 1851 Census included a question about this for the first time, and the results, published early in 1854, disturbed commentators, who realised that across the nation less than half the population regularly attended church. Attendance was even lower in urban districts, including London, where pews for just 46 per cent of the population were available, and only half of those were occupied on Sundays.[19] Of an estimated population of eighteen million in England and Wales, the number attending Anglican churches on Census day, Sunday 30 March 1851, was nearly four million, while over a million Methodists, half a million Baptists, and 305,000 Catholics were counted. This left about twelve million inhabitants who did not take part in any form of religious worship.[20]

Other denominations had small figures, but some could claim recognition and influence quite disproportionate to their numbers. Prominent among these were Unitarians and Swedenborgians, both active in Bloomsbury by mid-century, as was the reforming West London Synagogue of British Jews, established in Burton Street in 1842 to bring together London's Sephardic and Ashkenazi congregations and to introduce sermons in English rather than in garbled Hebrew.[21] A new religious group also appeared in the Census, adherents of the Catholic Apostolic Church, whose central 'cathedral' was formally opened on Christmas Eve 1853 in the south-west corner of Gordon Square. The worshippers here were known as 'Irvingites', since their branch of Christianity had grown out of the sermons, writings, and personal influence of the Revd Edward Irving, for whom a huge Scottish Presbyterian church had been built in Regent Square on the eastern fringes of Bloomsbury in the 1820s. The beliefs of the charismatic Irving were radical; his preaching laid down a challenge to complacent orthodoxy by attracting large numbers. Irving's brief decade in London before his early death was one of the most talked about phenomena of the age.

Dissenting churches were not the only ones to be built at this time. In recognition of the rapid expansion of London, a number of Anglican churches were built to cater for the inhabitants of newly developed areas, including Bloomsbury. At the same time as the Scottish church was being built for Irving in the still developing north-eastern corner of Bloomsbury, a new Anglican church, St Peter's, went up in the same square. Opened in 1826, it was designed in classical style by William and Henry Inwood, the architects a few years earlier of the Anglican St Pancras New Church, built in Greek revival style with huge female figures holding up its columns, on the corner of Upper Woburn Place and the New Road.[22] The incumbent of St Peter's, Regent Square, William Harness, was horrified by the opening opposite his fine new church in 1827, one year after his own, of the equally imposing National Scottish Church, built by William Tite on the model of York Minster to accommodate Irving's huge following, which had completely outgrown the previous Scottish Church in Hatton Garden. Irving brought crowds of worshippers to Regent Square, and large numbers of gawping spectators, newspaper reporters, and others who wished to hear for themselves the 'speaking in tongues' which went on in Irving's establishment and which Harness felt obliged to preach against in his own church.[23] Irving briefly transformed the landscape of religion as practised in Bloomsbury, and in doing so attracted the attention of both the local and the national press.

Edward Irving, born in Annan, Dumfriesshire, in 1792, had been a divinity student at Edinburgh and schoolmaster in Kirkcaldy, where in 1816 he met and befriended his fellow townsman Thomas Carlyle. Both young men were to move to London in the 1820s and both made an impact on metropolitan, national, and – in Carlyle's case – international intellectual life. After a slow start Carlyle became the most influential writer in Britain following his commanding essays in the *Edinburgh Review*, his unusual work of satire and enthusiasm *Sartor Resartus* (1834), his dramatic *French Revolution* (1837), and the attack on urban squalor and misery, *Past and Present* (1843). Through his correspondence and friendship with Ralph Waldo Emerson, he became equally famous in America.

Meanwhile, Irving, more charismatic as a speaker though less so as a writer, gained instant fame as a Presbyterian minister on his arrival in London in December 1821, but fell from grace almost as fast a few years later. His death at the age of forty-two in 1834 left it unclear whether he would have continued to hold sway over the religious beliefs of his followers or alienated ever more of them through his extreme prophetic pronouncements and toleration of 'speaking in tongues'. His chief legacy was the Catholic Apostolic Church, established by some of his associates. His friend Carlyle, though he shook his head over Irving's vanity, praised him in an article a few weeks after his death as 'the freest, brotherliest, bravest human soul mine ever came in contact with', and partly blamed London society's insatiable greed for novelty for turning Irving's head and then abandoning him in order to move on to the next spectacle:

Fashion cast her eye on him . . . Fashion went her idle way, to gaze on Egyptian Crocodiles, Iroquois Hunters, or what else there might be; forgot this man, – who unhappily in his turn could not forget. The intoxicating poison had been swallowed; no force of natural health could cast it out.[24]

In 1821 Irving had accepted the invitation to become Presbyterian minister of the small Caledonian Chapel in Cross Street, Hatton Garden. He so pleased the elders and congregation during the four-week trial period that they offered him a salary of £250 a year, with half the seat rents, another £250, in addition. He wrote jubilantly to Carlyle in April 1822 that with the 'security of £500 a year' he would be able to 'entertain you yet in London as every honest hearted fellow should be entertained'.[25] On this preliminary visit Irving lived in Everett Street, east of Russell Square; after his ordination at Annan in June 1822 he returned to London to take up his ministry, renting 'three very good, rather elegant rooms' at nearby 19 Gloucester Street, just off Queen Square. He described 'this part of town' as 'very airy and healthy, close to Russell Square, not far from the Church, and in the midst of my friends'.[26]

The combination of Irving's appearance – he was well over six feet tall, strongly built, with a full head of black hair and a handsome face, marred only by a squint – his theatrical manner of speaking, and his genuine religious enthusiasm won him immediate success with his small congregation of London Scots. His repute soon brought greater numbers to the chapel. Politicians and aristocrats turned up to hear this eloquent preacher; thirty-five coroneted coaches were counted on one occasion and a 'line of carriages often extend[ed] from the church door down Hatton Garden almost to Holborn'.[27] Carlyle recalled attending services at Hatton Garden while staying with Irving in the summer of 1824. He described 'the potent faculty at work, like that of Samson heavily striding along with the Gates of Gaza on his shoulders'. The attendance was large, though not as large as it had been during Irving's first months in London a couple of years earlier:

> The doors were crowded long before opening, and you got in by ticket: but the first sublime rush of what once seemed more than popularity, and *had been* nothing more, – Lady Jersey 'sitting on the Pulpit steps', Canning [then foreign minister], Brougham, Mackintosh [reforming Whig politician], etc. rushing, day after day, – was now quite over, and there remained only a popularity of 'the people'. . . At sight of Canning, Brougham, Lady Jersey and Co. crowding round him, and listening week after week as if to the message of Salvation, the noblest and joyfullest thought (I know this on perfect authority) had taken possession of his noble, too sanguine, and too trustful mind: 'That Christian Religion was to be a truth again, not a paltry form, and to rule the world, – he, unworthy, even he the chosen instrument!'[28]

This was written with hindsight, but even at the time Carlyle saw that his friend was susceptible to flattery and likely to be charged by some with being a religious mountebank. 'Like another Boanerges he is cleaving the hearts of the Londoners in twain', he reported to his brother in December 1822, 'acting so as to gain universal notoriety.'[29] So successful was Irving that plans were already afoot, a few months after his arrival, to build a larger church to accommodate his listeners; he wrote to a friend in Scotland that December in terms which demonstrate that in his reminiscence Carlyle caught his friend's tone of voice precisely:

> Already my Church overflows, & many are the testimonies which are brought to me of happy effects from my preaching[.] I have dispensed the sacraments to more communicants than have ever before sat down in the place. And there are [*sic*] already £3000 subscribed to build a new church which will be finished in less than a year to contain 2000 people and cost towards £10,000. But that above all which gives me happiness, is the liberty I enjoy of testifying without any restraint my full conception of that blessed Gospel of which I am the unworthy minister.[30]

The church authorities hoped that through Irving's inspired preaching some of the large number of Scots in the capital could be brought to worship; it was estimated that there were at least 100,000 potential worshippers, while accommodation in Presbyterian chapels amounted to just 5,000 seats, and actual attendance at the Hatton Garden chapel before

Irving's appointment had languished at about fifty.[31] Irving and the elders calculated in February 1827 that not even 1 per cent of Scots in London attended church.[32] William Tite's grand Gothic design was chosen and the new church was built between 1824 and 1827 at the large cost to the congregation of £21,000, including purchase of the site in Regent Square.[33] Irving was to bring his sizeable following with him to the eastern reaches of Bloomsbury.

Irving had a mission to revitalise the spiritual life of the nation, and he worked himself into an early grave in the endeavour. He was a religious radical who stepped outside the rules of his denomination by questioning the Scottish Church's Calvinist doctrine of predestination, by asserting the human nature of Christ on earth against the Presbyterian orthodoxy that Christ was incapable of sin, by returning to the prophetic books of the Old Testament and finding there material for his belief in the imminent end of the world and Christ's return to glory on the Day of Judgment, and finally by allowing – though never himself manifesting – the 'gift of tongues' in Regent Square. Between 1828 and 1833 he was twice tried for heresy, first by the London Presbytery, whose jurisdiction he refused to accept, and then by the presbytery in his birthplace Annan.[34] All this time he retained a faithful following, though inevitably he lost some members of his flock along the way. His radicalism did not extend to politics; he opposed Catholic emancipation and electoral reform, and quickly left the founding committee of the University of London when he saw that it was not going to be an academy professing dissenting religious beliefs.

For five years, however, he brought life and a kind of light to the far north-eastern corner of Bloomsbury. Though Regent Square had been laid out in 1820, no houses were built on it until 1829.[35] By the 1830s residents of the square included solicitors, barristers, architects, a surgeon, and a judge.[36] But when Irving's church opened in 1827, the surrounding small streets, bordering Gray's Inn Road, were not on the whole populated with lawyers, doctors, or even striving merchants, but with the working poor, whom Irving visited during his ministry, though his congregation continued to consist mainly of the middle-class professional people he had attracted at Hatton Garden. When the foundation stone was laid on 1 July 1824, the event was a momentous one for participants for whom a trip to the still undeveloped Regent Square was surely a novelty. *The Times* reported that 1,700 tickets had been issued for the occasion. The Duke of Clarence was due to lay the foundation stone but was indisposed on the day. Those who did attend included the Earl and Countess of Breadalbane, Earl Gower, the Earl of Rosebery, Countess Conyngham, and 'a number of Scotch nobility and gentry'. A 'sumptuous dinner' was held later in the Freemasons' Tavern. According to *The Times*, 'the crowd was great throughout the day, but not the least accident occurred'.[37]

Equally grand was the opening ceremony on 11 May 1827. Once again attendance was by ticket, but, as *The Times* reported,

> the crowd even exceeded expectation. For a considerable time the carriages, of which there was great abundance, were prevented from approaching the doors; and it was with the greatest difficulty that those who had tickets succeeded in getting within the doors. On entering the church, in which about 1,600 or 1,700 can be accommodated, we found it, at half-past eleven o'clock, uncomfortably filled: shortly after that hour, the crowd without succeeded in forcing open the outward doors, and a most tremendous rush took place ... By the exertions of the police, who attended in great numbers, the greater part of the intruders were ejected, after they had loudly asserted their right to remain in a place of public worship.[38]

Most of the 'notables', however, did not attend the church regularly after this. 'The world of fashion', according to Regent Square's historian, John Hair, 'had largely fallen away from Mr Irving', either put off by his increasingly urgent prophesying or, as Carlyle thought, tired of the novelty, and perhaps also discouraged by the unfashionable location.[39]

Irving had divided observers from the start. For every admirer of his pulpit rhetoric there was a sceptic, and many who began as admirers recoiled as Irving became more heterodox in his opinions. The barrister Basil Montagu and his socialite wife, who held regular salons in their home at 25 Bedford Square, had early become devotees. In July 1823 they took Irving to Highgate to meet Coleridge, who went to hear his new acquaintance preach at Hatton Garden, and reported to a friend that this 'super-Ciceronian, ultra-Demosthenic Pulpiteer of the Scotch Chapel' was 'the present Idol of the World of Fashion'.[40] Irving fell under the spell of Coleridge's famous oratory; Coleridge was impressed by Irving too, and was pleased to have a volume of Irving's *Orations* dedicated to him in 1825 from 'a disciple to a wise and generous teacher'. The Sage of Highgate attended the first Sunday service at Regent Square after the opening.[41] But his ardour had cooled by 1827, when Irving was preaching millenarianism, and in 1830 he commented on 'Mr Irving and his unlucky phantasms', joking that 'while other Scotchmen were content with Brimstone for the Itch, Irving had a rank itch for Brimstone'.[42]

Among the scoffers was *John Bull*'s Theodore Hook, who was quick to describe the 'scrambling, pushing, and squeezing for admission' to hear 'a great, brawny Scotchman' talk 'the most detestable nonsense that ever came from human lips'.[43] And Hazlitt, who paid Irving the compliment of including him among his character portraits in *The Spirit of the Age* (1825), enjoyed analysing the paradox of a clergyman 'spouting Shakespeare' from a 'Calvinistic pulpit', particularly when the clergyman in question looked like a prize fighter and spoke pugilistically too. Enlarging the metaphor, and drawing sly attention to Irving's squint, Hazlitt wrote:

> He literally sends a challenge to all London in the name of the KING of HEAVEN, to evacuate its streets, to disperse its population, to lay aside its employments, to burn its wealth, to renounce its vanities and pomp; and for what? – that he may enter in as the *King of Glory*; or after enforcing his threat with the battering-ram of logic, the grapeshot of rhetoric, and the cross-fire of his double vision, reduce the British metropolis to a Scottish heath, with a few miserable hovels upon it, where they may worship God according to *the root of the matter* [Hazlitt's italics].[44]

Though Irving's expulsion from Regent Square in 1832 was on account of his belief that Christ took on sinful human nature while on earth, it was the 'manifestations' by members of his flock, beginning in 1831, which held the attention of the wider world. Examples of speaking in unknown tongues held to be ancient biblical languages, along with apparent miracles and saintliness, first appeared amongst the congregation of one of Irving's followers in the west of Scotland in March 1830.[45] Some members of Irving's congregation, including the Bloomsbury lawyer John Bate Cardale, went to Scotland to investigate, reporting back on the apparent genuineness of the manifestations. In April 1831 Cardale's wife Emma 'spoke in the spirit' at home in Bedford Row.[46] Soon Cardale's sister Emily was speaking in tongues at prayer meetings held in both the Cardale house and Irving's home.

Affairs moved swiftly, until in October 1831 a Miss Hall spoke 'in tongues' at a service in Regent Square during which Irving delivered a sermon on 'the extraordinary gifts of the Spirit'.[47] The press and other curious folk beat a path to the church, with *The Times* declaring on 29 October that Irving was likely to be ejected by the church authorities and blaming him for encouraging 'the screams of hysterical women, and the rhapsodies of frantic men'. 'We warn sensible people who frequent the

Caledonian Chapel – lately converted into a miracle-shop – that these
follies are contagious'.[48] It was noticed that most, though not all, of the
members of Irving's congregation who spoke in tongues or 'in the Spirit'
were women, just as there was frequent mention of Irving's handsomeness
and vanity. An anonymous account in the *East Anglian Daily Times* of a
Sunday service at six in the morning in the snowy winter of 1831, though
not hostile, demonstrates why some thought him a fraud who used his gifts
to charm vulnerable women:

> Just as the clocks struck six, whilst the church was in complete darkness,
> the vestry door was heard to open and Mr Irving entered with a small,
> but very bright reading lamp in his hand. It shone upon his face and
> figure as if to illuminate him alone. He had on a voluminous dark blue
> cloak with a large cape which he loosened so that the cloak formed a
> kind of background to his figure. When he reached the reading desk, he
> stood for a few moments in silence, his face pale in the light of the lamp,
> his long, dark curls falling upon his shoulder and with his eyes staring
> into the darkness of the building. There was no sound except the sleet
> beating against the windows.[49]

Carlyle had feared that mass hysteria might attend his friend's sincere yet
self-dramatising demeanour; Hazlitt had hinted at his attractiveness to
women as he stood in his pulpit, handsome and eloquent, at Hatton
Garden; and Henry Crabb Robinson entered a note in his diary in May
1825, written in shorthand for secrecy, to the effect that there was gossip
about Irving's lack of 'personal' (i.e. sexual) holiness.[50] Crabb Robinson did
not believe the rumour, and there is no evidence to suggest that Irving was
anything other than honest in his personal as well as his professional dealings. He was increasingly troubled by the happenings in his own church,
though apparently powerless to stop them, as he felt unable to declare
manifestations – which he had encouraged by his own announcements of
the imminence of the Second Coming – to be false. He had set the brooms
fetching water from the Rhine without knowing the words to end the spell.
    The press continued to report the goings-on at Regent Square until
spring 1832, when Irving was tried by the London Presbytery for his heresy
on the nature of Christ. On 27 April he spoke in his own defence for over
four hours, claiming – truthfully – that over a thousand people had been
converted by his ministry.[51] The presbytery ordered him to be removed
from the church immediately, and he took 800 of his congregation with
him, leaving only 200 behind to shoulder the large debt still owed for the

building.[52] Irving preached his last sermon at Regent Square on 3 May 1832. The following day he rented a nearby hall at 277 Gray's Inn Road, opened a few years earlier as a horse stable and bazaar and now used by the socialist and co-operatist Robert Owen for his Society to Remove the Cause of Poverty and Ignorance. As *The Times* pointed out on 5 May, Irving and Owen

> will thus hold forth from the same place, and exhibit, perhaps, the strangest conjunction that ever design or accident produced. The former will give his 'new readings' of the Apocalypse, with occasional interludes on the 'tongues'; and the other his 'new view of society', with a little fiddling and a sixpenny hop, 'for the benefit of the working classes'.[53]

At the Horse Bazaar, or Royal London Bazaar as it was also called, Irving seemed to be taking part in the kind of spectacle that some speculative builders and entrepreneurs were attempting to establish in this difficult north-east corner of Bloomsbury. The architect James Elmes welcomed the bazaar in his 1827 book *Metropolitan Improvements; or London in the Nineteenth Century: being a Series of Views, of the New and Most Interesting Objects, in the British Metropolis & its Vicinity: from Original Drawings by Mr Thos. H. Shepherd. With Historical, Topographical & Critical Illustrations.* The building was, he wrote, 'a noble structure of quadrangular form, with a spacious arena in the centre', accommodation for 'about two hundred horses, and galleries for more than double that number of carriages', as well as a large building with a room 'capable of containing *upwards of one thousand persons!*' He also noted that there was a plan to convert the adjacent field 'into a handsome square and gardens, *à la Tivoli*, with a superb theatre, to be called the *Panarmonion*', 'the whole projected by Professor Lanza'. These establishments would, he believed, 'combine to render this part of the metropolis a principal object of attraction with the fashionable world'.[54]

Though Signor Lanza advertised the opening in March 1830, he was declared bankrupt a few months later; the whole Panarmonion project collapsed early in 1832 when another of its promoters, the architect Stephen Geary, also went bankrupt.[55] The area never became a place of fashionable resort, despite further plans for it, including the erection of a sculpture of St George killing the dragon at Battle Bridge, the crossroads of the New Road and Gray's Inn Road. At first the junction was to be called St George's Cross, but the name was changed to King's Cross to honour (or flatter) first George IV and then, after his death in June 1830,

William IV.[56] King's Cross Station was built across the New Road in the early 1850s, by which time the monument had been demolished.

Neither Irving nor Owen stayed very long in the Horse Bazaar; both had left by the end of 1832, Irving for a house in Newman Street, west of Tottenham Court Road, which Cardale took for him on a thirty-three-year lease. The building had been an art gallery and now served as both church for Irving's flock and home for his family. Irving's fame was such that 1,600 people attended the first service, according to *The Times* in its report of the opening on 19 October; among the named attenders were John Bate Cardale of Bedford Row and Henry Drummond 'the banker and Surrey magistrate'.[57] These two men were to be prominently involved in the establishment of the Catholic Apostolic Church, the idea for which had been conceived by Drummond, who held annual conferences on prophecy at his home in Albury, Surrey, from 1826 to 1830, which Irving and Cardale attended. By 1833, when Irving went to Annan to defend himself (unsuccessfully) against the presbytery there, Cardale had been created the first 'apostle' of the group; with his prophesying and manifesting wife Emma and sister Emily, he had begun to dominate an exhausted and ailing Irving. Cardale ordained Irving as 'angel', an inferior position to that of apostle, in April 1833, and Irving found himself outranked in a movement for which he had been the chief inspiration.[58]

In September 1834 Irving left for Glasgow, intending to convert people there to his apostolic beliefs. He was already ill with consumption and bowed down by work, by the loss of four of his children in childbirth or infancy, and by worry about the dissension among his Newman Street flock, who were arguing about the credibility of some of the manifestations in their midst. By November he was so ill that he wrote farewell letters to his congregation, humbly declaring himself to have been guilty of 'bringing in that sin for which the hand of the Lord hath long lain heavy upon us' and seeing his illness as divine punishment, though he still believed in principle that God was behind the 'gifts' of the spirit and that the manifestations were a sign that God intended a return to the direct inspiration experienced by the original apostles, this to be a prelude to the Last Judgment and the coming of the millennium of Christ's reign on earth.[59] He died on 7 December, and was buried in the crypt of Glasgow Cathedral.

The obituaries and sermons on his passing were generous, recognising his sincerity and the astonishing gift of making converts, while regretting his excesses. Irving had been a phenomenon. He had attracted society's elite to Hatton Garden and Regent Square; he had preached to thousands in fields around London during 1832; his congregations at Regent Square reached 2,000, though some of that number were inevitably curious observers; in Kirkcaldy in June 1828, at a service he took at the church of his father-in-law John Martin, 2,000 people crowded into the building, a gallery collapsed, and in the ensuing panic more than thirty people died.[60] In December 1830, aghast at the reform agenda of the new Whig government under Lords Grey and Melbourne and eyeing the Paris revolution of that year anxiously, Irving and his elders drew up a petition to the king for a national fast. He and three others presented the petition to Melbourne, praying in the anteroom during their long wait; on Melbourne's arrival Irving told him forcefully that it was his duty to present the petition to the king, after which he knelt in prayer again.[61]

Many, many Londoners went to hear Irving at least once. In December 1831 Elizabeth Barrett reported to a friend the account given to her by her father, a regular attender at Regent Square:

> Four thousand persons are assembled every Sunday at Mr Irving's chapel, – two thousand sitting, and two thousand standing; and after his fervent extempore prayer, he folds his arms in his black gown, & exclaims in his majestic manner, & deep solemn voice, 'I wait, until it please the Holy Ghost to speak unto us by the mouth of his servants'. Then comes the unknown tongue: the most terrific sound, Papa says, that he ever heard or expects to hear. 'Believe it, or do not believe it – you must be awed by it.' He was present at the first exhibition, – women shrieked and fainted, & there was a general rush towards the doors . . . All London was & is, in a state of excitement. Everybody acquits Mr Irving of being intentionally deceptive, – and some people acquit the exhibitors – but there is not so much unanimity in the latter decision.[62]

Irving's effort at religious revival and enlightenment in eastern Bloomsbury was unfortunately mixed with fanaticism and dubious outbursts of hysteria, so that his ministry remained, as his sorrowing friend Carlyle saw, a passing fad, a mere spectacle, instead of inculcating a moderate and lasting spirituality at a time of great national change. Carlyle himself, brought up like Irving a strict Calvinist, had moved from belief in any specific doctrine or sect towards a kind of theism, a trust in 'natural supernaturalism', in the world as a book written by God for human beings to read and interpret.[63] Carlyle's own 'prophetic' writings, directed against uncaring and inactive bureaucracy in state religion and parliamentary talking-shop alike, had a wider influence on the Victorian generation than his friend's lengthy sermons and volumes of interpretation of biblical prophecy. However, in the decades after Irving's early death, a whole new church arose partly as a result of his influence. Its outward symbol was, and remains, the enormous, imposing, mysterious central London building of the Catholic Apostolic Church which went up in the south-west corner of Cubitt's Gordon Square, on land at the back of University College London, in the years 1850 to 1853.

Early in his time in London, Irving had come to the attention of Henry Drummond, a wealthy member of an old Scottish aristocratic family and partner in Drummond's Bank in Charing Cross. Drummond was an enlightened Tory who supported land reform and endowed a chair of political economy in Oxford in 1825. He was against political reform, however, and alarmed at the principles behind the movement for educational reform, especially the secular principles applied at the godless college in Gower Street. When invited in 1828 to subscribe to the new university by one of its founders, James Loch, he replied bluntly:

> My dear Sir,
> There is no reason whatever why you should not apply to any body you please to support the London University; but you could not have made trial upon a worse subject than me. Although all my partners share my sentiments respecting it, yet none has as often had occasion to denounce it in public as I have; & it is quite useless for me therefore to bring the subject before them . . . Your brother Council-man [Zachary] Macaulay, & J[ohn] Smith & L[or]d Auckland have all made similar applications, & with similar success.[64]

(Drummond did subscribe for a share in King's College London in 1830, and his bank donated £200.[65])

In 1817 Drummond had begun to devote his attention to religion; he became active in the London Society for Promoting Christianity among the Jews, saving it from bankruptcy, and in 1819 he bought Albury House, a country mansion near Guildford in Surrey, where he held his advent meetings from 1826 to 1830 for like-minded colleagues to discuss the prophetic books of the Bible. He and Irving published three volumes of *Dialogues on Prophecy* in 1828–9, describing these Albury conferences. About forty men attended the meetings, of whom two-thirds were Anglicans, many of them clergymen, while some, like Irving, were Presbyterians, and others came from different dissenting sects.[66] Drummond and Irving sometimes clashed, because the former, though a religious enthusiast, had a sarcastic manner and authoritative tone which Irving disliked. Irving took Carlyle to dinner at Drummond's London home in August 1831, when Carlyle was visiting the capital to try to find a publisher for *Sartor Resartus*.[67] Carlyle lodged with Irving's brother George in Woburn Buildings, off Upper Woburn Place, from where he reported to his wife Jane that Drummond was 'a very striking man, taller and leaner than I, but erect as a plummet, with a high-carried quick penetrating head; some forty-five years of age: a singular mixture of all things; of the Saint, the Wit, the Philosopher, swimming if I mistake not in an element of Dandyism.'[68]

Among those at the dinner was Spencer Perceval, son of the assassinated Prime Minister of the same name and a Tory MP, who became in December 1833 one of the twelve apostles of the emergent Catholic Apostolic Church. Perceval, too, supported conversion of Jews; he responded to Isaac Lyon Goldsmid's request in 1831 for his support of a bill to go before parliament to abolish Jewish disabilities on the model of the abolition of Catholic disabilities by trying to convert him:

Dear Sir, I do not despise the Jew ... They knew not the voice of the Shepherd of Israel & the things that pertain to their peace were and are hid from their eyes ... Pray read the 10th of Romans and believe me dear Sir I trust yr. sincerely willing servant for Jesus Christ[']s sake, S. Perceval.[69]

Perceval worshipped in Irving's church; Mary Hall, one of the first speakers in tongues at Regent Square, was his family's governess.[70]

By the time Irving died in December 1834, a number of the men who attended both Irving's church and Drummond's conferences had been appointed – had in effect, as a new body, appointed one another – apostles of the new dispensation, not yet called the Catholic Apostolic Church. They were led by Cardale, the Bloomsbury lawyer who, with his wife and sister, began the 'speaking in the Spirit' which moved in the course of a few months during 1831 from their home in Bedford Row into first the vestry at Regent Square and then the church itself. Cardale and his family had been members of the Anglican congregation of their local church, St John's, Bedford Row. Its minister, the Revd Baptist Wriothesley Noel, whom Cardale consulted after his wife Emma and sister Emily spoke in tongues in April 1831, refused to accept the divine inspiration of the Cardale family's experiences, upon which they left his church to join Irving's in Regent Square.[71]

Soon after they had all moved to the former picture gallery in Newman Street in October 1832, Cardale himself spoke 'in prophecy', and on 7 November Drummond called him to be the first apostle. A month later Cardale ordained Drummond as 'angel' of the Albury congregation, and so began the hierarchy of the Catholic Apostolic Church, with the creation of twelve apostles and under them angels, then evangelists, and below these priests, deacons, and later deaconesses. In September 1833 Drummond was called by Cardale to be the second apostle. (To a hostile article written by the Oxford cleric Edward Pusey in 1855 Cardale defended the inevitable circularity of the ordaining process, describing how each member had acted under spiritual guidance in conformance with his sincerely held belief that God had called him.[72]) By 1835 all twelve had been appointed. All but one were wealthy middle-class professional men. Three were lawyers: Cardale, Francis Woodhouse, and Thomas Carlyle (not Irving's friend, later the Sage of Chelsea, though like him a Scot); two, Nicolas Armstrong and Henry Dalton, were Anglican clergymen; one, William Dow, was a Scottish Presbyterian minister who had been deposed, as Irving had; Henry King-Church was a clerk in the Tower of London; John Tudor, editor of the group's quarterly journal, the *Morning Watch* (1829–33), was a writer and artist; Drummond and Frank Sitwell were landowners; Perceval was an MP. Duncan Mackenzie, a chemist and elder at Irving's church, was lowest in the social order.[73]

The group, which resisted being called a sect, since its members in many cases still belonged to established churches and thought of themselves as holding the true apostolic beliefs from which the established churches had strayed, spent the next twenty years at Newman Street and Albury, where Drummond rented houses on his estate to Catholic Apostolic Church members. In 1835 the apostles gathered at Albury for the 'separation' – a summons to create seven churches in London and to undertake worldwide conversion. Following the Book of Revelation, they constituted themselves apostles for twelve spiritual 'tribes', each associated with a part of the world. Cardale took England (and so became the driving force for the building of the great church in Gordon Square), while Drummond became responsible for Scotland and the Protestant part of Switzerland.

Thomas Carlyle was assigned north Germany, where he had by far the greatest success of all the apostles. Meanwhile his namesake in Chelsea, well known as the great admirer of Goethe and German literature, kept his good humour through correspondence with several people who mistook him for the apostolic Thomas Carlyle. To Christian Bunsen the Chelsea Carlyle wrote in 1843 that he was not the man who had written a book on the German nobility. 'T. Carlyle the Angel has more than once got me into scrapes,' he wrote. 'He is, I believe, a zealous, very well-intentioned man', 'an "Angel" at Albury, in short; and I am no Angel anywhere!'[74]

Cardale, by far the most active member, widely read in ancient and modern languages and in church history of East and West, and since 1833 retired from his solicitor's practice, devised a liturgy which came into use in the Catholic Apostolic churches throughout England in 1843. He wrote a number of books and pamphlets, mostly anonymously, including a book of regulations.[75] As apostle for England, he did not have to travel abroad to spread the word, but remained at Albury, where he lived with his growing family – the 1841 Census shows him there with his wife, sister-in-law Frances Plummer, nine children, and their governess – and directed operations.[76] By early 1847 he had bought Bedford House to the north-east of Tavistock Square, one of the three adjoining houses which had been created in the 1820s out of Burton's original Tavistock House.[77] From here he set about consolidating the church.

The group wished to build a 'cathedral' in central London to act as a focus for the growing congregations. One member, John Prescott Knight, an artist who had studied in Henry Sass's school in the early 1820s, and who had been since 1848 a deacon at Newman Street,[78] published *On Building a Church for Divine Worship: A Discourse delivered by One of the Deacons of the Central Church, 3rd November 1850*. The discourse was addressed to Newman Street's 'Holy and beloved Brethren in the Lord'. Knight reminded the flock that 'for many years past, it had been in all our hearts to build a House for the name of the Lord' and that they had been appealed to from time to time 'to make offerings' towards a building fund. Now, he told them, they had to leave Newman Street, 'for the parties who own the property will neither allow us to purchase it, nor will they renew our lease'.[79]

What was urgently needed was 'a Central or Cathedral Church, such as would not only afford space for the worship and services of this congregation, but also accommodation for the congregations of the Seven Churches at their monthly meetings'. As no freehold ground large enough had been found, they had acquired 'a suitable and convenient' leasehold site in the south-west corner of Gordon Square. The Duke of Bedford as landowner and Thomas Cubitt as leaseholder agreed to this otherwise prohibited use of Bedford land because of Cubitt's difficulty in finding takers for the houses he was now building on the west side of the square, twenty years after he had begun developing the north and south sides.[80] The site was leased for ninety years from Michaelmas 1850 at £290 per annum, with the possibility of renewal for three further terms of thirty years. In 1919, long after the church ceased to hold full services, the Bedford Estate agreed to sell it the freehold for £10,000.[81]

In his address to the flock in 1850, Knight added that £11,000 had already been raised for the new building, but that a total of £30,000 would be required for the large church they envisaged. Though it might seem odd that a religious group which ardently believed that the millennium was due soon – so much so that they made no provision for the replacement of apostles who died – should aim to build a huge church, Knight explained the motive in terms of countering the 'cathedrals of Mammon' which were rising all around. By this he meant shops and banks, and also the engineering projects on roads, railways, rivers, and oceans, modernising efforts welcomed by men like Brougham and Lardner, but which Knight and his colleagues looked upon with fear, as made by man, not God:

> What gigantic roads and costly machinery, annihilating time and space – passing under rivers – through mountains – over valleys – leaping over apparently insurmountable barriers, by suspending in mid-air iron galleries of stupendous proportions, through which are hurried thousands of tons of merchandise and thousands of living men, while beneath great ships are borne on the bosom of the waters! Truly, these may be called the cathedrals of Mammon . . . May we not herein learn a lesson to stimulate our own *devotion*?[82]

With Euston Station not five minutes' walk due north of Gordon Square and King's Cross in process of being built, Knight might well have had them in mind as he spoke and wrote, though it was the accessibility offered by these same railway termini, situated along the New Road, which rendered Gordon Square attractive as a location for the desired 'central' cathedral of Catholic Apostolicism.

The money to build was raised through donations and subscriptions from the Newman Street congregation. Cardale was the principal figure. He took on the task of creating the liturgy, deciding on the vestments, the calendar, the order of service, the use of incense, the form of the burial service, even details such as whether 'a Deacon might wear a Stole over both shoulders in preaching' (a question asked of him in March 1854) – everything, in fact, which was required for this new church. He borrowed elements from different established churches to do so.[83]

An architectural plan sent in by John Raphael Brandon and Robert Ritchie, architects known for their Gothic church buildings, was adopted.

Brandon had written on early English ecclesiastical architecture, and was himself a member of the Catholic Apostolic Church; he donated the oak tabernacle on the altar at Gordon Square.[84] Work began towards the end of 1850 on the main part of the building, for which the estimated cost was £13,000. Gatehouse, cloisters offering accommodation to officers of the church, and preaching chapel – costed at an extra £7,000 – were to wait until more money had been donated.[85] Though the plan was ambitious, slate was chosen for the roof because it was cheaper than lead.

Despite a certain amount of scrimping and saving, the building which went up between the end of 1850 and December 1853 was a magnificent one. Built in Bath stone and modelled on Westminster Abbey – even the seating at the Abbey was copied, though as a temporary money-saving measure the seats from Newman Street were initially transferred to Gordon Square[86] – the new church did indeed look like a cathedral. However, shortage of money and the urgent requirement to move out of Newman Street and into Bloomsbury meant that the tower was left unfinished and the west end of the church curtailed and built of brick instead of stone. Again, the plan was to complete these elements when finances allowed. Apparently finances never did allow, for the church remains incomplete in these details, though at various points stained glass and other interior improvements were added.[87]

Some of those who had been with Irving at Newman Street now lived close to their great Bloomsbury church. Cardale himself was in Tavistock Square, and Irving's widow Isabella lived close by at 53 Burton Crescent (now Cartwright Gardens).[88] Isabella's daughter, also called Isabella, born in the year of her father's death, was to marry a member of the Catholic Apostolic Church, the historian Samuel Rawson Gardiner, in January 1856. Gardiner gave an account in 1858 of the Gordon Square church's financial situation in that year. The building had cost £37,000, of which £34,500 had by then been paid.[89]

The new church in Gordon Square was opened with a service on Christmas Eve 1853. It attracted a lot of publicity, partly because of its sheer size and the unusual use of a site on Bedford land for a large public building. The *Morning Chronicle* drew attention to it as early as January 1853 during the final phase of building, noting, without reference to the incongruity, its proximity to University College London. The author of the short article attempted to give a flavour of the sort of service to be conducted in the new church:

Those who are in the habit of passing through Gordon-square, at the back of the London University, must of late have been struck by a building of huge proportions now rearing itself, and rapidly approaching completion. It is in the cathedral style, the architecture being gothic. This building is intended for the followers of the late Rev. Edward Irving, who since his decease have much altered their form of conducting public worship. They call themselves the Holy Catholic and Apostolic Church. The service is conducted much in the same manner as the Roman Catholic, being liturgical and intoned, with frequent genuflexions and changes of posture by the priests who conduct the service. The vestments worn by the priests are as gorgeous as those worn by the Roman Catholic priesthood. They recognise various orders in their Church, such as apostles, prophets, evangelists, pastors, and deacons . . . They believe that the power of working miracles still remains to the Church, and that Christ will shortly appear and reign with his saints for a thousand years in the Millennium.[90]

This description is roughly accurate, though the comparison with Roman Catholic practices was not welcomed by the Catholic Apostolics, who, mainly in the person of Cardale, were at pains to explain that they did not consider themselves a sect of any kind. It is not surprising that they should be linked to Roman Catholicism, since not only did they wear gorgeous vestments, devised by Cardale, and practise some similar rites, but Roman Catholicism itself had recently received a boost from the controversial reintroduction of its hierarchy in England with Cardinal Wiseman at its head. Thomas Carlyle (not the apostle) told his brother in November 1850 that there was a great fuss, with 'Burn the Pope', 'Kick the Pope's bottom', and 'No Popery!' scrawled on walls and pavements.[91]

A further reason for the interest in the Gordon Square church was the reporting of the religious Census of 1851 in January 1854, just in time to show that the Catholic Apostolic Church, along with some other dissenting churches, enjoyed relatively healthy numbers compared to the Church of England. Cardale and other members took advantage of the coincidence to advertise themselves. The youngest apostle, Francis Woodhouse, published an anonymous pamphlet in 1854, entitled *The Census and the Catholic Apostolic Church*, in which he presented his church as a solution to desperate divisions among Christian sects:

The publication of the Census, showing the decline of the Established Church, the increase of dissent, and the rise of the Catholic Apostolic

Church; the opening for public worship of the edifice erected by this body in Gordon Square, its architectural propriety, its beautiful proportions, and its appropriate fittings-up, affording a marked contrast to the general character of modern ecclesiastical edifices around, whether belonging to the Established Church or to others ... the increasing notice which their Liturgy, and certain other printed documents, emanating from them, has attracted; all these things combined, seem to be drawing the attention of religious persons, of all parties, to the title of the whole Christian body to the name of Catholic Apostolic Church, and to the evil state of division, which the many names, the conflicting professions, and the discordant practices, of the Christian community in this land bespeak.[92]

The reference here to the 'marked contrast' between the Gothic Gordon Square church and other modern churches 'around' suggests disapproval of the 'unchristian' style of the equally imposing St Pancras New Church, located only five minutes' walk to the north-east of Gordon Square. The desire of the Catholic Apostolics to return the Anglican Church to its early roots made their choice of the Gothic style a logical one. The building of their church happened to coincide with the rise of the new Houses of Parliament in Westminster, designed by Charles Barry and Augustus Pugin (a Catholic) in medieval Gothic style. The Gothic was in fact coming into favour for both secular and religious buildings as a reaction to what was increasingly seen as the austere, classical, 'pagan', and 'gloomy' uniformity of Georgian London, the London – and in large measure the Bloomsbury – of Burton and Cubitt.[93]

At the opening of the church in Gordon Square, Cardale, as first apostle, delivered the address, which was published as *A Discourse delivered in the Catholic Apostolic Church, Gordon Square, on the Occasion of Consecrating the Altar, and Opening the Church for Public Worship, Christmas Eve, 1853.* Lawyer-like, he set about answering any objections which might be made about the magnificence of the building. If any of the flock hoped to make others envious or to show off the 'lofty grandeur of this temple' in order to attract admiration and enhance their own reputations, 'be assured that God will search out the thought of your heart, and will punish your sin'. The initial plan had been to stay in Newman Street, but when that failed and they were obliged to look for a new site, the one they found in Gordon Square 'could [not] be secured, except the building erected on it had been of some architectural pretension'.[94] In other words, the Bedford Estate had stipulated that the building must be a fine one.

'Brethren, your motives have not been those of vulgar ostentation', Cardale assured his listeners. Then he addressed the vexed question of whether they constituted a sect, or a set of 'Irvingites':

> We are not a sect. Our brethren, misjudging and misinterpreting our words, our actions, and our position, may seek to cast us off. But still we cleave to them, to all that are in Christ Jesus our Lord, to the One Catholic church from which we refuse ever to separate. We abjure the names of men: we count it an injury and cruel scorn that the name of any man should be applied to us. We claim no exclusive name . . . We are here to testify to the work of God, in restoring the ordinances with which He endowed the Church at the first . . . The gift on the day of Pentecost of some men to be apostles, some prophets, some evangelists, some pastors and teachers, is a fact. The restoration of them is a fact . . . You are here, that you may warn the baptized people of God of the near approach of the day of glory and blessedness dawning upon the Church, the day of terror also and of judgment advancing upon the world.

Moreover, he told them, 'your retention of the rites of the Catholic Church will be imputed to you as a paltry imitation of Roman ceremonials'; they must rise above all such attacks and resist the tendency of others to stigmatize them with a nickname.[95] He also made it clear that Irvingism had been left behind, especially the speaking in tongues which had begun in earnest in Bedford Row and Regent Square.

The newspapers carried accounts of the opening which were obviously informed by Cardale himself and some of his colleagues. The *Morning Chronicle* described the event in terms very close to those used by Cardale in his address.[96] On 23 January 1854 it quoted the 1851 Census return to the effect that there were thirty-two Catholic Apostolic chapels in England, with a total of about 6,000 members, adding that churches had also been established in Scotland, Ireland, Germany, Switzerland, France, and America.

Controlled from the new central church in Gordon Square, the Catholic Apostolic body grew until by 1900 it was calculated that there were about 30,000 members worldwide. The proselytising abroad varied in success, with Switzerland and France yielding about 300 members between them, America about 230, Holland and Belgium seven, and Italy and Spain none, while Russia, Poland, and India were too far away for a personal visit to be feasible. Only north Germany could be counted a success, with the apostle Carlyle 'gathering' just over a thousand.[97] Indeed, the movement in

Germany continued to be active into the twenty-first century, partly as a result of a schism which occurred among the German members in the 1860s. A breakaway group called the New Apostolic Church allowed ordination of new apostles on the deaths of the original ones and hence facilitated a continuation of full worship, which the mother church did not countenance.

In England no provision had been made for replacing apostles, as the group expected the Second Coming to happen in the lifetime of the original apostles. But in 1855 three of them died – Mackenzie, Carlyle, and Dow – followed in 1859 by Perceval, in 1860 by Drummond, in 1861 by Tudor, in 1864 by Sitwell, in 1865 by King-Church, in 1877 by Cardale, and finally, in 1901, by Francis Woodhouse. The church in Gordon Square, and other churches in London and England, carried on with prayer meetings but had no way of keeping up their religion fully. Still waiting for the Second Coming, they entered the time of 'silence' noted in the Book of Revelation as preceding the apocalytic destruction of the earth,[98] refusing all the while to allow historians – even from among the members of the church – access to their records.[99]

Though Cardale moved away from Bloomsbury in October 1854, returning with his large family to Albury, where Drummond had built a house for them at Cardale's request,[100] he remained the driving force behind the whole church in England and its central cathedral in Gordon Square. For three years Dickens was his next-door neighbour, the novelist having moved back to Bloomsbury from Devonshire Terrace, near Regent's Park, in the autumn of 1851. Dickens took Tavistock House, previously home to the London High School after John Walker's ejection from the University of London school on Gower Street in 1832, and more recently of Dickens's friend the artist Frank Stone and his family. The Stones handed over Tavistock House, the most westerly and the largest of the three adjoining villas, to Dickens, themselves moving to Russell House, the most easterly, with Cardale the middle neighbour in Bedford House.

Dickens, having taken the remaining forty-five-year lease on the house, engaged in a polite correspondence with his new neighbour Cardale about arrangements for a shared pathway. There was a little restrained skirmishing about who was to pay for what; Dickens confided in Stone in September 1851, shortly before moving in, that 'Mr Cardale seems a very good sort of man, but is evidently "fussy"', and so it had taken longer than anticipated to get his agreement.[101] In May 1852 Dickens apologised to Cardale, who had complained of one of Dickens's servants allowing others to use the key to the gate leading east from the houses into Burton Street.[102]

One might have expected that Dickens, with his great curiosity about people and places, would find much to comment on with reference to his neighbour Cardale and the Catholic Apostolic Church in nearby Gordon Square, but only one reference is extant. In a letter of 20 April 1854 to W.H. Wills, his assistant on *Household Words*, Dickens announces drolly:

> My neighbour's, Mr Cardale's, daughter married this morning [it must have been one of the first weddings to take place in the Gordon Square building], and I obliged to leave home at what the newspapers always call 'an early hour of the morning' to avoid distraction. All the women and girls in my house, stark mad on the subject. Despotic conjugal influence exerted to keep Mrs Dickens out of the church. Caught putting bonnet on for that purpose, and sternly commanded to renounce idiotic intentions. Bride reported by our Confectioner (envious and a Roman Catholic) to have the gift of Tongues. It probably will disappear now; being, as I take it, a manifestation of what may be called uterine religious sentiments [i.e. hysteria].[103]

What Cardale made of the famous flamboyant novelist, journalist, and enthusiastic amateur actor living next door to him is not recorded.

The Catholic Apostolic Church was a strange phenomenon; its members wished, like Irving before them, to reform the religious spirit of the country, and in terms of the numbers of worshippers they attracted they could count themselves successful. They also managed to finance their movement (though not enough to finish the Gordon Square church), as one of the regulations drawn up by Cardale was that every member must pay a tenth of his or her gross income.[104] Since some were wealthy – in the case of Algernon Percy, sixth Duke of Northumberland, husband of Henry Drummond's daughter Louisa, fabulously so – the movement was able to keep afloat.[105]

The apostolic lawyers, clergymen, and landowners were easy prey to mockers who saw only quackery in their serious, self-sacrificing, and scholarly beliefs. Theodore Hook, still dashing off comic social novels in the 1840s, introduces in *Peregrine Bunce; or, settled at last* (1842) a scoundrel whom Peregrine meets when out walking in Regent's Park. Montclaire is a mesmerist, but tells Peregrine that he has left that calling. 'What's your vocation now?' asks Peregrine. 'I'm an angel,' replies the other solemnly:

A saintly gentleman whom I picked up a short time ago in an Islington omnibus, and who afterwards happened to hear me preach in the streets on the subject of the Millennium, introduced me to an Irvingite who frequents the chapel at Newman Street; and I made such an impression on this excellent individual by my familiar acquaintance with the Unknown Tongues, that he procured me the appointment of one of the seven angels of the chapel in question; so now I stand at the altar on Sundays with a brazen candlestick in my hand, and am supported by a small subscription among the brethren, till I am permitted to officiate as preacher. I must confess, I felt a little foolish at first, when I did duty as an angel with a big brass candlestick stuck between my fingers; but I soon got used to it; besides, were it not so, one must not quarrel with one's bread and butter . . . And besides, I live in hopes; for the methodistical line is a very promising one, and sometimes one can contrive to pick up a rich, devout widow, or old maid. I am told that several wealthy ladies attend the New Jerusalem; and should I get tired of doing duty as a cherub in Newman Street, I think it very likely that I may be tempted to try my fortune among some of these.[106]

The New Jerusalem Church, embracing the mystical beliefs of Emanuel Swedenborg, operated on the fringe and so could be readily associated by the irrepressible Hook with both mesmerism and Catholic Apostolicism. In the 1790s the New Jerusalem Church had occupied the very chapel in Cross Street, Hatton Garden, which was taken over by the Scottish National Church, where Irving first came to fame in 1822. Its members also built a church in north-east Bloomsbury, the New Christian Church in Argyle Square.[107] In 1851 it had three churches, the ones in Hatton Garden and Argyle Square, and one in King's Cross; by 1896 there were eight Swedenborgian churches in London.[108] Members of the New Jerusalem Church believed, like the Catholic Apostolics, that the millennium would come, but, unlike them, not that it was imminent.

Connected to the New Jerusalem Church, but separate from it constitutionally, was the Swedenborg Society, which had been founded in 1810 with the intention of publishing Swedenborg's works in English and furthering appreciation of his philosophy. The Society was from the first based in Bloomsbury. Its prime mover was the homoeopathic doctor James John Garth Wilkinson, who lived and practised between 1835 and 1847 in Store Street, just off Bedford Square, and who attended mesmeric experiments at John Elliotson's house in 1839–40, on one occasion in company with Dickens.[109] In its early days the Society met at 47 Devonshire Street, off Queen Square; by the late 1830s it was renting Burton Street Hall for meetings and lectures, and in 1854 it took premises in Charlotte Street, near Bedford Square and Great Russell Street.[110]

While there were eight Swedenborgian churches in London at the end of the nineteenth century, the Catholic Apostolic Church's symbolic seven, though still in existence, were becoming inactive. The problem was the lack of apostles to lead the congregations, with only Woodhouse still alive, and Woodhouse's own death came in 1901. Church members still exist, but they remain hidden from view. The millenarian enthusiasm sparked by the charismatic and tragic Irving, and taken to extremes by those who followed him, had no lasting influence on religion in London, or in Britain as a whole. The marvellous 'cathedral' built in Gordon Square, on the other hand, today leased in part by the Church of England, dominates the south-west corner in all its unfinished grandeur, evidence in stone of the ambitious aim of its founders to bring renewed spirituality to a rapidly developing nation.

CHAPTER SEVEN

A 'Quasi-Collegiate' Experiment in Gordon Square

THE CATHOLIC Apostolic Church's adjoining neighbour on the west side of Gordon Square is a Tudor Gothic building erected in 1849, the year before Brandon's church was begun. It too belongs to the history of Nonconformist religion in Bloomsbury, though of a very different kind. Called University Hall, it was built as the first hall of residence for students of University College after money was raised among London's Unitarians. Unitarianism, or Socinianism as it was also called, with its minimalist beliefs and rituals, was almost as far as it was possible to be doctrinally from the Catholic Apostolic Church. Back in the days of Henry Drummond's Albury conferences, one discussion of 1830 was summed up as resistance to the 'abuses' in the Church of England, among which was 'amalgamation with Socinians and Heretics'.[1]

Both groups claimed reforming instincts in religion. As large public buildings of architectural merit, their headquarters symbolised not only the influence of their respective forms of dissent in mid-century, but also the truth that even the Duke of Bedford's Bloomsbury estate was coming under pressure to allow the erection of institutions where private residences had been intended. Because Gordon Square was largely undeveloped on the west side, it happened that representatives of these two opposing religious groups were enabled to erect their institutions next door to one another. From 1853 they shared a party wall (about which they held protracted discussions for several years).

The aim in founding University Hall was to fill two gaps in the facilities offered by University College, namely accommodation for students and the opportunity for religious worship and theological lectures for dissenting, rather than unbelieving, students of the godless college. Some founders of University Hall even thought that, through co-operation with University

College in the teaching of certain subjects, the Hall might become the
country's leading college for the training of dissenting ministers. This
return to the idea cherished by Irving and other dissenting ministers when
the university itself was being planned in the mid-1820s brought trials and
travails to the Hall itself, not to mention tensions with University College,
with which it shared a boundary at the back, where the playground of
University College School was located.

The idea for the Hall came after the passing of the Dissenters' Chapels
Act in 1844, which granted Unitarians and other non-Anglicans legal
rights to their chapels and endowments. A meeting of dissenters in July
1844 agreed to celebrate the passing of the Act by establishing 'some
permanent memorial, educational or otherwise, to perpetuate in the most
useful form the great principle of unlimited religious liberty'. One of the
most active members, the elderly non-practising lawyer Henry Crabb
Robinson, a member of the council and various committees at University
College, helped to steer his fellow dissenters towards the decision taken at
the July 1844 meeting that the best plan was to

> ensure to the youth of the Non-Subscribing Dissenters, a full participa-
> tion in the educational advantages of University College, London,
> together with that general theological knowledge, which is equally
> beneficial both to laymen and divines ... At the present time, the
> majority of Non-Subscribing Dissenters in the large towns and country
> districts of this country are reluctant to avail themselves of the establish-
> ment of University College, on account of the want of a suitable place
> of academical residence for their sons in the Metropolis.[2]

A 'Hall or Academical Institution near to University College' of this kind
would comprise 'numerous sets of rooms adapted for lodging and private
study, as well as a lecture-room, a general room for students, a library, and
apartments for a resident Superintendent or Principal'.[3] As if to signal this
function, the chosen style of the building which was eventually erected,
designed by University College's current (and first) professor of architecture, Thomas Donaldson, was reminiscent of the Tudor buildings of the
residential colleges of Oxford and Cambridge.

It was agreed that the hall of residence should be built in close proximity
to University College and, reflecting the allegiance of the founding
committee, that 'Theological Instruction' would be given. This decision, as
well as causing suspicion among the secularists at University College, was
to prove as much of a disadvantage to University Hall as that taken twenty

years earlier by the Gower Street founders *not* to include religious instruction of any kind had been to the university, which had to struggle against Church-and-State prejudice and *John Bull* name-calling in its earliest years.

Where in the case of the university there had been disagreements over the recruitment of professors – should all clergymen be excluded from appointments, or only Church of England clergymen, or should the posts be open to anyone, clergyman or not, of any religion? – the issue facing University Hall was that its founders did not agree clearly on whether its primary function was as a hall of residence for University College students or as an institution which would take some Gower Street students and teach them theology of a non-denominational but dissenting kind. An effort to marry the two aims was expressed in the inscription which went up on the wall of University Hall when it was built:

The objects of the founders of this hall were

To provide for students of University College London the accommodation and social advantages of college residence

To provide a place where instruction without reference to creed should be permitted in theology and other subjects not taught or not wholly taught in University College and disavowing all denominational distinctions and religious tests to maintain the sanctity of private judgment in matters of religion.[4]

The statement is an attempt to suggest openness about the particular religious opinions to be held at the Hall; the wording was no doubt carefully chosen in order to avoid alienating University College's council. But some in Gower Street suspected a desire to introduce theology by the back door, and, worse, the Hall committee's good intention to preserve 'the sanctity of private judgment' was soon tested in arguments about who should be appointed principal, what his religious beliefs should be, and what his duties would entail.

As Donaldson's Tudor Gothic building rose in Gordon Square during 1848, after £10,000 had been raised, the auguries were good. The founders could not have hoped for a better site: an undeveloped plot adjoining the north-east boundary of University College land. A reasonable arrangement was entered into with Francis Russell, seventh Duke of Bedford, who, while wishing to retain the residential character of the area, permitted University Hall to be built as an educational establishment on condition that no public worship be carried on there and no boys under the age of fifteen be resident.[5] The lease on the land had been purchased from the previous Duke by Thomas Cubitt, who still had many undeveloped sites in the square on his hands, as the building boom ended and middle-class families chose to live further west and south in Marylebone, Pimlico, and Belgravia.

The stipulation about not holding public services was intended to avoid toing and froing by large numbers of non-residents. The policy was to keep up the appearance of private housing even when the Bedford Estate found itself having to accommodate something other than a family residence. In 1830 the University of London School had been required to take down its brass plate from 16 Gower Street, and the Bloomsbury Savings Bank was allowed in 1836 to occupy a house in Montague Street, by the side of the British Museum, only on condition that a waiting room in a passage next to the building be made accessible to customers before the bank opened in the morning, in order to prevent 'such persons from congregating in the street', 'thereby annoying or disturbing the inhabitants'. The only advertisement permitted to the bank was a discreet notice of banking hours at the side of the door.[6]

In 1848 the Hall's founders took the lease on the Gordon Square site for ninety-one years at £197 10d. per annum, with an option 'on payment of £2,900, within ten years, to purchase the freehold, his Grace's moiety of the rent, and the reversion of Mr Cubitt's interest, under an act of parliament to be obtained for the purpose'; or, alternatively, 'without an act, to take a lease for a thousand years, at a peppercorn rent'. In 1855 the latter option was taken.[7]

Though the Gordon Square site was perfect for the new hall of residence and there were good relations with the architect Donaldson, with whom Crabb Robinson did much of the negotiating over the plans, shuttling between his house in Russell Square, committee rooms at University College, and meetings about University Hall, the fact that all the £10,000 raised in advance was needed for the building, and the sheer size and grandeur of the building itself, when its founders could not be sure of filling it, caused the cautious Crabb Robinson to worry. His diaries recount the discussions of the committee, detailing the difficulties encountered by the fledgling institution.[8] He was painfully aware of the damaging differences of opinion among the promoters of the establishment. 'My apprehensions of our ultimate failure increase every day,' he wrote in October 1848.[9] Two years earlier, when subscriptions were being raised, he had thought that some of his fellow committee members were overly sanguine in assuming the money would easily be found:

We are opposed in the North where alone there are wealthy Unitarians. In the rest of the country there are few and money is elsewhere more scarce than in manufacturing countries or individuals are less liberal. At this meeting . . . there was . . . considerable difference of opinion on the point whether prominence should be given to the opportunities afforded for teaching U[nitarian]s as well as facilities for partaking of the benefits of University College. The clergy and laity feel differently on this point. Even the name is not agreed on. Some would avow and some conceal the U[nitarian]ism.[10]

As Crabb Robinson foresaw, the fact that some founders wished to advertise and others to downplay the Unitarianism of the proposed institution was fundamental to the Hall's early problems. One difficulty was its relationship with a powerful committee in Manchester of governors of Manchester New College, the country's leading training college for independent ministers. The College had been founded in 1786, had moved to York in 1803 and back to Manchester in 1840, but, though well endowed, was struggling to attract enough students.[11] It had considered moving to London in 1829, when some of its members realised that the new University of London would compete with it for dissenting lay students (though not for trainee clergymen), but a majority had voted to stay in Manchester. Now with the plan for University Hall under way, the subject of a merger, or at least cohabitation, in Gordon Square was raised.

Both the London committee and the Manchester committee were split on the desirability of joining forces. University Hall needed the support of Unitarians in the north-west – Manchester was a stronghold – in order to finance the building of the hall and also to fill its rooms with the sons of dissenting families. But the founders did not want to be taken over by the training college, and they knew that the godless college in Gower Street would not be keen on being closely associated with such an institution. For their part, the authorities of Manchester New College were anxious that it might lose its dissenting and training identity; they were also wary of associating themselves with the godless college.

After six years of toing and froing, with Crabb Robinson and other members of the University Hall committee visiting Manchester and resolutions being painfully worked out on both sides, Manchester New College moved to London towards the end of 1853 to share the building in Gordon Square. As Crabb Robinson saw all too clearly, the move was a reluctant response to overwhelming circumstances, namely the opening in October 1851 of Owens College (later Manchester University) on the same open principles as University College London, and the fact that by this time the professors of Manchester New College were 'more numerous than the pupils', there being six students and eight professors.[12] The two institutions did not merge; they lived together uneasily, each guarding its identity and functions, until in 1882 Manchester New College took over the administration of University Hall completely, selling the building in 1889 on the eve of its own removal to Oxford.

Crabb Robinson's fears about the split nature of the University Hall committee were soon realised as it argued in the early days of 1849 over the appointment of its first principal, some insisting on a Unitarian while others, including Crabb Robinson, thought such an appointment would send a signal that this was a sectarian establishment and would therefore be likely to make the Hall unattractive to the larger body of (actual and potential) University College students. By June 1850, near the end of the first year of the Hall's existence, he was ruminating gloomily on the 'unpopularity of Unitarianism, both with the religious and the anti-religious'. 'It offends the Rationalists by the admission of a supernatural element', and 'the orthodox are offended by the attempt we make to combine the spiritual and moral elements of religion with the minimum of supernaturalism'.[13] In January 1852, when the first two principals had already resigned, with the third soon to follow suit, and the number of students in residence was not only disappointing but rendered the institution financially unviable, Crabb Robinson despaired. The problem, he wrote in his diary, was that the founders had not known clearly what they wanted and that there was 'not a single able man of business to place at our head and manage us'.[14]

The first three principals of University Hall, though short-lived in the post, were among the most interesting and intelligent young men of the time. They were representative of an emerging class in the mid-nineteenth century, that of the non-Anglican, non-establishment metropolitan intellectual. This group consisted of two types: Nonconformists of the first generation for whom it was possible to be involved in higher education through taking degrees and in due course professorships at University College London, and men in self-imposed exile from one of the older universities, former Anglicans who had abandoned their adherence to the established Church after their beliefs became unsettled by findings in geology and biblical criticism.

Three such men took up the post at University Hall in its earliest years. The first two were disaffected Oxford men. They were Francis William

Newman, born in 1805 in Bloomsbury, the younger brother of John Henry
Newman; and Arthur Hugh Clough, born in 1819, a fellow of Oriel
College, Oxford, and writer of poetry of faltering faith under the pseudonym 'Dipsychus' ('in two minds'), in which he employed the anxious
double negative, as in 'Say not the struggle naught availeth'. The third was
one of the most brilliant of the first generation of students to graduate at
University College London, the son of a Nonconformist minister, Richard
Holt Hutton, who was later to become a leading literary critic and editor of
the *Spectator*.

The pressing need in the summer of 1848, when building was about to
begin, was to appoint the first principal. The choice fell on Francis
Newman. While his older brother had become the leader of the Tractarian
Movement in Oxford in the 1830s and eventually converted to Catholicism,
Frank had moved in the other direction, towards Unitarianism. Having
given up the Church of England, he was unable to pursue at Oxford the
academic career for which he was so obviously suited. In 1836 he became
a Baptist; he then married a member of the Plymouth Brethren and
embraced Unitarianism before becoming non-aligned to any particular sect.
Manchester New College took him on as a teacher in 1840. When the chair
of Latin became vacant at University College in 1846 after Thomas Hewitt
Key had given it up to be sole headmaster of University College School,
Newman was appointed. His reputation as a brilliant undergraduate at
Oxford went before him; at University College he was famed for his
extraordinary cleverness and learning, knowledge of several languages, and,
over the years, a number of seriously held enthusiasms, including dedication
to the causes of Italian and Hungarian freedom.[15]

His students remembered a brilliant man characterised by eccentricity of
dress and shyness in social situations. One, Walter Bagehot, told his
mother of a 'queer party' at Newman's house in December 1847 at which
the men and women gathered in separate rooms, with Newman 'peering
through the folding doors at the ladies'.[16] Another, Roger Fry's father
Edward, noted Newman's 'devout Theism', but thought him irritable.[17] His
communications with University College were precise, even pedantic; in his
first report on his Latin classes in December 1846 he noted that 'the
attendance was good & punctual' until it began to snow and 'then the
skating began' (in Regent's Park), after which, he complained, attendance
dropped.[18]

Crabb Robinson had been a member of the appointing committee for the
Latin chair at University College in 1846 and was pleased that this man
with the double first in classics and mathematics from Oxford was now

joining University Hall. At the laying of the foundation stone of the Hall on 20 July 1848, Newman delivered the inaugural address, thrilling Crabb Robinson with 'the skill with which he asserted, without offence, the power of forming an institution open to all opinions whatever, even Jew and Mahometan'. Crabb Robinson congratulated the younger man on managing to conciliate everyone. 'It resembled, as I told him, the egg-dance of Mignon, in "Wilhelm Meister",' the diarist noted.[19] Newman had declared in his speech that the principles of University College and University Hall were the same:

> Each regards it as an impertinence to inquire into the religious opinions held by any of its members. Each, therefore, holds its doors open not only to Christians of every name, but to Jew and Mohammedan, to Parsee and Hindoo. There is no exclusion in either, and no prying into anyone's creed . . . When you appoint for yourselves a professor, you will not choose him by his creed, though certainly by his freedom to follow truth. You would (I believe) far rather select a learned and large-hearted man opposed in detail to your opinions, than one less accomplished or more narrow-minded, whose creed might yet be more in unison with that of the majority of you.[20]

The liberal Crabb Robinson may have been delighted by this compliment, but other founders of the Hall were less so. Young Walter Bagehot, a recent classics graduate of University College and member of University Hall's council, showed more shrewdness; describing the occasion to his fellow alumnus Charles Roscoe a few weeks later, he referred to his former tutor's appointment:

> The only objection that any one could have to Newman as the head of a religious institution is that his own religion is such a thoroughly bad one. What he says about the magnanimity of founding an institution independent of opinions is marred to me by my being convinced that if the Council *had* known his creed they would never have appointed him.[21]

It was not long before Newman resigned, though not because of Unitarian suspicions about his faith; he and his wife were unhappy with the architectural plans for the Hall, which would require them to live at closer quarters to the students than they liked. Bagehot guessed that the chief objection came from Maria Newman. He told his father that Newman 'invented a mass of architectural reasons about a staircase and a roof', but the real reason 'seems to be that Mrs Newman jibbed. She did not like housekeeping on a large scale I suppose and the commissariat is not exactly her line.'[22] Newman's resignation came in November 1848, several months before the Hall was due to open. His reply to Crabb Robinson, who had been asked to persuade him to change his mind, was that his objections to certain aspects of the original plans had been 'passed over as if they had not been made', and that it was now too late to make changes unless they were to 'pull down & rebuild the whole south wing'.[23] Like Bagehot, Crabb Robinson thought the real reason was Mrs Newman's membership of the Plymouth Brethren, which would have made her a 'very unfit mistress of an establishment for boarding young men'. But he regretted the loss of Newman, who had overcome the objections to his 'extreme liberal' opinions through 'the éclat of his name'.[24] On the other hand, Newman was an increasingly controversial figure who unerringly sowed discord wherever he went. He was soon to publish books relating his changing religious beliefs and his recent progress towards an individualist Nonconformism which pleased no one.[25]

The council, needing to find a principal before the Hall opened in October 1849, turned to a younger man, another whom Crabb Robinson had encountered in discussions at University College appointing commit-tees. In November 1848, just days before Newman's unexpected resignation letter arrived, twenty-nine-year-old Arthur Hugh Clough had been placed second in the contest for the chair of English language and literature, losing to the eloquent Scottish independent minister and erstwhile disciple of Edward Irving, Alexander John Scott. (Clough would get the job next time round, in 1850, when Scott resigned from University College to become principal of the new Owens College, which opened in Manchester the following October.) The members of University Hall turned to Clough.

So it was that when University Hall opened in the autumn of 1849, its first principal was Clough, protégé of the late Dr Arnold at Rugby School and his tutors' favourite student at Oxford. Crabb Robinson was charmed by him and not at all unhappy that Clough was not a Unitarian, though he noted that others on the University Hall council were doubtful.[26] A problem arose almost immediately, however, when negotiations over his appointment began in January 1849 and Clough declined to read daily prayers as part of his duties. He apparently told his friend Matthew Arnold, who told his mother, who in turn told Crabb Robinson, that 'quitting Oxford because he will not conform, it would be absurd to become a U[nitarian] conformist'.[27]

Clough was, in fact, a semi-reluctant self-exile from Oxford, tortured by doubts about the Thirty-Nine Articles, especially Article 18, which states that only those who believe in Christ will be saved. He felt unable in conscience to continue as a fellow of Oriel College, despite the elaborate attempts of the Provost of Oriel to persuade him to stay.[28] His poem, *The Bothie of Toper-na-Fuosich: A Long-Vacation Pastoral*, was published to some acclaim in November 1848, as he prepared to leave Oxford and waited to hear if University Hall wanted him. He wrote to one of the Hall's founders, Philip Le Breton, saying he did not feel 'competent to undertake the conduct or superintendence of any prayers', though he would 'feel every disposition to facilitate devotional arrangements'. Finally, he avowed with that frankness which was so attractive to Crabb Robinson, if not to some of his colleagues: 'I do not account myself to have made up my own mind, and should be shy of meddling with those of other people.'[29]

This letter was read out at the council meeting of 11 January 1849, when Crabb Robinson was absent in the Lake District visiting the Wordsworth and Arnold families as he did every New Year. Without him, the council came to the initial decision that it could not appoint Clough, given the 'difficulties' he had expressed with regard to the duties of the principal, but it was agreed to postpone the final decision for a week. In the meantime Crabb Robinson returned to speak up for Clough, who was beloved of his close friends the Arnolds. Other opinions were sought, including that of the most influential Unitarian in the country, the Liverpool minister James Martineau, who knew Clough well.[30] This was favourable enough to persuade the council to appoint him.

As well as having the support of Martineau and Crabb Robinson, Clough was fortunate to have fallen in with his contemporary, Bagehot, who also became an ally. Bagehot boasted from his own quarters in nearby Great Coram Street to his fellow University College graduate, Richard Holt Hutton, that he and Roscoe had been instrumental in getting Clough appointed. As former students of University College, they were being consulted by the council on the best way for University Hall to provide for the needs of its charges; they attended council meetings, and Bagehot acted as a go-between when relations between Clough and the founders appeared on the brink of breaking down. He told Hutton that he and Roscoe had had 'endless fun' talking over the committee until they voted for Clough 'nem. con.' 'After this we think that the council must succumb in future to what the junior members think fit to exact,' he added.[31]

Clough was reluctant to be wooed, or at least he did not like being pumped about his religious views or his willingness to take daily prayers. He wrote boldly but not unreasonably to one of the founders, Edwin Field, that the fact that the Book of Common Prayer was 'not a part of my religion' did not prove he had 'no religion, & no sympathy for people's religious wants':

> Among those wants, indeed, at the present day, I should be inclined to place that of having one's devotions left to themselves. I feel myself therefore to be not only recognizing but consulting the religious interests of the young men when I say that personally I do not wish for Common Prayer in your Institution. I w[oul]d rather it did not exist. If you choose to make the experiment, well & good; – but my own attendance *could* merely be a matter of conformity & I must have it quite open to myself to act as I find it best, with regard to the amount of that attendance.

The letter concludes defiantly, and somewhat disingenuously:

> Nothing but a very decided interest & sympathy in your plan w[oul]d have induced me to forego [*sic*] the enjoyment of two years of retirement which I had promised myself & which I still covet. On other points the Council must judge. I will only add that if they do not think my views suitable to their object, I shall be very glad to assist in seeking for a person better fitted, & I dare say that such may be found at Oxford.[32]

We might ask how a young man in his position – his father, a failed cotton manufacturer, had died in 1844, and Clough had duties towards his mother and sister – could possibly afford the luxury of 'two years of retirement'. It may also be imagined that the last carelessly thrown out suggestion, that a better-fitted person might be found in Oxford, would hardly go down well with Field and the others after the difficulties they had experienced first with Newman and now with Clough himself.

Nonetheless, Clough was appointed to the 'new quasi-collegiate institution', as he described it to an Oxford colleague.[33] 'Alea jacta est', he wrote on 15 February 1849. Showing his awareness of Theodore Hook's old nickname for University College, he added, 'I have accepted the Stincomalean position.'[34] By the end of October he was resident in Gordon Square, writing to his friend Tom Arnold, brother of Matthew and himself in self-imposed exile from Oxford – in his case in New Zealand – to complain about the narrow-mindedness of the Unitarians amongst whom he was now moving. One of them, he reported, had been taken on to read the daily prayers at the Hall which Clough himself had declined to do.[35]

Donaldson had been instructed to build rooms for thirty and to include in his plans a sketch of two wings at the back which might be built in future to accommodate another twenty.[36] Only eleven students enrolled for the first year. They were aged between sixteen and nineteen, and most had already begun their courses at University College. Five were the sons of subscribers; there was the son of a coal merchant from Swansea, the son of an independent minister in Bath, the son of George Courtauld of the famous silk manufacturing firm, and the son of Dr James Manby Gully, founder of the famous water cure establishment in Great Malvern. No doubt in order to help fill the empty rooms, Edwin Field, honorary secretary of the Hall, sent his son Rogers there, though he lived in nearby Hampstead.[37] The committee had tried to entice the sons of dissenting acquaintances from outside London, but so far without much success.

Clough paid little attention to his eleven students, clinging to his old Oxford friendships and taking full advantage of the permission granted by the Hall's founders to have some of his old university friends, including Francis Palgrave and Matthew Arnold, to breakfast from time to time, as he told Tom Arnold in October 1849, just after his tenure had begun. He also foresaw that his stay might not be long, 'believing that in the end I shall be kicked out for mine heresies' sake'. 'For intolerance, O Tom, is not confined to the cloisters of Oxford or the pews of the establishment, but comes up like the tender herb – partout.'[38]

Crabb Robinson tried to make Clough feel at home by inviting him to the literary breakfasts he held in his bachelor quarters in Russell Square. Bagehot was often invited too, and remembered these occasions irreverently when reviewing a selection of Crabb Robinson's diaries, published in 1869, two years after his death. 'Old Crabb', as he called him, 'was for many years both on [University College] senate and council; and as he lived near the college he was fond of collecting at breakfast all the elder students – especially those who had any sort of interest in literature.' On these occasions Bagehot and the other young men found Crabb Robinson rather too talkative – he would repeat his anecdotes, bringing in too much Schiller and Goethe, and forget to provide food – but he gave the old man his due by summing up the unusual breadth of his experience and acquaintances:

Mr Robinson had known nearly every literary man worth knowing in England and Germany for fifty years and more. He had studied at Jena in the 'great time', when Goethe, and Schiller, and Wieland were all at their zenith; he had lived with Charles Lamb and his set, and [the poet Samuel] Rogers and his set, besides an infinite lot of little London people; he had taught Madame De Staël German philosophy in Germany, and helped her in business afterwards in England; he was the real friend of Wordsworth, and had known Coleridge and Southey almost from their 'coming out' to their death. And he was not a mere literary man. He had been a *Times* correspondent in the days of Napoleon's early German battles . . . Such a varied life and experience belong to very few men, and his social nature – at once accessible and assailant – was just the one to take advantage of it.[39]

Clough's appointment to the chair of English at University College in December 1850, after Alexander Scott had been offered the job at Owens College, seemed to promise better things for him, not least because Clough's modest University Hall salary of £150 per annum would now be supplemented by a proportion of student fees. But that, too, was hardly a success. Very few students presented themselves for English – still a new subject for university teaching – and Clough, a reluctant lecturer, made little impression.[40] Crabb Robinson attended his final lecture on the history of English literature, pronouncing it admirable as far as substance went, but 'so ill delivered' that it gave him little pleasure.[41]

University Hall did not flourish under Clough. In March 1850, some six months after the Hall's opening, Crabb Robinson told him frankly that the general feeling in the Hall, which he himself shared, was that Clough was not taking an active enough part in its affairs.[42] By October 1850, when the second session at the Hall was getting under way, still with too few students and an unhealthy bank balance, Crabb Robinson confided to his diary: 'Our Principal is very amiable but he wants energy . . . A man I very much like but wish away.'[43] Though it was not Clough's fault that the Hall did not attract enough students to fill its rooms and balance the books, the inevitable break came when he was asked in October 1851 to give advice about how to attract greater numbers and replied in a terse letter to council that he was 'unable to offer any suggestion'.[44] The following month he informed council that he was a candidate for a classics chair at the new university in Sydney, and was told in return that he must resign at Christmas so that they could find a replacement for the New Year. He did not get the Australian post, but he did resign from University Hall, where he had felt uncomfortable and had hardly fulfilled his duties with zeal.

Clough's time as a reluctant recruit to the London educational scene was not quite as bleak as was sometimes made out, not least by himself. His time in London was not a happy one, but neither could he be said to have experienced much contentment before (or after) it. Lines from his poem *Mari Magno* are sometimes quoted to characterise the London period from the end of 1848, when he resigned his Oxford fellowship, to autumn 1852, when he set off for America to try his luck there. The lines are:

> He has a life small happiness that gives,
> Who friendless in a London lodging lives,
> Dines in a dingy chop-house, and returns
> To a lone room, while all within him yearns
> For sympathy, and his whole nature burns
> With a fierce thirst for some one – is there none? –
> To expend his human tenderness upon.

While most of Clough's poetry reflects the events and emotions of his own life, this scene does not really represent his London sojourn. He endured no 'London lodging', 'dingy chop-house', or friendlessness. Though he did not get on with his masters at University Hall, he enjoyed eight rooms on two floors of the building, where he was able to have friends to stay.[45] After his resignation at Christmas 1851, he was offered continued accommodation in Hall until the end of the session; he chose to move out in February 1852 to lodgings in nearby Caroline Street, just off Bedford Square, until leaving Britain in October. These lodgings may have been modest, but here, too, he was not abandoned by his London friends.

One of the first to blame the London experience for Clough's unhappiness was an Oxford contemporary, James Anthony Froude, who resigned his own fellowship a few months after Clough resigned his, also because of religious scruples. Froude later described Clough's shift to London in melodramatic terms. In his widely read biography of Thomas Carlyle, published in the early 1880s, Froude brought to its highest pitch the sanctification of Clough which was being carried on by well-meaning friends, saddened by Clough's early death in 1861 at the age of forty-two and frustrated by what seemed to them his unfulfilled poetic ambitions, not to mention his lack of success in finding a career in either England or America. When Carlyle met Clough in the spring of 1849, Froude wrote, the older man formed the highest opinion of his new acquaintance:

> His pure beautiful character, his genial humour, his perfect truthfulness, alike of heart and intellect – an integrity which had led him to sacrifice a distinguished position and brilliant prospects, and had brought him to

London to gather a living as he could from under the hoofs of the horses in the streets – these together had recommended Clough to Carlyle as a diamond sifted out of the general rubbish-heap.[46]

Though it is true that Clough bravely gave up his Oriel fellowship without having a definite job to go to, he was hardly to be compared, as Froude almost suggests he should be, with Jo the crossing-sweeper in *Bleak House* or with any of Dickens's other vagabonds. He had friends in London with whom he could lodge and who were in a position to help him find something, among them his Oxford friends Matthew Arnold, Frederick Temple, and Francis Palgrave, all at this time landing on their feet in (admittedly establishment) educational circles in London.[47] He had good relations, too, with older men including Carlyle, Crabb Robinson, Richard Monckton Milnes, and the Italian nationalist Giuseppe Mazzini. There were also at least two acquaintances, young men from dissenting back-grounds who had studied at University College and were associated with University Hall, who were his intellectual equals, namely Hutton and Bagehot. Hutton later recalled that Bagehot was fascinated by Clough and was keen to do all he could during Clough's time at University Hall 'to mediate between that enigma to Presbyterian parents – a college-head who held himself serenely neutral on almost all moral and educational subjects interesting to parents and pupils . . . – and the managing body who bewildered him and were by him bewildered.'[48]

The truth of Clough's time in London is more nuanced than is often supposed, though it must be accounted a failure in terms of his professional career. For this Clough himself was partly to blame, as a damaging indecisiveness combined with a streak of aggression to make him ill at ease in his surroundings. The rest of the blame can be placed on the inevitable clash of attitude and opinion between a man still pining for some aspects of his previous life in orthodox Anglican Oxford and a somewhat unbending and righteous group of dissenters with a serious educational mission in London. From the beginning Clough had struck a cynical note in his letters when describing his dealings with the founders of University Hall, though he saw that he was partly responsible for the misunderstandings and awkwardnesses that occurred. He talked revealingly in letters to Tom Arnold about his 'situation here under a set of mercantile Unitarians' being 'in no way charming', and of 'being set down amongst uncongenial people', the passive mood suggesting that he had no agency in the matter of his own career.[49]

Yet he did get on well with the few students he had at University Hall; in March 1852, soon after he left, 'the good young people at University

Hall' gave him a present of a silver teapot, milk jug, and sugar bowl with an inscription. 'Mightily ill-deserved is all that I have to say in return,' he confessed, 'and I really am half-sorry and three-quarters ashamed.'[50] He was obviously a better tutor than he was a lecturer. Those who took a class on Aristotle that he gave to a small group from University College remembered him fondly. The historian Thomas Hodgkin described these classes as 'with the possible exception of De Morgan's lectures' the 'most stimulating and fruitbearing' of his whole University College career; Clough 'often used the Socratic method, and invited us to discuss in dialogue with him the debateable points raised by Aristotle'.[51] Hodgkin's friend Edward Fry, who lodged at the time in the same house as Bagehot, 6 Great Coram Street, also attended the Aristotle class, recalling:

> Four of us (Hodgkin being one) formed a small class and read the greater part of the *Nichomachæan Ethics* with him, and perhaps no class was ever more enjoyed by me or added more to my store of thought and to the cultivation of the habits of my mind. I used from time to time to breakfast with Clough and meet there some of his Oxford friends . . . and it is needless to say that Clough, with all his strange reticences and hesitations (if I may so speak), was very interesting to me.[52]

The unfortunate fact was that, though Clough was liked, admired, and wondered at by so many contemporaries, he was unable to achieve professional success. He certainly left no very positive recollections of his three years in London half-heartedly attempting to help with the education of dissenting youth. His place as principal of University Hall was taken by Richard Holt Hutton in February 1852.

Hutton was the perfect choice. He was a brilliant prize-winning alumnus of University College School and University College, where he had founded the College Debating Society with Bagehot in 1843. On graduating in 1845, he had intended to read for the Bar, but first went to study theology at Bonn and Heidelberg, returning in 1847 to prepare for the Unitarian ministry at Manchester New College.[53] Unsure about his vocation for the ministry but still a practising Unitarian, he accepted the invitation in November 1849, at the age of twenty-three, to take prayers in University Hall, since Clough declined to do so; he also tutored the resident students in mathematics and was given the title of vice-principal. Having taken over the principalship from Clough, he was forced to resign in June 1852, after barely five months in the post; he was suffering from serious inflammation of the lungs, and sailed for the West Indies in October.[54] Crabb Robinson's diary summed up his feelings at this time about the 'ill-fated institution': 'Newman an avowed unbeliever, Clough of doubtful faith, bro[ugh]t with great personal attractions, only harm to the Hall, and now Hutton retires from ill health.'[55]

Hutton agreed with Bagehot that when they were undergraduates, before the opening of University Hall, the lack of residential accommodation for University College students was a disadvantage, but he remembered in a memoir of Bagehot written in 1877 that, despite the lack of a collegiate society at University College, it matched and even outdid Oxbridge in other respects. Recalling their student days from 1841 to 1845, he wrote:

> I am not at all sure that University College, London, was not at that time a much more awakening place of education for young men than almost any Oxford college ... Indeed, in those years London was a place with plenty of intellectual stimulus in it for young men, while in University College itself there was quite enough vivacious and original teaching to make that stimulus available to the full ... [O]f this, at least, I am sure, that Gower Street, and Oxford Street, and the New Road, and the [squares of Bloomsbury], were the scenes of discussions as eager and as abstract as ever were the sedate cloisters or flowery river-meadows of Cambridge and Oxford.[56]

This picture of London university life echoes the half-mocking prediction the young Disraeli had made in 1826 in *Vivian Grey* that 'in the course of a century' things in the London university might be 'as fair, and flourishing', as in 'the most leafy bowers of New College gardens'.[57]

At University Hall itself, Hutton, as vice-principal, had supported Clough in his small attempts to liberalise the somewhat strict regulations imposed on the student residents by the Hall's over-anxious council. In January 1850 they wrote a joint letter to the newly convened theological committee suggesting that the complete course of lectures in theology which the committee proposed to start would be too much for the University College students, who already had so many lectures in Gower Street, in subjects from classics to maths to modern languages, that they could 'scarcely fit them all in', let alone find time (even if they had the inclination) for these extra theology lectures in University Hall.[58] Their letter was not heeded, and Clough wrote again in February to repeat that what these young men, many of them only sixteen or seventeen, most needed was teaching in small groups rather than more lectures. He showed some irritation, reminding council that no new lectures should be given 'without previous reference to your Principal', a sharp remark which no doubt did nothing to improve his sticky relations with those founders who had been against his appointment from the start.[59] Hutton supported Clough, writing in March 1851 that the students needed personal tuition to supplement the lectures they received at University College.[60]

The teaching of theology, the pet wish of some of the founders, hardly got off the ground in any case, as University Hall was in crisis. Only twelve students were in residence during its third session, 1851–2, and there were fears that it might have to close at the end of the summer. When Hutton had to go abroad for his health in June 1852, his father, Dr Joseph Hutton, was asked to come over from Dublin to take charge of the Hall for the remainder of the session.[61] The council then made one more attempt to set the institution going with the appointment in August 1852 of William Benjamin Carpenter, another son of a Unitarian minister. Carpenter had studied medicine at University College London before taking his degree at Edinburgh – the qualification which saw him appointed to the British Museum's Swiney lectureship – and had been since 1849 professor of medical jurisprudence at University College.[62] He was the first married man to take the job of principal, and he could be counted a success, as he continued in Gordon Square until 1859, and helped the Hall to survive.

The appointment of Carpenter, together with the reluctant arrival of some teachers and pupils from Manchester New College in 1853, saved the Hall from closure, but it continued to suffer from lack of money and from disagreements about its purpose. Not enough lay students presented themselves; probably Crabb Robinson was right when he speculated that one of the reasons for this was the perception that the Hall was narrowly Unitarian, a perception that was intensified by the arrival of the Manchester group, led by their principal John James Tayler, who was followed in 1857 by their most respected preacher, James Martineau.

Carpenter did his best. He oversaw the protracted arrangements for accommodating Manchester New College, and was also in charge of raising the funds in 1855 to buy the lease from the Bedford Estate before the ten-year term was up. It was Carpenter, too, who negotiated with the solicitors of the trustees of the Catholic Apostolic Church as it rose next door during 1852–3. In November 1852 the council noted that 'a window was being placed in the building now in the course of erection adjoining the Hall premises, so as to overlook the ground belonging to the Hall', and a long correspondence ensued about the party wall linking the church's cloisters, which were being built for the accommodation of its clerical personnel, and the Hall, which was concerned that its privacy at the back should be respected. That issue was finally settled in February 1860, a year after Carpenter resigned.[63]

What the inhabitants of the neighbouring establishments thought of one another is not recorded, except for a little 'Irvingite' joke made by Crabb Robinson at the dinner held in the Hall's 'spacious dining hall' after the annual meeting on 7 July 1853, as the erection of the church for their new ecclesiastical neighbours entered its last few months. Crabb Robinson was speaking in favour of bringing Dr Williams's Library with its historical collection of dissenting literature to Gordon Square, perhaps to adjoin University Hall on the vacant plot immediately to the north. It might, he speculated, be erected 'in white stone, to match the edifice on the other side belonging to those who boast of making use of an unknown tongue', a remark which brought him a laugh from the assembled diners.[64]

The fact that Carpenter had a wife and young children in the principal's quarters helped to make the Hall more homely than in Clough's time. The principal installed an organ, which he played at the musical soirées he and his wife initiated.[65] As a forward-thinking biologist and enthusiastic populariser of the microscope who made a contribution to science through his lectures at University College and his much-reprinted work, *The Microscope and its Revelations*, first published in 1856, he offered in October 1854 to give a lecture at University Hall on the topic.[66] As Swiney Lecturer from 1847 to 1851, he also helped to bring University College into closer connection with the British Museum.

Under Carpenter, the number of resident students at University Hall rose to eighteen in 1853, but this was no thanks to Manchester New College. Its principal, Tayler, lived nearby at 22 Woburn Square, and when Martineau left Liverpool for London in 1857 he took a house in Gordon Street, to the north of Gordon Square. At first not one of the Manchester students lived in the Hall. In November 1854 Carpenter told the council that only two Manchester New College students were now in residence and that there was 'little intercourse' between them and the Hall students. It appears that Manchester New College was reluctant to bring its divinity students into close contact with the lay students of University College.[67]

Carpenter sometimes struggled. He was an unbending disciplinarian, complaining to council of minor breaches of discipline by some students and demanding that fines be levied on those who failed to attend the morning roll call.[68] In May 1856 he took on the registrarship of the University of London in addition to his University Hall post. The Hall's finances were still precarious. A loan of £300 was raised and an appeal launched.[69] There were ongoing wrangles with Manchester New College, which was reluctant to pay more than £100 a year towards the upkeep of the Hall in return for its staff and students having access to the public rooms, where they held their own lectures and could enjoy the Hall's facilities. Showing some impatience, University Hall's council told the Manchester representatives in November 1856 that £100 was not enough, given the advantages they gained from the Hall's position in London, and specifically in Bloomsbury, near to University College: 'You not only are placed in the very locality for your purpose, but are exempt from all further charge for Taxes (and our local taxation is extremely heavy), repairs, fuel, cleaning & attendance.' If the Hall had been able to fill its vacant rooms with Manchester New College students, the question of raising the annual contribution would not have arisen. Moreover, 'we have every reason to believe, in several instances students have been deterred from joining the Hall, in consequence of the intimate connection between it and Manchester New College: an impression having thus gone abroad that the institution was of a sectarian character'.[70]

The Hall was caught in a bind: it had failed to attract enough students to fill the rooms initially, a failure attributed by some – Crabb Robinson among them – to its being perceived as a narrowly Unitarian establishment; in order to fill the rooms and restore financial health, it had welcomed Manchester New College to London, only to find that owing to a lack of co-operation from the newcomers there were still empty rooms and money troubles, while their arrival had actually increased the reputation for sectarianism which had put off non-Unitarians in the first place.

Of the small number of applicants who came forward when the post of principal was advertised after Carpenter's resignation in 1859, the one chosen was, surprisingly, Edward Spencer Beesly, a twenty-eight-year-old assistant master at Marlborough College, a school in Wiltshire founded in 1843 for the sons of Church of England clergymen. Beesly was another graduate of Oxford. Like Newman and Clough, he had moved away from Anglican orthodoxy while there, but in his case it was to follow the new creed of positivism, the 'religion of humanity' promulgated by Auguste Comte and embraced in at least some of its aspects (mainly its historical view of Christianity and conviction that the modern or 'positivist' age was one of a scientific, post-Christian society) by, among others, John Stuart Mill, George Henry Lewes, George Eliot, and Harriet Martineau. Beesly had come under the influence of his tutor at Oxford, Richard Congreve, who was to open the first British Church of Humanity in Bloomsbury in 1870.

The appointing committee did not know about his as yet nascent positivism – he joined the Positivist Society in 1869 – and in their report of the interview to which they had summoned him described his views accurately enough as those of a practising Anglican, but one who 'appears to have, for some time, desired a position of greater intellectual and religious freedom than are [sic] consistent with holding office in an Ecclesiastical Foundation, and to have therefore entertained the idea of connecting himself with University College'. His testimonials stressed his academic achievements and his 'peculiar power of directing and influencing youth'.[71] The committee appointed him unanimously, and in 1860 he also got the chair of history at University College.

With the appointment of Beesly, the Hall had once again chosen an unusual, talented, and in this case politically reforming man to manage its students. Beesly soon became well known both as a positivist and as a supporter of workers' rights and the efforts of trades unions to uphold and improve those rights. In 1870 he joined Congreve's positivist group at the newly opened centre in Chapel Street (now Rugby Street), just to the east of Great Ormond Street, where the quasi-religious ceremonies of the 'religion of humanity' were held. His unorthodox religious and political beliefs brought him into conflict with the council of University Hall, which must have wondered how it had happened that once again a man with different, and to them offensive, views had joined them.

At first, however, Beesly was a popular choice. He was active in keeping up the numbers of resident students; indeed in June 1862 he was able to report to council that, with twenty-seven resident students, the Hall was full for the first time since its opening.[72] A popular professor at University College, Beesly was also keen to improve facilities for the students of the Hall. He worked hard to get a racquets court built for them in the face of difficulties with the agents for the Duke of Bedford, who quoted the strict terms of the lease about buildings and their use. Crabb Robinson had given £1,000 anonymously in 1860 for this purpose, and Beesly persevered with his requests to the Bedford Estate, which refused out of the usual anxiety about noise and nuisance to the neighbours, inhabitants of the houses Cubitt had finally managed to build on the west side of Gordon Square, north of the Hall. Negotiations continued until 1864, when Beesly and his committee gave up trying to get permission from the Bedford Estate and turned to University College, offering them the £1,000 if a racquets court could be built on College land for the joint use of College and Hall students. The final arrangement in July 1864 was for a racquets and adjoining fives court to be built 'on the south part of the Gymnastic

Ground, & on a small part of the play Ground of the Junior School', the building to remain the property of University College but to be under the management of Beesly as principal of University Hall.[73]

At much the same time Beesly was joining forces with the residents of the Gordon Square houses adjoining the Hall to the north to force the removal of a cow yard situated in the mews at the back of the Hall's grounds; in October 1862 they began proceedings after an act had been passed to require cow keepers to apply for licences. Together the occupants of the square's buildings opposed the granting of licences to the three cow keepers on the grounds of noise and smell. The residents were successful, though Beesly had to report two of the cow keepers to the authorities for not leaving by the appointed deadline of June 1864; the two were fined £5 each and left in December.[74] The cow yard was soon replaced by a timber yard, and in 1877 by a mattress warehouse for 'Messrs Shoolbred', the large furniture company which had its shop on Tottenham Court Road.[75] Beesly was also kept busy by his millenarian neighbours to the south; in May 1868 he noted the 'annoyance caused by persons in the building' who were 'in the habit of throwing refuse of various kinds into the Hall grounds' despite numerous complaints.[76]

Not only were there more student residents at the Hall under Beesly, but they now represented an interesting variety of backgrounds. In addition to Nonconformists and friends and relatives of founders, there were a number of foreign students and some who were taking the Indian Civil Service examinations.[77] Beesly's efforts to make the Hall attractive to students were helped by the generosity of Crabb Robinson, who died at his home in Russell Square in February 1867, aged ninety-one, leaving a fund consisting of £3,200 in stocks and shares to the Hall he had done so much to bring into existence, with the instruction that it should be used to promote the comfort of the students. Council acknowledged the 'respectful and affectionate remembrance' in which he was held on account of his 'unswerving attachment to truth and freedom' and his 'generous interest in liberal and unsectarian education' during 'an unusually long life'.[78]

Crabb Robinson was one of the most active figures in the history of Bloomsbury's reforming institutions. This aspect of his long career has been partially obscured by his fame as a diarist, diner out, and friend of genius. In truth, he was a great benefactor of University College, University Hall, and also the Ladies' College established in Bedford Square by his friend Elisabeth Jesser Reid in 1849, the same year as the Hall.[79] In the very years in which he was so assiduous in his attempts to help University Hall establish itself, from 1847 to the early 1850s, he was also the heroic prime mover in the plan to bring the sculptor John Flaxman's famous casts to University College.

Flaxman, whose classical sculptures gained him fame throughout Europe, had been among the founders of the Swedenborg Society in London in 1810. Despite his international reputation, he left his sister-in-law and adopted daughter Maria Denman only debts on his death in 1826. His studio and effects were seized by creditors and many of his models and casts were sold off, until a group of admirers, including Crabb Robinson, stepped in to conserve his remaining works. They raised money to build a gallery to exhibit the casts and sculptures. Crabb Robinson was assiduous in getting subscriptions and in persuading Maria Denman, who was inclined to raise objections to every plan, to allow University College to house the exhibits in a specially commissioned gallery.

The Flaxman Gallery, located under the dome of University College, was designed by Thomas Donaldson at the same time as he was planning University Hall. From November 1847, when the agreement regarding the gallery was brokered, until 1851, when the Flaxman Gallery was finally opened, Crabb Robinson kept the process alive, negotiating tirelessly with the demanding Miss Denman and with the College, which was keen to house the casts of the great sculptor but struggling as usual with financial difficulties.[80] Crabb Robinson was rewarded for his efforts by seeing the Gallery open in April 1851 to universal praise.[81] He is named in the Latin inscription in the Gallery as its chief enabler. The part he played in the founding of University Hall was also memorialised. A marble bust of him by G.E. Ewing was acquired for the Hall in 1874, and an elaborate fresco was painted on the walls of the dining hall by Edward Armitage after Crabb Robinson's death, featuring him sitting, pen in hand, surrounded by life-size figures of thirty-four of his most distinguished friends, English and German, including Flaxman, Blake, Wordsworth, Coleridge, Southey, the saturnine Edward Irving, and the blessed Goethe and Schiller.[82]

Living the comfortable life of a retired lawyer on a private income in Russell Square, Crabb Robinson was in his seventies in the late 1840s, when these new ventures were started. He was, however, extremely active, moving around Bloomsbury from meetings at University College to discuss professorial appointments and to bring the Flaxman casts and sculptures to the College, to encouraging Mrs Reid in the early days of her Ladies' College in Bedford Square, to discussions about the planning and management of University Hall. A typical day's business would thus take him on a tour of educational Bloomsbury, from his home in Russell Square to Bedford Square to see Mrs Reid, to Gower Street to talk to Donaldson or appoint a new professor, to Gordon Square to observe progress on the building of University Hall, and back home to Russell Square.

In spite of his elderly bachelor ways, Crabb Robinson was one of the more liberal and open-minded managers of University Hall. He was, however, made nervous by Beesly's socialism. His diary of 15 October 1861 reads:

> Accompanied Beesly to the University Hall. The dinner (at the opening of the session) was numerously attended. The Principal (Beesly) addressed the young men simply and pleasingly. His really best character is that of a teacher; every one seems to like him. But he is extreme in his opinions, and I fear this may interfere with his usefulness. He is going to attend a meeting of bricklayers, and says they conduct business better than scholars.[83]

On 2 July 1867 Beesly spoke at a public meeting at Exeter Hall in defence of protesting Sheffield steel workers, some of whom had resorted to violence. He attracted negative press coverage, with *Punch* calling him 'Professor Beastly' on 13 July. Both University College and University Hall were embarrassed by his activities. At University College Sir Francis Goldsmid, son of Isaac Lyon Goldsmid, moved that Beesly be removed from his chair, on the grounds that his speeches showed him 'unfit to be entrusted with the instruction of young men in History', but the motion was defeated by twelve votes to three after the intervention of George Grote.[84]

Meanwhile at University Hall motions to unseat Beesly were discussed at several meetings between July and December 1867, when it was finally accepted on a close vote that Beesly was 'equally entitled with all others to enjoy that principle' enshrined in the first clause of the constitution of the Hall, namely 'the great principle of unlimited religious liberty, and the right of private judgment' on all matters of opinion.[85] Three members of council resigned as a result of the decision not to act against Beesly, but he was safe. He continued with his political activities, coming across Karl Marx at trade union meetings, and corresponding with him in 1867–8.[86] He wrote a favourable account of Marx's activities in the *Fortnightly Review* in November 1870, praising the work of the International Working Men's Association and declaring that Marx, 'in his acquaintance with the history and statistics of the industrial movement in all parts of Europe is, I should imagine, without a rival'.[87] Marx described Beesly as 'ein sehr tüchtiger und kühner Mann' (a very capable and bold man) despite being obliged by his

Comtist beliefs to hold 'allerlei Crotchets' (all sorts of crotchets).[88] They were friendly enough for Beesly to invite Marx to dinner at University Hall on a number of occasions.[89] Marx accepted one such invitation on 23 April 1869, when, as he told his daughter Eleanor, Beesly's brother-in-law and fellow positivist Henry Crompton was also a guest. Marx's daughter Jenny visited Beesly's wife Emily in October 1871.[90]

In 1880 the Hall was faced with expensive drainage work to improve sanitation; by October of that year the number of resident students had dropped to only seven. (It is not clear exactly why numbers had decreased, though the momentous abolition of religious tests at Oxford and Cambridge in 1871, allowing dissenters to graduate at the two ancient universities for the first time, undoubtedly played a part.) The Hall was facing financial collapse once more and Beesly offered to resign at the end of the session. He was asked to stay for one more year while the council tried to get Manchester New College students to fill some of the empty rooms. During Beesly's final year, 1881–2, the Hall's founding society dissolved itself, transferring the Hall to Manchester New College, which now took over the building completely, on the understanding that it should be permitted to sell the property if it wished to leave Gordon Square. The trustees would be free 'to accept any offer by or on behalf of University College London or other educational Institution which the Trustees may consider reasonable although such offer may not be of the amount which might be realised by public sale'.[91]

This was not quite the end of University Hall as a residence for students of University College, however. The trustees encouraged them to apply for rooms and paradoxically brought relations with University College closer than they had ever been by persuading Henry Morley, the energetic and popular professor of English at the College, to take over as principal. He was to be the last in the interesting and distinguished line of principals the Hall managed to appoint in its forty years of existence, and the most reforming educator among them.

Meanwhile Beesly moved out of Gordon Square to a house in Finsbury Park in 1882, having done good service for University Hall for over twenty years, despite his socialist and Comtist views. He continued as professor of history until 1893 and taught Latin at the Ladies' College in Bedford Square, as well as being active among the British disciples of Comte. In 1869 he had married Emily Crompton, daughter of a judge and sister of Henry Crompton. Together with Crompton, an alumnus of University College School, and Frederic Harrison, Bloomsbury-born and a friend of Beesly's at Oxford, Beesly helped Britain's leading Comtist Richard

Congreve open the country's first positivist centre in 1870. They leased a small hall in Chapel Street, close to the Working Men's and Working Women's Colleges in Great Ormond Street and Queen Square, respectively, where both Harrison and Beesly gave classes.[92] Congreve moved with his family to 17 Mecklenburgh Square to be near the Chapel Street hall. All three of his followers were socialists as well as positivists, using their expertise – legal in the case of Harrison and Crompton, historical in the case of Beesly – to support trade unionism and becoming involved with international socialism.

Beesly wrote to Marx in June 1871, at the time of the Paris Commune, to underline his political agreement and defend his positivism:

> I know very well that you are radically opposed to us Positivists nor do I suppose it to be at all likely that you will ever alter your views. The one point we & you have in common is our indignation against the individualist theories of the propertied classes & their anti-social conduct.

He goes on to say that 'all the English Positivists' are 'ardent supporters' of the Paris Commune.[93]

At Chapel Street the positivists taught English to refugees from the Commune, translated Comte's *System of Positive Polity* in four volumes (1875–7), and began to build up an English version of Comte's 'religion of humanity', which turned the original 'scientific' positivist theory of the current age as a post-religious one into a new religion with rituals of its own such as baptism, prayers to humanity, and a new calendar based on the lives of secular 'saints' including Homer, Aristotle, Dante, Gutenberg, Shakespeare, and Descartes.[94] The building, known as the Positivist School, was used for free evening classes for children and adults, who were given instruction in reading and writing, drawing and singing. Not many attended, and these classes were discontinued in 1877.[95] The following year Beesly and Harrison broke from Congreve's ever more ritualistic 'religion'; they set up their own centre, Newton Hall, just off Fleet Street, while Crompton stayed faithful to Congreve, succeeding him at the Church of Humanity on Chapel Street, as the Postivist School was now called, after Congreve's death in 1899. Adherents of the religion of humanity had decreased by then, and despite a reunion in 1916 between both branches, the church on Chapel Street finally closed in 1932, two years before its lease expired.[96]

The building still stands, its address now 20 Rugby Street. Its history illustrates a distinguishing feature of nineteenth-century British education and religion, namely the often uneasy and experimental coming together of scientific and intellectual progress with unorthodox religious theories and practices. Such combinations are seen in Bloomsbury in Elliotson's use of mesmerism in medical practice; the phenomenon of homoeopathy with its claim to scientific rigour but reputation as a pseudo-science; De Morgan's rejection of orthodox religion but openness to spiritualism in his later career (in 1863 he contributed a supportive preface to his wife Sophia's book embracing spiritualism);[97] the lawyerly mind of Cardale combined with his enthusiastic embracing of millenarianism; and Beesly's progressive socialism alongside his adherence to some of the spiritual aspects of Comte's postivism. Beesly's successor at University Hall, Henry Morley, was a more straightforward example of the progressive educator who did not bring religion, either orthodox or unorthodox, into his vocation as a teacher.

Though he did not come to live in Bloomsbury until he took over the management of University Hall in 1882, Morley already had many connections with the area. He collaborated on Dickens's weekly newspaper *Household Words* from 1851 to 1859, when Dickens was living in Tavistock House; in 1855 he proselytised for the first kindergarten in England run by the German exiles and followers of Friedrich Froebel, Johannes and Bertha Ronge in Tavistock Place;[98] and he held the chair of English language and literature at University College London from 1865 until 1889, when he retired from both the College and the Hall.

Born in Hatton Garden in 1822, the son of a doctor, Morley attended from the ages of ten to twelve a Moravian school at Neuwied on the Rhine, where he was impressed by the kindness of the teachers and the lack of flogging.[99] He studied medicine at King's College London from 1838 to 1843, and set up a partnership with another doctor in Shropshire, which was dissolved in 1848 when his partner proved to be unlicensed. Morley was left with £700 in legal debts which he took several years to pay off. He had been engaged to the daughter of a Unitarian family since 1843, but was unable to marry until 1852, when his finances were finally put on a sound footing.[100] Thereafter he attended a number of Unitarian chapels in London with his wife.

His admiration of the Moravian school he had attended in Germany – he had previously been at more than one private school in England where flogging was normal – for its refusal either to use corporal punishment or to proselytise for its own religious views made him want to introduce this 'right way of teaching' to England.[101] In 1849 he opened a day school, first in Manchester, then in Liverpool, on the same humane principles, gaining the support of Unitarians in the two cities. In the same year he responded to a cholera outbreak in England by writing on public health for John Forster's *Examiner* newspaper and, through Forster, wrote for the newly founded *Household Words*. He was now earning £200 a year from his school, but was still paying off his debt and he was aware of the precariousness of private school-keeping. He therefore accepted an invitation from Dickens, who was impressed by his articles, to come to London to be his regular assistant editor on *Household Words* at a salary of five guineas a week. Morley rented lodgings in Camden Square until his wedding in April 1852, when he took a house in Hampstead.[102]

Morley was one of the first visitors to Tavistock House when Dickens moved there in November 1851, on completion of some lavish alterations he had commissioned from Thomas Cubitt. Dickens's new recruit described an evening party at the house in December 1851, noting some unusual features:

His study leads out of the drawing-room by a sliding door, and on the study side of that door and on a corresponding panel he has what Carlyle would call 'shams' – bound backs of books which have no bodies or insides – mock shelves between glass, for the rows on which he has amused himself over the invention of a series of ludicrous titles, such as 'Godiva on the Horse', 'Hansard's Guide to Refreshing Sleep', 'Teazer's Commentaries' (for Caesar's), and so on.[103]

Among the scores of articles Morley wrote for *Household Words* was 'Drooping Buds', co-written with Dickens in April 1852 to welcome the new Hospital for Sick Children on Great Ormond Street. He contributed an essay on 'Infant Gardens', published on 21 July 1855, in which he describes in detail the kindergarten system devised by Friedrich Froebel, with its then revolutionary method of teaching through play, and alludes to an educational exhibition held in St Martin's Hall from July to September 1854, when the Ronges lectured on the system. He recommends their recently published *Practical Guide to the English Kinder Garten*, and tells his readers that they 'may see an Infant Garden in full work' by visiting the Ronges' house at 32 Tavistock Place.[104]

Morley was appointed professor of English at University College in December 1865. Here he was a popular lecturer, talking extempore instead of reading from notes, as Henry Solly, his former student, now son-in-law, recalled; he presided over a huge increase in the numbers studying English from fifty-two in 1865 to 108 in 1872. A further peak of 191 students was reached in 1878, when women were first admitted to full degree status at University College, a great move forward in education for which Morley had personally worked tirelessly. (Though women's colleges were founded in Oxford and Cambridge in the latter decades of the nineteenth century, and some provision was made for examinations, they did not acquire full degree status until 1920 in Oxford and 1947 in Cambridge.[105])

Morley gave over twenty lectures a week to the young men of University College, for which he was dubbed 'Professor More and Morley' by *Punch*, and from 1868 he lectured up and down the country for the newly established Ladies' Educational Association, the forerunner of the University Extension Movement and of higher education for women. One typical week's work, in January 1870, saw him lecture at University College from Monday to Thursday, give evening lectures on Thursday evening in Bradford, Friday morning lectures to women at Bradford's Mechanics' Institute, Friday afternoon lectures in York, Saturday morning ones in Huddersfield, then return home on Saturday evening.[106]

In a memoir called 'Pioneers of University Extension', written in 1891, Morley recalled how, with his University College colleague Carey Foster, professor of experimental physics, he gradually gained permission to give lectures to women inside the College itself, rather than in rooms in Harley Street and elsewhere which they had taken for the first sessions begun by the London Ladies' Educational Association in March 1869. Morley taught literature and Foster science, and in the session 1871–2 'prejudice was so far removed that, with the consent of the council of the college, we brought all the classes into our lecture-rooms', getting the co-operation of other colleagues and thereby increasing the number of women's classes offered from eight to twenty-one. 'We then moved step by step in the next successive sessions' until 'by gradual experiment extended over ten years, all the old prejudices' were conquered, and women were admitted on the same full degree terms as men.[107]

This indefatigable pioneer of extending higher education to women was persuaded to become principal of University Hall when it came under the management of Manchester New College in 1882. While his wife remained at their home in Hampstead, Morley and his son Forster shared the task of spending nights in Gordon Square. Morley made this partial sacrifice of home life because he was convinced, as Bagehot and Hutton had been, of the importance of a collegiate experience for young men. According to Henry Solly, who had himself been a resident at University Hall in 1871–2, Morley felt it was a pity that 'men might come to lectures, and sit side by side, hardly exchanging a word, and then separate and see no more of each other'.[108]

Just as he succeeded in increasing the numbers reading English at University College, so Morley managed against the odds to raise the numbers living at University Hall. In 1884 pressure for places was so great that the original Donaldson plan for a possible extension of the accommodation was put into action, with a new building erected at the back.[109] Solly recalled how varied the residents were at this time. There were students of Manchester New College, 'whose numbers were comparatively steady', and in addition 'a considerable body of candidates for the Indian Civil Service', some medical students, 'and a miscellaneous body of men training for various professions connected with art, science, law, engineering, and education'. How different life in University Hall was from the glum early days of Clough and his immediate successors; how Henry Crabb Robinson would have delighted in this late-flowering success of the institution as the liberal, open, miscellaneous society he had hoped to see it become. Solly continues:

> I remember French, German, Spanish, American, Hindoo, Parsee, Burmese, Cingalese, Japanese, Negroes. This mingling of many types was one of the circumstances on which Professor Morley relied most as a means of creating a vivid social life . . . Life in the Hall was never dull. In addition to the general interplay of mind with mind, each department was organized on its own democratic basis. The library and the reading-room had their separate committees; there was an excellent debating society, and, chief of all, an important body, known as the House Committee, whose resolutions were moved, seconded, and carried concerning matters great and small, down to the cooking of puddings and the making of beds.[110]

From 1884, when the extra building opened, until 1887, the Hall was continuously full, all fifty-three rooms being occupied by students, a 'remarkable advance' on the situation in 1882 when Morley took over, when there were only fourteen residents. A report read out to a University College council meeting in May 1889 attributed the improvement in numbers to 'Professor Morley's personal popularity, and the efforts which he made to secure the University College connection'.[111] By September 1888, however, there was another falling off, and the Hall made a loss of nearly £300. At this point Manchester New College began plans to move to Oxford, where a building was erected for them during 1889. The idea was to associate the college with the University of Oxford, now that religious tests had been abolished there.[112] Morley urged University College to buy the Hall in order to carry it on as a hall of residence for its students; the College council had the building valued at £12,000 and offered £10,000, intending to spend £2,000 on repairs and redecoration.[113]

To Morley's frustration, University Hall refused the offer. Instead of asking University College to increase its bid, the trustees accepted a higher one from Dr Williams's Library, which wanted to move its collection – based on the 7,000 items bequeathed by the leading dissenting minister Dr Daniel Williams on his death in 1716 – from its current Bloomsbury address, a smaller building in Grafton Street (now Grafton Way). Morley drew attention both to the original constitution of the Hall, which stated its purpose as a residence for students of University College, and to the agreement struck between the trustees of University Hall and those of Manchester New College when the latter took over the building in 1882, that in the event of its leaving Gordon Square, it could offer the Hall to University College at a price below its market value. He was bitter about the failure, calling it an example of the way in which 'the judgment of the best men can be warped by party zeal'.[114] The annual report of University College in February 1890 described 'with regret' the failure to buy the Hall, noting that since the sale to Dr Williams's Library there was 'not at present a Hall of Residence for men Students coming from a distance'. Attempts had been made to obtain 'by purchase or on lease a house or houses which they might establish as a Hall of Residence', but without success.[115]

By an irony which pained Morley, University College's women students already had a hall of residence, which he had helped them secure. He had actively supported the philanthropic educationist and suffragist Annie Browne in 1882 when she opened 1 Byng Place, next door to the Catholic Apostolic Church in the extreme south-west corner of Gordon Square; by 1887 the two adjoining houses, Nos. 2 and 3, had been added and the title College Hall adopted. One of College Hall's two superintendents, Rosa Morison, told Henry Solly that she 'could not talk to [Morley] about the success of College Hall and the good work it was doing for the women students; he felt so deeply the contrast with the failure of his own efforts for the men'.[116] Morley retired from University College in 1889 after twenty-three years, as well as leaving University Hall as it prepared to move to Oxford. The Gower Street council expressed its thanks for his 'constant attention to the welfare of the students, for his efforts in the cause of University Education', and in general for his 'promotion of the best interests of the College'.[117] In 1891 a medal was struck in his name and funds raised to award it to the best students in English.

With Morley's distinguished contribution as its final principal, University Hall came to an end. It had started with educational philanthropy but discordant views about the scope of its concerns; it was unfortunate in its early principals, Newman, Clough, and Hutton, all of whom were failures at the Hall, though extraordinary men. William Carpenter steadied the ship, and was followed by the clever radical Edward Beesly, who gave long service and brought some colour to the establishment, not least by inviting Karl Marx into the building. Finally Morley made the Hall what its most active founder, Henry Crabb Robinson, had wanted it to be, namely a welcoming place of residence and society for students pursuing their courses at the adjacent University College.

During its happiest years, the Hall hosted several new kinds of student, not just young Englishmen from dissenting families – though that was novelty enough in the earliest days – but in due course foreigners from countries far and wide, as well as students taking exams for the ever-expanding Indian Civil Service. Its leaders in their different ways represented a new sort of professional man, pushing on the Gower Street idea of a university education either separated completely from religious affiliations or chiefly dissenting, but accommodating different religions (especially once Turks, Burmese, Japanese, and others became residents in the later years), and – for the first time – bringing such disparate groups together socially. Some of the Hall's principals were progressive by conviction – Beesly and Morley are the best examples – while Clough, an exile from Anglicanism, found himself there more by circumstance than by conviction.

In its forty years of existence the Hall had mixed fortunes, and its closing as a hall of residence was a disappointment to its supporters, though the building continued to be called University Hall and almost immediately became the first home of another pioneering educational venture, that of Mary Ward to bring both useful knowledge and leisure activities to the poor of the neighbourhood in 1890, when Dr Williams's Library rented her a few rooms.[118] In this way, the Hall continued to be the chosen location for educational and social experiment.

CHAPTER EIGHT

Educating Women

ELISABETH JESSER Reid, the woman who inaugurated higher education for women in Britain, was a long-term Bloomsbury resident who naturally turned to her acquaintances among the professors at University College and University Hall, including Hutton, Carpenter, and Beesly, to help her with her new college, established in Bedford Square in 1849, the same year in which University Hall opened. Though she often despaired about the future of her college, it survived to become Bedford College and a constituent part of the University of London. Without help from the men of Gower Street and Gordon Square she might have failed. Instead, against the odds, she started women on their way towards full educational parity with men.

Early in 1849 she brought together a group of men and women to discuss the founding of a ladies' college which would offer lectures to girls and women in the same subjects and to the same standard as those delivered to young men at the English universities. A wealthy Unitarian, she was on friendly terms with many of the men involved in the teaching and management of University College London, and a close friend of Henry Crabb Robinson. Because she relied on Gower Street professors to teach at her establishment, it was desirable that she should find a location in Bloomsbury. In a letter to her friend Sophia De Morgan, wife of Augustus De Morgan, written while plans were progressing towards the opening of the college in October 1849, Elisabeth Reid thanked her for helping in the search for a suitable house. 'I think I mentioned G[rea]t Ormond Street where are some large houses vacant,' she wrote. The location would be convenient, though the professors might object to its being rather far from Gower Street. 'Can't you persuade the Professors the exercise is good for them? A good *run* from one College to another?'[1]

By September a house nearer to Gower Street had been found and taken, namely No. 47 (now 48) on the south side of Bedford Square, on land owned by the Bedford Estate. The prospectus for the Ladies' College stated that Bedford Square had been 'chosen as a suitable situation, from its being in the centre of a populous and wealthy neighbourhood, where such advantages as this College affords will be particularly valued', though in one of her letters to Sophia De Morgan Mrs Reid had been doubtful. She thought a more easterly location (like Great Ormond Street) might be better, largely because a college for women had already been started the previous year in Harley Street, not far to the west of Gower Street. This was Queen's College, opened in March 1848 by Frederick Denison Maurice as a Church of England establishment connected with the Governesses' Benevolent Institution with the intention of giving young women a proper training to be governesses. Maurice, who lived in Queen Square, was an Anglican clergyman and professor first of English literature and history, and from 1846 of theology, at King's College London. His beliefs were not entirely orthodox. When he questioned the Anglican doctrine of eternal punishment in his *Theological Essays*, published in 1853, he was obliged to resign his theology chair. The following year, as the central figure in the movement known as Christian Socialism, in which he was joined by Charles Kingsley and Thomas Hughes, he set up the Working Men's College in Red Lion Square.[2]

Mrs Reid's plan for a college seems to have been discussed at an early stage by some of the Gower Street professors, who, presumably with her approval, invited Maurice to join forces with them. Maurice wrote to Alexander John Scott, the former Irvingite and professor of English at University College, about a meeting that had been held in Gower Street to consider 'in what way we could honestly and with mutual advantage work together' in the event of a new college for women being formed. He stressed his conviction that there was no feeling of 'rivalship or jealousy' on either side between the professors at Queen's College and those planning a non-denominational college. Maurice claimed to be immune to 'the discredit we might possibly incur by mixing ourselves up with University College professors', fearless in the face of the probability that he would be exposed to 'attacks from the religious world', and yet mindful of the wisdom of the two parties keeping 'distinct'. His dislike of Francis Newman's religion made him particularly nervous:

Those who have attended my lectures on the Scriptures – our kind friend, Mrs Reed [*sic*], for instance – know, though the last thing I have ever thought of has been to attack ... Mr Newman, yet that I have formally, distinctly, consistently, vehemently arrived at working out an idea diametrically the opposite of that which is set forth [in Newman's works].[3]

It would therefore seem inconsistent, he continued, if he were to take part in the 'establishment of a teaching' which, if Newman were prominently involved, would 'seem to point another way'. Maurice, with his inherited adherence to Anglicanism, albeit an idiosyncratic form of it, was keen to stay clear of the altogether unorthodox Gower Street people. He therefore gave a qualified welcome to the new plan, which he agreed would offer 'substantial, honest teaching for girls', but he felt that his own college did the same for Anglican governesses, and thought it wiser not to join forces with Mrs Reid's colleagues.[4]

It is likely that Mrs Reid was relieved at Maurice's polite refusal to make common cause, for she was not convinced that he would be a good teacher for her students. Having attended some of his lectures at Queen's College, she was alert to the 'charm in the man's earnest devout spirit', as she told Sophia De Morgan; she left the lectures 'with a certain calm raised feeling that makes one sensible of having breathed a good moral atmosphere'. On the other hand, he preached the Atonement, in which she as a Unitarian did not believe, and she noticed that the younger girls at Queen's College found his lectures dull and could not understand them. She was also afraid that Maurice might foist some of his Anglican friends on her; one of these, Richard Chevenix Trench, professor of divinity at King's College London, gave lectures on the New Testament at Queen's College which she declared 'trash & dark as midnight'.[5] All in all, then, it was a good thing that Maurice himself was not keen to lecture at Bedford Square.

Elisabeth Reid was determined that her college would differ from Queen's by being non-denominational and by offering education to a higher standard. She also wanted to be in charge of her brainchild, rather than let it be subsumed into another, different, women's college, one led by men. She described her project in a letter of 1860 as her 'dream from childhood'; her aim was to use education for the 'elevation of the moral and intellectual character of Women', and she was prepared to sink her own money into the venture, though she optimistically thought of her initial investment of £1,500 as a loan.[6] Her college was thus to be different from, and not in direct rivalry with, Queen's College, which she actively supported, as did many of her colleagues in the founding of the Ladies' College. Though determined to strike out into new educational territory,

she was keen to learn what she could from the experiences of Harley Street
and to give credit where it was due. As she wrote to Sophia De Morgan
early in 1849:

> They bought a ten years remainder of 67 Harley St for £1000 advanced
> by the Governesses' Institution. If there is nobody else to do a similar
> aid, I will do it with pleasure. Their Sec[retar]y a very worthy man Revd
> Laing, is one I would avoid, he delights in a fuss & a flourish & flings
> money to the right & left like a prince . . . I am persuaded it is greatly
> for our good to be as unobtrusive as possible, even the less of
> Advertisement the better. When they advertise the Opening Day at
> Harley St one line giving notice of that in B[edford] Sq[uare] may be
> enough & this, too, would show their co-operation.[7]

Something of Mrs Reid's inexperience and inconsistency is seen here –
qualities much commented on by her friends, though they also praised her
benevolence and good intentions – in the odd idea that a new educational
venture should not advertise itself. She was soon complaining that not
enough students came forward, and that professional men were not as
supportive as she had hoped, which suggests that she ought to have done as
much advertising as possible, not as little. A strange attraction to secrecy,
allied to possessiveness about her project, emerges also in her letter of 1860
to two young women whom she was then naming as her trustees, women
who would carry on the College when she retired, which she did in 1863
from ill health, and after her death, which occurred in 1866. Her letter
refers to the topical subject of the American slave question.

As an adherent of philanthropic causes, she supported Harriet Beecher
Stowe and the anti-slavery movement, acting as hostess to Mrs Stowe on
her visit to England in 1853 and offering accommodation in her house in
1860 to Sarah Remond, the first black woman to tour Britain to lecture on
slavery and, it seems, also the first black woman to study at the Ladies'
College.[8] In appointing her trustees she alluded to the 'Underground
Railway', the secret channels by which American abolitionists helped slaves
to escape to freedom in Canada:

> My earnest wish is, that the whole proceeding may be as an Underground
> Railway, differing in this from the American U. R., that nobody shall
> ever know of its existence. You will thus be saved all importunity and
> much vexation of various kinds . . . Within three months of my decease
> you two must appoint a third, to share in all your powers and labours,

and bound likewise to secrecy. If either of the Three marry or remove to such a distance as to make the actual supervision of our College difficult, it will be only just to resign the Trust to other hands previously.

The Two cannot appoint again. I think better to confine it to Ladies for ever, and I am certain that if Two Men are chosen it will become a job [a public position used for personal gain or political advantage] and a sinecure.[9]

Though the enthusiasm for secrecy was hardly likely to help the future of the college, and the instructions to her young friends Jane Martineau and Eliza Bostock could be seen as obstructive rather than enabling, Mrs Reid did have some reason for her suspicion and bitterness. As a Unitarian, she was, like her friend Henry Crabb Robinson, aware of being outside the mainstream, a position which partly invigorated and partly frustrated her. As a widow whose husband had died in 1822, only a year after the marriage, she felt the helplessness of her situation and resented the need to rely on men to support her causes. If she had seen Maurice's letter to Scott, she would have been incensed at the assumption that it was the Gower Street professors themselves who were setting up this new college for women.

Despite making mistakes and alienating some potential supporters with her bluntness of speech and over-sensitivity, she managed to set on foot the first establishment for the higher education of women twenty years before Emily Davies started Girton College in connection with Cambridge University. And although she was obliged to have men on her council and as professors, she insisted that women be represented on the governing body, in contrast to Queen's College, which was run for women by men. The Ladies' College became therefore the first institution to include women on its council. Renamed Bedford College in 1859 and later incorporated into the University of London, it provided three students who achieved first-class honours in the university in 1881, the first year in which women could graduate in England.[10]

Elisabeth Reid owed her residence in Bloomsbury to the fact that in 1821 she had married John Reid, a doctor practising from his home at 6 Grenville Street, off Brunswick Square. As a Nonconformist Reid had studied medicine at Edinburgh in the 1790s, where he was a contemporary of Roget and another friend, the Unitarian John Bostock, father of the Eliza Bostock who helped Mrs Reid found the Ladies' College and was one of those entrusted with taking over the concern. The Reids, the Rogets, and the Bostocks were near neighbours, the Reids in Grenville Street, the Rogets in

Bernard Street and from 1843 in Upper Bedford Place, and the Bostocks also in Upper Bedford Place.

Most of the men and women who met at the first general committee of the new college in June 1849 were Unitarians or Nonconformists. All were in some way progressive rather than conservative, especially on the topic of education. Mrs Reid had appointed three male trustees to manage her loan of £1,500. One was Erasmus Darwin, older brother of Charles, who had studied medicine at Edinburgh in the 1820s but did not practise; he was in poor health and lived a bachelor life on inherited wealth. Darwin's cousin Hensleigh Wedgwood was also a trustee, while his wife Fanny was a founding member of the women's committee and one of the first Lady Visitors, whose task was to attend some of the lectures as chaperones to the young ladies. The Wedgwoods, though now living in fashionable Regent's Park, knew Bloomsbury well, having lived until 1845 at 16 Gower Street (the house in which the University of London's school had its unhappy start in 1830).[11] The third trustee was a young lawyer, Thomas Farrer.

Among the committee women and Lady Visitors were Sophia De Morgan and Lady Romilly, whose husband John was Roget's cousin and second son of the unfortunate Sir Samuel Romilly. (John had been sixteen when his father took his own life at the family home in Russell Square in 1818.) Also on the committee was Ann Scott, wife of Alexander John Scott, one of the first professors to agree to teach at Bedford Square. Anna Jameson, author of a number of works on women, travel, and art, was another supporter, though she had very little money and lived with her mother and sisters in Ealing, rather far to the west of Bloomsbury. Elisabeth Reid admired her, suggesting half in jest to Sophia De Morgan that Mrs Jameson might be invited to give lectures on 'the History & Literature of the Fine Arts' at the college:

> Could anything be so delightful? I believe no woman can hear such now, but there is a woman so pre-eminently qualified to give them that artists sit at her feet & court her criticisms, – while her speech w[oul]d put fancy & feeling into dry bones. Why should not Mrs Jameson be invited to that department? she is very shy, which ranks as an impediment, but her heart & soul are with us in desire for improved education. Her best work would make our fortune, we should open so brilliantly![12]

Anna Jameson did not, alas, become the first female professor in Britain. No one was hired to teach art history until 1854, when Gottfried Kinkel joined. Previously professor of art history at the University of Bonn, he was now a political refugee who had given some well-attended lectures at University College.[13]

If Mrs Reid was sensitive to the charge, identical to that facing the University Hall committee at exactly the same time, of wanting to open a Unitarian establishment, a letter to Mrs De Morgan from Anna Jameson during the planning stage confirmed her anxieties. Mrs Jameson warned that there were 'public & private attempts to throw discredit on this new institution by representing it as sectarian & not in Harmony with the Harley Street college'. She urged that 'such false impressions should be removed as soon as possible'.[14]

The female supporters were willing to give practical help. They included Lady Noel Byron, widow of the poet, philanthropist, convert to Unitarianism, and a friend of Henry Crabb Robinson and Sophia De Morgan. Lady Byron sent Mrs De Morgan a list of aristocratic ladies who might be asked to support the project.[15] Ann Scott arranged to visit Queen's College to see how they managed things there. One of the women at 67 Harley Street, Emily Taylor, told Mrs Scott that the Ladies' College should be cautious about arrangements for musical instruction:

[M]y experience would lead me to doubt whether you will not do better by choosing a capital female Teacher for the Piano Forte . . . If you fix, *first*, on a celebrated Professor of Harmony, you must allow him to make all the musical arrangements, and, depend upon it, a woman will then never be chosen, but if a Professor recommends, as is very likely, young men for Teachers, you will have the trouble of providing someone always to be present.[16]

The same was true, she added, of language teaching. Women should be appointed as assistants to the professors both to avoid the need for constant chaperoning and out of simple justice, since music and modern languages were among the few subjects in which women, hitherto excluded from studying most academic subjects, might actually have some competence. Emily Taylor here touches on a point made by Emily Davies in her short but hard-hitting book, *The Higher Education of Women*, published in 1866. Picking up the threads of discussion from Mary Wollstonecraft's *A Vindication of the Rights of Woman* (1792), and more recently George Eliot's *Westminster Review* articles during the 1850s and her piquant comparison of the different educational experiences offered to Maggie and Tom Tulliver in *The Mill on the Floss* (1860), Emily Davies writes with sharp appreciation of the irony that boys are routinely taught only the 'dead languages', as if that were a useful preparation for travel abroad as part of their profession and for 'go[ing] into offices where they have to conduct foreign correspondence', while girls are taught modern languages, though they 'rarely see a foreigner'.[17]

Another woman involved in the project was Louisa Goldsmid, niece and daughter-in-law of Isaac Lyon Goldsmid. The most scholarly of Mrs Reid's female supporters was Anna Swanwick, a woman of thirty-five who had been taught by James Martineau when her family attended his Unitarian chapel in Liverpool in the 1820s. She had visited Germany, and learned Greek, and by 1849 had begun to make a reputation as a translator from German literature, including the plays of Goethe; in the 1860s and 1870s she translated the complete dramas of Aeschylus. She lived with her mother first in Tavistock Place and from 1845 in Woburn Square, from where she started a school for poor children over a shop in the Colonnade, the cobbled passage between Bernard Street and Guilford Street leading into Grenville Street.[18]

Anna Swanwick's niece recalled:

She used to relate how, when visiting the poor streets round Tottenham Court Road on her errands of mercy, she frequently met little girls carrying babies, and looking as if they had nothing to interest them. She accosted some of these, and asked if they went to school, to which they invariably replied, 'Oh, no, the boys go to school – mother wants me to mind the baby!'[19]

Anna called on the girls' mothers and persuaded them to bring their daughters for lessons two evenings a week, at first at her home and then in a rented room in the Colonnade. A former pupil recalled her experience:

My remembrance of dear Miss Anna Swanwick dates back as far as 1847. In or about that year, I was admitted as a pupil in a school which she opened in conjunction with other ladies. The classes were held in a room over a shop in the Colon[n]ade (a quaint old-world place now demolished). The room was large, we were thirty-six in number, that was our limit, and vacancies were readily filled by waiting candidates. Our curriculum was poor compared with the present School Board Code [School Boards were established under the Elementary Education Act of 1870], nevertheless what we learnt was *well* learnt.[20]

The novelist Mary Elizabeth Braddon, who lived in Mecklenburgh Square and set a number of her novels partly in Bloomsbury, describes the

Colonnade in *Eleanor's Victory* (1863) as a bohemian corner where hard-up but respectable middle-class women give piano lessons for a living:

> The place popularly known as the Pilasters is one of the queerest nooks in London. It consists of a row of tumble-down houses, fronted by a dilapidated colonnade, and filled with busy life from cellar to attic. But I don't believe that the inhabitants of the Pilasters are guilty of nefarious practices, or that vice and crime find a hiding-place in the cellars below the colonnade. The retreat stands by itself, hidden between two highly respectable middle-class streets . . . Small tradesmen find a home in the Pilasters, and emerge thence to work for the best families in . . . 'the Squares'.
>
> Here, amongst small tailors and mantua-makers, cheap eating-houses, shabby beer-shops, chimney-sweeps and mangles, Signora Picirillo had taken up her abode, bringing her faded goods and chattels, the remnants of brighter times, to furnish the first-floor over a shoe-maker's shop. I am afraid the shoemaker was oftener employed in mending old shoes than in making new ones, but the Signora was fain to ignore that fact, and to be contented with her good fortune in having found a very cheap lodging in a central neighbourhood.[21]

Until early 1842 Elisabeth Jesser Reid herself lived in her comfortable house in Grenville Street at the eastern end of the Colonnade; like Anna Swanwick, she appears to have exercised educational philanthropy among her poor neighbours. During the 1830s she converted some rooms above one of the Colonnade shops 'into a library and reading-room', where Roget, among other friends, gave lectures. Occasional concerts were held, and 'the management of the library and reading room (which also formed the lecture room) was in the hands of the members, consisting mainly of the working classes, apprentices, &c., each of whom were introduced on the recommendation of two members'.[22] By 1870 the Colonnade, despite the best efforts of the Foundling Estate on which it stood, had become a slum; Booth's 'poverty map' of 1889 classifies it as dark blue ('very poor', 'inhabited principally by casual labourers and others living from hand to mouth') edged with black ('the lowest grade', 'loafers and semi-criminals – the elements of disorder').[23]

Anna Swanwick and her mother were among the first Lady Visitors at the Ladies' College; they also enrolled for classes in order to show solidarity with Mrs Reid. Anna took ancient history, moral philosophy, and elocution in 1849–50.[24] Thirty years later she was asked to present the first women graduates from Bedford College to receive degrees from the Chancellor of the University of London, and in 1884 she was elected Visitor to the College, the first woman to take up the position initially held by Erasmus Darwin.[25]

There needed to be a large number of Lady Visitors, three of whom were to sit on the College council, and the rest to take it in turns to accompany the students at lectures. Twenty-one were found, but this aspect of the early higher education of women caused problems, partly because the rota was complicated, so that misunderstandings arose about who should attend which classes at what time, and partly because the professors felt resentful of what they saw as unnecessary interference by these women.[26] A letter from Ann Scott to Sophia De Morgan during preparations indicates that there were doubts even about having unmarried men on the committee. There were two such men, Thomas Farrer and William Shaen, aged twenty-nine and twenty-seven, respectively. Shaen was a Unitarian lawyer who had been one of the earliest pupils at University College School, and had studied at University College London and Edinburgh. He was involved in a number of reforming causes, including the anti-slavery movement and female education and suffrage, and he helped Mazzini set up a school for Italian children in London. He later offered his legal expertise during the setting up of the London School of Medicine for Women in Bloomsbury in 1874.[27]

Despite difficulties, the College opened in October 1849, its declared aims including the firm statement that 'no question whatsoever is to be asked as to the religious opinions of a pupil, nor is any pupil to be required to attend any theological lectures which may be given'. A draft prospectus to this effect was drawn up by Augustus De Morgan; from our knowledge of his disapproval of some decisions taken by University College in connection with the faith professed by candidates for its chairs, we can guess that the declaration met with his full approval.[28] The College did not escape controversy completely, however. Of the first twelve professors who agreed to teach (most of them for no fee), five were clergymen and three of those were Anglicans. Two, John Brewer and Charles Nicolay, were professors at King's College London: Brewer taught classical literature, while Nicolay, who gave the inaugural lecture in Bedford Square in October 1849, lectured in geography. They were named in the first prospectus of the Ladies' College as professors of biblical teaching (Nicolay) and modern history (Brewer). But in the event neither actually taught at Bedford Square, as their principal at King's, Richard Jelf, refused them permission to teach at this non-Anglican establishment.[29]

Most of the other professors walked down Gower Street to Bedford Square from their jobs at University College. De Morgan taught mathematics, but left at Easter 1850 because of pressure of work, though Mrs Reid, probably unfairly, put his resignation down to frustration at not being paid; part of the reason is likely to have been impatience with the level of knowledge of maths shown by the girls.[30] William Carpenter, later principal of University Hall, had just been appointed to his chair in medical jurisprudence at University College, and he too left Bedford Square at the end of its first year, pleading overwork. Alexander John Scott was a successful teacher of moral philosophy and literature at the Ladies' College until he resigned early in 1851 on being appointed principal of Owens College in Manchester. While at Bedford Square, he attracted twenty-three students to his philosophy classes and fifteen to his English literature classes in the first term. German was also popular, taught by Adolf Heimann, since 1848 professor of German at University College and the friend, through his wife Amelia, of Christina Rossetti.[31]

Other classes attracted small numbers, fewer than ten in the first year for Italian, geography, natural history (Carpenter's subject), and even vocal music, which was taught – rather against the advice of Miss Taylor of Queen's College – by the famous John Hullah, composer and professor of vocal music at King's College London and also at Harley Street.[32] Drawing classes were given by Francis Cary, son of the Dante translator and British Museum employee Henry Cary. The younger Cary had taken over Henry Sass's famous drawing school on the corner of Charlotte Street in 1842.

The intake of students, or pupils as they were at first called, was miscellaneous, since the committee had decided to admit girls 'over the age of twelve',[33] which was hardly conducive to study at the higher educational level. In effect, however, most of them seem to have been grown-up women. Only sixty-eight students enrolled for the first term (as against 200 at the opening of Queen's College eighteen months earlier),[34] and a number of those were friends of Mrs Reid. Lady Romilly attended classes on the Bible during the Lent Term, Eliza Bostock and Jane Martineau took classes in French and drawing, and maths and English, respectively. Barbara Leigh Smith signed up for a number of classes. In 1854 she was to set up her own experimental co-educational school and she went on to co-found Girton College with Emily Davies in 1869; on her death in 1891 she left £1,000 to Bedford College.[35]

One name on the register for 1850–1 was that of Marian (or Mary Ann) Evans, who enrolled for maths, taught by Frank Newman after De Morgan's resignation, and Latin, taught by the Revd Bennett Johns.[36]

Later famous as the novelist George Eliot, Marian Evans had recently arrived in London from Coventry after the death of her father; she was a lodger at 142 Strand, the house and workplace of the radical publisher John Chapman, for whom she translated German works and edited the *Westminster Review*.[37] Another early student was Dickens's thirteen-year-old daughter Katey; her father paid £1 11s. 6d. for her to attend drawing classes from her home, Tavistock House, during the Easter Term of 1853, and £4 14s. 6d. for the whole of the following session.[38] Katey became an artist, moving in Pre-Raphaelite circles and marrying the painter Charles Collins, younger brother of Wilkie Collins.[39]

Elisabeth Reid herself attended English lessons given by Scott at the beginning of the second session, and from January 1851, briefly, by Thomas Wilson, who was to cause the first resignations since the two King's College professors had been instructed to withdraw before the college opened. Others attending in 1850–1 were Barbara Leigh Smith's friend and fellow feminist Bessie Rayner Parkes, who studied political economy under Newman,[40] and Henrietta Le Breton, daughter of the Unitarian minister Philip Le Breton, one of the chief founders of University Hall and himself a member of the council of the Ladies' College from 1854 to 1860.[41] Among these younger women – all in their early twenties – was Frances Martin, born in 1829, an early student at Queen's College, Harley Street, who joined the Ladies' College in 1850 to study moral philosophy and English literature with Scott.[42] She was such a successful student that she was asked to take charge of the school which was added to the Ladies' College in January 1853, and was later involved in the founding of the Working Women's College in Queen Square.

Though Mrs Reid was perversely disinclined to advertise her new institution, some publicising was done. Professor Scott's name and position at University College were useful to the Ladies' College, and in December 1849 his first two lectures were published by University College's publisher, Taylor, Walton, and Maberly of Upper Gower Street. An advertisement in the *Daily News* announced '*Suggestions on Female Education: Two Introductory Lectures on English Literature and Moral Philosophy*, delivered in the Ladies' College, Bedford-square. By A. J. Scott, A.M., Professor of the English Language and Literature in University College, London.'[43] A month later, on 17 January 1850, the same newspaper, of which Dickens had been the first editor, and which was a reliable friend to progressive educational experiments, published an 'outline of a Lecture delivered by the Rev. William Elliott, M.A., at the Ladies' College, Bedford-square, yesterday', on 'Modern History, considered as the Development of Laws discoverable in the Bible'. 'The lecture room was crowded, and the audience appeared to take the deepest interest in the lecture.'

At the beginning of the second session, in October 1850, the *Standard* newspaper offered its support to the college with an article entitled 'Ladies' College, Bedford-Square', which began:

> The Rev. B.G. Johns, Latin professor at this institution, and head master of the Grammar School, Dulwich, delivered an introductory lecture to the pupils of his class and several visitors and strangers at the Ladies' College on Saturday last, upon the Latin language and literature ... [He] combatted the absurd and now almost entirely exploded arguments of those who talk of the difference in the capacities of men and women, as rendering them unfit to bear similar treatment, and the danger of extending female pedantry ... The founders of the Ladies' College would have it raised above the mere idea of a school. It was to be a college in the sense of being the place where associated students were to be gradually moulded and fashioned into a higher, purer, and nobler stature of intellect.[44]

This endorsement was heartening, especially coming from an Anglican clergyman at a boys' public school.

If the modest numbers who turned up for teaching by this group of distinguished experts disappointed Mrs Reid's dearest hopes, the ugly disagreements which arose in the spring of 1851 turned disappointment to despair. On Scott's resignation in preparation for his move to Manchester, Thomas Wilson was taken on to teach English, and also geography and astronomy. He had been a curate in Norwich, but had resigned from the Church of England in 1847 because of doubts about the Thirty-Nine Articles. In 1850 he published *Catholicity, Spiritual and Intellectual: An Attempt at Vindicating the Harmony of Faith and Knowledge*, dedicated in fulsome terms to his friend Carlyle, whom he described as 'an Example of Transcendent Genius Hallowed by the Purest Life and Worthiest Work'.[45] Carlyle wrote on New Year's Day 1851 of having had 'Tom Wilson (growing more and more a *radical* reverend now)' as a visitor on Christmas Day; he wrote again on 20 February, by which time Wilson had begun his lectures in Bedford Square, of his being 'about to burst forth into heterodox *preaching*, I believe'.[46]

Members of the council of the Ladies' College appear at first not to have known about the recent book, which expressed a vague, non-denominational Christianity influenced by Carlyle. Lady Romilly (daughter of the Bishop of Chichester) raised objections to Wilson's heterodoxy, suggesting to her fellow council members that in the interests of the College – which was already believed by many to be Nonconformist and would be damaged by having someone who seemed barely to be a Christian at all – he be asked to resign. On 5 March 1851 the council drew up a resolution, supported by all except Fanny Wedgwood and Francis Newman:

> The Council, with extreme regret, finds that some of those who united in inviting Mr Wilson to accept his appointments were most imperfectly aware of the nature of his published opinions. In consequence, they are ashamed to feel that they have elected him prematurely and unwisely for the interests of the College; and they are led to confess this to him candidly, knowing how little they have to offer to his acceptance; in order that he may consider whether he would be disposed to relieve them from their difficulty by resigning.[47]

To this plea they added a weaselly explanation that the objection to his views was that they destroyed the balance of opinion represented in the College, as they were too similar to those of Newman. The latter had recently published his own book, *Phases of Faith* (1850), detailing his shifts from Anglicanism to Unitarianism and on to a non-sectarian general belief in the individual's direct relationship to God. This work was now attracting unwelcome public attention, and the council panicked about the adverse effect it would have on the College's reputation. Though his colleagues persuaded Newman not to resign immediately – Wilson went in March as requested – they were probably relieved when did so he in June.[48]

In Francis Newman they lost a polymath, a brilliant teacher of maths, Latin, ancient history, and political economy; much later George Eliot recalled 'the awe I had of him as a lecturer on mathematics at the Ladies' College'.[49] He was also a man who constantly attracted controversy. In June 1850 Crabb Robinson noted that Mrs Reid was 'not hopeful', being 'sensible that Newman's Phases of Faith will do a great deal of harm' to her college. In April 1852 he described a visit to Mrs Reid's house, where Newman was once again the topic of conversation. 'It is a sad fact', wrote Crabb Robinson, 'that Mr Newman has been the ruin of the Ladies' College and the main occasion of the bad success of our University Hall.'[50]

There is no doubt that Newman could be a difficult colleague. He was fearless in expressing his opinion, and when the council of the Ladies' College begged Wilson to resign in March 1851, he sent it a sharp, sarcastic letter of protest, which gave several reasons for his anger:

1. Because I see nothing in Mr Wilson's published theological views that is opposed to the best interests of our institution . . .

2. Because it is an extreme & dangerous use of power, hitherto quite uncontemplated among us, to call on a Professor to resign on the ground of his religious opinions.

3. Because the doctrine of *balancing Creeds* among the Professors, by which this novel proceeding has been justified, involves in practice a great deal which is unintelligible, absurd, & pernicious, & which soon must destroy any institution by discord, if it is really & consistently acted upon.[51]

Newman takes the balancing argument to apply also to members of council, commenting that the previous year, 'as a member of the Board, I voted for Mrs Goldsmid and Mr Shaen', but that next time 'I shall not be able to do so with the same satisfaction, without first interrogating them, & the previously elected members, on their respective Creeds'. As for advertising for teachers, that will become a farce:

Imagine such an Advertisement as this: 'Wanted, a Professor of Physical Geography . . . who must not be a Deist, nor a Puseyite, nor a Unitarian, nor a Roman Catholic. A liberal Churchman or Quaker will be acceptable, if not too deep in Rationalism.'

Finally, Newman declares that there is no prospect of conducting the affairs of the College properly 'until the doctrine of balancing Creeds be fundamentally renounced' and one of two courses taken, namely '*either* to draw up the scheme of a Creed which it is expected that *all* the Professors will hold, *or* to take no notice of Creed, as such', except in the case of 'avowed teachers of technical Theology'.[52] Having made his colleagues thoroughly uncomfortable with his impeccable logic, Newman left in the summer of 1851.

The new college carried on, though Mrs Reid was constantly fearful of failure and fretfully aware that others were not as enthusiastic about it as she was. Her young friend Eliza Bostock told her more than once that she expected too much and alienated people by her tactlessness; and Crabb Robinson, who did his best to encourage her with good wishes, books, and the occasional donation of money, told her frankly in 1863 that he had often seen her make a 'mistake into which ardent & generous natures are ever prone to fall', that of 'mistaking a warm wish that a thing could be done, an approbation of the object if attainable, for a belief in the attainability & a readiness to concur in measures for securing it'.[53] Eliza Bostock thought Mrs Reid was too ready to let the College be associated with Unitarianism and that she was inclined to 'assert the rights of conscience' above the 'rights of women', when the latter should have been her main concern.[54] She scolded Mrs Reid soon after Newman's departure:

> You are quite taken by surprise at the want of interest that other people show in what appears to you of paramount importance, but you should consider that most good benevolent people have their own engrossing schemes, their own hobbies to ride & that the human mind being limited there is no space for your ideas to gain admission . . . I think you sometimes do harm rather than good by your very warm expressions about it, both because sober English folk have a great dread of enthusiasm & are apt to take a grudge against things & people that are over bepraised, as they think. Now certainly your expressions are much stronger than what other people are in the habit of using . . . If the professorships are only filled with regular steadily working men, there can hardly be a doubt of success, but dear Mrs Reid, you must take patience & take things quietly that the grain of mustard seed may have time to grow.[55]

Eliza was right. Newman was soon replaced by the energetic Alexander Bain, a young man who had left school at the age of eleven to learn the weaving trade from his father, but who had sought an education in the evenings at his local Mechanics' Institution in Aberdeen, and had attended the university there, graduating joint top in classics, maths, science, and philosophy in 1840. He had stayed on as a lecturer until 1845, when he failed to be elected to a chair because of his religious scepticism. After arriving in London in 1848 to help Edwin Chadwick's work on the sanitary commission, he took over Newman's secretaryship to the council at Bedford Square in 1851 and for three years taught moral philosophy and geography with great success (presumably keeping diplomatically quiet about his lack of religious faith).[56] In 1855 he married Frances Wilkinson, the Lady Resident at the Ladies' College, and soon after that he became an examiner for the University of London.

Poor Mrs Reid never stopped worrying about her college. In 1856 she realised that the institution was not likely to become self-supporting and that it would not attract large donations. In thanking Crabb Robinson for

a gift of £50, she noted bitterly that a Mr Carter, a solicitor whose daughter
was a student at the College, was the only other man to have given as much.
At this point she reluctantly turned her initial loan of £1,500 into a gift.[57]
She was consoled by Crabb Robinson, who had been an inside observer
both at University College in its early days and from 1849 at University
Hall. He tried to get her to put her disappointment about the Ladies'
College into a wider perspective:

> You have written under a sense of disappointment at the faint success
> your generous undertaking has enjoyed. This is a natural sentiment, but
> it should be resisted, if it threaten to interfere with the vigorous contin-
> uance of the requisite exertions . . . Our University College set on a
> broader foundation still stands but on a single story. We set an example
> of a reformed scheme of education. And in fear of our success, those
> originally opposed to us followed our example in more than one place
> [i.e. King's College London and Durham University]. And those
> colleges have succeeded. I individually have rejoiced at this. And should
> the reformed Oxford & Cambr[idge] Universities who have stolen
> our thunder hurl it against us I shall not grieve at their prosperity.
> Without our University which humbly consented to become a mere
> College in name, the reforms in those old establishments would never
> have been adopted. And this is honour enough to justify self-applause.
> May not you, dear friend . . . say the same, or what resembles this
> boast?[58]

The reference to reforms at Oxford and Cambridge relates to the removal
of some restrictions attaching to scholarships and the like; major reform, in
the shape of the abolition of the legislation which required graduates to sign
the Thirty-Nine Articles, did not come until 1871. Crabb Robinson
continued, protesting that Mrs Reid was wrong to complain of the 'disre-
gard of *female* education by *men*', but agreeing with her that, as was also the
case at University College and University Hall, the 'fierce opposition from
the clergy' was shocking. Nevertheless, the Ladies' College did survive,
partly thanks to a decision similar to that taken by the first University of
London in Gower Street in 1830 when it too looked likely to be a failing
concern, namely to open a school to attract greater numbers and to be a
nursery to feed pupils through to the more advanced institution.

The school was opened in January 1853, some of the rooms at 47
Bedford Square being given over to it. Girls from the age of nine were
admitted, and, as in University College School, German was taught as well

as French and Latin, with writing, arithmetic, drawing, geography, and singing the other subjects of study. Frances Martin, former student and devoted follower of F. D. Maurice, was appointed to run the school. Mrs Reid was delighted with her, declaring her 'the loveliest and perhaps, the most gifted woman I know'. Crabb Robinson, too, found her 'a very interesting young person'.[59]

The next change was the taking of the lease on the neighbouring house, 48 Bedford Square, which was done in 1860. Up to thirteen students began to board in No. 48, transferring from Mrs Reid's old house, 6 Grenville Street, which she had turned into a boarding house for students of the College in 1852, having moved out herself ten years earlier after the death of her mother.[60] Eliza Bostock oversaw the students' move and spent many nights in 48 Bedford Square herself, while the young women were under the supervision of a live-in helper. As was the case in the early years of University Hall, the social life of the resident students was not much catered for. Former boarders recalled the house having 'a rather Spartan air', though the 'beautiful mahogany doors' and Adam mantelpieces of these fine late-eighteenth-century houses were appreciated.[61]

Lunch was apparently eaten standing up, and consisted of bread and butter with treacle or cold meat, rather in the fashion of the female colleges at Cambridge in the 1920s noted with such crafty irony by Virginia Woolf in *A Room of One's Own* (1928). 'The lamp in the spine does not light on beef and prunes' followed by dry biscuits and washed down with water, she writes of a collegiate dinner in Fernham (i.e. Newnham) College, contrasting this meal with the sumptuous lunch she had enjoyed as a guest at a men's college which included soles spread with 'a counterpane of the whitest cream', partridges served with 'a retinue of sauces and salads', and a dessert 'which rose all sugar from the waves', while throughout the meal 'the wine-glasses had flushed yellow and flushed crimson'. The spine on this occasion had been lit with 'the subterranean glow which is the rich yellow flame of rational intercourse'.[62] Here, in a nutshell, was the difference between the social life of the men's colleges at the ancient universities and that experienced not only in their poorer women's colleges, but also, eighty years earlier, in the unendowed godless college on Gower Street and its spartan cousins University Hall and the Ladies' College.

The extension of the College's space into the adjoining house could be considered a triumph, since it happened only after the kind of battle with the agents for the Duke of Bedford which leaseholders wishing to carry on educational establishments always faced. When the College sought to renew the lease on No. 47 in 1857, the Duke's agent refused on the familiar grounds that the lease did not permit the use of the premises as a school. Appeals were made and the school continued, though not without fears that the lease would not be further renewed. Francis Russell, the seventh Duke, finally agreed personally, after three years of delaying a decision, that the College could remain in the houses, subject to the same sorts of rules as those invoked in 1830 at 16 Gower Street and in 1849 at University Hall. No brass plate was to be put up and pupils were not to go into the Bedford Square garden.[63] Henry Crabb Robinson sympathised with Mrs Reid during the protracted negotiations with the Duke's agents. He recalled how the council of University Hall 'had the same spirit to encounter' with respect to the garden in Gordon Square:

> At first, in our lease, there was introduced an actual *forfeiture* if any one of our pupils went within the gardens . . . as it might alarm puritanical maidens. And we are prohibited from having public worship in the Hall. But [the Duke] ought to feel the difference between a college for young men & women.[64]

The school did help put the College on a sounder footing financially, though there were again worries about impending insolvency in December 1864, when the treasurer, William Shaen, reported that expenditure exceeded receipts. Mrs Reid had expressed her fear in 1860 that the College might get swallowed up by the school, and it was 'to avert this fatal retrogression' that she had installed her trustees as managers, enjoining them to keep the interests of the higher institution always at the forefront of their minds.[65] Her fears looked like being justified, as Frances Martin, though a successful headmistress of the school, raised hackles in the College itself with her forcefulness, her inclination towards Anglicanism, and her possessiveness about her pupils. She was accused of keeping girls in the school who were ready to move on to the College. In return, Miss Martin resented what she saw as interference from those heading the College. With Mrs Reid in her seventies and no longer concerning herself with the day-to-day business at Bedford Square, her trustees Eliza Bostock, Jane Martineau, and a third trustee, Eleanor Smith, were the managers.

On Mrs Reid's death in April 1866, the professors suggested raising money for an entrance scholarship in her name, and Eliza Bostock and Jane Martineau set about raising money. Henry Crabb Robinson gave £25, as did Erasmus Darwin, but Mrs Reid's sister disapproved of the scholarship idea as 'not sufficient to be considered as a *personal memorial*', and so in the end nothing was done. Crabb Robinson remembered his friend as a woman who 'made both friends & foes' by her 'zeal which was sadly injudicious in its operations', but he was sorry that no scholarship in her name had been set up, since without her enthusiasm and determination there would have been no Ladies' College at all.[66]

Her younger friends had given willing support and appreciated her earnest desire for female education, especially Eliza Bostock, who encouraged her even while she made frank criticisms of Mrs Reid's vehement ways. We catch a glimpse of Elisabeth Jesser Reid, for once outside her Unitarian and Bedford Square circles, in a letter of Jane Carlyle. The picture is not a flattering one. A lively birthday party for Nina Macready, daughter of the actor-manager and friend of Dickens, was held on Boxing Day 1843, with Dickens himself performing astonishing magic tricks. Jane Carlyle recounts meeting Mrs Reid there:

> You would have laughed to have heard her as I did trying to *indoctrinate* one of Dickens's small children with *Socinian benevolence* – the child about the size of a quartern loaf was sitting on a low chair gazing in awestruck delight at the reeking plum-pudding which its Father had just produced out of 'a gentleman's hat' – Mrs Reid leaning *tenderly* over her (as benevolent gentlewomen understand how to lean over youth) said in a soft voice – *professedly* for *its* ear but loud enough for mine and everybody else's within three yards distance – '*Would* not you like that there was such a nice pudding as that in every house in London tonight? I'm sure *I* would'! – The shrinking uncomprehending look which the little blowzy face cast up to her was inimitable – a whole page of protest against *twaddle*! if she could but have read it![67]

In a contest for the most witty, lively, and intelligent letter-writer, Jane Carlyle would win hands down against Elisabeth Reid; but it was the humourless yet philanthropic and determined Mrs Reid who forced through real progress in the struggle for the higher education of women.

The Ladies' College was renamed Bedford College in 1859, then removed from its original buildings in 1874 to take over premises in York Place, near Baker Street, after the Bedford Estate managers informed the trustees that the expiring lease on No. 48 Bedford Square would not be renewed.[68] Its subsequent history was one of steady progress until its future was secured by the introduction of degrees for women at the University of London in 1878 and the incorporation of the College into the newly constituted university in 1900.[69] The school had been discontinued before the end of 1868, when Mrs Reid's three trustees, who did not get on with Frances

Martin and wished to separate the two establishments and concentrate on the College, told the council that, as lessees, they had decided there was not space enough in the two houses for both school and college.[70]

A second generation of feminists attended Bedford College after its removal from Bloomsbury. These included the daughters of reforming Bloomsbury residents, among them Philippa, daughter of one of the leaders of the women's suffrage movement, Millicent Garrett Fawcett of 2 Gower Street; Janet (later Trevelyan), daughter of Mary Ward, doyenne of Russell Square and prime mover in the establishment of the Passmore Edwards Settlement in Tavistock Place; and Annie, daughter of Philip Wicksteed, a Unitarian minister who had lived in University Hall as a student of University College in the 1860s, lectured widely for the London Society for the Extension of University Teaching during the 1890s, and was a colleague of Mary Ward and John Passmore Edwards in founding the Tavistock Place Settlement.[71]

While Bedford College was still in its first home in Bedford Square, it numbered among its Lady Visitors two women who would go on to establish the teaching of women in Cambridge. Emily Davies, co-founder and first mistress of Girton College, was a Lady Visitor for the year 1863–4, and Anne Jemima Clough, known as Annie, the sister of Arthur Hugh Clough, and as diffident as he but more determined to make a difference in the world of education, was a Lady Visitor from 1866 to 1870, when she became the first principal of Newnham College.[72] An opportunity to push reform in female education even further was unfortunately turned down by Bedford College council in 1865, when Millicent Fawcett's sister Elizabeth Garrett (later Anderson), newly qualified to practise medicine after being the first woman to be admitted to the examination of the Society of Apothecaries, offered to teach physiology. The council, still made up of many more men than women, decided that physiology was an unsuitable subject for girls.[73]

After the closure of the school, some of the young women who were students and teachers at Bedford Square went on to start girls' schools and colleges of their own. Frances Martin's Anglicanism had caused difficulties with the trustees of Bedford College, and she disagreed with them, and with Emily Davies, over whether women should receive the same kind of higher education as men – Frances believing they should have a separate syllabus strong on religious and moral training. The closing of 'her' school in Bedford Square infuriated her; she wrote to her friend the publisher Alexander Macmillan in May 1868 that she would like to 'put a gigantic extinguisher over the existing so called colleges for ladies and all the ladies above forty interested in them'.[74] She was already involved with Elizabeth Malleson's Working Women's College, established in Queen Square in 1864, later showing her independence again by splitting from the management there to start her own successful College for Working Women in the area now known as Fitzrovia, across Tottenham Court Road from Bloomsbury.[75]

One of Frances's helpers at the Bedford Square school, Lucy Harrison, co-founded a school in 1870 in Gower Street, where she lived at No. 80.[76] She had been a student at Bedford Square for two years from 1861; in 1866, when she was twenty-two, Frances Martin asked her to stand in for a sick teacher, and she stayed on, giving classes in Latin, English, and natural history, until the school closed. She also helped at the Working Women's College, where one of the male teachers, Arthur Munby, described her as good-looking, 'buxom', and looking 'like a more intelligent dairymaid'. At a soirée there in 1866 she '*whistled* an elaborate accompaniment of a song which her sister sang and played'. 'I never heard a lady whistle before,' Munby mused.[77]

The movement for improving the education of women and girls during the second half of the nineteenth century was inevitably a patchwork of networks and pressure groups which did not always harmonise with one another. The issue was sometimes dealt with in conjunction with agitation for general education; after all, until the Education Act of 1870, a primary education was not guaranteed to boys any more than to girls, and both secondary and higher education were still by no means open to all boys and young men.[78] Where women took up the cause of education exclusively for their own sex, they sometimes differed about whether what was wanted was equal access to the same education and examination as for men, as advocated by Emily Davies and the three trustees of Bedford College, but not by Frances Martin. Anne Clough, founder with Henry Sidgwick of Newnham College, disagreed with Emily Davies, her opposite number at Girton College, seeking during her early days at Newnham a gradual acceptance of women and petitioning Cambridge University to institute special examinations for them.[79]

Sometimes female education was discussed as part of the larger movement for women's political and civil rights; in their *English Woman's Journal*, published from 1858 to 1864, Bessie Rayner Parkes and Barbara Leigh Smith – since her marriage in 1857 Barbara Bodichon – agitated for equal education, decent working conditions for working-class women, a broadening of the employment possibilities for women, and equal property rights.[80] The National Association for the Promotion of Social Science, founded in 1857, accepted papers from women at its congresses; one by

Emily Davies on 'Medicine as a Profession for Women' was read out at the Association's meeting in June 1862. A friend of Miss Davies, Emily Faithfull, was a member of its committee, along with Bessie Rayner Parkes. In the same year Miss Faithfull, having taken lessons from a compositor, started the Victoria Press, which employed only women as compositors and proofreaders. For its first two years it was based at 6 Great Coram Street (where Walter Bagehot had lodged a decade earlier). Emily Faithfull described the enterprise and its location in a paper given to the Social Science Association in August 1860 and published in the *English Woman's Journal* in October:

A house was taken in Great Coram Street, Russell Square, which, by judicious expenditure, was rendered fit for printing purposes; I name the locality because we were anxious it should be in a light and airy situation, and in a quiet respectable neighbourhood . . . The opening of the office was accomplished on the 25th of last March. The Society for Promoting the Employment of Women apprenticed five girls to me at premiums of £10 each . . . In April we commenced our first book . . . I have at this time sixteen female compositors.[81]

Despite the success of the press, and the approval of its name by Queen Victoria, the National Union of Printing and Paper Workers did not admit women as members until 1904.[82] Meanwhile, Emily Faithfull went on to become the first woman to join the Women's Trade Union League in 1875 and acted as treasurer of a girls' club in Lamb's Conduit Street, a little to the south-east of Great Coram Street.[83] The Society for Promoting the Employment of Women also had one of its premises in Bloomsbury; founded in 1859 by Barbara Bodichon, Jessie Boucherett, and Adelaide Procter, it hired rooms for teaching book-keeping and law-copying in Queen Square. One of the pupils there, Mary Harris Smith, later became the first female chartered accountant.[84]

Societies for furthering women's interests proliferated.[85] Branches of the Ladies' Educational Association were established in the later 1860s in London, Edinburgh, and Leeds, among other centres. Henry Morley not only lectured for the Association up and down the country, but ensured that University College was welcoming to the London branch. In 1873 the London executive committee included Fanny Wedgwood, Millicent Fawcett, Elizabeth Malleson of the Working Women's College, and Lady Crompton, mother of the positivist lawyer Henry Crompton. A prospectus of classes to be offered at University College during the 1873–4 session states that 'the object of the Classes is to place within reach of ladies (not under the age of seventeen) a course of higher instruction similar to that offered to the students of the College'. The convenience of the Bloomsbury location is stressed:

> The College is close to the Gower-Street Station of the Metropolitan Railway and to the intersection of the Lines of Omnibuses between North, West, and Central London, which pass along Tottenham-court road and the Euston road. It is also near the Terminus of the North-Western Railway, and but a short walk from the St Pancras and King's-cross Stations of the Midland and Great Northern Railways respectively.[86]

Among the teachers listed in this prospectus are Morley for English literature, Adolf Heimann for German, and Beesly for history. Their classes were offered until women were admitted to University College on the same terms as men in 1878.

The greatest headway for women was made in two subjects: art and medicine. Bloomsbury, especially Gower Street and Queen Square, was at the centre of much reforming effort in these fields. Though middle-class girls had always been encouraged to learn drawing as part of their preparation for life, the professionalisation of the subject for women arose in conjunction with improvements in printing technologies, the interest in the decorative arts awakened by the Great Exhibition of 1851, and an increasing sense of the importance of finding suitable employment for middle-class women who were not supported financially by father, brother, or husband. The Censuses of 1851 and 1861 showed a surplus of women in the population, a problem which led to much concerned comment. Some observers, such as William Rathbone Greg in a famous article published in the *National Review* in 1862, 'Why are Women Redundant?', suggested emigration as the solution to the surplus of 500,000 women, while others, mainly women, argued for the urgent extension of employment opportunities at home for both middle-class and working-class women. Harriet Martineau wrote 'Female Industry' for the *Edinburgh Review* in 1859; Frances Power Cobbe published 'What Shall We Do With Our Old Maids?' in *Fraser's Magazine* in 1862; and Jessie Boucherett suggested 'How to Provide for Superfluous Women' in an essay of 1869.[87]

In 1837 a Government School of Design had been founded with the aim of raising the standard of British manufacture; the school became closely involved with plans for the Great Exhibition opened in Joseph Paxton's great

Crystal Palace in Hyde Park in May 1851. The full title of the Exhibition, organised by the civil servant Henry Cole and encouraged by Prince Albert, was The Great Exhibition of the Works of Industry of All Nations. Industrial design and innovation were shown off to the six million visitors to Hyde Park for the five-month duration of the Exhibition, with the objects on display ranging from the largest known diamond, the Koh-i-noor, to new designs for locks, daguerreotypes, an automatic machine for counting votes, various uses of cast iron, as well as handicrafts from across the world.[88]

A female department of the Government School of Design was added in 1842, known first as the Female School of Design and later as the Female School of Art, under which name it became well known a decade later in its premises in Gower Street. Unlike the male school, which was largely intended for artisans (the Royal College of Art catering for young gentlemen wishing to become painters and sculptors, rather than designers of manufactured objects), the female school was established, according to its committee of management, partly 'to enable young women of the middle class to obtain an honourable and profitable employment'.[89] Women could not study fine art until the founding of the Slade School in University College in 1871, but they were now included in practical training. One reason for this was the recognition that those who had no support from father or husband needed to find employment; another was the acceptance that women would naturally know something about home decoration and could therefore, if properly trained, help to 'improve ornamental design in manufactures by cultivating the taste of the designer'.[90] At first the female school shared limited quarters in Somerset House with the main (male) school, but in 1848 it was moved across the Strand to some cramped rooms above a soap manufactory in the maze of narrow streets around Holywell Street, famous for its second-hand clothes shops and pornographic book-shops.

The unsuitability of this arrangement attracted scandalised attention, not least in Dickens's *Household Words* in March 1851. In 'The Female School of Design in the Capital of the World', Richard Henry Horne, a sub-editor on the paper, wrote:

[A]s to the suitability of its locality for respectable young females, I may ... venture to state – with no power to use any exaggeration that can surpass the fact – that it is in the close vicinity of several gin-shops, pawn-shops, old rag and rascality shops, in some of the worst courts and alleys of London, and in a direct line with two narrow streets [Holywell Street and Wych Street, both swept away at the end of the century by

the building of Aldwych], which, as disgraces, cannot be surpassed by
the worst quarter of any metropolis in the world.[91]

The school was run by the accomplished painter Fanny McIan, who lived
with her husband Robert, her assistant at the school, at 9 Great Coram
Street. Sixty-five female students attended in the dirty, dark rooms above
the soap shop in 1848–9.[92] At the end of 1852, after much lobbying by
Fanny McIan, the female school was moved to more respectable quarters at
37 Gower Street, while the examination department moved to South
Kensington; from this time the school was known as the Gower Street
School. It moved once more, to another Bloomsbury location, 43 Queen
Square, at the end of 1860.[93] The *Leader* newspaper ran an advertisement
for the school in its new Gower Street location in January 1853, announcing
that elementary drawing classes for females would open, as directed by the
Board of Trade, on Monday and Wednesday evenings from 6 to 8 p.m. The
entrance fee was two shillings; instruction for one month three shillings, for
three months seven shillings, and for six months ten shillings.[94]

In 1860 it was calculated that nearly 700 women had been through the
courses at the school since its removal to Gower Street.[95] Fanny McIan had
retired on a pension in 1857 after the death of her husband, and Louisa
Gann took over as head. The school faced a crisis in 1860, when the
government announced that it was withdrawing its financial support of
£500 a year and that the institution would have to become self-supporting.
An impressive number of articles praising the work of the school, deploring
the loss of funding, and appealing for help appeared in the early months of
1860. *The Builder* described the school as 'ably conducted' and 'one of the
most successful schools of art in the kingdom', with 118 students. On
28 April 1860 the same paper announced: 'The Royal Academy, we are
glad to hear, has unanimously voted £50' to help.[96] The success of the
school, especially in training respectable middle-class women, many of
them the daughters of clergymen and doctors, to gain 'honourable and
profitable employment' and to support themselves when their fathers had
died or failed in business, was stressed by an article in the *Leader* in
March.[97] Similar articles appeared in the *Art Journal* and the *Spectator*, and
in *Macmillan's Magazine* F. D. Maurice reminded readers of the original
aims of the school and claimed the successful fulfilment of those aims
to date.[98]

The school planned to raise money to buy premises or a site on which to
build near the current Gower Street address.[99] Both the *Builder* and the
Leader declared the location 'convenient for the North and West of

London, as well as for the City',[100] an opinion heard often during the second half of the century about the erstwhile 'desert' lying to the north of Great Russell Street, since the arrival of railway stations along the New Road, or Euston Road, as this part was called from 1856, had rendered Bloomsbury accessible from all directions. Subscriptions were sought, bazaars held, and exhibitions of the women's paintings arranged in conjunction with the Royal Society for the Encouragement of Arts, Manufactures and Commerce, or Royal Society of Arts for short. Its periodical, the *Journal of the Society of Arts*, announced in June 1860 that a *conversazione* was to be held to raise funds 'for erecting a building for this School of Art'. By permission of Queen Victoria, the Koh-i-noor diamond, 'which has been re-cut since the Exhibition of 1851', was to be shown.[101]

No suitable premises in Gower Street were found, and by December 1860 the school had moved to a fine eighteenth-century house on the south side of Queen Square, No. 43. The *Builder* claimed that these premises were 'in many respects better adapted for the school than those in Gower-street' and expressed the hope that 'its permanency' might be established here.[102] Its immediate neighbour, No. 42, was the home of the College of Preceptors, founded in 1846 to regulate the training and examining of teachers; in 1864 these two institutions, already set amongst a group of innovative hospitals and nursing homes, many founded and run by women, were joined at No. 29 on the east side of the square by the Working Women's College.[103]

Back in Gower Street, the Slade School of Fine Art was opened in 1871 in the recently built north wing of University College. Felix Slade had left money for fine art professorships to be established in his name at Oxford, Cambridge, and University College. The London Slade School accepted women from the start, and almost from the beginning the classes were mixed. Edward Poynter, the first Slade professor, addressed the vexed question of life (i.e. nude) models in his inaugural address, conceding that there was 'unfortunately a difficulty which has always stood in the way of female students acquiring that thorough knowledge of the figure which is essential to the production of work of a high class'. 'I have always been anxious to institute a class where the half-draped model might be studied,' he said. 'It is my desire that in all the classes, except of course those for the study of the nude model, the male and female students should work together.'[104] Scholarships were open to women as well as men, and in the early years women students outnumbered men.[105]

Over the years the Slade School produced many good female artists, one of its first successes being the children's book illustrator Kate Greenaway.

An early scholarship winner in 1874 was Evelyn Pickering, who later married Augustus De Morgan's son William, an alumnus of University College School and University College itself as well as the Royal Academy school. William De Morgan, a follower of William Morris, became a celebrated experimental potter and ceramicist connected to the Arts and Crafts movement.[106]

At the same time, further down Gower Street, just north of Bedford Square, another pioneering female artistic enterprise was flourishing. Agnes Garrett, sister of Elizabeth Garrett Anderson and Millicent Fawcett, lived at 2 Gower Street with her cousin Rhoda. In 1874 they set up the first female interior decorating business, called A. & R. Garrett House Decorators. After suffering many rejections, they had been taken on as apprentices by two enlightened men, Daniel Cottier, a Scottish glass painter who himself had worked his way up by attending classes at the Working Men's College, and the architect John McKean Brydon.[107] The women received commissions mainly from friends and relatives – they decorated parts of Elizabeth Garrett Anderson's New Hospital for Women, built on Euston Road in 1890 – but they were successful enough to rent in 1879 a warehouse for their goods in Morwell Street, a small street located between Bedford Square and Tottenham Court Road, then the heart of London's furniture-making and furniture-selling quarter. Heal's, Maples, and Shoolbred all had their premises on Tottenham Court Road.[108]

The Garretts' own house in Gower Street was decorated with William Morris's famous 'Trellis' wallpaper, and their designs for wallpaper were clearly influenced by him. Fireplaces, tiles, painted ceilings, and window glazing at 2 Gower Street were done by the cousins in Queen Anne revival style. These were featured as illustrations to their book, *Suggestions for House Decoration in Painting, Woodwork, and Furniture*, published in 1876 and so successful that it went through six editions in the next three years.[109] Early in the book they make a strong claim that the best houses in Bloomsbury (they name Bedford Row in particular) are better constructed than similar houses in South Kensington. They even express the hope that the westward direction of travel for those going up in the world might be reversed, and that 'the fashionable world may one day return and live in the houses which were built in the solid and unpretentious style so much in accordance with the best characteristics of the English people'.[110]

In 1888 a new venture had its beginnings at a meeting in 2 Gower Street. Rhoda Garrett had died in 1882, followed in 1884 by Millicent's husband, Henry Fawcett, the Cambridge professor of economics and agitator for higher education for women, and Millicent had brought her daughter

22 Portrait of Edward Irving preaching by Andrew Robertson, 1823. Irving, a charismatic Scottish Presbyterian minister, attracted crowds to the church built for him in Regent Square, where he allowed 'speaking in tongues' by members of his congregation.

23 Eleven of the twelve apostles of the Catholic Apostolic Church, founded in the 1830s, which opened its specially commissioned 'cathedral' in Gordon Square in 1853. The prime mover and chief apostle, the Bloomsbury lawyer John Bate Cardale, is the figure in front of the table on the right.

24 Photograph of the Catholic Apostolic Church, Gordon Square, designed by John Raphael Brandon and opened in 1853.

25 Russell House (left), Bedford House (centre), and Tavistock House (right), photographed in 1900 by Catherine Ward. John Bate Cardale of the Catholic Apostolic Church lived in Bedford House in the early 1850s, with Charles Dickens as his next-door neighbour in Tavistock House.

26 Engraving of Henry Crabb Robinson in 1861, aged eighty-six, by William Holl from a photograph by Maull & Co. A bachelor and retired lawyer who lived in Russell Square, Crabb Robinson was involved in the founding of the University of London (later University College London), University Hall in Gordon Square, and the Ladies' College in Bedford Square.

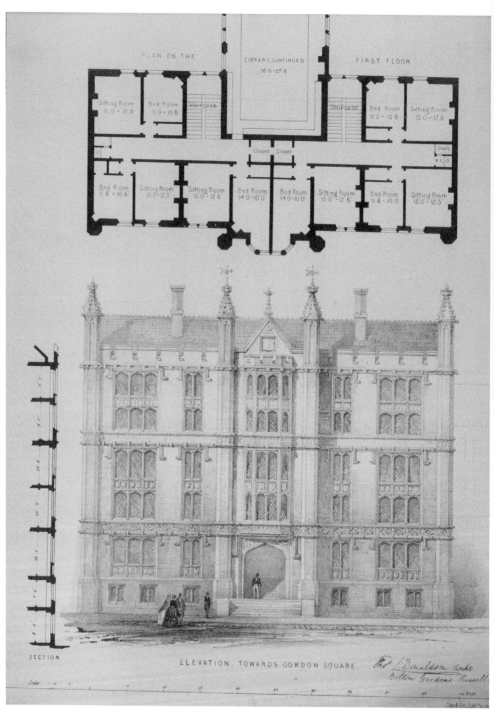

27 Design by Thomas Donaldson for University Hall (now Dr Williams's Library), Gordon Square, 1848. The building was opened in 1849 as a hall of residence for University College London students, finished to a slightly simpler neo-Gothic design by Donaldson, professor of architecture at University College.

DECORATION OF FLAXMAN GALLERY, UNIVERSITY COLLEGE
GOWER STREET.
CARRIED OUT BY MESS^RS. GREEN AND ABBOTT, OXFORD ST.
FROM THE DESIGN BY PROF. F. M. SIMPSON, F.R.I.B.A.

28 Design by F.M. Simpson for the decoration of Thomas Donaldson's Flaxman Gallery (opened in 1851), University College London, *c.*1922. The gallery of sculptures by John Flaxman was acquired for University College by the efforts of Henry Crabb Robinson.

29 Photograph of the Flaxman Gallery, University College London.

30 Interior of the Church of Humanity, Chapel Street (now Rugby Street), near Great Ormond Street. The hall was taken in 1870 by the leading English positivist Richard Congreve, supported by Edward Beesly and Frederic Harrison.

31 Henry Morley c.1847, aged 25. Morley became Dickens's editorial assistant on *Household Words*, in which he wrote favourably of the kindergarten system; he later became professor of English at University College London, where he pioneered the teaching of women, and principal of University Hall in Gordon Square.

32 Edward Matthew Ward's portrait of Dickens in his study in Tavistock House, 1854. Dickens lived here from 1851 until 1860.

33 The Ladies' College, 47 (now 48) Bedford Square, founded by Elisabeth Jesser Reid in 1849.

34 Elisabeth Jesser Reid, founder of the Ladies' College, Bedford Square.

35 Photograph of the Colonnade, off Herbrand Street. The small cobbled street still has some of its older houses, including the Horse Hospital on the corner of Herbrand Street.

36 Photograph of 42 and 43 Queen Square. From 1855 to 1887 No. 42 housed the College of Preceptors, the first professional body for the training of teachers; the adjoining building, No. 43, was home to the Female School of Art from 1861 until the early twentieth century.

37 Female students at the Slade School of Art, University College London. The north wing of University College was built to accommodate the Slade School, which was founded in 1871 and accepted male and female students from the beginning.

38 Elizabeth Garrett (later Anderson), *c.*1865, the first woman to obtain a licence to practise medicine in Britain, and the first to become a member of the British Medical Association.

39 Aquatint of Queen Square from the north, published in Ackermann's *Repository of Arts*, 1 September 1812. The square was developed in the early eighteenth century and named in honour of Queen Anne; the north side was left undeveloped, to allow residents an uninterrupted view north to the villages of Hampstead and Highgate, until the Foundling Hospital began to develop its estate in the 1790s.

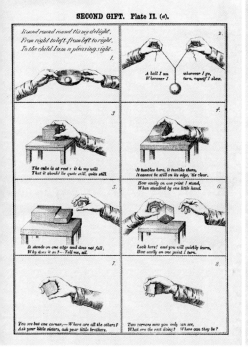

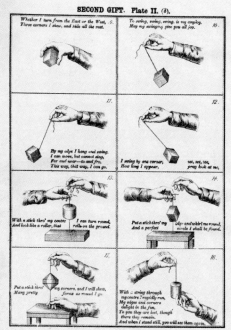

One-fourth of the children hide themselves, representing cuckoos, and sing "Cuckoo, cuckoo." The rest promenade singing the song, and representing the companions of the cuckoos seeking them. As the words indicate, they find each other; when they are glad and promenade together, singing the chorus.

VI.
FISHES.

One-fourth of the children form a circle, representing the banks of a fish-pond; the remainder move about in the centre, representing fishes swimming, as in position 7.

Those forming the circle move round in proper time, singing the song.

When they sing "Now diving," the fishes change their motions extending their arms, as in position 5. They bend the body, or stand erect, as the words indicate.

This exercise is of great use in the development of the muscles of the trunk, particularly the chest.

VIII.
SOLAR SYSTEM.

The tallest child stands in the centre of the room, to represent the sun, holding in his hand as many ribbons as there are planets, each longer than the other.

The smallest child represents Mercury, and, taking hold of the shortest ribbon, moves round the sun, to represent his annual motion: during this circuitous motion he turns round upon his heels, extending the hand that holds the ribbon over his head, to imitate his diurnal motion. While Mercury is making his revolution all the children forming a circle round the room, sing the first verse. As the song ends the next child in size represents Venus, and, taking hold of the second ribbon, imitates Mercury, who still continues his revolutions. The song is repeated,—" Venus" being substituted for "Mercury" in the second line. At the end of the song a third represents the Earth, and "Terra" is substituted for "Venus." A fourth represents Mars, and "Mars is moving" is substituted for "Mercury moves." A fifth represents Jupiter; a sixth Saturn; a seventh Herschel; an eighth Neptune: the names being substituted for "Mercury," as before.

The last time the song is repeated, while all the planets are moving, the words " Planets move," are substituted for "Mercury moves."

This game is intended to familiarize the children with the motions of the heavenly bodies. The ribbons convey the idea of their attraction to the Sun, and their different distances. Their movements round the Sun represent the planet's annual motions in their orbits; and the movements of each upon his heels educes the idea of the planet's diurnal, or daily, motions.

40 Illustrations in Johannes and Bertha Ronge, *A Practical Guide to the English Kinder Garten* 1855. The Ronges were German political exiles who settled in London in 1851 and opened the first kindergarten in England at 32 Tavistock Place in 1853.

41 Mary Ward in 1898 from a photograph by Ethel Ward. She wrote bestselling novels in the 1880s and 1890s under the name Mrs Humphry Ward and she was the prime mover of the Passmore Edwards Settlement, built in Tavistock Place in 1897 to offer after-school play to the poor children of the area and evening clubs and classes for their parents.

42 Portrait by Felix Moscheles of John Passmore Edwards, the self-made newspaper proprietor and philanthropist who funded Mary Ward's project for the cultural and educational settlement on Tavistock Place which bore his name.

43 Extract from Passmore Edwards's letter to Mary Ward, 3 November 1894, showing his disappointment at the location chosen for the settlement for local poor people, the relatively affluent neighbourhood of 'kid-glovish' Russell Square.

44 The Passmore Edwards Settlement (now Mary Ward House), Tavistock Place, designed by two Bloomsbury architects, Cecil Brewer and Arnold Dunbar Smith, and opened in 1897. The illustration, by C. Henzell-Ashcroft, was published in *The Building News*, 19 October 1900.

Philippa to live with Agnes in Gower Street. With Agnes continuing her architectural and interior decorating work and Millicent a leading light in the women's suffrage movement, their house became a headquarters for reforming women and their supporters. The new plan was to build in Bloomsbury a block of purpose-built flats for single middle-class women earning their own living in London away from the family home. Two such blocks had been built in Chelsea in 1882 and 1888, and Millicent and Agnes were at the centre of the newly founded society, the Ladies' Residential Chambers Ltd. Agnes's former master Brydon was hired as architect for the block, which was built in Chenies Street, linking Gower Street and Tottenham Court Road, just north of Bedford Square.

Among those who held shares in the Ladies' Residential Chambers company in its early years were Millicent, who presided over the opening of the block in May 1889, Agnes Garrett, Louisa Gann, principal of the Female School of Art in Queen Square, and the Garretts' near neighbour Fanny Wilkinson of 6 Gower Street, the first professional woman landscape gardener.[111] (Both No. 2 and No. 6 Gower Street were thus being used for business and professional purposes, against the strict terms of the Bedford Estate lease, though the Garretts and Fanny Wilkinson with her bookbinder sister Louisa were discreet enough not to put up brass plates on their doors advertising their respective trades.[112])

One of the first residents of Chenies Street was typical of the generation of young, or youngish, middle-class women who were trying to make a respectable career in London. Adeline Sergeant's father, a Methodist minister, had died in 1870, at which time she had a scholarship to study at Queen's College, Harley Street; her mother died a year later, and she became a governess in Kent, then moved to Dundee to work for the *People's Friend* newspaper, which serialised some of her stories. In London from 1887, she became a prolific novelist as well as journalist, living first in a boarding house on Euston Road, then in Torrington Square, before moving into the Ladies' Residential Chambers. During her eleven years in Chenies Street she became co-secretary of the Recreative Evening Schools Association in the St Pancras district and manager of an evening school in the area.[113] Many of her novels concern young women making their way in Bloomsbury, which she describes as the favoured location for journalists, artists, and professors, though she agrees with the architectural orthodoxy of the late nineteenth century in giving her opinion that the houses in Bedford Square are 'dull and respectable' and that Gower Street is not only long but also 'unlovely'.[114]

In *Anthea's Way* (1903), Adeline Sergeant describes the Chenies Street flats as being 'occupied by women of various ages and capacities', some 'fairly rich' and others 'poor', living in 'large or small flats according to their means' and having meals together 'at a fixed price, in one big dining-room in the basement'.[115] An interview with her in 1893 notes the 'imposing block of red-brick mansions' with their brass plate outside, the electric button which summons the porter, and the twenty-two self-contained flats in the building. Adeline Sergeant's apartment on the first floor is described in detail, with its blue and white walls, its Japanese screen, oriental draperies on the couch, 'Persian rugs of subdued tints', bookcases, pots of flowers – lilies of the valley, ferns, and palms – and a large Arabian brass salver. She told her interviewer, Helen Black, that the other flats were occupied by, among others, 'a busy journalist', an artist, a young musician, a schoolmistress, and two 'practising medical women'.[116]

Just as so much medical innovation had taken place earlier in the century in Gower Street and Queen Square, so now medical education and practice for women were pioneered in Bloomsbury. The oldest of the talented Garrett sisters, Elizabeth, and the one who gained the most lasting fame, led the way. With extraordinary tenacity, and fully supported by her father, a wealthy Suffolk grain merchant, she fought to become the first female doctor to qualify in Britain. Elizabeth Blackwell had been the first to practise, having qualified in America in 1849, where she had emigrated with her family as a child; she returned on a visit to London in 1858 to have her name entered on the new Medical Register established under the provisions of the Medical Act, passed to regulate medical practice and discourage charlatans.[117] She was the first woman doctor on the register. Elizabeth Garrett, who as a young woman in her early twenties met and was inspired by Elizabeth Blackwell on her London visit, was the second woman to enter the register, after she obtained a licence to practise from the Society of Apothecaries in 1865. The Society allowed her to take its examination only under threat of legal action from her father; it moved to close the inadvertent loophole in 1868, making it impossible for more women to qualify by stating that only students registered at recognised medical schools could enrol, safe in the knowledge that all the medical schools at that time rejected women. Much the same thing happened with the British Medical Association, to which Elizabeth Garrett was admitted as a member in 1873 after having taken her MD at Paris, the first woman to qualify there. The Association voted in 1878 not to admit any more women, and she remained the only one for nineteen years.[118] But in the meantime medical education for women had been put on a proper footing in London.

Elizabeth Garrett, who married James George Skelton Anderson in 1871, lived in Marylebone, not Bloomsbury, but she was connected with the area not only through her sisters and cousin but also through the founding in 1874 of the London School of Medicine for Women in Henrietta Street, just off Brunswick Square and close to the Foundling Hospital, on whose estate it stood. Though the new institution was supported by Elizabeth, who agreed to lecture there, it was not her idea. She was utterly determined to win her way through and over all obstacles, but she did not think that a separate medical school, established by women for women, was the best way to bring about equal opportunities, since the existing all-male hospitals, medical schools, and university medical faculties could continue to ignore and exclude women from mainstream medicine. It was Sophia Jex-Blake, living at the time in nearby Bernard Street, who started the women's school in 1874, after attempting and failing to get a full medical education in Edinburgh, where she had enrolled as a student with four other women in 1869, only to be thwarted by opposition from both the professors and fellow students.

Sophia Jex-Blake was as tough-minded as Elizabeth Garrett, and could claim the success of her London medical school after early struggles, but she clashed with colleagues and lost friends and influence by her tactlessness. At eighteen she had bulldozed her father into letting her study at Queen's College, confiding to her diary in September 1858 that she had staged a fit of hysterics to frighten him into submission. In Harley Street she studied mathematics, English composition, French, history, natural philosophy, astronomy, theology, and church history under F.D. Maurice and R.C. Trench; less than three months after starting as a student, she was asked to tutor other girls in maths. In January 1860 she took book-keeping lessons from her contemporary Octavia Hill, who wrote of her that she was 'a bright, spirited, brave, generous young lady, living alone, in true bachelor style', and that 'it took me three nights to teach her'.[119] By March 1861 she was lodging with Octavia Hill's family in Marylebone; Octavia is described in the 1861 Census as an artist, her sister Miranda as a governess, and Sophia Jex-Blake as a teacher of arithmetic.[120]

After many struggles in London and Edinburgh to get a medical education, Sophia eventually obtained her MD from Bern and then Dublin in 1877. Meanwhile, she had obtained the lease of 30 Henrietta Street in September 1874, spent a night there, then moved her residence to 32 Bernard Street on Friday 9 October, and opened the London School of Medicine the following Monday.[121] She invited the celebrated scientist and supporter of Darwin, Thomas Henry Huxley, to join the board of her school, and after the MPs James Stansfeld and Russell Gurney had pushed a bill through parliament in 1876 enabling recognised medical bodies to accept women, she persuaded the Royal Free Hospital on nearby Gray's Inn Road to agree to affiliation with the London School of Medicine for Women. This meant that women could at last combine study at a medical school with practice in an accredited hospital.[122]

Relations between the two pioneering women, Sophia and Elizabeth Garrett, were strained. Both were obstinate and self-confident. Some observers accused Elizabeth of being hard – Francis Newman called her arrogant and cold, and Arthur Munby had been struck by her coolness as well as skill when he observed her 'tying up the toes of a live frog, whose foot was to be inspected under the microscope' at the Working Women's College in Queen Square in 1866. Munby described her then as 'a young woman of 25 or so [she was twenty-nine], well drest in black silk, with soft full chestnut hair & an open pleasant face, with, one fancies, something of a professional look about it already'.[123] One of the earliest students at Henrietta Street, Jane Waterston, remembered her as 'very clever' but with 'a hardness about her' and 'certainly a godlessness that is painful to see'. 'She is frank and honest, but hard and politic too, a great deal of Mr Worldly Wiseman about her.'[124]

It is true that Elizabeth was indifferent to religion, and certainly she could be sharp. She was annoyed by Sophia Jex-Blake's strident ways (Jane Waterston was even more unflattering about Sophia in her recollections, saying she could not bear her and that she was not a good doctor), and clashes occurred between the two. Sophia Jex-Blake's invitation to Elizabeth to join the council of the new school in Henrietta Street was expressed in graceless, not to say aggressive, language:

If I kept a record of all the people who bring me cock-and-bull stories about you, and assure me that you are 'greatly injuring the cause', I might fill as many pages with quotations as you have patience to read, but, beyond defending you on a good many occasions, I have never thought it needful to take much notice of such incidents, still less to retail them to you. Nor do I much care to know whether or no certain anonymous individuals have confided to you that they lay at my door what you call 'the failure at Edinburgh', – inasmuch as the only people really competent to judge of that point are my fellow-workers and fellow-students . . . I never said it 'did not signify' whether you joined the Council (though I did say that I believed the School was already tolerably certain of success). I think it is of very great importance, both for your credit and ours, that there should, as you say, be no appearance of split in the camp, and I should greatly prefer that your name should appear on the Council with Dr [Elizabeth] Blackwell's and those of the medical men who are helping us.[125]

While Sophia battled, Elizabeth Garrett carried all before her. To add to her 'firsts' in breaking down barriers to the medical profession, she was also the first woman to be elected by Marylebone voters to her local school board set up under the Education Act of 1870. She headed the poll with a huge 47,858 votes, beating twenty-one other candidates.[126] In 1908, after she had retired to her Suffolk home town of Aldeburgh, she became the first woman mayor in Britain. The council at the London School of Medicine for Women had chosen her as dean in 1883, after Sophia Jex-Blake, angry that she had not been elected secretary of the school she had founded and spent three years establishing, had retired in 1877, hurt, to Edinburgh, where she once more set about opening a medical school for women.[127]

Before her marriage Elizabeth Garrett had opened first a dispensary for women and children near her Marylebone home in 1866, then the New Hospital for Women in 1871, consisting of ten beds opened above the dispensary, staffed exclusively by women, inescapably at this time unregistered women with foreign medical qualifications. A larger site on Marylebone Road was found in 1874, and in 1890 the hospital moved to a purpose-built building, planned by Agnes Garrett's mentor John McKean Brydon and decorated and furnished by Agnes herself, on the northern side of Euston Road, diagonally opposite St Pancras New Church.

Brydon had been tasked with finding a suitable location, and he considered several sites on the Bedford Estate south of Euston Road – more middle-class and respectable than the area immediately to the north – but could find none that would offer enough light and air. He and Elizabeth had also looked at several large houses in both Marylebone and Bloomsbury, but, as she explained, 'everywhere the landlord objected to a hospital' on the grounds that queues of poor women and their babies waiting for the outpatients' clinic to open were not attractive to property-holders in the neighbourhood.[128] The custom-built New Hospital for Women, built by Brydon and renamed the Elizabeth Garrett Anderson Hospital in 1918 after the death of its founder, was staffed exclusively by women, who were chosen from among the increasing ranks of graduates of the London School of Medicine for Women; it continued as a women-only establishment until the 1980s.[129]

After some complex and exhausting battles, middle-class women had by the end of the century achieved equality with men in education. The University of London admitted women to non-medical degrees in 1878, and the first woman to graduate MD from the university was Mary Scharlieb in 1888. She had studied at the London School of Medicine for Women after its affiliation with the Royal Free Hospital. Elizabeth Garrett Anderson named Mrs Scharlieb her successor as surgeon at the New Hospital on her retirement at the end of 1892.[130]

Progress had been made through the efforts of determined individuals, from the amateur and sometimes despairing Elisabeth Jesser Reid to the single-minded and professional Elizabeth Garrett Anderson, with others such as Fanny McIan and Louisa Gann making a success of art education, and Sophia Jex-Blake, though difficult and divisive, achieving her aim of opening a school of medicine for women. They were helped by the support of enlightened men, including a few liberal members of parliament, some of them reforming lawyers, a professional group which supplied a large proportion of those involved in founding Bloomsbury's progressive educational institutions.

Efforts were also being made from mid-century to reach out educationally to the poor, the disadvantaged, the working-class, and to very young children. The Mechanics' Institutions and the Society for the Diffusion of Useful Knowledge had led the way in the 1820s and 1830s. The emphasis then had been on improving child and adult literacy, but also on teaching working men the new science and technology associated with the coming of steam. Now efforts were made in various Bloomsbury locations, and in neighbouring Fitzrovia, to offer education mainly in the arts and humanities to groups of both men and women of a slightly different sort – skilled handicraft workers, clerks, shop assistants, tailors, people like those who inhabited the Colonnade in Braddon's novel *Eleanor's Victory*. While most of the instructors were middle-class professionals, some working-class students became involved in the self-help aspect of these endeavours. Co-operation was a key concept as the attention of educationists shifted towards those groups in society, children and working-class adults, who were yet to be brought into the brave new world of progressive education.

CHAPTER NINE

Christian Brotherhood, Co-operation, and Working Men and Women

THE YEAR 1848 was a momentous one for European politics, with uprisings in many continental cities following the example set by French liberals and reformers in Paris in February 1848, when large crowds took to the barricades and a (short-lived) revolutionary government was installed. In March middle-class radicals and working-class protesters joined forces against their governments in Berlin, Vienna, and other cities across Europe. London saw no revolution, but fear of contagion induced Lord John Russell's Whig government to prepare carefully for events on 10 April 1848, the great day of protest planned by the Chartist movement. A demonstration was to be held on Kennington Common, south of the Thames, followed by the delivery to parliament of a huge petition – said by the Chartists to contain nearly six million signatures – demanding the implementation of the six points of the People's Charter, including universal male suffrage, secret ballots, and the abolition of property-owning qualifications for MPs.

Upwards of 80,000 'special constables' were sworn in for the day to protect London against rioting. Significant public buildings, including Somerset House and the British Museum, were strongly defended, as the Chartist delegates gathered for their march, many assembling at their usual meeting place, the Literary and Scientific Institution in John Street, near Fitzroy Square, while those from outside London who arrived by train from the north at Euston Station rallied in Russell Square before marching to Kennington.[1] Henry Crabb Robinson observed 'great numbers of unarmed people' gathering 'in pairs' outside his window at 30 Russell Square at 9.30 a.m.[2] At the British Museum the erstwhile firebrand Panizzi mustered 250 men from among both the Museum staff and the workmen undertaking Smirke's enlargements in order to defend the building. He sent out patrols from time to time, who reported back that some 2,000 Chartists had marched off from Russell Square at about eleven o'clock, and that they were unarmed. At midday beef, bread, and beer were brought over from the Museum Tavern across the road to feed the garrison.[3] The event was peaceful, and was seen by most observers as spelling the end of Chartism, more especially the militant 'physical force' element within the movement.[4]

A perhaps unexpected outcome of 10 April was the founding of an apolitical, but educationally far-reaching, movement known as Christian Socialism, at 21 Queen Square, the Bloomsbury home of Frederick Denison Maurice. The training college for governesses which he had started with his sister Mary in Harley Street had opened earlier in the year, with Maurice as principal. One of his young friends, and a recruit to Queen's College, where he taught literature and history when he was in London, was Charles Kingsley, recently appointed to a Church of England living in Hampshire. Inclined to radicalism, Kingsley sympathised with Chartism and with the miserable conditions of both the urban and the rural poor, about whom he wrote in his 'condition-of-England' novels *Yeast* (1848), in which he described poverty and absentee landlordism in the countryside, and *Alton Locke* (1850), the story of the trials of an oppressed London tailor, poet, and Chartist who takes part in the events of 10 April. In the chapter entitled 'The Tenth of April' Kingsley's ambivalence about Chartism is evident; he supported the movement, even calling himself a Chartist in pamphlets and articles at this time, but in the novel he expresses through his working-class hero a sense of relief that 'the practical common sense of England' has prevented the protesters from starting a revolution.[5]

On the day itself the radical young clergyman came up from Hampshire specially to observe the demonstration. Maurice had given him a letter of introduction to another of his younger 'disciples', the idealistic and devout barrister John Ludlow, whom Kingsley persuaded to accompany him on to the streets of London. At the end of their day's wanderings, Kingsley and Ludlow visited Maurice in Queen Square, where it was agreed that Christian Socialism – in contrast to atheistic socialism or political radicalism – was the way forward in improving the lot of the working class. A revival of the co-operative principles practised twenty years earlier by Robert Owen, but with Christian faith now underpinning them, was planned, first through the publication of a weekly penny newspaper, *Politics for the People*, which Maurice and his friends managed to launch in less than a month, and by the end of 1848 through offering evening classes to working men in a tiny alley near Maurice's house, Little Ormond Yard, just south of Great Ormond Street.[6] They were joined by two other young admirers of Maurice, Tom Hughes, later famous as the author of *Tom Brown's Schooldays* (1857), who regularly attended Maurice's sermons at Lincoln's Inn, where Hughes was studying for the bar, and Frederick James Furnivall, also a trainee lawyer at Lincoln's Inn. Furnivall had spent two years at University College London from the age of sixteen, studying German, chemistry, Greek, history, natural philosophy, botany under John Lindley, and mathematics with Augustus De Morgan, before taking his BA degree at Cambridge.[7]

Maurice had been told by the rector of his local church, St George's Bloomsbury, that a corner of this generally wealthy parish, Little Ormond Yard, was so squalid that even policemen would not venture there alone at night, so it was here that the group began the night school for local working men which was the forerunner of the much bigger, and longer lasting, venture they shared a few years later, the Working Men's College.[8] Furnivall asked his father, a wealthy doctor, for some money to set up the little school. Ten pounds was sent, along with a warning, which went unheeded by the son: 'With Ragged Schools, Socialism, or any other ism, you really have no business at all ... Don't play at Law and work at School teaching.' Furnivall spent the money on desks and chairs, and on 21 September 1848 the school opened, ready to teach reading, writing, and arithmetic to the working men who lived or worked in the dim streets and mews of eastern Bloomsbury.[9] Louisa Twining, a member of the Twining tea family and founder of a number of philanthropic ventures in and around Queen Square in the 1860s, recalled in 1893 how she had visited poor families – mainly Irish – in Little Ormond Yard, 'one of the worst slums of that neighbourhood' until it was swept away in 1882, and how she had climbed the outside staircases to the upper floors, where she had to stoop under the low roofs in the tiny rooms.[10]

Maurice's group soon became involved in the founding by journeyman tailors of an association which met early in 1850 at the Hall of Association in Castle Street, near Oxford Street. Together they formed the Society for Promoting Working Men's Associations, which differed from Mechanics' Institutions by having a greater element of self-government and an educational mission that was less secular and utilitarian in outlook than Birkbeck's organisations. Maurice's group disliked the idea, promoted with such vigour earlier in the century by Brougham and his colleagues in the Society for the Diffusion of Useful Knowledge, that knowledge was power. Where Brougham, Lardner, and others had taken pleasure in working out mathematical problems, welcoming advances in the design of steam engines, and teaching men to understand political economy as a way to better themselves and improve their conditions, the Christian Socialists were more concerned to bring a moral and spiritual dimension to the education of the working class, to express and inculcate a love of beauty in art, architecture, and literature. While they talked of co-operation and brotherhood, they thought patriarchally.

This more overtly Christian turn now taken by the movement for widening education among all classes soon led to a fruitful alliance with John Ruskin, who was becoming increasingly influential through his proselytising for artistic pride amongst craftsmen, using the model of medieval guilds, and his promotion of Gothic architecture, especially in *The Stones of Venice* (1851–3). Ruskin offered to teach art at the Working Men's College when it opened at 31 Red Lion Square in October 1854, and his classes were one of its greatest successes. In the 1860s the Christian Socialists also came into close contact with William Morris, who was beginning to put such ideas into practice in his decorating company, known as The Firm, which started, like the Working Men's College before it, in Red Lion Square, and continued, following physically in the College's footsteps, in Queen Square, just round the corner from the College's second home in Great Ormond Street.

The Bloomsbury locations of the Working Men's College and The Firm were geographically and socially distinct from the airy spacious squares of the Bedford Estate. Here was a less solidly middle-class area in south-east Bloomsbury, at a point where a number of estates bordered one another, with the result that maintenance and upkeep were not in the hands of one careful estate manager such as those employed by successive Dukes of Bedford. This part of Bloomsbury had been developed much earlier than the land to the north and west; ownership was shared by Gray's Inn, the Doughty and Rugby estates, and the Bedford Charity (connected to the town of Bedford, not the Russell family).

Red Lion Square, home of the Working Men's College from 1854 to 1857, had been developed by Nicholas Barbon as early as 1684 and had once been a smart residential area, popular throughout the eighteenth century with professional men and their families. After the development of the Bedford Estate from 1800, however, Red Lion Square rapidly became less residential. By the mid-nineteenth century it was home to a large number of institutions, which had been able to settle there because of the lack of restrictions on commercial and non-residential tenants. Robert Owen had moved his London Co-operative Society to the square from Burton Street in the 1820s; the Blind Indigent Visiting Society was at No. 20 in the 1840s; the Adult Deaf and Dumb Institution was at No. 26;

and in 1850 No. 27 was the headquarters of both the Ladies' Society for Promoting the Mental Improvement and Religious Welfare of Jewesses and the Society for Promoting Industry and Religious Instruction amongst the Jews of Both Sexes.[11] These last two organisations were strategically placed, as the small streets immediately surrounding the square were apparently notable for Jewish residents. Thackeray writes in *Vanity Fair* of Mr Davids of Red Lion Square, one of Rawdon Crawley's 'numerous creditors', and Dickens refers in an essay in *Household Words* in August 1853 to moneylenders and bill-discounters, 'Mosaic Arabs [Jews] and others, usually to be seen at races, and chiefly residing in the neighbourhood of Red Lion Square'.[12]

The square was also famous – or infamous – as the location of the Mendicity Society, established at No. 13 in 1822. Founded to stop begging in the streets of London, the Society operated somewhat illogically by doling out charity to beggars on condition that they immediately leave the area, and prosecuting those who failed to comply. It was soon attacked by *The Times*, which suggested in 1824 that the large donations it received were being spent on the secretary's bonus rather than on beggars. An action for libel was brought against the newspaper, with Brougham among the counsel for the Society.[13] Theodore Hook was quick to respond with ridicule in one of his early stories, 'Martha, the Gypsy', in *Sayings and Doings* (1824). A magistrate living 'in the vicinity of Bedford-square' is described as 'a subscriber to the Mendicity Society, an institution which proposes to check beggary by the novel mode of giving nothing to the poor'.[14] In 1843 the recently founded *Punch* gave a brief account of the current state of begging in London in an article entitled 'The Mendicity Market (From Our Red-Lion-Square Correspondent)'.[15]

Great Ormond Street and Queen Square had also been developed in the late seventeenth and early eighteenth centuries, on land owned in part by Rugby School and in part by the Curzon family. No. 45 Great Ormond Street, the address of the Working Men's College from 1857, was on the north side of that street, next door to the Hospital for Sick Children, which in turn was adjacent to the Homoeopathic Hospital on the corner of Great Ormond Street and Queen Square. As with Red Lion Square, sales of land and changes of ownership made it easy for institutions to take over gradually from family residences as the nineteenth century progressed, though Queen Square was still partly occupied by middle-class professionals in the 1840s. Maurice himself moved his family there in 1846 in order to be relatively near both his then places of work, King's College on the Strand and Lincoln's Inn. He wrote contentedly three days after he had moved to 'this very quiet and antiquated square'.[16] In 1865 (by which time the Maurice family had moved to a larger house in Russell Square) William Morris brought The Firm, with its workshops, office, and showroom for the furniture, wallpaper, tapestries, fabrics, and illuminated manuscripts produced there, from Red Lion Square to No. 26 Queen Square; he and his family came to live above the shop. The skilled workmen employed by Morris at both Bloomsbury addresses of The Firm belonged to the class for whom the Working Men's College was chiefly intended.

The origins of the College lay partly in the limitations of the arrangements at the Hall of Association in Castle Street. According to Tom Hughes, looking back in 1886, the ideals of association and co-operation were not translated into practice in the meeting rooms of the associates. Classes went on there until 1854, with Maurice teaching history and Shakespeare, Hughes grammar and English literature, and Ludlow French. Professor Hullah of King's, Queen's, and the Ladies' College taught singing, while a working man, Walter Cooper, later one of the first students at the Working Men's College, lectured, appropriately enough, on 'The Life and Genius of Burns'. But Maurice became disillusioned by the 'squabbles and idlings and swindlings and incompetence of the workmen in the London Associations', deciding that they had to be properly educated before they could be expected to co-operate.[17] Out of the experiments at the Hall of Association and Little Ormond Yard came the more coherent foundation of the Working Men's College, based on Maurice's belief that a kind of brotherhood could be forged across classes under inspired spiritual leadership.

Until the end of 1853 Maurice held a chair in theology at King's College London, but his increasingly unorthodox Anglicanism caused problems with the principal, Richard Jelf, who had already prevented two of his staff at King's from teaching at the Ladies' College. After the publication of *Theological Essays* in 1853, in which he doubted the doctrine of eternal punishment, Maurice was dismissed from his post. With characteristic scrupulousness (and perhaps a touch of theatricality) Maurice immediately resigned from Queen's College also, not wishing to damage it by the accusation of unorthodoxy which now attached to him. His leadership at the Hall of Association was acknowledged by his being presented there, in December 1853, with a testimonial from the fourteen committee members, signed by another 953 working men, deploring the actions of the authorities at King's College and declaring their 'affectionate regard' for Maurice and their gratitude for his efforts 'to improve their condition and introduce a higher and purer tone into their daily life'. The committee, consisting of three tailors, two pianoforte makers, two shoemakers, two engineers, a smith, a lithographer, a compositor, a carpenter, and a 'watch-case joint finisher', concluded by asking Maurice to become the 'Principal of a Working Man's College'.[18]

Helped by the young professional men – Ludlow, Furnivall, Hughes, and to a lesser extent the non-Londoner Kingsley – who already looked up to him as their 'master', Maurice set up his Working Men's College in October 1854. Like Elisabeth Reid, though for different reasons, he was an unlikely pioneer of a progressive educational establishment. While Mrs Reid was hampered by her touchiness and the inevitable lack of both education and organisational experience, Maurice, though clearly a guru to some, was unintelligible to others. Hughes and Ludlow revered him, as did Furnivall, though he crossed swords with Maurice on more than one occasion in discussions about the management of the Working Men's College. Three of the married men in Maurice's circle – Kingsley, Hughes, and the publisher Daniel Macmillan – named their sons Maurice in his honour. Hughes wrote in 1873, soon after Maurice's death, that he had been 'a man sent from God', and Ludlow said he was 'the only man for whom I have ever felt a sense of reverence'.[19] Elizabeth Malleson was inspired by his example to found her complementary Working Women's College. The precocious young Octavia Hill heard him preach and was overwhelmed by his spiritual bearing, as was Louisa Twining, who remembered his services at Lincoln's Inn Chapel: 'It was not reading, but praying the prayers, and, in all the years since, never have I heard it equalled for solemnity and deep fervour'.[20]

Others, like Mrs Reid of the Ladies' College, had their doubts. Among the sceptics was Ruskin, who, though happy to help at the new Working Men's College from the start, thought Maurice a woolly sentimentalist, while Matthew Arnold later wrote sharply of Maurice's published theological writings that he 'passed his life beating about the bush with deep emotion and never starting the hare'.[21] History has rather taken Arnold's view; Maurice appears to have been more charismatic in the flesh than in his prolix and sometimes impenetrable writings, which take scrupulousness in debate to such an extreme that no identifiable position seems to have been reached.[22] Nonetheless, it was thanks entirely to Maurice that the Working Men's College was founded at 31 Red Lion Square. Maurice had rented rooms in the building in 1851 for a Needlewoman's Association which had failed. Louisa Twining describes this ephemeral venture in her autobiography; the idea was to cut out the middleman and allow the seamstresses to sell their work directly to customers, 'orders being sent by ladies or by shops'. Louisa undertook to go there two or three times a week to read aloud to the women as they worked. 'I cannot remember how long this plan lasted', she wrote, 'but like all other such partial efforts, it failed to accomplish any permanent result'.[23] In 1854 Maurice made the Red Lion Square rooms available for the new college.[24]

Maurice was not the first in the field. He and his supporters heard of a 'People's College' which had been founded by a dissenting minister in Sheffield in 1842, and obtained information about its origins.[25] But the Red Lion Square venture differed from previous attempts, and from Mechanics' Institutions, in Maurice's insistence on Christian brotherhood as its motive force. In a circular for his new college he wrote:

> The name College is an old and venerable one. It implies a Society for fellow work, a Society of which teachers and learners are equally members, a Society in which men are not held together by the bond of buying and selling, a Society in which they meet not as belonging to a class or a caste, but as having a common life which God has given them and which He will cultivate in them.[26]

In spite of these words, Maurice was not in favour of a fully democratic constitution. In the *Scheme of a College for Working Men*, which he drew up in February 1854, he declared that

> the pupils should feel themselves a part of the College, adopted into it from the first, any of them capable of holding offices in it hereafter. But I would not let them have the least voice in determining what we shall teach, or not teach, or how we shall teach. We may have social meetings with them; we may have conversations with them individually; but no education will go on if we have general tumultuous assemblies to discuss what has been done or what is to be done. We who begin the institution must claim authority over it, and not hastily resign our authority, however we may admit others by degrees to share it . . .[27]

This caution was no doubt a result of his experience of meetings in the Hall of Association. The plan was that he and his helpers – most of them idealistic young middle-class graduates of Cambridge – would run the College with the willing co-operation of the students, but the latter would not be part of the governing body, at least at first. Ludlow and Furnivall disagreed with this, but Maurice won the argument, and the College started with a council consisting wholly of teachers; students were gradually to be added until they made up at most one third of the council. In the event, student representation remained much smaller than this, at two out of twenty-eight members in 1860 and six out of fifty-three in 1870.[28]

Another young Cambridge graduate and student of Lincoln's Inn, Arthur Munby, who joined the teaching staff in 1858 to give Latin classes, noted wryly in March 1859 that Furnivall wanted to read John Stuart Mill's new book, *On Liberty*, with his class, but that Maurice 'objects to it as a contemporary book on an unsettled question' – the very reason Furnivall, who favoured letting students on to the council, as well as introducing social events such as dancing and Sunday outings for both men and women, wished to introduce the subject. 'F will kick', Munby wrote in his diary, 'but Maurice will conquer: for all submit to him, not because he is *Principal* but because he is *Maurice*.'[29] Four years later, in May 1863, when it had been agreed that three students should be elected to the council, Munby noted with amusement how the students immediately proposed a different set of rules, under which the council would be, in Munby's words, 'swamped' with 'innumerable students'. At this, 'all our liberal "radical" members suddenly changed to conservatives & aristocrats in spite of themselves'. Maurice's response was characteristic:

> Maurice at the head of the table had been chafing for long under his sense of this: and at length he rose, as chairman, and losing not indeed his temper but his judgement, broke into one of his most fitful, earnest, pathetic harangues. He was no longer Principal, he said; the College was at an end; class had been set against class, the very principle of cooperation and brotherhood on which we – all men – stood, had been violated; let us confess to the world that we were a failure, a sham – that there was no divine centre of unity among us! He sat down, his frame quivering . . . and his face electrical with noble but unreasonable emotion.[30]

The crisis was averted by a restatement of the agreement that a maximum of a third of the council should be made up of students. Maurice's personality had once again asserted its influence.

The 'brotherhood' of *teachers*, at any rate, despite temperamental and intellectual differences, did hold together. The group was fortunate in attracting members of another brotherhood, the Pre-Raphaelites, formed in Gower Street in 1848, some of whom came to the College to teach art. It was the combative and sometimes divisive Furnivall who secured the Pre-Raphaelites' champion, Ruskin, as drawing master; Furnivall took it upon himself to hand out copies of Ruskin's chapter 'On the Nature of Gothic Architecture' from *The Stones of Venice* to the first students who enrolled. According to his own account, Furnivall realised that 'the working-men we wanted to reach didn't like parsons, and knew little or nothing of Maurice – who had written nothing to "fetch" them', and so he secured both Ruskin and his chapter for the introductory meeting of those interested in the new college. The meeting was held in Covent Garden and attracted 600 people.[31] Ruskin, showing characteristic generosity, not only gave Furnivall his permission to reprint the chapter on Gothic architecture, 'saying, if you like, "by the author's permission for the Workmen's College"', but added, 'If you lose by it, I will stand the loss; if you make anything, give it to the college funds.'[32]

Through Ruskin, his young protégé (and recipient of many unreturned 'loans') Dante Gabriel Rossetti joined the staff of the new college in January 1855. He described the first of his Monday-evening classes to a friend on 23 January; he had been engaged to teach 'the figure, quite a separate thing from Ruskin's, who teaches foliage'. 'Ruskin's class', he added, 'has progressed astonishingly, and I must try to keep pace with him.'[33] Rossetti was soon urging his friends, from his fellow artist Ford Madox Brown to curious aristocrats such as Lady Bath and Lord Ashburton, to come and observe his classes in Red Lion Square.[34] A year or two later another two young friends, Edward Burne-Jones and William Morris, also started teaching at the College. The latter two shared lodgings in Red Lion Square from 1856 to 1858, taking over rooms previously rented by Rossetti at No. 17. (They moved there from Upper Gordon Street on the Bedford Estate, between Gordon Square and Euston Road. Georgiana Burne-Jones, Edward's wife, later recalled that Red Lion Square was 'dark and dirty, but much more interesting than Upper Gordon Street, where the houses were so exactly like each other' that Edward once got halfway upstairs, shouting to his landlady for dinner, before realising that he was in the wrong house.[35])

The establishment opened at 31 Red Lion Square with 120 students, the number rising to 174 in the summer term of 1855. Ruskin left in 1858, but other artists in his circle had taken over, including Rossetti, Ford Madox Brown, and Burne-Jones.[36] One student, John Emslie, who went on to be a pupil-teacher at the College, told Georgiana Burne-Jones that whereas Ruskin insisted on making his students draw in only black and white for a long time, to ensure that they understood the properties of light and shade before they moved on to the use of colour, the showman Rossetti allowed them to paint with colours straight away.[37] Rossetti was appreciated for his kindness and his love of art. 'Art was his religion,' recalled one pupil; 'he never talked Mauriceism.' That he was not noted for his punctuality or reliability is made clear by an entry in the suggestions book for 1857 requesting 'that Mr Rossetti attend regularly'.[38] Rossetti was teaching in Great Ormond Street one Monday evening in February 1862; he returned home late at night to find that his wife and muse Lizzie Siddal had taken an overdose of laudanum, from which she died in the early hours of the following morning.[39]

The removal of the College to Great Ormond Street in 1857 was necessitated by the expiry of the lease on 31 Red Lion Square; according to R.B. Litchfield, an early teacher at the College and its first historian, Maurice gave £500 towards leasing the new building.[40] Maurice's foundation has been a lasting success. The College moved from Great Ormond Street in 1904, handing over the building to its neighbour, the Hospital for Sick Children, which was expanding, and in 1905 reopened in its new building, Crowndale Road, north of Euston and King's Cross stations, where it remains.[41] From the earliest days the College's students were representative of London's skilled working class and the growing class of white-collar workers. In 1854 45 per cent were handicraftsmen, 20 per cent clerks, and 11 per cent shopmen and warehousemen.[42] One or two made their way on to the council; of these George Tansley worked his way up to become Dean of Studies and was accorded the rare distinction in 1888 of having an honorary MA degree conferred on him.[43]

Until his death in 1872, Maurice held sway. He disapproved of some innovations introduced by Furnivall and other more radical members of staff. Dance evenings and Sunday outings did not fit with Maurice's idea of propriety, though he objected less to Tom Hughes's introduction of social evenings of singing, which involved both women and men, as well as popular lessons in boxing for the men. Maurice himself offered Bible readings on Sundays, stressing that attendance was not obligatory; Monday evenings were given over to the topic of health, a 'long-neglected' subject which now seemed vital after the serious cholera outbreak of 1852.[44] But the Bible readings were not well attended, whereas Furnivall's Sunday outings for men and women to Hampstead Heath and other open spaces as far afield as St Albans, a round trip of over forty miles, proved unsurprisingly popular.[45] While holidaying outside London in August 1858, Maurice wrote to Ludlow of being troubled by the Sunday outings led by Furnivall, which had been seized on mischievously by the 'Sunday League' activists agitating for leisure activities to be extended to Sundays. His view was that 'a Working College, if it is to do anything, must be in direct hostility to the

Secularists – that is to say, must assert that as its foundation principle which they are denying'. On the other hand, 'it must also be in direct hostility to the Religionists – that is to say, it must assert the principle that God is to be sought and honoured in every pursuit, not merely in something technically called religion'. Caught in this bind, he concludes: 'I have failed grievously, perhaps utterly, to make my meaning understood', and suggests, not for the first or last time, that perhaps he should resign his position. Of course his friends dissuaded him.[46]

Maurice did not disapprove of allowing women on to the premises; indeed he instigated some (separate) classes for women in 1855, delivering the first lecture himself on 21 May on the 'Plan of a Female College for the Help of the Rich and the Poor'.[47] Unlike the men's classes, which were held in the evening so as not to interfere with the working day, the women's were scheduled for the afternoon, with the inevitable result that they attracted not so much working women as married women of the middle or lower-middle classes. These lessons, of which there is little record, attracted about forty women at the beginning, rising to seventy in 1858, but were discontinued in 1860 after some unexplained 'difficulties' arose in connection with them.[48] In his prospectus for the classes, Maurice acknowledged freely that they were aimed at ladies, rather than working women. The idea was to 'bring different classes more into fellowship with each other, which should educate ladies for occupations wherein they could be helpful to the less fortunate members of their own sex'. They were lectured to by men on history, the Bible, domestic economy, and health, and by women on writing, needlework, geography, and arithmetic.[49] The magazine of the Working Men's College carried some articles arguing for mixed classes in 1859–60, but there was not enough support for such a change to be made.[50]

What little we know about the women's classes comes from the reminiscences of Octavia Hill and her circle. Remarkably, Maurice invited the precocious seventeen-year-old Octavia to become secretary of the women's classes early in 1856 and to teach arithmetic lessons herself. Octavia lived near Fitzroy Square, and was already, with her mother and sisters, teaching girls, many of them not much younger than herself. She was also a disciple of Ruskin, who sent her to the National Gallery and the Dulwich Picture Gallery to copy paintings for him. After hearing Maurice preach, she fell under his spell too, rejecting Ruskin's view, as reported by her sister Emily, that Maurice in his writings 'seemed like a man who did not see clearly, and was always stretching out, moving in the right direction, but in a fog'.[51] (Emily Hill was later to marry Maurice's son Charles Edmund, who became Octavia's first biographer.)

Born in December 1838, Octavia was the daughter of James Hill, a corn merchant and supporter of Robert Owen's co-operative socialism, and his third wife Caroline, redoubtable daughter of the redoubtable Thomas Southwood Smith, sanitary reformer, controversial candidate for a philosophy chair in the late 1820s, presider over the dissection of Bentham's body in 1832, and owner of the latter's mummified body until he made a present of it to Gower Street. Caroline Southwood Hill brought up six stepchildren from her husband's first two marriages, as well as bearing five daughters of her own between 1836 and 1843; she and her husband wrote radical journalism and ran an infant school on Pestalozzian principles at their home in Cambridgeshire. In 1840 James Hill was declared bankrupt; a few years later he suffered a nervous breakdown and, on the advice of John Conolly, the progressive expert in nervous diseases who had taught briefly in Gower Street, henceforth lived apart from his family until his death in 1871.[52]

Caroline moved with her younger daughters to London, where Southwood Smith helped her to bring them up. All of them became involved in teaching, and in the 1860s Octavia, with financial help from Ruskin, started her pioneering work of renting properties and letting them at reasonable cost to poor tenants who had hitherto suffered overcrowding and insanitary conditions at the hands of slum landlords. Her early achievements as a teenager educated entirely at home by her mother were remarkable. She had just turned thirteen when Mrs Hill was invited, at the beginning of 1852, to be manager of the Ladies' Guild. This was a co-operative crafts workshop for girls established by Edward Vansittart Neale, a lawyer and admirer of Maurice who took part in the various movements and societies gathered at the Castle Street Hall of Association in the early 1850s. The Ladies' Guild rented a house at 4 Russell Place, near Fitzroy Square. A detailed report of the new venture appeared in February 1852 in the friendly *Daily News*, explaining that the Guild would train young women to apply Eliza Wallace's patent method of making ornamental glass for inlaying into tables, adding to panelling, and making stained-glass windows.[53] Miss Wallace's glass-painting technique had been exhibited to acclaim at the Great Exhibition of 1851, and a number of newspapers welcomed not only the new decorative method, but also the employment of women and girls in such skilled trades.[54]

Thirteen-year-old Octavia became her mother's helper, being put in charge of some young female toymakers at the Guild. She and her mother moved into 4 Russell Place, where Octavia had responsibility for book-keeping, design, and pricing. Dickens published an article by her mother in

Household Words in May 1856, in which she describes the work done by the girls and their teenage manager:

> There is a large, light, lofty workshop . . . in which are occupied about two dozen girls between the ages of eight and seventeen. They make choice furniture for dolls' houses. They work in groups, each group having its own department of the little trade . . . A young lady whose age is not so great as that of the majority of the workers – only whose education has been infinitely better – rules over the little band; apportions the work; distributes the material; keeps the accounts; stops the disputes; stimulates the intellect, and directs the recreation of all.[55]

In June 1852, the Ladies' Guild was announced as one of the many associations of workers that banded together with the tailors at Castle Street (another was the North London Needlewomen in their headquarters at 31 Red Lion Square, the house rented for them by Maurice).[56] Octavia had by now met Maurice and his friends; she wrote enthusiastically to her older sister Miranda, 'Mr Furnivall I admire more and more the more I know and read of him'. As for Ludlow:

> Certainly there is not (excepting Mr Furnivall) such a person in the whole world. He has the largest, clearest, best-balanced mind joined to the truest most earnest wish to help the working classes I ever met with (of course excepting Mr Furnivall's).

She had been reading Ludlow's 'Christian Socialism and its Opponents' and Kingsley's 'Cheap Clothes and Nasty', which had 'made a deep impression on me. How delightful the History of the Working Tailors' Association is!' She added, 'Do you know I have a post at the Guild? I have to give out the stores and am responsible for them', signing herself 'Your own loving little sister, OCKEY'.[57]

Maurice offered to take a Bible class for the toymakers at the Guild, but when he got into trouble with the Anglican authorities over his *Theological Essays* some of the churchgoing female supporters of the Ladies' Guild threatened to withdraw their support if he were allowed to carry out his promise. Caroline Hill protested. Her defence of Maurice led to her dismissal from the Ladies' Guild towards the end of 1855, and the Guild closed a few months later.[58] Octavia reported to her sister Florence in February 1856 that the Guild's 'foundations are rocking', but with financial support from Vansittart Neale she herself kept the toymaking going for the next fifteen months, encouraging the girls to learn branches of needlework so that they did not become unemployed on the closure of the Guild.[59]

It was at this point that Octavia, aged seventeen, was asked by Maurice to be secretary of the women's classes at the Working Men's College and to teach arithmetic there. She was to be paid £26 a year and to do two hours' work a day at the College.[60] Luckily for her, Vansittart Neale had taken a room for the toymaking in Devonshire Street, just off Queen Square, not far from Red Lion Square, and scarcely five minutes' walk from the Working Men's College's new location from 1857.[61] By 1859 Octavia had added a third part-time job to her load: she was giving French and drawing lessons at another pioneering establishment, Barbara Leigh Smith's Portman Hall school, a co-educational primary school set up in Marylebone in 1854 on non-denominational principles.[62] Here Octavia met not only Barbara Leigh Smith, now Madame Bodichon, but also Elizabeth Whitehead, now Mrs Malleson, the chief teacher at the school. Octavia told her sister Miranda in 1860 that the school was looking for a full-time female teacher at £100 per annum, and suggested that Miranda might try for the post: 'I do think . . . that you would find Mme Bodichon and Mrs Malleson delightful people to work under.'[63] Maurice was asked his opinion, which was against Miranda taking a full-time position at a school where there was no religious instruction or practice.[64]

In the event the Portman Hall school was closed by its founder in 1864 so that she could concentrate on the campaign for female suffrage and the educational work which would lead to her co-founding Girton College for women five years later. Elizabeth Malleson was given the Portman Hall equipment for use at the new establishment she was founding, the Working Women's College, which she opened with the help of her husband Frank, a wine dealer, in October 1864.[65] They took a seven-year lease, at £110 a year, on a house on the east side of Queen Square, No. 29, and began their college on the same lines as those of the Working Men's College just round the corner. Naturally they looked to Maurice's colleagues to help with teaching and organising. Maurice himself gave the occasional Saturday evening lecture, as did Tom Hughes.[66] Octavia Hill taught for the new college, along with George Tansley, R.B. Litchfield, and Arthur Munby – the last-named with particular enthusiasm, being an admirer and photographer of working women in their rough working clothes and a man who lived with a servant, Hannah Cullwick, whose existence he kept secret from his colleagues even after he married her in 1873.[67] It is from Munby's diary that we learn most about the day-to-day activities of the Working Women's College.

Though Elizabeth Whitehead had been educated at a Unitarian school and her marriage in 1857 to Frank Malleson was conducted by Frank's father in James Martineau's chapel in Little Portland Street, she approved of Barbara Leigh Smith's avoidance of all religion in her Portman Hall school. She was a supporter of Furnivall's dances at the Working Men's College, writing to him in October 1859 to say how pleased she had been 'to see y[ou]r circular of the "Four Dances". The place has our most hearty sympathy – it is so right and good that working men & women sh[oul]d have pleasant intercourse together.' The dances were discontinued in January 1861, after Litchfield had written an article in the *Working Men's College Magazine* objecting to the attention to 'wreaths and white waistcoats' as inappropriate.[68] Munby recounted the meeting of the College council 'on the dance question' on 25 January, when 'Furnivall defended himself', Munby and others were for 'compromise and peace', while Hughes and Ludlow were 'severe and indignant'.[69]

In February 1864 the Mallesons had a party of friends at their home in St John's Wood, where the plan for a Working Women's College on the same principles as the Men's was discussed. Munby was there, as were Litchfield and Tansley from Great Ormond Street, Mrs Tansley, 'and six young ladies who had offered to teach'. Elizabeth later recalled the start of her college, giving full credit to Maurice's example. Her enterprise owed 'humble allegiance to Mr Maurice's educational ideas':

I, as honorary secretary [her husband Frank was treasurer] to what was, I suppose, a provisional committee, wrote to many leaders of liberal thought: gifts of furniture, books and pictures as well as of money resulted. Mme Bodichon, John Stuart Mill, George Eliot, Dr Martineau, Harriet Martineau, Vernon and Godfrey Lushington, Miss Anna Swanwick were amongst those who first helped us, and within a few months we were able to take the lease of a large old Queen Anne house in Bloomsbury. Mr Maurice had demonstrated in actual practice the truth which educators insist upon in theory, viz., that instruction is a part, and a part only, of education; that bread-winning should not absorb the whole time of workers, but that adult life should command the continuance of varied learning; that a college of workers should offer to the many-sided nature of man many-sided opportunities of growth and development and means of culture; and should also be a centre of mutual help to students of various gifts, leisure and social opportunities.[70]

The prospectus announced that classes would be held in the evenings, and 'the instruction given will be designed to meet the needs of the several classes of women who are at work during the day'. No one would be turned away; some would go into preparatory classes, while others would go straight into advanced classes. 'On Saturday evenings free lectures to the students on subjects of special interest will be provided as opportunities occur.'[71] An impressive list of eminent men, and a few women, gave these occasional lectures, including Maurice and Hughes from the Working Men's College. Among the regular teachers were Octavia Hill and Arthur Munby, who taught Latin. Another was Sheldon Amos, from 1869 professor of jurisprudence at University College London, who married the resident Lady Superintendent of the Working Women's College, Sarah Bunting, in 1870 and taught on democracy and government.

William Morris, 'a most generous neighbour' who settled on the same side of Queen Square, helped with decorating the College and lent some drawings by Burne-Jones to adorn the coffee room.[72] The positivist Frederic Harrison, of the Church of Humanity which soon opened just round the corner in Chapel Street, Thomas Henry Huxley, Robert Louis Stevenson, and two employees of the British Museum, Reginald Stuart Poole, Keeper of Coins and Medals at the Museum, and Charles Newton, Keeper of Greek and Roman Antiquities and later professor of classical archaeology at University College, were among those who came to help the cause of educating working women.[73] As for Elisabeth Jesser Reid's establishment for middle-class girls and women in nearby Bedford Square, Elizabeth Malleson was not only aware of her fellow Unitarian's activities; she gratefully accepted books from Mrs Reid, and two of her own sisters attended the Ladies' College.[74]

Munby's diary for 22 November 1865, shortly after the beginning of the second session, records that on coming to teach his Latin class he had looked at the book

in which the women enter their names, occupations, &c, in Miss Harrison's office downstairs. There one reads of 'Kate Appleton, *Telegraphic Clerk*'; 'Emily Holdsworth, *Corrector of the Press*'; 'Charlotte Frank, *Medical Student*'; 'Jane Orris, *Tobacconist*'; 'Louisa Cook, *bootmaker*'; 'Emma Wilson, *barmaid*'; 'Lucy Gearing, *waitress*'; 'Ann Smith, *domestic servant*'. But most are milliners, shopgirls, or 'at home'. There are 2 medical students, 2 barmaids, 1 waitress; and 4 servantmaids, all of whom however are sent by mistresses interested in the college. Not a few married women too. 310 names entered since the College opened; 170 now at work there. Home by 10. Many of the girls come from far – as from Pimlico, Islington, &c; and many walk home alone after class.[75]

According to Elizabeth Malleson's report for this second session, 1865–6, over 200 women were then enrolled, of whom fifty-six were dress-makers or milliners, forty were shop assistants, thirty were needlewomen, fifteen were domestic servants, five were secretaries or book-keepers, while the largest number – seventy – were teachers. Presumably this last figure is explained by the fact that teacher training, especially for women, was not yet fully established, and that many women felt they were in need of extending their own education in order to be competent teachers of others.[76] Elizabeth Malleson herself felt like this; from the age of fifteen she had helped to educate her ten younger siblings without having had more than basic schooling.[77] One who had plenty of confidence was Elizabeth Garrett, whom Munby met at a 'Conversazione of the Working Women's College' in January 1866, observing on that occasion her cool handling of a live frog.[78]

Munby had begun his Latin class 'with trepidation' in October 1865. He took note not only of the physical attributes of the female students and teachers, but also of the differences between the two colleges for working people at which he was employed:

Found Miss Harrison, the pretty superintendent, at her desk, with rosecoloured ribbon in her hair; and student girls lounging in the saloon-like coffee room; and Mrs Tansley, duenna to my class. Neat & comfortable was my classroom; neat tables & papers; neat little table for me, well-arranged with neat penwipers, inkstand, name books & so on. Woman's careful eye & facile hand everywhere; whilst we of the men's college, after ten years experience, are rough & careless and untidy as schoolboys. There were seven pupils, all girls of 20 or so; respectably & plainly drest [sic]; probably shopgirls & the like. Most had left their bonnets & shawls downstairs. They sat facing me, & answered ques-tions & took notes; behaving with quiet frankness; not giggling, nor yet too grave. Not one (they said) knew anything of Latin: so I discoursed of the why & wherefore, & they seemed interested & fairly intelligent.[79]

To the question which naturally arises, namely why would these women wish to learn Latin? Munby gives no answer here, though a couple of years later he notes that a new girl in his class '*begged* to join because she is employed at Powell's glassworks in painting inscriptions on churchwindow glass, & she wants to know what they mean: the inscriptions being mostly in Latin'.[80]

Munby's obsession with working women led him to admire Clough's 1848 poem, *The Bothie of Toper-na-Fuosich*, in which the hero, an impressionable Oxford student not unlike Clough himself, falls for the attractions of a buxom Highland girl he sees digging potatoes and washing clothes. Munby met Clough at a party given by Richard Monckton Milnes in 1859, and described him then as 'a grave gentlemanly man, handsome, grey-haired, with [an] air of fastidious languor about him'. Soon after Clough's early death in November 1861, Munby was at another evening party, where Clough's 'charming' *Bothie* was discussed. 'My theories of women, my love of college reminiscences, of scenic description, of hexameters, are all satisfied by it to the utmost,' he noted.[81] At one of the social evenings in the coffee room of the Working Women's College he tried out some lines of the poem on the students and the 'three or four' ladies present, with less than satisfactory results:

I opened the talk with a short speech about the nobleness & noble effects of robust and hardhanded labour, for women as well as for men; and read an apropos passage from the Bothie: and then they, or rather the ladies & one or two only of the students, commented & questioned: the net result being, of course, that these lower middle class London girls showed themselves quite unable to realize the charm of rustic women & rustic work, or even to see that of service and its work & dress, though they professed not to be above working. But I put it very feebly and ill; partly because they are not the right sort of girls, being but weakly stitchers and strummers; & partly for that I could not say out frankly all I knew [i.e. from his experience of living with his maidservant lover].[82]

Small wonder that a middle-class Cambridge graduate could not convince working London girls of the attractions of outdoor physical labour – and more especially the attractions of the female participants in it – so keenly felt by him and by the Rugby School and Oxford educated Clough before him. But even if his interest in being involved in the education of working women had its unhealthy aspects, Munby did more in the way of pioneering education for groups other than the exclusively male, middle-class type than Clough had managed during his couple of years in dissenting

University Hall. Munby was an energetic teacher at both the Working Men's and the Working Women's Colleges, and he also belonged to the circle dedicated in the 1860s to extending university education to women at Oxford and Cambridge. His diary of 11 February 1869 records 'a conversation-party in Blandford Square at Mme Bodichon's' where he joined 'a small & agreeable gathering of cultivated and accomplished women', including Elizabeth Malleson, Emily Davies, one of the founders of Girton College that year, and Clementia Taylor, an agitator with Barbara Bodichon for female suffrage. Another entry in March 1870 notes his attendance at 'a meeting of the Women's Suffrage Society at the Hanover Square Rooms', chaired by 'my friend Mrs Taylor' and attended by Millicent Fawcett, who gave a 'logical and calm' speech.[83]

Munby was one of a large minority of the council of the Working Women's College which disagreed with the decision in 1874 to turn the College into a co-educational establishment. Elizabeth and Frank Malleson had more than once suggested a merger with the Working Men's College. From 1870 some of the classes at the Men's College were opened to students of the Women's College, so when the seven-year lease on 29 Queen Square came up for renewal the following year, the Mallesons thought the colleges could merge. However, as the council at the Men's College in Great Ormond Street did not agree, the lease was renewed and the colleges carried on separately.[84] But Elizabeth was not satisfied with having her women attend only a few classes in Great Ormond Street, where they were not made to feel welcome:

> Step by step we assumed the usual uncomfortable position of malcontents and reformers. Some tentative mixed classes with the Working Men's College had been tried, but the women students admitted to these felt their presence one rather of sufferance than equality, and the experiment was scarcely successful.[85]

Munby recorded a council meeting at Queen Square on 10 December 1873, at which twenty-five men and women 'of various classes' discussed whether men should be admitted as students. '[Sheldon] Amos & the Mallesons strongly in favour of this: others, like myself, anxious to keep the College for women only. Result nil, and general chaos.'[86] Eventually the Mallesons 'carried the majority of our council with us in the change we desired in the college', and at a meeting held in October 1874 at St George's Hall, Langham Place, with 'Thomas Hughes speaking among others', the Queen Square college's name was changed to the cumbersome 'College for

Men and Women, with which is incorporated the Working Women's College'.[87]

The name soon became just the College for Men and Women, but confusion was caused (and has continued among historians) by the immediate setting up of a rival college by the minority group which split from the Queen Square people. This group was joined by Munby, along with George Tansley and his wife from the Working Men's College, Frederic Harrison, and the unrelated Lucy Harrison so admired for her good looks by Munby. It was led by Frances Martin, who had followed her stint as headmistress of the school belonging to the Ladies' College by joining the staff of the Working Women's College. Always dedicated to teaching women separately, she now founded a women-only college, of which she became the honorary secretary.

The breakaway institution found a home at 5 Fitzroy Street (later moving to No. 7); it was called the College for Working Women and it outlasted its Queen Square parent, carrying on as Frances Martin College after the death of its founder in 1922 and finally merging, somewhat ironically, with the Working Men's College in 1966.[88] The first annual report of the new college at Fitzroy Street named among the occasional lecturers for 1874–5 not only Frederic Harrison, but also Tom Hughes, the King's College professor John Brewer who had almost started teaching in Bedford Square, and the Revd John Llewelyn Davies, brother of Emily Davies.

Students in Fitzroy Street numbered over 400 by the end of the first session. They included 153 milliners and needlewomen, thirty domestic servants, twenty-two shop assistants, and twenty-four warehouse women and machinists. The most popular classes were in grammar, followed by singing, then geography and Latin. Among those who subscribed amounts of between £1 and £10 were people we have encountered in connection with other efforts in the field of women's education, including the Ladies' College, the Working Women's College, and the London School of Medicine for Women – founded in 1874, the same year as the new College for Working Women. These supporters included Elizabeth Garrett Anderson, Erasmus Darwin, Lucy Harrison, Frederic Harrison, Tom Hughes, Harriet Martineau, Arthur Munby, Anna Swanwick, Fanny Wedgwood, and – a new name – Thackeray's daughter Anne.[89] Like Elizabeth Malleson before her, Frances Martin acknowledged her debt to Maurice; she concluded her article, 'A College for Working Women', published in *Macmillan's Magazine* in 1879, with a tribute to her late mentor, recalling 'with ardent and grateful affection the honoured name of Frederick Denison Maurice'.[90]

Back in Queen Square, the newly co-educational college also gained numbers, according to Elizabeth Malleson. Sheldon Amos and his wife were members of the council, as were Reginald Stuart Poole and Clementia Taylor.[91] Frances Sitwell, unhappily married and the object of Robert Louis Stevenson's love (she later married Stevenson's friend Sidney Colvin, Keeper of Prints and Drawings at the British Museum), was appointed secretary of the College for Men and Women. In an article in *The Academy* on 10 October 1874, Stevenson himself welcomed the new arrangements at 29 Queen Square, arguing that under the old female-only system the number of students was 'necessarily so limited that there was a certain waste of power, especially in the higher subjects, which will, it is hoped, be now no longer the case'. The Saturday evening lectures for the present session, he added, would be given by Henry Morley, professor of English at University College, F.J. Furnivall of the Working Men's College, and Charles Newton of the British Museum. 'To all who have the higher culture of the working-classes truly at heart, this announcement cannot fail to be of interest', Stevenson concludes his article.[92]

In what appears to have been an unpublished prospectus for the new co-educational college, Stevenson characterised the whole square as a place dedicated to good causes:

> Queen Square, Bloomsbury, is a little enclosure of tall trees and comely old brick houses, easy enough to see into over a railing at one end . . . It seems to have been set apart for the humanities of life and the alleviation of all hard destinies. As you go round it, you read, upon every second door-plate, some offer of help to the afflicted. There are hospitals for sick children . . . There is something grave and kindly about the aspect of the Square that does not belie the grave and kindly character of what goes on there day by day.[93]

Stevenson haunted Queen Square, not only because he taught classes there, but also because he hoped to catch frequent sight of Frances Sitwell both in the College and at the nearby lodgings she took at this time, after separating from her husband. By July 1874 she was living in rooms in Brunswick Row, a little alleyway in the north-west corner of the square.[94] In a story written in 1885, *The Dynamiter*, Stevenson returns to this location, lodging his protagonist here. In his description he echoes both his own earlier words and also those published in *Household Words* thirty years earlier about the dozing, quiet, half-forgotten square. Like Dickens and his colleagues, Stevenson sings its praises as the now-famous location of progressive institutions, including increasing numbers of colleges and hospitals catering particularly for children and for the poor:

> Mr Harry Desborough lodged in the fine and grave old quarter of Bloomsbury, roared about on every side with the high tides of London, but itself rejoicing in romantic silences and city peace. It was in Queen Square that he had pitched his tent, next door to the Children's Hospital, on your left hand as you go north: Queen Square, sacred to the humane and liberal arts, whence homes were made beautiful [by William Morris and The Firm at No. 26], where the poor were taught [in the Working Women's College at No. 29], where the sparrows were plentiful and loud, and where groups of patient little ones would hover all day long before the hospital [the Alexandra Hospital for Children with Hip Disease, located at No. 19 on the west side, where it had been founded in 1867 by two nurses from the Hospital for Sick Children in Great Ormond Street] . . .[95]

To these allusions he might have added the institution founded by Louisa Twining at the house she took in 1866, No. 20 Queen Square, which she opened as St Luke's Home for the care of epileptic and incurable women, an extension of her previously established house for the elderly and incurable in New Ormond Street.[96] Louisa described her Queen Square house as 'a charming and spacious mansion of Queen Anne date, with a noble old staircase, offering just the accommodation required, with a large garden at the back, and fine trees', and 'an old conduit of some centuries ago, an interesting stone passage leading to a well, which was often explored by visitors'.[97] As well as running a number of homes, visiting workhouses, and becoming involved in the Metropolitan and National Nursing Association, which was started in Queen Square in July 1875 before moving to 23 Bloomsbury Square a few months later,[98] Louisa Twining was an amateur artist. She executed at least one drawing of the square, and on retiring from St Luke's Home in 1882 she gave away some of her pictures to various institutions in which she had an interest, including the Working Men's College.[99]

The College for Men and Women continued with the Mallesons in charge until 1882, when Elizabeth's ill health made them give up; it carried on until 1901, when the house became the property of the National Hospital for Nervous Diseases next door.[100] Without the Mallesons to drive it on, the College closed its doors at this point, rendered redundant by the continued success of the Working Men's College round the corner (which had once more refused to merge in 1889–90) and the thriving condition of the College for Working Women in nearby Fitzroy Street.[101] In any case, by the beginning of the new century there were many methods of getting an education in Britain, partly thanks to the private efforts of men like Maurice and women like Elizabeth Malleson and Frances Martin, not to mention Brougham, Birkbeck, Campbell, and Elisabeth Reid many years earlier, and partly as a result of the recent catching up of the state in educational provision. Successive Education Acts from 1870 brought children into universal schooling, the University Extension Movement gave instruction at a higher level to working adults, and the opening of university degrees and of medical training to women at last brought them parity with men.

In its early years the co-educational college at 29 Queen Square had welcomed another pioneering educational movement with its roots in Bloomsbury, that of the Froebelian kindergarten. The minutes of some early meetings of the Froebel Society, established in November 1874 in the Kensington home of one of its leaders, Beata Doreck, to found colleges to train women in the teaching methods of Friedrich Froebel, show that the Society recognised the potential usefulness to its own activities of both the College for Men and Women in Queen Square and the Hospital for Sick Children round the corner in Great Ormond Street.

At a meeting on 27 April 1875, the committee of the Froebel Society agreed to set up a course of about six months to train children's nurses. Residence for such nurses at the Hospital for Sick Children would be advisable, and classes in household economy and the preparation of food for children could be held at the College for Men and Women, 'where rooms could be had at a small rent, as the College only requires them in the evening'. 'A few infants & young children from the neighbourhood' might be brought in for the purpose of such training. Notes from subsequent meetings indicate that classes were indeed held at 29 Queen Square, though nothing more is said about the Great Ormond Street Hospital or how children were found on whom to practise.[102]

One of the movement's leaders, Maria Grey, an agitator for the improvement of women's education in general as well as for the extension of the kindergarten system in Britain, appears to have been a member of the council of the College for Men and Women at this time. She spoke at a meeting of the College council in November 1875, praising its attempts at co-education, but complaining that 'when a male teacher gave place to a lady the male students showed a tendency to drop off, as if they were still possessed by the antiquated idea of the inferiority of women as teachers'.[103]

Annoying though this was, Maria Grey and others realised that the teaching of young children was the area in which teacher training for women would be most acceptable to society at large. State provision of education for children of pre-school age was still lacking, and it was once more due to the enterprise of private individuals that this gap came to be filled; once more, too, such innovation originated in Bloomsbury.

CHAPTER TEN

Work and Play in Tavistock Place

T HE FOUNDING of the Froebel Society in 1874 in Kensington marked the bringing of the kindergarten system into the mainstream of British education. The Education Act of 1870 smoothed the way by making provision for elementary education for all children, though it was not until a second Act of 1880 that education from the ages of five to ten was made compulsory. But Friedrich Froebel's system of teaching very young children through play, song, dance, and outdoor pursuits had been introduced in Britain twenty years earlier, when Johannes and Bertha Ronge set up the first kindergarten for children aged three to seven, briefly at their temporary home in Hampstead, and then in a house they took at 32 Tavistock Place, on the north side of the road, a few houses east of Tavistock Square.

The Ronges arrived in London in March 1851. Johannes Ronge was a religious as well as a political exile. He had been a Catholic priest when, in an echo of Luther's attacks on indulgences and the exhibiting of relics for money, he objected publicly to the showing of the so-called 'Holy Coat of Trier' (said to be the coat belonging to Jesus for which the Roman soldiers drew lots) by the Bishop of Trier in 1844 in a fund-raising drive to complete his cathedral building. According to one account, half a million people made the pilgrimage to see the relic.[1] Excommunicated for denouncing this, Ronge founded a modern liberal Roman Catholic sect, the Freie Gemeinde (Free Community) in Hamburg in 1846, took part in the short-lived political revolution of 1848 in Berlin, and finally came to England after the closing down of the school he had opened in connection with his religious sect. In London he soon met Karl Marx and a number of other German exiles.[2] Marx's wife Jenny described hearing Ronge's 'German Catholic organ tones' at a London banquet attended by German exiles in 1852. Marx himself mocked the title Ronge was widely given of 'the modern Luther'; and Johanna Kinkel, wife of another prominent exile, Gottfried Kinkel, occasional lecturer in art history at University College London and the Ladies' College, noted enviously that Ronge was doing quite well in finding converts and supporters.[3]

It was true that Ronge attracted a good deal of press attention, particularly that of the liberal and radical press, including the *Daily News*, established in 1846 with Dickens as its first editor. The editor from 1851 to 1854 was Frederick Knight Hunt, founder in 1839 of the *Medical Times*, in which he had supported John Elliotson and mesmerism, and who now gave a lot of space to Ronge, allowing him to write long accounts of the persecution faced by him before his escape and now by his followers in Germany and Austria.[4] Ronge was invited to lecture in Newcastle upon Tyne about the state of religion in Germany by the artist and friend of Dante Gabriel Rossetti, William Bell Scott. The *Newcastle Courant* reported his talk on 23 January 1852. Rossetti himself wrote a poem, 'Johannes Ronge', in which he addresses his subject as a hero, a seeker after truth, and now a wanderer as a consequence of his boldness.[5] But Christina Rossetti, introduced to the Ronges by Scott, wrote to her brother William Michael in July 1852 that the couple 'did not in the least take my fancy'.[6]

She was not alone in disliking or disapproving of Ronge. After the publication of his attack on the Bishop of Trier, he had been sent supportive letters by British religious groups, including leading Unitarians such as James Martineau and John James Tayler, and when he came to England in March 1851 he was welcomed by the Unitarians and invited to speak in their pulpits. However, as one young member of the church later recalled, his egotistical demeanour and personal cricumstances 'completely demolish[ed] the illusive ideals which they had formed from reading the descriptions of his admirers'.[7] Not only did it become clear that Ronge's 'New Catholicism' was really a kind of humanism (he denied original sin, for example), but people were put off by stories about his marriage. It was not until August 1851 that he and Bertha were married, and a child was born two months later. Bertha was the unhappily married mother of six children, the youngest three of whom came to London with the couple, and the fact of her divorce and their late marriage did not go down well in religious circles in London.[8]

In spite of this social setback, the Ronges managed to bring the kindergarten system to Britain; Bertha had trained under Froebel in Hamburg, and together with her husband she started a small school in Hampstead. By the summer of 1853 they had moved into town, taking a house in Tavistock Place, where at first they combined Johannes' meetings proselytising for his brand of religious humanism and Bertha's infant school. They succeeded in attracting the attention of a number of newspapers, which reported their doings, usually in a friendly manner. *Lloyd's Weekly Newspaper*, for example, carried an account in July 1853 of the renting of 32 Tavistock Place:

> The Humanistic community, established by Mr Ronge, the German religious reformer, took the premises of the house, 23 [*sic*] Tavistock-place, Tavistock-square, to hold there their weekly meetings of *cultus* and general instructions. On the 14th inst., a gentleman was engaged in painting the solar system on the ceiling of the meeting-hall, adjoining the garden.[9]

Another observer fills in further details of the building and its use by Ronge:

> He held forth there on a Sunday evening; and he had many followers – foreigners, of course – both here and in America. The place in which he met his friends was in a private residence. Two rooms thrown into one formed the chapel. There was a desk for the speaker and benches for the hearers. A few garlanded busts of Milton, Byron, and others adorned the room. Above us was a blue ceiling, with a plan of the solar system. The object of the association was to bring into action the higher religious ideas which have sprung from the development of science, philosophy, art, and civilization in general, to found the groundwork for a higher period of cultivation.[10]

The similarities with the rituals and beliefs practised in the Church of Humanity in the Chapel Street hall taken by Richard Congreve and others in 1870 are striking. The writer of this piece, James Ewing Ritchie, described Ronge's appearance:

> He had a pleasing expression of face, dark hair, dark eyes, dark moustache and beard. He spoke English very creditably, and in German had a rapid flow of language, and harangued with considerable force. I must own that, the victim of priestly hate, I was not surprised to find him at war with all priests, or that, driven from the Church of his fathers by its sham and lies, he was somewhat shy of Churches and sceptical as to creeds.[11]

It was Bertha who was responsible for setting up and advertising the kindergarten, which turned out to be a longer-lasting success than her husband's Sunday-evening humanistic meetings under the painted ceiling. She impressed British educationalists with her contribution to an Educational Exhibition organised by the Society of Arts in St Martin's Hall in Covent Garden from July to September 1854. On 1 September she gave a lecture at the Exhibition 'On Infant Training (Kindergarten)', describing the origins of the system in Germany and its practice in her home in Tavistock Place, and 'illustrat[ing], by means of a class of pupils, the songs and games with which the children were taught'.[12]

A letter by Johannes was published by the supportive *Daily News* in July 1854, drawing attention to the exhibition and especially to the kindergarten system. He explains briefly the principles of Froebel, 'the adoption of such means as will call forth the creative powers of the child and develop harmoniously and freely all his faculties, at the same time making the means of development the source of his greatest enjoyment'. Froebel's so-called 'gifts' are outlined, a successively more complicated set of toys intended to arouse the child's curiosity from an early age and increasingly to promote the understanding of shapes, colour, number, the motion of bodies, and the construction of objects by encouraging play with balls, cubes, sticks, string, and other everyday objects. Ronge ends by inviting readers to 'come and judge for themselves' the merits of the system at his home in Tavistock Place.[13]

Both Ronges frequently travelled the country lecturing, he on the suppression of his church in Germany, she – usually to acclaim – on the kindergarten movement. Their appearances were regularly noticed in the regional press.[14] In Manchester members of the large Unitarian community hosted them, which is probably how Elizabeth Gaskell, whose husband William was a leading Unitarian minister in the city, came to know about the kindergarten in Tavistock Place. Her correspondent Dickens, living a stone's throw from the Ronges in Tavistock House, replied to her mention of it, assuring her in February 1855 that

> Mrs Dickens shall be duly instructed about the Child-Garden, and will see it, I am sure, with pleasure and interest. There was a certain Baroness here the other day, who was strongly interested in some such system. She was a German Baroness, and lived (I suppose) in a Castle somewhere – to which stronghold she has returned.[15]

The woman Dickens alludes to casually here is Baroness Bertha von Marenholtz-Bülow, a disciple of Friedrich Froebel who promoted the Froebelian system across Europe through visits and publications until her death in 1893.[16] There is no further mention of the Tavistock Place kindergarten in Dickens's letters, but *Household Words* soon gave the Ronges their best advertisement when it carried a detailed account of the system in July 1855. It was written by Henry Morley, who had a particular interest in the subject because of his own education in Germany and his subsequent establishment of schools on free principles in Liverpool and Manchester (where he got to know the Gaskells) before joining *Household Words* in 1851.

Morley's article leans heavily on Baroness von Marenholtz-Bülow's book, *Woman's Educational Mission: Being an Exploration of Frederick Froebel's System of Infant Gardens*, published in an English translation in 1854, during her visit to Britain. The flowery language of the German original, reflecting Froebel's adaptation of German idealist philosophy to education, is presented without irony by Morley, though it probably put Dickens off. Morley explains why the system is called 'Infant Gardens'. Paraphrasing the Baroness, he writes:

> The first sproutings of the human mind need thoughtful culture; there is no period of life, indeed, in which culture is so essential. And yet, in nine out of ten cases, it is precisely while the little blades of thought and buds of love are frail and tender, that no heed is taken to maintain the soil about them wholesome, and the air about them free from blight. There must be INFANT GARDENS, Froebel said; and straightway formed his plans, and set to work for their accomplishment.[17]

Despite the sentimental vocabulary, the basic kindergarten idea – so revolutionary in the days before education was extended to children of primary school age, let alone those aged three to seven, and when children who did receive schooling were put in rows and subjected to rote learning and corporal punishment – eventually entered the mainstream of education in Britain, as elsewhere.

Morley finishes his article with a reference to the educational exhibition of the previous summer and to Bertha Ronge's current practice of the system at 32 Tavistock Place, where, he says, anyone 'may see an Infant Garden in full work by calling on a Tuesday morning between the hours of ten and one'. He also recommends the Ronges' recent book, published in English, *A Practical Guide to the English Kinder Garten* (1855). An article in the *Monthly Christian Spectator* in August 1855 also advertises Bertha Ronge's establishment, where the solar system on the ceiling is used for a game of song and dance, with the children representing the movement of the planets. The anonymous author quotes a letter received by Bertha from a Mr Mitchell, a government inspector of schools, saying he was so impressed by the system that he had made a special reference to it in his report.[18]

Having begun the movement in Britain, including helping to set up a well supported school in Manchester in 1857,[19] the Ronges left England, Bertha returning to Germany in ill health in 1860, and Johannes joining her the following year after an amnesty had been declared for political exiles. Their establishment at 32 Tavistock Place continued under the management of two German sisters recruited to help, Minna and Rosalie Praetorius; the latter's name and the Tavistock Place address appear in the list of members of the newly founded Froebel Society in November 1874.[20] The movement had new life breathed into it at this time, with the opening by the Froebel Society of a training school for kindergarten teachers in May 1879 at 31 Tavistock Place (divided from No. 32 by Woburn Chapel), to which Caroline Bishop, a Unitarian who had studied the Foebelian system in Germany, was appointed principal.[21] The system was now in mainly English hands. Two sisters, Emily Shirreff, President of the Froebel Society from 1876 until her death in 1897, and her older sister Maria Grey, were in the vanguard of both the kindergarten movement and various organisations which were springing up to promote female education. Together they founded the Girls' Public Day School Company in 1872; they started the Teachers' Training and Registration Society in 1876, and Maria opened her own training college for women teachers in 1878 in Bishopsgate, absorbing the Tavistock Place kindergarten training college into her college and moving the merged organisations to Fitzroy Street in 1883.[22]

The Froebel Society resolved itself into a council in 1884, electing to its board the young Claude Goldsmid-Montefiore, grandson on his mother's side of Isaac Lyon Goldsmid and a member of the liberal Jewish community which had started the West London Synagogue of British Jews in Bloomsbury's Burton Street forty years earlier. In 1895 the Froebel Educational Institute for training teachers was opened in West Kensington.[23] By this time the kindergarten method was accepted everywhere. The Ronges' astonishingly detailed *Practical Guide*, full of line-drawn illustrations of the toys and equipment recommended by Froebel, and of songs and musical exercises to accompany the educational games, had gone through nineteen editions by 1896. The newspapers were now full of advertisements both seeking and offering trained kindergarten nurses; *The Times* alone carried over 500 such notices in the decade 1881–90, where a mere twenty-one had appeared between 1861 and 1870. The movement had become an integral part of the expansion of opportunites in education and training, especially for women, in the last decades of the nineteenth century.

In 1900 the Froebel Society's Registry for Kindergarten Teachers was located at 4 Bloomsbury Square, next door to the headquarters of the College of Preceptors, the chief organisation for the training of teachers – both men and women – for children of all ages. If the kindergarten system had to struggle for twenty years against a background of unregulated and incomplete schooling until successive Education Acts from 1870 achieved compulsory free schooling for children nationwide, the movement for training teachers also took half a century to force through. This movement, begun in 1846 by a Brighton schoolmaster, was from the start located in Bloomsbury, where it remained, moving three times to larger accommodation within the area.

Henry Stein Turrell of Brighton set up a provisional committee which met in February 1846 at the Freemasons' Tavern in Great Queen Street, Covent Garden. The plan was to instigate 'a legally authorized or corporate body or college, consisting of persons engaged in tuition', who would apply qualification tests to assistant masters in the first instance. The need for regularisation of the profession was clear at a time when any quack or undischarged bankrupt (such as the John Walker who had so embarrassed and horrified the members of the University of London council when he was headmaster of their first school in Gower Street) could set up a school and call himself a schoolmaster.

Offices for the new college were taken in Great Russell Street; among those who agreed to sit on the board were John Romilly MP and the brilliant mathematician associated with University College, James Joseph Sylvester.[24] Women were admitted in 1849; two years earlier a journal of the College, the *Educational Times*, was launched. By 1850 it had a charter, had already granted a number of diplomas, and had begun to examine not only masters and mistresses, but pupils as well. In 1860 there was a plan to compile a register of accredited teachers, on the model of the Medical Register, which reformers such as Thomas Wakley of the *Lancet* had finally achieved in 1858 to put a stop to quack medical practices.[25] Strong opposition came from university graduates and masters of endowed schools, however, and the battle for a teachers' register was not won until 1899.

By 1848 the College was in premises at 28 Bloomsbury Square, just along the road from Great Russell Street; in December 1854 it took the second and third floors and the basement of 42 Queen Square, on the south side (where in 1860 it acquired as its neighbour the Female

School of Art).[26] Like the College for Men and Women a few steps away
on the east side of the square, the College of Preceptors rented out its
rooms to the Froebel Society.[27] At No. 42 Queen Square the College
appointed the first professor of education in the country, Joseph Payne, in
1873. Five years later it was decided that the accommodation was too
cramped and a building fund was started, as was the search for another suitable building or site, preferably in 'a central and easily accessible situation'.
Bloomsbury was therefore favoured, though a site was considered in South
Kensington in 1882 (thought by some members of the College council to
be 'too remote'), another near Victoria Station in 1883, and one in
Westminster in 1884.[28] None of these was deemed suitable, and in the end
the Bedford Estate manager told the officers of the College of an available
site on the south side of Bloomsbury Square; in December 1884 an eighty-
year lease was offered on the site of two houses in the square and a house
in Southampton Street (now Southampton Place) 'adjoining the rear of the
Bloomsbury Square houses, at an annual rent of £130'. This was agreed,
and a fine building of red brick and Portland stone, designed by Frederick
Pinches, was built, adorned with carved stone panels containing medallions
with the busts of great educators, from Locke and Milton to Matthew
Arnold, Pestalozzi, and Friedrich Froebel.[29] As had happened in Gordon
Square thirty-five years earlier, the Bedford Estate was prepared to countenance the building of a public institution as long as its intended use was
respectable and its architectural value indisputable.

The new building of the College of Preceptors was opened in March
1887 by the Prince of Wales; Sophia Jex-Blake's older brother Thomas,
headmaster of Rugby School, gave the address.[30] The chief organisation for
the regulation of the teaching profession thus remained in Bloomsbury, in
close proximity to the many progressive educational institutions operating
in Gower Street, Gordon Square, Tavistock Place, Queen Square, and
Great Ormond Street. The College of Preceptors building still stands in
Bloomsbury Square, though it is not used for its original purpose. That
purpose is continued in the University of London's Institute of Education,
the leading institution in Britain for educational research and training, from
its modern building in Bedford Way, Bloomsbury.[31]

Just as Tavistock Place had been the home of Britain's first kindergarten
and its first training school for kindergarten teachers, so it was the location
for another pioneering effort at the end of the century. In 1897 a fine new
building designed in the Arts and Crafts style was opened on the site of
two houses, 36 and 37 Tavistock Place, a few doors west of the Ronges'

establishment on land belonging to the Duke of Bedford and marking the border of his estate with that of the Foundling Hospital to the east and the Skinners' Company to the north.

The current Duke, Herbrand Russell, who succeeded his older brother George in 1893, was the eleventh. Fortunately for the founders of the Passmore Edwards Settlement which rose at this location in 1897, Herbrand had markedly different interests from those of his immediate predecessors. George had been tenth Duke for only two years, during which time his main interest was in the Woburn Estate rather than the family's London estates.[32] The father of both George and Herbrand, the ninth Duke, Francis Russell, had held the title from 1872 to 1891. Francis was a keen agriculturalist, carrying out fertilising experiments at Woburn but, according to the newspapers, neglecting his London estates.[33] Unlike many of his predecessors, he was not interested in parliamentary politics. He was a reactionary in the matter of removing the gates erected earlier in the century by Cubitt to stop traffic from trundling through the desirable streets and squares of the Bedford Estate. In 1890 parliament authorised the newly established London County Council to order the removal of London's many private gates and bars, five of which were in the Duke of Bedford's Bloomsbury, namely those on Torrington Place, Gordon Street, Endsleigh Street, Taviton Street, and Upper Woburn Place.[34]

For over thirty years there had been agitation inside and outside parliament for the removal of gates on sites such as the Bedford, Southampton, and Grosvenor Estates, in order to enhance metropolitan improvements and allow the traffic to flow. The Bedford Estate now delayed implementation of the regulation, possibly in part because of the death by suicide of Francis Russell at his London home in Belgravia in January 1891.[35] Naturally the middle-class residents of Bloomsbury's squares also disliked the idea of losing their peace, and some of them supported the Estate in its obstruction. A number of those living in the region of Gordon Square had signed a petition when threatened by the removal of the Gordon Street gate in 1879. On 20 November of that year owners and tenants of properties in Gordon Square, Gordon Street, Torrington Square, Byng Place, and adjoining streets, including Edward Beesly on behalf of University Hall, some residents of the cloisters attached to the Catholic Apostolic Church, and James Martineau of 5 Gordon Street, presented a printed *Memorial to the Chairman and Members of the Metropolitan Board of Works, against the Removal of Gates*. They argued that they had taken on leases which forbade trades, thereby ensuring that their neighbourhood remained quiet and residential. Because of the 'close proximity of three great railway termini' on

Euston Road, 'there cannot be any doubt that the effect of the removal of the gates would be to bring waggons, omnibuses and other vehicles of all kinds', as well as cattle and sheep, driving through their streets 'at all hours of the day and night'.[36] The residents won a reprieve on this occasion, but by 1893 all gates had come down in final accordance with the London Streets (Removal of Gates) Act of 1890, including all the Bedford Estate gates and the gate across Gower Street belonging to University College London, which was taken down, also after a struggle, in April 1893.[37]

While Herbrand possessed all his predecessors' caution about allowing the establishment on Bedford land of institutions with their public activities, comings and goings, potential noise nuisance, brass plates, and the consequent lowering of rental potential and attractiveness to lessees, he took a genuine interest in his Bloomsbury Estate (though he lived in Belgrave Square), and was inclined to London rather than Woburn philanthropy. He was elected a governor of the Foundling Hospital in 1897, and in 1900, when the Metropolitan Borough of Holborn was created, he became its first mayor. In 1894, with the ninety-nine-year leases of many of the Estate's buildings due to fall in, he sold sixty-nine houses in the streets immediately surrounding the British Museum so that it could expand to the north, netting £200,000 for them.[38] More altruistically, he proved himself extremely accommodating over the negotiations to build the Passmore Edwards Settlement. The Settlement's successful start was due partly to Herbrand's open-handedness and partly to the insistent charm of the most extraordinary Bloomsbury pioneer since Brougham. Herbrand Russell found himself on the receiving end of a large number of the most adroit begging letters from the formidable Mary Ward, known as Mrs Humphry Ward, bestselling novelist, niece of Matthew Arnold, and gracious hostess in her grand house in Russell Square.

Mary Arnold was born in Tasmania in 1851, the oldest of eight children of Tom Arnold, older brother of Matthew and son of Dr Arnold of Rugby School. Tom had gone first to New Zealand to try farming, but ended up teaching in Tasmania, where he married a staunchly Protestant wife. In 1856 Tom converted to Catholicism and was forced to leave his job.[39] He brought his family back to Britain, but spent the next five years 'of straightened means and constant struggles', as Mary remembered, living with a miserable wife and growing family in various 'dismal furnished houses' in Dublin, where Tom taught at the new Catholic University begun by his mentor John Henry Newman.[40] As the oldest child, Mary lived for the most part with her Arnold grandmother and aunts in the Lake District, where from 1858 to 1860 she attended a school in Ambleside run by Anne

Clough and her mother.[41] Both she and a former schoolmate recalled years later how badly the uprooted, insecure, and passionate little girl had behaved. She recalled bashing in a door panel with her fists 'in my fury when I was locked into the cloakroom for punishment', and her schoolfriend described her standing at the top of the stairs with a plate of bread and butter, throwing 'slice after slice smack in the face of the governess standing at the foot, finally hurling the plate after'.[42]

In 1865 her father converted back to Anglicanism, upon which the separated family came together again for an idyllic few years in Oxford, where he became a tutor at the university and his clever daughter moved among Oxford's learned men. (Tom Arnold returned to Catholicism and Dublin in 1876.) In 1872 Mary married Thomas Humphry Ward, a fellow of Brasenose College, and when he joined *The Times* in 1881, soon becoming its principal art critic, they moved to London. Here they found a house, as their daughter Janet Trevelyan remembered,

> in that comfortable Bloomsbury region, which was then innocent of big hotels and offices, and where the houses in Russell Square had not yet suffered embellishment in the form of pink terra-cotta facings to their windows. They found that the oldest house in the Square, no. 61, was to let, and in spite of the dirt of years with which it was encrusted, perceived its possibilities at once, and came to an agreement with its owner. A charming old house, built in 1745, its prettiest feature was a small square entrance-hall, with eighteenth-century stucco-work on the walls, from which a wide staircase ascended to the drawing-room, giving an impression of space rare in a *bourgeois* London house. At the back was a good-sized strip of garden shaded by tall old plane-trees and running down to meet the gardens of Queen Square, for No. 61 stood on the east side of [Russell] square and adjoined the first house of Southampton Row.[43]

Their house, built half a century before the rest of Russell Square, and demolished in 1905–11 to make way for the building of the Imperial Hotel, was to be the headquarters for the next ten years of Mary Ward's educational projects. First, though, she published articles, translations, and fiction, finding herself an overnight success with her second novel, *Robert Elsmere*, published in 1888. This work absorbs and transposes all her experience of her parents' unhappy marriage, the result of irreconcilable differences in their religious views, of the intellectual life of Oxford which she had enjoyed, of her wide reading in European literature, philosophy, and history, and of her fascinated and repelled response to her father's intermittent thraldom to the influential Cardinal Newman. Robert Elsmere is a clergyman who to the despair of his devout wife suffers doubts about the Thirty-Nine Articles; Elsmere leaves his pulpit in order to do social work among the poor in London's East End, where he dies of tuberculosis and overwork.[44]

Elsmere is modelled closely on an Oxford academic Mary Ward had admired, T.H. Green, one of the first non-clergymen to hold a fellowship after the liberalising of the rules at Oxford, rules which had earlier caused Clough to resign his fellowship on being unable to sign the Articles. Green was in favour of extending the franchise and he was active in movements to open university education to the working class and to women. His religious philosophy was one of Christian brotherhood not dependent on dogma or miracles; after his early death in 1882, his pupil and admirer Arnold Toynbee planned to carry out Green's social philosophy in the first London 'settlement'. Called Toynbee Hall, it was established in Whitechapel in 1883, after Toynbee's own untimely death, by his collaborator Canon Barnett, vicar of St Jude's, Whitechapel. Toynbee Hall was the first such institution set up by Oxford academics in a poor London neighbourhood, where – in a half-echo of the origins of Maurice's Working Men's College, but in this case by means of a residential establishment – young Oxford graduates lived in the settlement building, teaching and ministering to the poor of the locality. (The second such settlement, organised by the High Church Anglicans of Keble College, Oxford, and supported by Octavia Hill, was Oxford House, opened in 1884 to offer clubs and activities for working boys and men in another poor East End neighbourhood, Bethnal Green.)

In a further echo of Maurice, Mary Ward's hero in her novel founds the 'New Brotherhood of Christ'. Where Elsmere and his author differed from both Maurice and the Anglican founders of Toynbee Hall and Oxford House was in the non-denominational nature of their Christian belief. One of the most astute critics of *Robert Elsmere*, Richard Holt Hutton, late of University Hall, wrote of the novel's 'curious Arnoldian intensity of resolve to make people at once believe more than they did before, and reject more than they rejected before'.[45] Comparing Mary Ward's position to that of her uncle Matthew, Hutton recognises as 'Arnoldian' her acceptance of Christ as the type of the good man, while she remains unconvinced by all forms of Christian dogma. 'Nothing is clear', she had written to her father in 1873, 'except the personal character of Christ and [the] view of Him as the founder and lawgiver of a new society.' 'The more I read and think over the New Testament the more impossible it seems to me to accept what is ordinarily called the scheme of Christianity.'[46]

Having made her name and a large amount of money from the publication of *Robert Elsmere* – she later noted that half a million copies had been sold in America within a year, and that in Britain 'an edition of 5000 copies a fortnight was the rule for many months after the one-volume edition appeared'[47] – Mary Ward continued to write successful novels, but she also had the idea of putting into practice herself some of Elsmere/Green's social ideals. In February 1890 she held a meeting in her elegant Russell Square house of social reformers who included the venerable Unitarian of Gordon Square James Martineau, the Revd Stopford Brooke, her friend Lord Carlisle, 'and a group of other religious Liberals'.[48] Stopford Brooke was the minister of Bedford Chapel in Charlotte Street (later incorporated into Shaftesbury Avenue, just south of New Oxford Street), which the Wards attended. He was an unorthodox Anglican, who announced in a sermon in 1880 that he no longer believed in the Incarnation and was leaving the Church of England. As the chapel was a proprietary one and not consecrated for marriages and christenings, he was able to stay on among his faithful congregation, offering a 'modified edition of Anglican prayers', as Mary Ward described it in 1893.[49]

As one of those who met in her dining room in February 1890 recalled:

Mrs Ward was the moving and executive force; the rest of us were simply admiring and sympathetic spectators of her enterprise and zeal. It is delightful to recall her abounding activity and enthusiasm. Difficulties were overcome, criticisms answered, work was carried on with extraordinary devotion and skill . . . At last, early in March, 1890, a scheme for the establishment of a Settlement at University Hall, Gordon Square, in a part of the old building belonging to Dr Williams's Trustees, was agreed upon.[50]

Dr Williams's Library had just succeeded in taking over University Hall, to the bitter disappointment of Henry Morley, who had wanted University College London to continue to have it as a hall of residence. Now the trustees were willing to let some rooms to Mary Ward for her settlement, which was to be run, according to the circular she drew up, 'somewhat on the lines of Toynbee Hall', but with 'a religious aim', though one which would be undogmatic. 'The Hall will endeavour to promote an improved popular teaching of the Bible and the history of religion', and 'a special effort will be made to establish Sunday teaching both at the Hall, and, by the help of the Hall, in other parts of London, for children of all classes'.[51] As with the original founders of University Hall in 1849, the money to start the project came mainly from subscriptions among Unitarians, but just as Henry Crabb Robinson had worried forty years before that the Hall would be unpopular if it were associated exclusively with Unitarianism, so now Mary Ward argued against using the U-word in the circular, in the hope that her settlement would attract a wider set of subscribers.[52]

She was also conscious that Gordon Square (coloured yellow for wealthy in Booth's poverty maps) was a different kind of location from the other settlements, in their East End slums. This potential awkwardness is addressed directly in the circular:

> It is intended that the Hall shall do its utmost to secure for its residents opportunities for religious and social work, and for the study of social problems, such as are possessed by the residents at Toynbee Hall or those at Oxford House. There will be a certain number of rooms at the Hall which can be used for social purposes, for lectures, for recreative and continuation classes and so on. Though the Hall itself is in one of the West Central Squares, it is surrounded on three sides [she means north, east, and south] by districts crowded with poor. A room could be taken for workers from the Hall in any of these districts or in the Drury Lane neighbourhood. In addition, the Hall is close to Gower Street Station [on the underground, now Euston Square Station], so that it would be comparatively easy for the residents to take part in any of the organizations already existing in the East or South of London, for the help of the poor and the study of social problems.[53]

Despite her concern that the Settlement should not look too Unitarian, she persuaded Philip Wicksteed, the Unitarian minister of James Martineau's old chapel in Little Portland Street, to become the resident Warden at University Hall. He was reluctant because of his averred Unitarianism and his awareness of her averred desire not to be associated with Unitarianism, but, like everyone else who came into contact with her, he succumbed to her persuasive force. In fact, she was lucky in him, for Wicksteed, educated at University College School and University College in the early 1860s, and a student resident in University Hall from 1864 to 1867, under Beesly's principalship, was to save the new venture from failure by his common sense and lack of sectarian zeal.

The semi-acknowledged disadvantage of the location in Gordon Square for attracting the target audience of working people living in the poorer streets to the east, those living across Euston Road to the north, and the 'young men employed in the big shops of Tottenham Court Road',[54] was exacerbated by the time-honoured reluctance of the then Duke of Bedford, Francis Russell, to countenance noisy comings and goings, especially of children, in Gordon Square. He apparently objected to the mention in Mary Ward's circular of a school for boys and a playground attached to the settlement.[55] As a result, when the Settlement opened at the end of November 1890, the emphasis was on serious lectures for adults on the history of religion and the Old and New Testament, with talks on Dante by Philip Wicksteed and on English poets of the nineteenth century by Stopford Brooke.[56] Such activities were hardly likely to attract large numbers of poorly educated adults to the Hall.

It was a false start. Mary Ward was induced by the astonishing success of *Robert Elsmere*, with its personalised history of nineteenth-century religious doubt in the face of geology, evolution, and German biblical criticism, to give a very learned speech at the inaugural meeting, held on Saturday 29 November 1890 in the Portman Rooms, Baker Street. She ran through two hundred years of history in the questioning of traditional Christian faith, invoking Voltaire, D'Holbach, David Friedrich Strauss, and Tractarianism and Puseyism in Oxford in the 1830s. Stopford Brooke, in the chair, said that the new settlement would be 'not only a social and humanitarian, but a religious, experiment, which had been suggested by Mrs Ward's famous book'.[57]

The residents of the rooms rented in University Hall, as at London's other settlements, were young university-educated men, mainly lawyers, though among them were also two young architects, Cecil Brewer, born in Bloomsbury's Endsleigh Street, and his friend Arnold Dunbar Smith. There were eleven residents by 1892,[58] but by this time a number of them had become frustrated at the stuffiness of the Hall's activities; they were determined to reach out properly to the poor of the neighbourhood by providing them with more attractive fare than that on offer in Gordon Square. For this purpose they took matters into their own hands, casting about for another location in which to carry out activities not catered for by Mary Ward in University Hall.

On 14 February 1891 the following notice appeared in the *Pall Mall Gazette*:

A circular has just been issued stating that after taking a careful survey of the district within a radius of a mile of Gordon-square it has been decided to take over Marchmont Hall, Marchmont-street, W.C., for the purpose of social work. The buildings, which are situated in a district singularly wanting in institutions designed to elevate the social and intellectual life of the people, consist of a large room, and three smaller rooms. It is intended to establish a reading-room and club for men, and a club and gymnasium for boys. There is no Free Library in the district, and it is therefore intended to form a library at the hall, which it is hoped will serve as a centre for art exhibitions, provident societies, employment bureau, and other special objects not provided for in the district. The residents of University Hall, who have thus set their hand to practical work, appeal for £150 to meet the expenses of the first year, this sum including the cost of alterations and necessary additions, &c.[59]

The prime mover in this frank attempt to do the social work which seemed not to be a priority of Mary Ward and her friends was a lawyer resident in University Hall, Alfred Robinson. Marchmont Hall was a small building squeezed between two houses on Marchmont Street, which runs from north to south across Tavistock Place, from Cartwright Gardens (then known as Burton Crescent) in the north to Bernard Street in the south, one block to the east of Tavistock Square. In fixing on it, Robinson and his colleagues were taking the Settlement out from its genteel location in Gordon Square to a much more crowded and deprived part of Bloomsbury, though it was only a five-minute walk from one to the other. Marchmont Street belonged partly to the Foundling Hospital Estate – the part south of Tavistock Place – and partly to the Skinners' Company – the section north of Tavistock Place, where Marchmont Hall was located at No. 94. It was close to the troublesome north-eastern boundary of the Bedford Estate, where Tavistock House and the adjoining Russell and Bedford Houses suffered the nuisances frequently alluded to in the reports of the Bedford Estate managers, especially towards the end of the century. Marchmont Street was one of the few streets in Bloomsbury where shops, particularly those selling food and household wares, were licensed. From at least the 1810s both the Foundling Estate and the Skinners' Company had permitted residents to turn their ground floor parlours into small shops, though strict regulations were applied as to the style of shopfront which was allowed in these buildings, built for the two estates by James Burton in the early years of the century.[60]

Marchmont Hall was a success. It welcomed women and girls as well as men and boys; the atmosphere was undaunting and the tone of the activities distinctly democratic. A printed sheet written by Robinson entitled

'Marchmont Hall. What are we driving at?' describes the Sunday evening lecture schedule planned for the Hall. The subjects would include history, literature, labour questions, the lives of great men. All would 'concern work-a-day people'. 'We believe in the freedom of the human spirit – that each man has the right to work out his own relations with the Power behind the world.' 'We believe in Democracy.' Another sheet, 'Marchmont Hall Songs', underlines the left-wing credentials. The song sheet contains the words to Burns's 'A Man's a Man for a' That', Walt Whitman's 'Come, I will make the continent indissoluble' (from *Leaves of Grass*, 1872), Charles Kingsley's 'The Day of the Lord is at hand, at hand' (from *Poems*, 1889), and William Morris's 'I heard men saying, Leave hope and praying' (in *Chants for Socialists*, 1884).[61]

Despite the fact that the premises were 'ill-built, ill-ventilated, insanitary', according to one contemporary account, and 'little more than a shed' with a leaking roof at the centre of 'a very drab neighbourhood', according to the later reminiscences of a settlement worker, Marchmont Hall soon became crowded with working people and their children.[62] It was immediately clear to Mary Ward and Wicksteed that University Hall was no match for Marchmont Hall in attracting those whom they wished to help. Mary Ward was reluctant to give up the predominantly religious tone of the offerings in Gordon Square, but her Unitarian colleague pointed out in a remarkable letter to her, written on 1 March 1891, barely two weeks after the press announcement of the acquisition of Marchmont Hall, that Robinson and his supporters were on the right track:

My Dear Mrs Ward,
I have slept on it, and spent a few hours in the country on it, and had an hour's talk with Mr Darbishire on it, and given it all my very best and most anxious thought, and in the main I am clear.
    1st: We cannot get good work out of men unless we give them their heads.
    2nd: I firmly believe that (with possibly one or two exceptions) the men are not actuated by any want of sympathy in their unwillingness to enter into any pledges [i.e. to teach 'a broad religion' at Marchmont Hall, as requested by Mary Ward], but simply by a desire to know more of the people and their wants before they commit themselves.
    3rd: That they are setting about the special work they contemplate in a spirit that has every promise of doing us all the greatest credit and that if the question is not forced there is every prospect of a growing sympathy on their part; whereas if they are pressed for a pledge they will

either give it under a sense of constraint which will be deplorable or refuse it which would be a scandal, and indeed a declaration of war fatal to our scheme.[63]

To her credit Mary Ward saw the sense in this, and backed down from a confrontation with the University Hall residents. The two halls carried on separately for another two years, during which time Mary Ward visited Marchmont Hall to give talks and joined in the social outreach activities. According to one voluntary worker, writing in the *In Memoriam* booklet prepared by the Settlement in 1921 to commemorate her achievements, she threw herself into this work. She 'brought in the rough women from Derry Street [a tiny street in the poor north-eastern corner of Bloomsbury, near Gray's Inn Road], who came reeking of drink', the helper, Mrs Gray, recalled, adding, 'Nothing was too small for Mrs Ward's interest; she was the head and tail of all the work that went on.'[64]

By 1893 it had become clear that the accommodation in University Hall was too big and too expensive, at a rent of £300 a year, for the relatively small number of residents and attenders at lectures, while Marchmont Hall, rented for £45 a year, rising to £60, which could squeeze in a maximum of 150 and was visited by many more, was too small to fulfil its plans.[65] The sensible thing was to merge the two endeavours, and for this Mary Ward decided that a completely new building was required. If Robinson and his friends could bring along the working people from Marchmont Hall whom they had attracted where she could not, she would do what she did best, namely use her name, her connections, her determination, and her charm to raise the necessary money. She set about this task in earnest early in 1894.

Herbrand Russell, eleventh Duke of Bedford, was one powerful man she drew into her plan. As a prominent resident of Russell Square until January 1891, when she moved reluctantly to 'terribly "smart"' Grosvenor Place on the earmarking of her old house for acquisition and eventual demolition to make way for the Imperial Hotel, she had met the Duke socially and was on easy terms with him. She also turned her attention to a man she did not yet know personally, the wealthy and famously philanthropic newspaper magnate John Passmore Edwards, who lived at 51 Bedford Square. Neither the Duke nor Passmore Edwards could resist her unstoppable requests, though both tried from time to time.

In February 1893 Alfred Robinson resigned as a resident of University Hall, as he wished to get married; despite his differences with Mary Ward,

he continued his connection with the Settlement, acting as her solicitor in
the negotiations over a site for the new building. Wicksteed also resigned at
this time, giving up his wardenship at University Hall in order to devote
more time to his lecturing for the London Society for the Extension of
University Teaching. He was replaced by John Russell, formerly a master at
University College School.[66] Things went on as before at both Marchmont
Hall and University Hall, but meanwhile Mary Ward looked around for a
good location for her new settlement and at the same time set about seeking
financial support. She made her first approach to Passmore Edwards in a
letter of 17 March 1894 written from her holiday address in the Italian lakes:

> Dear Sir – I have long had it in my mind to write to you to ask whether
> it would be possible for you, amid all the kind & generous things you do
> for the poor of London, to help us with our 'Settlement' at University
> Hall . . . We have reached the utmost limits of what can be done in our
> tiny rooms at Marchmont Street, . . . & University Hall itself is not the
> best home we c[oul]d find for a 'Settlement' of the sort. Our men want
> to be close to their work, as they are at Toynbee, & we want larger
> premises in every way for the social side of it. We have now 100 paying
> Associates of Marchmont Hall, of the working class, most of them
> much attached to the little place, & to the Warden & Residents of
> University Hall. We feel that we have in them a nucleus wherefrom to
> start a new work in the neighbourhood on a larger scale . . . We cannot
> however find either buildings or site *close* to Marchmont Hall. The
> Bedford Estate has been searched in vain, & we feel now that we must
> cross the Euston Road & settle ourselves in Somerstown where there is
> a thick working-class population, where such a 'Settlement' seems to be
> really wanted . . . We want a concert room to hold some 400 or 500
> people, a gymnasium, a reading room, two or three class rooms, a coffee
> bar, &c. . .[67]

This appeal was unsuccessful. Passmore Edwards replied that he could
not help, as he was too much committed with other benefactions. She
wrote to him again in May, not begging for money but asking his advice
about locations, and was rewarded with a reply offering to give the £4,000
she had previously requested, on condition that somebody else provided a
suitable site. As she had no doubt anticipated, he was keen on a location in
the poor Somers Town region.[68] It soon became clear, however, that social
work of the kind envisaged was already being undertaken in Somers Town,
and when Mary Ward turned again to the obvious landowner, the Duke of

Bedford, he took a lively interest, offering a number of possible sites on his Bloomsbury estate.

During the summer and autumn of 1894 Mary Ward was required to bring all her tact and charm to bear as she corresponded with these two very different men. Coming from his poor childhood as the son of a carpenter in Cornwall, self-educated through reading articles in the *Penny Magazine* of the Society for the Diffusion of Useful Knowledge, and self-made through his acquisition of newspapers, Passmore Edwards had a poor opinion of aristocratic landowners, not least the ninth Duke of Bedford, whose plans to expand Covent Garden Market had required Edwards to move out of his business premises there in 1884.[69]

On first coming to London in 1845 Edwards had joined various reform movements; he was anti-slave-trade, anti-Corn-Laws, against the so-called 'taxes on knowledge', including the stamp duty on newspapers, anti-capital-punishment, anti-war, pro-temperance. He became the proprietor of a number of specialist and reforming newspapers over the years, landing in debtors' prison in 1852 when some of his many ventures failed, but paying back his debts in full and going on first to make a success of the *Mechanics' Magazine* and then, at the end of 1868, launching *The Echo*, the first half-penny London evening newspaper aimed at working-class readers. Soon after this he began his course of philanthropy, giving money over the next forty years to build and support more than seventy public buildings – libraries, hospitals, convalescent homes – mainly in Cornwall and London.[70]

In his privately printed autobiography, *A Few Footprints* (1905), Edwards reached for the language of the Society for the Diffusion of Useful Knowledge which had impressed and influenced him seventy years earlier in order to explain his enthusiasm for free libraries in particular:

Public libraries are, in my opinion, entitled to public support because they are educative, recreative, and useful; because they bring the products of research and imagination, the stored wisdom of ages and nations, within the easy reach of the poorest citizens . . . because they encourage seekers after technical knowledge, and thereby promote industrial improvements; because, being under the public eye, they are economically conducted; because they teach equality of citizenship, and are essentially democratic in spirit and action, in as much as they are maintained out of the public rates and subject to public control.[71]

Having received the offer of £4,000 from Passmore Edwards in May 1894, Mary Ward asked the Duke of Bedford if he could help with possible sites. He wrote to her several times over the summer, sometimes from his London house in Belgrave Square, sometimes from Woburn Abbey, to which he invited her for lunch, and sometimes from his Scottish holiday home, sending word of sites on his land where the leases were due to fall in, and getting his estate manager, Alfred Stutfield, to draw up plans and show her round.[72] One possibility was the Russell Institution on Great Coram Street, which Stutfield reported to be in a decline not only from its all too brief heyday as a place of elegant resort in the early years of the century, but also from its second life as a literary and scientific institution, where Roget, among others, had given lectures, and Crabb Robinson had read newspapers and written letters on his way home to Russell Square. As Stutfield wrote in his report for the Duke in August 1894, 'the tide of fashion' had long since 'flowed Westward', and the Institution was now 'used as a Club which has a Membership of about 80', not enough to pay for the upkeep of the building. It might be adaptable to Mrs Ward's purposes, but there was a problem in the shape of a wine merchant, who leased the basement and might demand a large sum to move out.[73] Mary Ward sensibly rejected this option; in the event the Institution was demolished in 1897 after the lease fell in.

She was more interested in a second offer, that of a site just to the north of the Russell Institution, on the corner of Little Coram Street (later incorporated into Herbrand Street) and the south side of Tavistock Place. She told the Duke that it might be best – and she guessed that Passmore Edwards would prefer it – if she chose land where a new building could be erected 'exactly adapted to our wants'.[74] The Duke agreed, especially as this corner site was faced by some blocks of model housing, or 'artisans' dwellings', as he called them, across the road on the east side of Little Coram Street, which, unlike the west side, was not on Bedford land. 'It might therefore be desirable', he wrote, 'in reconstructing the block to make both sides of Little Coram St convenient for the same class of resident.'[75]

The blocks he describes were on land sold in 1882 by the Foundling Estate to the Peabody Trust, which administered the legacy of the American banker and philanthropist George Peabody. The Peabody Buildings were put up in 1884 in an effort to restore respectability to the immediate area of Little Coram Street, which had 'greatly degenerated' and become a slum.[76] In 1860 Samuel Hadden Parkes, senior curate at St George's Bloomsbury, concerned at the cramped conditions of poor people living in Little Coram Street – he put the number at 1,700 – started a local 'working man's flower show' in the street, encouraging the residents to grow and exhibit geraniums 'as a means of cheering their lives and inducing habits of care, prudence, and forethought'.[77] (So successful were the annual summer flower shows started by Parkes that in 1863 the venue was moved to Russell Square, with the approval of the Bedford Estate.) Mary Ward's interest in Little Coram Street had been piqued before her negotiations with the Duke of Bedford began. Her most recent novel *Marcella*, published in April 1894, had for its heroine a district nurse who visits the poor of Bloomsbury, while herself living in 'Brown's Buildings', Mary Ward's fictional name for the very Peabody Buildings alluded to by the Duke.[78]

On 1 November 1894 Herbrand Russell wrote to offer Mary Ward 10,000 square feet of land at the corner of Little Coram Street for £5,000; he thought he could help her to get any remaining tenants out without it costing too much. She replied the next day, thanking him, saying that the location 'will suit us in every way', and suggesting that her solicitor Alfred Robinson should meet with the Bedford Estate manager Stutfield as soon as possible to begin the arrangements.[79] But she was rejoicing too soon. Her next letter was to Passmore Edwards on the same day, 2 November. With characteristic frankness she told him that she had been 'just about to send you in great cheerfulness the enclosed letter from the Duke of Bedford, when your own letter came, – which has of course made me anxious'.[80] Edwards had written to oppose her dealings with the Bedford Estate:

> Personally I have a strong objection to paying rich landlords very big prices for the privilege of building institutions for the public good and particularly landlords like the Duke of Bedford whose family has done so little for a district from which they gather such a rich rental ... Humanity has claims on me wherever it exists and particularly its poorer portions; and what pleased me most in your first letter to me was the suggested site for the proposed Institution. You proposed a Toynbee Hall for North London. Now your suggestion seems more of an establishment for central London. That appears to me to be a deviation from the original intention and a step backward. I should have thought that there were places where building land would be cheaper and where such a settlement as you propose would be more useful than the corner of Tavistock Place.[81]

In her reply, having indicated her alarm at his opposition, Mary Ward managed both to apologise and to defend herself and the Duke, and finally she adroitly offered a reason for going ahead with the Tavistock Place site which he, with his concern for doing the best thing for the working people who would attend the Settlement, could hardly reject:

> In the first place let me say that I imagine there can be no question in this case of 'paying rich landlords very big prices'. Mr Robinson our solicitor tells me that the sum of £5000 for which the Duke now proposes to sell us the Little Coram St site will in all probability not pass the Duke's trustees. The Duke Mr Robinson thinks will have to put his own hand in his pocket to satisfy the claims of the estate. The sum at which he now offers the site is less than half his agent's original estimate . . . The Duke, as far as he himself is concerned, is really making a large contribution to the scheme. As to the site itself, I am very sorry that I had no idea you would have any objection to it. I thought that Mr Russell [current Warden of the Settlement at University Hall] had explained to you when he met you in the summer that it would be much better for us to stay on the Gordon Square side of the Euston Road, & as close to our Marchmont Hall people as possible.

She continues by confessing that she had not realised that it was 'a sine qua non with you that it should be north of the Euston Road', and she describes the problems over the Somers Town location she had first mooted: no freehold land had been found; the secretary of the landowner, Lady Henry Somerset, had told her that there were already other social projects in the area; and, finally, the Marchmont Hall people had urged her to establish her settlement near them, and emphatically *not* across Euston Road. She assures Passmore Edwards that the new site will bring 400–500 working-class people to the Settlement. 'We find the district *packed* with working people.'[82]

It seems odd that Edwards, living nearby, was not aware of the crowded working-class area immediately surrounding this site to the north, south, and east. He made one more complaint, writing to her the next day, 3 November, to reiterate his concerns. The choice of site was 'infelicitous'; more suitable ones could surely be found in the region south of Oxford Street, in Soho, or near Drury Lane. A settlement so near Russell Square would be 'kid-glovish and Russell Squarish'.[83] But he gave way, and plans went forward for taking the site. The contract was signed on 7 March 1895 between Stutfield and Robinson.[84] A competition for designs for the new building was already under way, and naturally Mary Ward managed to persuade one of the most famous architects of the day, Norman Shaw, to be the judge.[85]

She was determined to name the settlement after its main benefactor; Passmore Edwards replied to this suggestion on 23 March 1895 saying it looked 'egotistic' to use his name, but that if it was going to be used, he would prefer 'Passmore Edwards Hall' to just 'Edwards Hall' – 'there are so many Edwards [sic] in the field'. In his impulsive way, he continued in the same letter to say that she could pledge him to £7,000 rather than the original £4,000, '& if you will insist on calling it the "Passmore Edwards Settlement" I must insist in [sic] increasing my donation to £10,000'.[86] This was princely, and timely too, as costs were outrunning the amounts coming in from Mary Ward's efforts at supplementing Edwards's generosity by appealing for small contributions from friends and acquaintances. By the time the Passmore Edwards Settlement opened, unofficially in October 1897, followed by a grand formal opening in February 1898, Passmore Edwards had raised his contribution to £14,000 (and the Duke of Bedford had given £1,500, as well as offering generous terms on the lease).[87] *The Times*, fed stories by Mary Ward and happy to give details of the progress of the Settlement and its founders, the famous novelist and the famous philanthropist, carried over 200 articles and notices about the Passmore Edwards Settlement between June 1894 and the end of 1898. But the Settlement was not in the end built on the site on the corner of Little Coram Street and the south side of Tavistock Place. So many problems arose, with costs rising and tenants reluctant to leave their properties, that the Duke of Bedford agreed to cancel the contract and shift the arrangements to a site on the north side of Tavistock Place, just across the street from the Little Coram Street corner site.[88]

The new site was a vacant plot; it covered the area of a house, No. 37, previously occupied by the astronomer Francis Baily, who had measured the Earth's density here in 1838–42 with a grant from the Royal Astronomical Society; at the back it adjoined the garden of the soon to be demolished Tavistock House.[89] In due course the Duke of Bedford allowed the Passmore Edwards Settlement to use the former Tavistock House garden in addition to the back garden of the Settlement itself. In 1899 he said that 'we must have an inscription on the mulberry tree which grew in Dickens's garden'; and in 1902, when Mary Ward started her vacation school for children during the summer holidays, he permitted the use of the garden every afternoon from 1 June to 30 September, stipulating that in the first instance such permission was for one year only. 'I am obliged to say this year only because if the *neighbours* raise any objection I must of course listen to them.'[90] (The mulberry tree was reported in 1931 to be 'rather tottering', 'propped up and carefully surrounded by iron railings'.[91] The whole garden of Tavistock House has since been swallowed up by the grounds of the British Medical Association; in the inner courtyard garden there is a small wall made from the bricks of Dickens's house.)

The site of No. 36 Tavistock Place, one door east of No. 37, also featured on the plans drawn up in August 1895 by the two winners of the architectural competition, the young University Hall residents Arnold Dunbar Smith and Cecil Brewer, as a garden space of 4,000 feet from front to back, and Mary Ward's solicitor negotiated an option to purchase the plot of No. 35 as well. This was the last house on the Bedford Estate; immediately to the east (with the Ronges' old house at No. 32 and the Froebel Society's No. 31 only a few houses along) the land was owned by the Foundling Estate. Behind, except for the Bedford-owned gardens of the erstwhile Tavistock, Bedford, and Russell Houses, the landowner was the Skinners' Company.[92]

Smith and Brewer's Arts and Crafts building duly went up on the north side of Tavistock Place. As it was being built *The Times* noted its progress, describing the design as one 'of great merit architecturally and original, though showing traces of Mr Norman Shaw's influence'.[93] The two architects, both in their twenties at this time, were disciples of Shaw, who practised from 29 Bloomsbury Square; they also had connections with the Art Workers' Guild, founded in 1884 to promote the interaction of art, design, and architecture. (William Morris joined the Guild in 1888 and was elected Master in 1892.) The Passmore Edwards Settlement building has been praised by architectural historians as 'one of the most charming pieces of architecture designed at that time in England', 'an inspired moment in British architecture', a 'wonderful example of a social ideal being expressed in architecture', and 'one of the best examples of the Free Style applied to a public building in the 1890s'.[94]

The building, still standing on the north side of Tavistock Place, is notable for its design details, which were intended to be both practical and decorative. The stone eggs surmounting the main entrance porch represent new beginnings; the east side of the building has three trees marked out in raised brickwork to represent the Tree of Life; everything from drainpipes to interior details such as ceiling cornices, fireplaces, and chair backs was designed to be both useful and beautiful. The *raison d'être* was that the building be inviting to its target membership, not off-puttingly imposing in the way of most public buildings, whether neoclassical like University College and the rebuilt British Museum or Gothic like the new Houses of Parliament. Inside there were public rooms, a library, a gymnasium, and a billiard room; upstairs were a flat for the Warden and a large hall for concerts and lectures, while on the second floor the residents had their individual rooms and their common room.[95]

The Passmore Edwards Settlement opened for business in October 1897 with a social evening consisting of a welcome speech by Mary Ward, refreshments, and songs ranging from works by Schubert to the traditional English song 'Cherry Ripe' and the 'March of the Workers' by William Morris (this last no doubt chosen by Alfred Robinson and the working-class members, known as Associates, who migrated from Marchmont Hall).[96] The Marchmont Hall people were represented on the managing commit-tees, as were a number of Mary Ward's friends, including the Duke of Bedford; her colleagues on the original University Hall committee, Stopford Brooke, the Earl of Carlisle, Philip Wicksteed, and James Martineau; the residents Alfred Robinson, John Russell, and the latter's replacement as Warden of the Settlement, R.G. Tatton. Added to these were some new recruits, middle-class Bloomsbury residents already involved in other progressive educational ventures such as Millicent Fawcett and Anna Swanwick, and, representing the Working Men's College, George Tansley.[97]

Mary Ward's daughter Janet later remembered how she, her sister Dorothy, and her mother's secretary Bessie Churcher were detailed to transfer to Tavistock Place the Saturday morning dance and play activities for children which had been started so successfully in 'that shabby little room' in Marchmont Street by Mary Neal, who also ran a club for factory girls in the slums of St Pancras. Janet's diary for Saturday 16 October 1897 describes how she and the other young women arrived at the Passmore Edwards Settlement at ten o'clock 'to superintend the children's play-hour, which we are now going to have every Saturday in the big hall'. She notes that it was 'perfect pandemonium', as they had not planned for the 120 or more children who turned up.[98]

This was the beginning of a hugely successful enterprise. Passmore Edwards need not have worried about the location; soon over 400 children were coming to the Saturday morning events, where they enjoyed singing, dancing, and gymnastics. Even more innovative – and necessary for the poor working people who lived in the Peabody Buildings opposite and in the crowded houses in the smaller streets to the east – were the facilities Mary Ward started offering on weekday afternoons. Recognising that the children of many working parents were cast adrift after school closed to wander 'aimlessly about the streets' between the hours of 5.30 and 7 p.m., while their parents were still at work, she opened the Settlement to them at these times. A year after the opening the numbers attending had reached

650 a week; by October 1899 the number was 900, and a few years later 1,200. Mary Ward had discovered and catered to a real need. By her energetic efforts, local schools were encouraged to join in such after-school activities; two of them, located in Manchester Street and Prospect Terrace in the extreme north-east corner of Bloomsbury, took their cue from her and set about offering after-school activities in their own buildings.[99]

Though the activities for adults – lectures on academic and practical subjects by such luminaries as Sidney Webb and George Bernard Shaw, concerts, women's clubs, mother and toddler clubs, free legal advice from the residents, domestic economy classes, chess club – were much valued, it was in the field of children's activities that Mary Ward was most pioneering. The astonishing numbers turning up for after-school play attracted the attention of members of parliament and the London County Council, and eventually such facilities became part of the British school system. The Education Bill of 1907 had a 'Mary Ward Clause' inserted into it which permitted local authorities to spend money on play centres and vacation schools, which increasing numbers decided to do.[100]

Mary Ward had been vindicated in her choice of location, and she had been right to defend the Duke of Bedford against Passmore Edwards's accusation of greed and self-interest. At every stage of the Settlement's evolution, she wheedled and reasoned the Duke into agreeing favourable terms and special consideration. After an exhaustive exchange of letters, the lease arrangements finally fixed on were generous. A document of January 1940 indicating that the Duke of Bedford's Trust wished to buy back the building (Herbrand was still Duke – he died in August 1940) describes the original agreement:

On the 14th March 1896 the Duke purchased from the Estate Trustees the Settlement building for the sum of £5,000, and on the 11th November 1899 the Invalid Children's School for the sum of £3,800.

It is believed that these transactions were entered into to enable the Duke to let the buildings to the Mary Ward Settlement at rents below those which the Trustees would be empowered to accept.

The Duke leased the Settlement for a term of 999 years from Christmas 1895 at the rent after the first 1½ years of £195 per annum. The Lease gave the Settlement the right to purchase at any time before 1915 for the sum of £6,500.[101]

The determined founder's insistence to a doubting Passmore Edwards that the area had enough poverty in it to satisfy his philanthropic ambitions was borne out by the sheer numbers who took part in activities at Tavistock Place for some decades to come.[102] At the grand formal opening of the building on 12 February 1898 the speeches by Mary Ward, Lord Peel, the Liberal MP John Morley, and Mary Ward's husband Thomas Humphry Ward stressed the fact that the Settlement stood at the meeting-place of rich and poor London. *The Times* of Monday 14 February reported the speeches at length; the previous Friday the paper had declared, 'London is about to be enriched by the addition of a new centre of educational and social life' to extend 'the diffusion of knowledge'. There followed a quotation from the end of *Robert Elsmere*, in which the dying protagonist sketches out his ideal of a settlement, an ideal which was now about to become reality in an area where, 'while many of the small shopkeepers and artisans are fairly well-to-do, there is a deplorable amount of poverty within a mile radius of the settlement buildings'.[103]

Two more innovations were added by the indefatigable Mary Ward. In 1902, having read an article in *Harper's Magazine* describing American vacation schools, she decided at short notice to open one at the Settlement. According to a speech given by one of her daughters in 1907, she forthwith started organising the first vacation school in Britain, which opened after four weeks of preparation at the end of July 1902, immediately attracting over 500 children a day. She staffed it with teachers 'mainly selected from the Secondary and Kindergarten Training Colleges'; in a few years there were ten vacation schools in London, following Mary Ward's example.[104]

It is hardly surprising that Mary Ward embraced the kindergarten system and incorporated its practices into her own activities for young children. She had been a member of the council of the Froebel Society as early as 1885.[105] The journal of the Society, *Child Life*, reported in October 1902 on the first vacation school at Tavistock Place, welcoming this 'experiment, an outcome of the ever-fertile brain of Mrs Humphry Ward', and describing with approval the 'clay-modelling, brushwork and drawing, paper-cutting, brick-building, and other forms of Kindergarten handiwork' which went on.[106]

Even more important than the vacation school and the evening play centres for after-school activities, however, was Mary Ward's founding of the first school in the country for disabled children. This she started in 1899, having approached the Duke of Bedford to ask if she could take up the option on the piece of land immediately to the east of the Settlement building at the same ground rent.[107] Janet Trevelyan recalled her mother's concern for disabled children in the years when the family lived in Russell Square and their garden looked on to the back of the Alexandra Hospital

for Children with Hip Disease. 'What "Diseases of the Hip" exactly were
was an obscure point to our childish minds', Janet wrote, 'but we knew that
our mother cared very much for the children lying there, [and] that all our
old toys went to amuse them.'[108]

A couple of short-lived experiments had been tried in this field, but Mary
Ward went further. She succeeded in opening her school on the ground
floor of the Settlement building on 28 February 1899 with twenty-five
children, and got the Duke of Bedford's permission to build on the
plot next door, for which purpose she set about fund-raising once more.
Thomas Barlow, a senior physician at University College Hospital and the
Hospital for Sick Children who took a special interest in rickets and scurvy
in children, donated a horse-drawn ambulance to collect the children from
their homes and deliver them back after their day at school. Mary Ward
talked the School Board into supplying special furniture and a paid
teacher.[109]

A second building, to the east of the original one, also designed by Smith
and Brewer, opened in 1903 to house the enlarged class of disabled children. Once again Mary Ward was leading the way, through a combination
of private philanthropy and fund-raising and her skillful, determined efforts
to involve the kind of public bodies and state institutions that would eventually take over complete responsibility for the education of disadvantaged
social groups. By a happy marriage of character and circumstance she was
able, and willing, to exploit every opportunity to encourage the establishment in its slow efforts during the last decades of the century to universalise
education and professional training. Where Brougham and his colleagues
had been obliged to engage in private enterprise to introduce educational
opportunities to groups neglected by the establishment, Mary Ward both
observed the direction of travel and put herself at its head, bringing private
endeavour and philanthropy into closer unity with public policy.

When Mary Ward died in 1920, having actively managed the Settlement
since its beginnings, as well as writing over twenty novels, many works of
non-fiction, plays, translations, and journalism, and sitting on large numbers
of committees, her children inscribed on her tombstone some lines from the
poem 'Come, Poet, Come!' by her father's old friend Clough. She herself
had quoted the same lines on the final page of *Robert Elsmere*:

Others, I doubt not, if not we,
The issue of our toils shall see;
Young children gather as their own
The harvest that the dead had sown.[110]

Interestingly and appropriately, however, the final line of the poem was omitted from the gravestone. It reads, in Clough's characteristically pessimistic tone, 'The dead forgotten and unknown'. He had feared this fate for himself; Mary Ward's children did not expect such an outcome for their formidable mother.

While Mary Ward is not quite the household name today which she ought to be in recognition of her achievements, her name does adorn two buildings in Bloomsbury. The Smith and Brewer building in Tavistock Place is called Mary Ward House and is now privately owned; the successor institution to the Passmore Edwards Settlement, renamed the Mary Ward Settlement in 1921, is the Mary Ward Centre, which moved from Tavistock Place to Queen Square in 1982. There, in the two handsome eighteenth-century houses on the south side of the square which were once home to the College of Preceptors and the Female School of Art, the Centre continues in the spirit of the original Settlement, offering classes in a wide range of subjects, academic and practical, as well as dispensing free legal advice, as its predecessor did from the beginning, and acting as a hub for local social activities.[111]

In her essay in the booklet compiled in 1921 in memory of Mary Ward, the Invalid School's first head teacher, Miss Milligan, remembered how its founder used to send 'rugs for ambulance and garden, toys for wet days', and 'hampers of fresh vegetables and flowers from her country home' in Hertfordshire. She was called 'the Fairy Godmother' by the staff and children.[112] Inevitably there were those who resented, envied, or criticised her gracious do-gooding, her privileged status, and her wealth, though the wealth was earned rather than inherited. She took herself seriously as a morally and socially concerned novelist in the mould of George Eliot, and, being a member of the Arnold family, she found it natural that she should be at the heart of the country's cultural life, leading from the front and promoting reform. Less radical politically (rather surprisingly, she became a leading figure in the Women's National Anti-Suffrage League in 1908)[113] than her predecessors in the educational reform movement which brought about the University of London and the Ladies' College, she nevertheless shared with Campbell, Brougham, Birkbeck, and others a genuine desire for the 'diffusion of knowledge'. The emphasis in the 1890s had shifted away somewhat from the earlier desire that knowledge should be 'useful' to a more general sense of the importance of moral and aesthetic as well as intellectual culture. The work of F.D. Maurice, Octavia Hill, and William Morris, and the arrival on the scene of institutions devoted to arts and crafts as well as technical and industrial teaching, had broadened the remit of educational reform. Through such figures, culminating in Mary Ward, the educational establishment itself came to embrace Bloomsbury's reforming ideas.

Nonetheless, like the founders of 'Stinkomalee', dubbed godless and vulgar by the Tory press in the 1820s, Mary Ward attracted the ire of some conservative observers in the 1890s. One of them, W.H. Mallock, was the author in 1877 of *The New Republic: or Culture, Faith and Philosophy in an English Country House*, a cheerfully wide-ranging satire on the pretensions of modern 'gurus', including Matthew Arnold. Following Thomas Love Peacock with his country house format, in 1899 Mallock published his satirical novel *The Individualist*, set mainly in the 'mysterious region' of Bloomsbury with its 'faded but stately façades and smoke-begrimed square gardens, islanded far off in the great Maelstrom of business'.[114] He parodies William Morris's *Chants for Socialists*, makes fun of the Comtists pursuing the religion of humanity in their dingy halls in Bloomsbury, and creates at the centre of his novel a charitable monster, the bestselling novelist and founder of a settlement, Mrs Norham:

> Mrs Norham was beyond all doubt a celebrity. She had written a novel with a purpose which, despite its length and its solemnity, had achieved an enormous circulation, and had raised her to the ranks of a prophetess. She was now surrounded by a clique of admiring worshippers who would have taken her, were that possible, even more seriously than she took herself.[115]

Mallock's protagonist is a hypocrite, always spouting altruism from the platform or the lay pulpit, while enjoying a privileged life of holidaying on the Riviera and hobnobbing with the liberal aristocracy. It is a good likeness of Mary Ward, except that she was no hypocrite; for every week she spent on holiday in the south of France or in her fine country house, she spent many more employing her 'fertile brain' on behalf of the less privileged sections of society. If she exploited her Arnold connections and her charm, she did so for very good reasons and with excellent results.

Epilogue

Not every reform or innovation in the social, intellectual, and cultural life of London in the nineteenth century had its origins in Bloomsbury. The area to the west of Tottenham Court Road, now known as Fitzrovia, could boast the Ladies' Guild run by Octavia Hill and her mother and Frances Martin's breakaway College for Working Women from 1874. Barbara Leigh Smith founded her co-educational school at Portman Hall in Marylebone; Elizabeth Garrett's hospital for women started in that area too, before moving to the edge of Bloomsbury in 1890. Queen's College, founded by F.D. Maurice in 1848 for the training of governesses, was in Harley Street. The Froebel Society started in a house in Kensington in 1874, though its first college was set up in Tavistock Place; Maria Grey's training college for kindergarten teachers was begun in Bishopsgate and continued in Fitzroy Street from 1883. In the last decades of the century South Kensington became home to a number of museums, though the British Museum remained the chief national institution; in the course of the nineteenth century it had become surrounded by new establishments with which it shared some of its aims and some of its personnel.

A striking example of the connections between Bloomsbury's institutions was Anthony Panizzi, influential librarian and designer of the famous Round Reading Room at the Museum. This fellow who came to England with a rope round his neck, escaping from an Italian death sentence, was one of many men and women who walked the streets of Bloomsbury and worked in its buildings, where they affected the life not just of the area, but of the nation. Panizzi is not generally considered in terms of his intimate and essential relationship with this ever-growing area of London and with other 'Bloomsbury' people, yet a large group of such figures did their pioneering work in Bloomsbury's streets and squares, in institutions often built especially to accommodate their activities, or in older houses which they adapted to the needs of their organisations.

Foremost among these was the extraordinary Henry Brougham, who offers an interesting comparison and contrast from the early part of the century with Passmore Edwards at the end. Brougham, 'Mr Big-Wig' to the satirists, and Edwards, dubbed 'Mr Greatheart' by the actor Sir Henry Irving when he laid the foundation stone for one of the many public libraries built with Edwards's money, both did huge amounts of good in their shared pursuit of educational improvement, but they operated in vastly different ways.[1] One used his brain, his pen, and his mouth (in court and parliament), and was forever catching the public eye, while the other worked more modestly, opening his purse at every opportunity for doing good.

Between these two came many other important residents and workers in Bloomsbury. There were brilliant and eccentric professors at University College, among them De Morgan, Robert Grant the zoologist, and Newman, as well as the disreputable Lardner. In mid-century there was F.D. Maurice, known as 'Master' by the Christian Socialist disciples who helped him with his College for Working Men in Red Lion Square and Great Ormond Street. Edward Irving and John Bate Cardale followed their earnest religious calling, in Regent Square and Gordon Square, respectively, as 'apostles' of a new religion. Their aim was to save Britain from irreligion, loss of faith, and materialism, while so many determinedly secular reformers, Brougham among them, appeared to be replacing traditional faith with a social and educational mission. Frederic Harrison and Edward Beesly embraced the religion of humanity, which they taught in their dingy hall in Chapel Street, while Beesly also taught history at University College and ran University Hall as a successful residence for its students.

John Elliotson combined medical excellence with a showman's experimentations with mesmerism; to his friend Dickens he was known affectionately as 'Blue Beard', and to Thackeray he was nothing less than a life-saver when the novelist fell seriously ill while writing *Pendennis*. From his home in Bedford Square another progressive medical man, Thomas Wakley, editor of the *Lancet* and scourge of quackery in the profession, supported the progressive techniques of Elliotson and his colleagues at nearby University College Hospital, before exposing the scandalous side of his erstwhile friend's enthusiasm for mesmerism. Robert Liston, the surgeon with the physique of a prize fighter, performed his pioneering surgical operations at University College Hospital.

Among the women who embraced reform, mainly seeking better working conditions or equal educational opportunities, some have remained relatively obscure. Though Elisabeth Jesser Reid was the first person to offer classes at university level to women in the houses she took in Bedford Square, she was hindered from making her name by an amateurishness and a sometimes less than logical way of doing things at the Ladies' College. Nonetheless, many girls and women benefited from her endeavours, some of them going on to run schools of their own, while others, like Anna Swanwick, were involved in the governance of the College as it prepared to become truly part of the higher educational establishment by joining the University of London in 1900. Better known to posterity than either Elisabeth Reid or Anna Swanwick is Octavia Hill, though she is more famous for her later achievements in the field of social housing and the founding of the National Trust than for her remarkable work as a teenager at the Working Men's College. Elizabeth Malleson, who set up the Working Women's College in 1864, is scarcely a household name, and even Mary Ward, the 'Fairy Godmother' of the Passmore Edwards Settlement with her 'firsts' – evening play centres, vacation school, and invalid school – is not celebrated now as she was in her lifetime. The pioneers of the Froebel Society, Emily Shirreff and her sister Maria Grey, are names known only to specialist historians, as are those of the two German exiles who brought the kindergarten system to Britain in the first place, Bertha Ronge and her husband Johannes, 'the modern Luther'.

In the field of medicine, specialist hospitals, and medical training for men and women, Bloomsbury has long been in the forefront, thanks to University College Hospital, the Hospital for Sick Children, Elizabeth Garrett Anderson's New Hospital for Women, and Sophia Jex-Blake's London School of Medicine for Women. Less well known are the many small hospitals and nursing homes set up by caring individuals, especially, as Robert Louis Stevenson pointed out, in the neighbourhood of Queen Square. Elizabeth Garrett Anderson's name lives on, as does her sister Millicent Fawcett's, in her case for her work on behalf of women's suffrage, but less so that of their other sister Agnes Garrett, who ran her ground-breaking decorating firm from her home at 2 Gower Street.

A host of other pioneers have made their appearance in this history of nineteenth-century reformers and their institutions. Not the least important, though not the best known today, is Henry Crabb Robinson, 'Old Crabb' as he was known to his more famous student Walter Bagehot. Robinson lived his long and useful life in Russell Square, the square at the very heart of intellectual Bloomsbury. He was there at the beginning of several ventures: University College London, University Hall, the Ladies' College. He was responsible for the preservation and display of the famous Flaxman sculptures under the dome of William Wilkins's 'godless' building on Gower Street. He gave both time and money, showing himself prepared to join committees, suffer setbacks and annoyances, and carry on in spite of everything. Though he complained in his copious diaries – the single most useful surviving record of Bloomsbury's intellectual life from the 1830s to the 1860s – he never gave up in the face of difficulties. Robinson was a member of the dissenting religious group which did most to broaden educational possibilities in nineteenth-century Britain, the Unitarians, who were so prominent on the boards and committees of the new institutions and who have not had the recognition they deserve for their enterprise.

All these, in their different ways, are heroes in the story of progress, a story which was captured imaginatively by an impressive roll call of novelists – Disraeli, Dickens, Thackeray, Trollope, Braddon, Stevenson, Gissing, as well as the now-forgotten Theodore Hook – some of them in favour of reform, others against, and all at some time inhabitants of Bloomsbury. The members of one family are sometimes represented as villains. Successive Dukes of Bedford, from John Russell, the sixth Duke, to Herbrand Russell, the eleventh, set up obstacles to those who wished to open schools, colleges, hospitals, or other public buildings on Bedford land, which covered such a large part of western Bloomsbury, including many of its most elegant squares. Their concern was to keep their properties respectable, both for the sake of the huge return in rents which they received (as Passmore Edwards grumbled to Mary Ward), and to keep their middle-class tenants happy.[2] The result of the strict conditions on their leases – no trades, no brass plates, no subletting, no public activities – was that most properties on the Bedford Estate remained in good repair, while houses on nearby estates like those of the Foundling Hospital and the Skinners' Company risked becoming dilapidated, with some small pockets turning into slums.

Some determined individuals and groups did manage to persuade the Russell family to countenance new buildings for their enterprises, especially at times when the housing market slumped. Astute Bedford Estate managers from Christopher Haedy to Alfred Stutfield steered their employers towards accepting such buildings, though on strict conditions concerning both their aesthetic value and their planned use. University Hall and the Catholic Apostolic Church in Gordon Square are handsome examples, and the Passmore Edwards Settlement on Tavistock Place is an exceptionally good building architecturally speaking, as well as offering a public service to a group – the poorer people of the neighbourhood – which the

Dukes of Bedford were on the whole anxious to keep out of their domain. In sanctioning the Passmore Edwards Settlement, at least one Russell – Herbrand – showed himself to be a positive force in the history of educational progress. He did not obstruct Mary Ward's plans; on the contrary, he took a good deal of trouble for her, as well as offering generous rental terms. Like his predecessors, he was prepared, no doubt partly out of enlightened self-interest, to accept public use of sites on his land, as long as the architectural style was prestigious, the specifications reasonable, and the aims of the lessee respectable. In Mary Ward he could be sure that all these conditions would be met, and he was generous in return.

In 1800 large parts of Bloomsbury, including the land running north of Great Russell Street up to the New Road, were still undeveloped. A hundred years later Bloomsbury was fully built up. Many of the area's nineteenth-century buildings are intact today, though some of its streets and parts of its squares have undergone change. The first major rebuilding occurred in the last years of the nineteenth century, as ninety-nine-year leases fell in and large houses such as Dickens's Tavistock House, Cardale's Bedford House, and the adjacent Russell House in the north-east corner of Tavistock Square, as well as those on the east side of Russell Square, including Mary Ward's house at No. 61, were demolished to make way in the one case for what is now the British Medical Association building, and in the other for large hotels. Other rebuildings took place during the twentieth century, mainly at the hands of the expanding University of London; the building of Senate House in the 1930s swallowed up most of Keppel Street, where Anthony Trollope was born (and where Dickens's father died in the home of his doctor on Census night 1851).[3]

No part of a city remains exactly the same over time in terms of its social and cultural demographic. As Thackeray pointed out in *The Newcomes*, Soho was a favourite residential choice of the rich and fashionable in the eighteenth century before it became associated with art-school bohemianism in the nineteenth century. Chelsea was a muddy village by the side of the Thames until the river was embanked in the later nineteenth century, after which it became a desirable residential area for the wealthy. As for Bloomsbury, its 'character' today as the centre of British intellectual and cultural life was attained in the nineteenth century, at the same time that the area was being developed physically. We have traced changes from the beginning of the nineteenth century to the end, noting how this quarter of London, intended as a residential area, became compromised, or invigorated, depending on one's point of view, by the introduction of public buildings, most of which were erected or adapted for educational purposes.

Today the area is still largely institutional, though certain modern developments, notably the Brunswick Centre next to Brunswick Square, and the return of some Georgian houses to residential use as flats, have made the area once more one of mixed use.

Bloomsbury, for all the changes it has undergone, is the heart of intellectual London, with more libraries, museums, and educational establishments than any other part of the city. The name 'Bloomsbury' is associated primarily in many minds with the literary and artistic 'group' which lived and worked in some of the area's squares in the first few decades of the twentieth century: Virginia and Leonard Woolf, Vanessa Bell, Duncan Grant, John Maynard Keynes. Without denying the intellectual and artistic importance of members of this small group of friends, we can identify a more comprehensive, and ultimately more significant, influence in the activities of an earlier set of Bloomsbury-based pioneers, men and women of the nineteenth century who fought against entrenched opinion and vested interests for universal education, from kindergarten to university, and for cultural opportunities for all.

Notes

Introduction: Surveying Bloomsbury

1. See Eliza Jeffries Davis, *The University Site, Bloomsbury* (London, 1936), p. 30; Richard Tames, *Bloomsbury Past: A Visual History* (London, 1993), pp. 8–9.
2. Peter Mark Roget to his sister Annette, 29 December 1800, D.L. Emblen, *Peter Mark Roget: The Word and the Man* (London, 1970), p. 54.
3. *Morning Chronicle*, 25 October 1826.
4. Rowland Dobie, *The History of the United Parishes of St Giles in the Fields and St George Bloomsbury* (London, 1829), pp. 142–3, 146.
5. See Catherine Durant, 'London's First Northern By-pass: Urban Development and the New Road from Paddington to Islington', *Camden History Review*, vol. 15 (1988), pp. 15–19.
6. For information on Burton's work in Bloomsbury, see Dana Arnold, *Rural Urbanism: London Landscapes in the Early Nineteenth Century* (Manchester, 2005), and Richard Clarke, Elizabeth McKellar, and Michael Symes, *Russell Square: A Lifelong Resource for Teaching and Learning* (Birkbeck Faculty of Continuing Education Occasional Paper, London, 2004).
7. See Hermione Hobhouse, *Thomas Cubitt: Master Builder* (London, 1971), pp. 20–37.
8. Ibid., pp. 68–9, 83–102, 116–66.
9. Ibid., p. 5.
10. See Chapters 8, 9, and 10.
11. Two books in particular have been helpful for my study of Bloomsbury: Donald J. Olsen, *Town Planning in London: The Eighteenth and Nineteenth Centuries* (New Haven, Connecticut and London, 1964, revised 1982), and another book by Olsen, *The Growth of Victorian London* (London, 1976). Other books with useful information about the history of London, and that of Bloomsbury in particular, are: James Elmes, *Metropolitan Improvements; or London in the Nineteenth Century: being a Series of Views, of the New and Most Interesting Objects, in the British Metropolis & its Vicinity: from Original Drawings by Mr Thos. H. Shepherd. With Historical, Topographical & Critical Illustrations* (London, 1827, reprinted 1978), Thomas H. Shepherd, *London and its Environs in the Nineteenth Century, illustrated by a Series of Views from Original Drawings* (London, 1829, reprinted 1970), Charles Knight, *Knight's Pictorial London* (London, 1851) and *Knight's Cyclopædia of London* (London, 1851), Thomas Beames, *The Rookeries of London* (London, 1852), John Timbs, *Curiosities of London* (London, 1855), George Clinch, *Bloomsbury and St Giles's: Past and Present* (London, 1890), Edward Walford, *Old and New London: A Narrative of its History, its People, and its Places*, 6 vols (London, 1873–8), of which vol. 4 deals with Bloomsbury, Walter Besant, *London in the Nineteenth Century* (London, 1909), E. Beresford Chancellor, *London's Old Latin Quarter, being an Account of Tottenham Court Road and its Immediate Surroundings* (London, 1930), John Lehmann, *Holborn: An Historical Portrait of a London Borough* (London, 1970), *The A to Z of Georgian London*, with

Introductory Notes by Ralph Hyde (London Topographical Society, London, 1982), Edward Jones and Christopher Woodward, *A Guide to the Architecture of London* (London, 1983, reprinted 1992), Roger Hudson, *Bloomsbury, Fitzrovia & Soho* (London, 1996), Bridget Cherry and Nikolaus Pevsner, *The Buildings of England: London 4: North* (London, 1998), Lynda Nead, *Victorian Babylon: People, Streets, and Images in Nineteenth-Century London* (London, 2000), Liza Picard, *Victorian London: The Life of a City 1840–1870* (London, 2005), Jerry White, *London in the Nineteenth Century* (London, 2007), *The London Encyclopædia*, third edition revised, ed. Ben Weinreb, Christopher Hibbert, Julia Keay, and John Keay (London, 2008).

12. See Gladys Scott Thomson, *The Russells in Bloomsbury 1669–1771* (London, 1940), pp. 20–2; Olsen, *Town Planning in London*, p. 146.
13. Olsen, *Town Planning in London*, pp. 100–1.
14. Ibid., pp. 205–7. The manuscript Booth Notebooks, with detailed descriptions of streets and their occupants and full notes of interviews with local vicars, doctors, nurses, and secretaries of charitable institutions, are held in the British Library of Political and Economic Science at the London School of Economics. These unpublished detailed notes are an invaluable source of material about the lives of Londoners. The 'poverty maps' themselves have been made available online (The Charles Booth Online Archive, http://booth.lse.ac.uk).
15. For the juxtaposition of the ordered and the random, especially as represented in nineteenth-century fiction, see Franco Moretti, *Atlas of the European Novel 1800–1900* (London, 1998), pp. 77–8.
16. Olsen, *Town Planning in London*, pp. 202–3.
17. 'Flunkeiana', *Punch*, vol. 28 (January–June 1855), p. 114.
18. Report, 11 December 1890, Middlesex Report Book vol. 2 (1883–1895), BE RB69, Bedford Estate Office, Woburn Abbey. All quotations from Bedford Estate papers are by kind permission of the Duke of Bedford and the Trustees of the Bedford Estate.
19. See Olsen, *The Growth of Victorian London*, p. 128.
20. Vanessa Bell, 'Notes on Bloomsbury' (1951), in *Sketches in Pen and Ink*, ed. Lia Giachero (London, 1997), pp. 98–9, 97.
21. Virginia Stephen to Violet Dickinson, 31 December 1903, *The Letters of Virginia Woolf*, ed. Nigel Nicholson, 6 vols (London, 1975–80), vol. 1, p. 119.
22. Virginia Woolf, *A Passionate Apprentice: The Early Journals 1897–1909*, ed. Mitchell A. Leaska (London, 1990), p. 246.
23. Noel Annan, *Leslie Stephen: The Godless Victorian* (London, 1984), pp. 3, 6–7.
24. Virginia Woolf, 'Phyllis and Rosamond' (1906), in *The Complete Shorter Fiction of Virginia Woolf*, ed. Susan Dick (London, 1958), p. 24.
25. Bell, 'Notes on Bloomsbury', p. 95.
26. Wilkie Collins, *Heart and Science: A Story of the Present Time*, 3 vols (London, 1883), vol. 1, pp. 16–17.
27. For Russell Square, see Chapter 5.
28. *The Times*, 19 March 1894.
29. R.S. Surtees, *Handley Cross; or, Mr Jorrocks's Hunt* (London, 1854, reprinted 1903), pp. 72–4.
30. Haedy's report, 25 May 1840, quoted in Olsen, *Town Planning in London*, pp. 110–11.
31. In 1857–8 Sir Rowland Hill's plan to divide London into ten postal districts was implemented; see British Postal Museum & Archive, www.postalheritage.org.uk.
32. Edwin Lutyens to his fiancée Emily Lytton, 12 February and 14 July 1897, *The Letters of Edwin Lutyens to his Wife Lady Emily*, ed. Clayre Percy and Jane Ridley (London, 1985), pp. 26, 50, 51.
33. Emily Hobhouse, 'Women Workers: How They Live, How They Wish to Live', *Nineteenth Century*, vol. 27 (March 1900), pp. 471, 477, 482, 483. For the Ladies' Residential Chambers in Chenies Street, Bloomsbury, see the UCL Leverhulme-funded Bloomsbury Project website, www.ucl.ac.uk/bloomsbury-project.
34. George Gissing to Algernon Gissing, 3 August 1881, *The Collected Letters of George Gissing*, eds Paul F. Mattheisen, Arthur C. Young, and Pierre Coustillas, 9 vols (Athens, Ohio, 1990–7), vol. 2, p. 55; George Gissing, *Workers in the Dawn*, 3 vols (London, 1880). See

also Richard Dennis, 'George Gissing (1857–1903): London's Restless Analyst', *The Gissing Journal*, vol. 40, no. 3 (2004), pp. 1–15.

35. *The Times*, 24 August 1894.
36. J.M. Barrie, *The Greenwood Hat, being a Memoir of James Anon 1885–1887* (London, 1937), pp. 9, 56. See Rosemary Ashton, 'Peter Pan and Bloomsbury', *Times Literary Supplement*, no. 5619 (10 December 2010), p. 15, and 'Barrie and Bloomsbury', in *Gateway to the Modern: Resituating J. M. Barrie*, eds Andrew Nash and Valentina Bold, to be published by the Association of Scottish Literary Studies (Glasgow, 2013).
37. Edward Verrall Lucas; see *ODNB* entry.
38. E.V. Lucas, *A Wanderer in London* (London, 1906, revised 1913), pp. 189–90.
39. See Chapter 2.
40. Confusingly, a new University of London was granted a charter in the same year, 1836; it came into existence originally as an examining institution for the two colleges, King's College and the newly renamed University College; see Negley Harte, *The University of London 1836–1986* (London, 1986), and Negley Harte and John North, *The World of UCL 1828–1990*, revised edition (London, 1991).
41. See Chapter 1.
42. See Chapters 7 and 8.
43. See Chapter 1.
44. See Chapter 7.
45. See Chapter 8.
46. See Chapter 9.
47. See Chapter 10.
48. The phrase 'March of Mind' originated in a poem written by Mary Russell Mitford in 1814 for a meeting of the British and Foreign School Society; it was taken up, with its variation 'The March of Intellect', in countless cartoons of the 1820s; see M. Dorothy George, *Hogarth to Cruikshank: Social Change in Graphic Satire* (London, 1967), pp. 177–82.
49. See Chapter 4.
50. See Alison Winter, *Mesmerized: Powers of Mind in Victorian Britain* (Chicago and London, 1998), p. 180; H. Hale Bellot, *University College London 1826–1926* (London, 1929), pp. 164–6.
51. See Chapter 4.
52. See Elizabeth Crawford, *Enterprising Women: The Garretts and their Circle* (London, 2002). The Elizabeth Garrett Anderson building on Euston Road has recently been saved from demolition and parts of it restored to create an exhibition area, the Elizabeth Garrett Anderson Gallery, by the new owners of the site, the Unison trade union. For a discussion of the hospital, and the London School of Medicine for Women, see Chapter 8.
53. See Chapter 5.
54. See Chapter 10.
55. See White, *London in the Nineteenth Century*, pp. 31–2; Beames, *The Rookeries of London*.
56. See George, *Hogarth to Cruikshank*, p. 169; Walford, *Old and New London*, vol. 4, p. 484.
57. See Chapter 5.
58. See Timothy Grass, *The Lord's Watchman: Edward Irving* (Milton Keynes, 2011); Rosemary Ashton, *Thomas and Jane Carlyle: Portrait of a Marriage* (London, 2002). For a discussion of Bloomsbury's alternative reforming churches, see Chapter 6.
59. See Chapters 6 and 7.
60. Haedy's 1852 report, *Annual Reports* vol. 3 (1848–1852), BE RB6, Bedford Estate Office, Woburn Abbey.
61. Ibid. For a detailed account of Haedy's work for the seventh Duke of Bedford, see David Spring, *The English Landed Estate in the Nineteenth Century: Its Administration* (Baltimore, Maryland, 1963).
62. See Chapters 1 and 3.
63. See Chapter 2.
64. John Passmore Edwards, *A Few Footprints* (London, 1905), p. 6.

Chapter 1 Godlessness on Gower Street

1. The institution began as the University of London, changing its name in 1836 to University College London, when a new University of London, the examining body for students of University College London and King's College London, came into existence. Throughout this book I will call the institution on Gower Street the University of London when the period referred to is that preceding 1836, and University College London from that date on.
2. See George, *Hogarth to Cruikshank*, p. 200.
3. *The Times*, 6 June 1825.
4. See Harte and North, *The World of UCL*, pp. 78, 231.
5. Thomas Campbell, 'Proposal of a Metropolitan University in a Letter to Henry Brougham, Esq.', *The Times*, 9 February 1825.
6. See W.A.C. Stewart and W.P. McCann, *The Educational Innovators*, 2 vols (London, 1968–9).
7. *John Bull*, 14 February 1825.
8. Quoted from Thomas Campbell, *The Pleasures of Hope*, Part 1 (1799).
9. *Life and Letters of Thomas Campbell*, ed. William Beattie, 3 vols (London, 1849), II, 446, 445, 449.
10. See Bellot, *University College London 1826–1926*, pp. 8–9, 11, 15–16.
11. *Life and Letters of Thomas Campbell*, II, 440–1.
12. See Cyrus Redding, *Literary Reminiscences and Memoirs of Thomas Campbell*, 2 vols (London, 1860), vol. 2, pp. 15, 20.
13. Thomas Campbell to Leonard Horner (Warden of the University of London), 21 January 1828, MS College Correspondence, UCL Special Collections.
14. The three men dominate volumes 10 (1820–1827) and 11 (1828–1832) of M. Dorothy George's *Catalogue of Political and Personal Satires preserved in the Department of Prints and Drawings in the British Museum* (London, 1952, 1954).
15. *Standard*, 8 February 1828.
16. See Chapter 2.
17. Harriette Wilson to Henry Brougham, 16 December 1827, *The Blackmailing of the Chancellor: Some Intimate and Hitherto Unpublished Letters from Harriette Wilson to her friend Henry Brougham, Lord Chancellor of England*, ed. Kenneth Bourne (London, 1975), p. 41. Harriette's letters to Brougham are in the Brougham Papers, UCL Special Collections.
18. George Vivian Poore, 'The History of University College', 14 June 1897, pp. 7, 9–10, College Collection A20 POO, UCL Special Collections. Poore is quoting from the famous diary of the Clerk to the Privy Council Charles Greville, *The Greville Memoirs 1814–1860*, eds Lytton Strachey and Roger Fulford, 7 vols (London, 1938), vol. 1, p. 195. The *Memoirs* were first published in 1874. For an account of the first fifty years of Brougham's life, see Chester William New, *The Life of Henry Brougham to 1830* (Oxford, 1961).
19. See Bellot, *University College London 1826–1926*, pp. 21–2, 213.
20. Thomas Carlyle to Jane Welsh (later his wife), 19 October 1825, *The Collected Letters of Thomas and Jane Welsh Carlyle*, eds C.R. Sanders, K.J. Fielding et al., 37 vols so far (Durham, North Carolina, 1970—), vol. 3, p. 391.
21. Zachary Macaulay to Thomas Chalmers, 17 January 1829, quoted in Grass, *The Lord's Watchman*, p. 146.
22. See [Henry Morley], 'A Short History of the College: II', *University College Gazette*, vol. 1 (22 October 1886), p. 27 (in UCL Special Collections).
23. See UCL Council Minutes, 23 March 1850, UCL Records Office.
24. The *Edinburgh Review* carried articles on the University of London in August 1825, February 1826, and September 1828. The article in February 1826 is thought to be by Macaulay, and the others by Brougham; see *The Wellesley Index to Victorian Periodicals 1824–1900*, eds Walter E. Houghton et al., 5 vols (Toronto, 1966–89).
25. Place Diary, July 1826, Bellot, *University College London 1826–1926*, p. 31.
26. The cartoon is in UCL Art Collections; it is reproduced in Harte and North, *The World of UCL*.
27. Bellot, *University College London 1826–1926*, pp. 33–4.
28. Ibid., pp. 34–5; see also the UCL Leverhulme-funded Bloomsbury Project website, www.ucl.ac.uk/bloomsbury-project.
29. For Wilkins's career, see R.W. Liscombe, *William Wilkins 1778–1839* (Cambridge, 1980).

30. See J. Mordaunt Crook, 'The Architectural Image', in *The University of London and the World of Learning 1836–1986*, ed. F.M.L. Thompson (London, 1990), p. 4.
31. *The Times*, 1 May 1827.
32. Redding, *Literary Reminiscences and Memoirs of Thomas Campbell*, vol. 2, p. 15. *The Times* reports the meeting on 2 July 1825, noting that 'Mr Brougham, who entered the room as Mr [John] Smith sat down, was loudly called for, and received with reiterated cheers'.
33. *The Creevey Papers: A Selection from the Correspondence and Diaries of the Late Thomas Creevey, MP*, ed. Sir Herbert Maxwell (London, 1903, reprinted 1933), pp. 169, 171.
34. See Harte and North, *The World of UCL*, pp. 25–9.
35. Liscombe, *William Wilkins*, p. 160.
36. 'The London University', *The Times*, 6 August 1828.
37. See [Henry Morley], 'A Short History of the College: II', p. 28.
38. See Harte and North, *The World of UCL*, p. 75.
39. See R.H. Dalton Barham, *The Life and Remains of Theodore Edward Hook*, 2 vols (London, 1849), vol. 1, pp. 147–81. See also Bill Newton Dunn, *The Man Who Was John Bull: The Biography of Theodore Edward Hook 1778–1841* (London, 1996).
40. See George, *Catalogue of Political and Personal Satires*, vol. 10, p. 426ff., for the many caricatures during 1824–5, when the mania was at its height.
41. 'Stinkomalee', *John Bull*, 26 December 1825.
42. *John Bull*, 21 April and 12 May 1828.
43. *Age*, 18 May 1828.
44. See George, *Catalogue of Political and Personal Satires*, vol. 10, p. 578.
45. *Morning Chronicle*, 19 July 1825, reprinted in *Selected Poems of Winthrop Mackworth Praed*, ed. Kenneth Allott (London, 1953), pp. 276–7.
46. Benjamin Disraeli, *Vivian Grey* (1826–7), ed. Lucien Wolf, 2 vols (London, 1904), I, 100–1.
47. 441 students matriculated at Cambridge in 1850; see www.cam.ac.uk/univ/history. Numbers at the University of Edinburgh between 1820 and 1850 varied from about 1,300 to 2,000, though far fewer, between 100 and 150, were awarded a degree in any one year; TS 'University of Edinburgh 1820–1920: Total Number of Matriculated Students and Total Number of Degrees Awarded', Edinburgh University Library.
48. See *Annual Reports*, 1829ff., UCL Records Office; Bellot, *University College London 1826–1926*, pp. 51, 175, 400.
49. *John Bull*, 4 May 1835, quoting the *British Magazine*.
50. See Sydney Smith to Lady Grey, 14 January 1835, *The Letters of Sydney Smith*, ed. Nowell C. Smith, 2 vols (Oxford, 1953), vol. 2, p. 601.
51. See the report of his speech at a meeting of the university in the *Morning Chronicle*, 25 February 1830.
52. See Bellot, *University College London 1826–1926*, p. 51.
53. See *Annual Reports*, February 1831, February 1832, and February 1833, UCL Records Office; Bellot, *University College London 1826–1926*, p. 176.
54. See Council Minutes, 2 June 1827, UCL Records Office.
55. Charles Darwin to William Darwin Fox, 24 October 1839, *The Correspondence of Charles Darwin*, eds Frederick Burkhardt et al., 18 vols so far (Cambridge, 1985—), vol. 2, p. 234. See also *The Autobiography of Charles Darwin 1809–1882*, ed. Nora Barlow (London, 1958), and Janet Browne, *Charles Darwin*, 2 vols (London, 1995–2002).
56. See the file '1830 Disputes re Warden', UCL Special Collections.
57. Augustus De Morgan to William Frend, 29 July 1831, Sophia De Morgan, *Memoir of Augustus De Morgan* (London, 1882), p. 40.
58. See *Annual Report*, February 1830, UCL Records Office.
59. See Council Minutes, 3, 10, and 17 February 1827, UCL Records Office.
60. Ibid., 17 February 1827. The archives of the Gilchrist Educational Trust, established in accordance with his will after his death in 1841, are in UCL Special Collections.
61. Education Committee Minutes, 19 November 1828, UCL Records Office; see also Bellot, *University College London 1826–1926*, pp. 42–3, 118–19.
62. See James Fernandez Clarke, *Autobiographical Recollections of the Medical Profession* (London, 1874), p. 305.
63. *Second Statement by the Council of the University of London, explanatory of the Plan of Instruction* (London, 1828), pp. 149–51, UCL Special Collections.

64. Conolly's letters to Horner and the Council from 1827 to 1831, and his letter of 11 April 1847 from Hanwell to C.C. Atkinson, are in the College Correspondence, UCL Special Collections.

65. See Mimi Romilly, 'Sir Samuel Romilly of Russell Square and his Descendants', *Camden History Review*, vol. 20 (1996), p. 6.

66. See Emblen, *Peter Mark Roget*, pp. 127–30; *The Times*, 3, 4, 5, 7 November 1818.

67. Emblen, *Peter Mark Roget*, pp. 138, 107.

68. Ibid., pp. 184–7.

69. Council Minutes, 3 February and 12 July 1827, UCL Records Office. Roget's letter withdrawing does not survive in the University College archives.

70. Emblen, *Peter Mark Roget*, p. 138.

71. Council Minutes, 10 and 17 February 1827, 5 January 1828, UCL Records Office.

72. Campbell to Lord Auckland, quoted in Bellot, *University College London 1826–1926*, pp. 43–4.

73. Education Committee Minutes, 27 October 1828, UCL Records Office.

74. Bellot, *University College London 1826–1926*, p. 176; Council Minutes, 7 February 1829, UCL Records Office.

75. Edward Miller, *Prince of Librarians: The Life and Times of Antonio Panizzi of the British Museum* (London, 1988), p. 49.

76. Panizzi to the Inspector of Taxes at Reggio, 10 May 1824, Louis Fagan, *The Life of Sir Anthony Panizzi, KCB, Late Principal Librarian of the British Museum, Senator of Italy &c, &c*, 2 vols (London, 1880), vol. 1, pp. 51–2.

77. See Margaret C.W. Wicks, *The Italian Exiles in London 1816–1848* (Manchester, 1937).

78. Campbell to William Roscoe the younger, 5 July 1823, published by Sydney Jeffery, *Times Literary Supplement*, 8 July 1944.

79. See Miller, *Prince of Librarians*, pp. 67–8; *The Times* commentated on the case from March 1826 to June 1827.

80. Council Minutes, 17 February 1827 (Pecchio), 10 March 1827 (Rossetti), 28 April 1827 (Foscolo), UCL Records Office. See also Wicks, *The Italian Exiles in London*, pp. 63, 130ff., 169.

81. See Constance Brooks, *Antonio Panizzi: Scholar and Patriot* (London, 1931), p. 46.

82. See Council Minutes, *passim*, 1827–8.

83. Antonio Panizzi to Leonard Horner, 19 April 1828, quoted in Miller, *Prince of Librarians*, p. 70. See also Wicks, *The Italian Exiles in London*, pp. 130–1, 266–9.

84. Council Minutes, 16 February 1828, UCL Records Office.

85. See Brooks, *Antonio Panizzi*, pp. 48–9.

86. British Museum Committee Minutes, 14 May 1831, vol. 12, p. 3352, British Museum Central Archive.

87. Brooks, *Antonio Panizzi*, pp. 48–9, 170–1.

88. See Chapter 5.

89. Fagan, *Life of Sir Anthony Panizzi*, vol. 2, p. 269; Miller, *Prince of Librarians*, p. 280.

90. Gabriele Rossetti's poem attacking Panizzi (1828) is quoted in Brooks, *Antonio Panizzi*, p. 177.

91. See Bellot, *University College London 1826-1926*, p. 42; Council Minutes, 16 February, 29 May 1828, UCL Records Office.

92. Council Minutes, 24 November 1829, UCL Records Office.

93. Joseph Hume to James Loch, 17 January 1830, Loch Papers, MS Add 131, UCL Special Collections.

94. Council Minutes, 20 and 27 March 1830, UCL Records Office.

95. Education Committee Minutes, 26 November 1828; Council Minutes, 24 July 1828 and 15 October 1830, UCL Records Office.

96. Original Letters and Papers, 10 May 1834, vol. 13, p. 3811 and 11 April 1835, vol. 14, p. 3966, British Museum Central Archive.

97. See the *ODNB* entry on Rosen.

98. Original Letters and Papers, 22 January and 20 April 1839, vol. 17, pp. 4973 and 5053, British Museum Central Archive.

99. See Frances J. Woodward, *Portrait of Jane: A Life of Lady Franklin* (London, 1951), pp. 83–5, 96–7, 102, 115, 124.

100. Book of Admissions to Reading Room (21 February 1828 and 15 March 1830), British Museum Central Archive.
101. Jane Griffin Diary, 16 February 1827, Woodward, *Portrait of Jane*, p. 149.
102. Council Minutes, 5 July 1830, UCL Records Office.
103. Woodward, *Portrait of Jane*, pp. 335–7.
104. *Abschrift eines Lebenslaufs des Ludwig von Mühlenfels* (extract of a curriculum vitae) sent to Bellot from the Foreign Office of Berlin, 11 April 1927, UCL Memoranda: Bellot (Box 1), UCL Special Collections.
105. Council Minutes, 15 October 1830, 30 July 1831, UCL Records Office; Bellot, *University College London 1826–1926*, pp. 121–2.
106. Bellot, *University College London 1826–1926*, pp. 120–1.
107. Education Committee Minutes, 22 May and 22 June 1827, UCL Records Office; Bellot, *University College London 1826–1926*, pp. 58–9.
108. Council Minutes, 14 November and 5 December 1829, 2 February 1830, UCL Records Office; Bellot, *University College London 1826–1926*, pp. 108–9.
109. See Bellot, *University College London 1826–1926*, pp. 339–41.
110. Agnes Fry, *A Memoir of the Rt Hon Sir Edward Fry, GCB, 1827–1918* (London, 1921), p. 42.
111. J.B. Benson, 'Some Recollections of University College in the Sixties', quoted in Bellot, *University College London 1826–1926*, p. 111.
112. See Bellot, *University College London 1826–1926*, pp. 57–8.
113. Council Minutes, 6 July and 10 November 1827, 21 January 1828, UCL Records Office.
114. Council Minutes, 10 and 15 May 1828, ibid.
115. Council Minutes, 14 August 1828, ibid.
116. *Morning Chronicle*, 8 July 1828; Bellot, *University College London 1826–1926*, p. 58.
117. Thomas Dale to Leonard Horner, 28 June 1828, MS College Collection: Professors: Dale, UCL Special Collections.
118. *The Times*, 28 June 1828.
119. Ibid.
120. Council Minutes, 10 July 1828, UCL Records Office.
121. Council Minutes, 9 August 1830, ibid.; letters of Dale to Horner, 28 June 1829, 13 March, 7 June, and 16 July 1830, and to Lord Auckland, 3 August 1830, College Collection: Professors: Dale, UCL Special Collections.
122. Council Minutes, 3 December 1831, UCL Records Office. For more of Lardner's career, see Chapters 2 and 3.
123. For discussions of the school and hospital, see Chapters 3 and 4.

Chapter 2 Steam Intellect: Diffusing Useful Knowledge

1. See *The Times*, 3 December 1824, for an account of the meeting to celebrate the first anniversary of the founding of the London Mechanics' Institution.
2. Henry Brougham, *Practical Observations upon the Education of the People, addressed to the Working Classes and their Employers*, 13th edition (London, 1825), p. 32. For studies of working-class education and literacy in the nineteenth century, see R.K. Webb, *The British Working Class Reader 1790–1848* (London, 1935); Thomas Kelly, *George Birkbeck: Pioneer of Adult Education* (Liverpool, 1957); and J.F.C. Harrison, *Learning and Living 1790–1960: A Study in the History of the English Adult Education Movement* (London, 1961).
3. See *The Times*, 19 May 1828.
4. For cartoons on the topic 'March of Intellect' or 'March of Mind' in the mid-1820s, see M. Dorothy George, *English Political Caricature 1793–1832: A Study of Opinion and Propaganda* (Oxford, 1959), pp. 208–13.
5. Karl Marx (with Friedrich Engels), *The Communist Manifesto* (1848; reprinted with an introduction by David McLellan, Oxford, 1998), p. 8.
6. William Thomas Moncrieff, 'The March of Intellect; or, Mechanical Academics', written in the 1830s and published in Moncrieff, *An Original Collection of Songs* (London, 1850), p. 45.
7. 'Address of the Committee', 1 June 1843, in Augustus De Morgan's own collection of SDUK papers, De Morgan Library, Senate House Library, University of London, [DeM] Z (B.P.328).

8. Ibid.
9. The most detailed study of the SDUK is the remarkable 4-volume University of London MA thesis by Monica C. Grobel, 'The Society for the Diffusion of Useful Knowledge 1826–1846 and its Relation to Adult Education in the First Half of the Nineteenth Century, alias "The Sixpenny Science Company" alias "The Steam Intellect Society"' (1933). Sales figures for the treatises are in vol. 3, pp. 681–3.
10. See Valerie Gray, *Charles Knight: Educator, Publisher, Writer* (Aldershot, 2006), especially Chapter 3, 'Knight and the Society for the Diffusion of Useful Knowledge: A Special Relationship (1827–1846)'.
11. See W. B. Clowes, *Family Business 1803–1953* (London, 1953).
12. See letter from Dugald Bannatyne to Thomas Coates, 3 June 1828, quoted in Grobel, 'The Society for the Diffusion of Useful Knowledge', vol. 2, pp. 386–7.
13. See Grobel, vol. 3, p. 681.
14. Brougham, *A Discourse of the Objects, Advantages, and Pleasures of Science* (1827).
15. *The Times*, 22 March 1827.
16. See George, *Hogarth to Cruikshank*, p. 178.
17. [William Heath?], *The Blunders of a Big-Wig; or Paul Pry's Peeps into the Sixpenny Sciences* (London, 1827), pp. 4, 13, 49, 51.
18. Thomas Love Peacock, *Crotchet Castle* (1831), Chapter 2.
19. *The Diaries of Charles Greville*, ed. Edward Pearce with Deanna Pearce (London, 2005), p. 62.
20. *The Times*, 30 January 1828.
21. See George, *Catalogue of Political and Personal Satires*, vol. 11, pp. 391, 447, 466–7.
22. See, for example, *Punch*, vol. 10 (January–June 1846), p. 248, vol. 16 (January–June 1849), p. 49, and vol. 19 (July–December 1850), p. 45.
23. *Morning Post*, 28 February 1828. A search through the British Library's database of nineteenth-century newspapers for the years 1826–1834 brought up 1,067 examples of the phrase 'march of intellect'.
24. Dionysius Lardner to Thomas Coates, 17 March 1829, SDUK Papers, UCL Special Collections; quoted in Grobel, 'The Society for the Diffusion of Useful Knowledge', vol. 1, pp. 163–5.
25. James Martineau, 'Biographical Memoranda', MS Harris Manchester College, Oxford; quoted in *ODNB* entry for Martineau.
26. UCL Special Collections has a petition dated 22 March 1838 from two students who were locked out and who gathered about seventy signatures supporting their complaint that they had paid for their tickets and were entitled to entry, and also pointing out that many students lived a long way from College and were not always able to be punctual (College Correspondence).
27. See Agnes Fry, *Memoir of the Rt Hon Sir Edward Fry*, p. 43.
28. See the De Morgan Collection, MS Add 7, UCL Special Collections.
29. For examples of William De Morgan's caricatures and sketches, see A.M.W. Stirling, *William De Morgan and his Wife* (London, 1922). The papers of the London Mathematical Society are in UCL Special Collections.
30. *Memoirs of Dr Robert Blakey*, ed. Revd Henry Miller (London, 1879), p. 75.
31. David Booth to the SDUK, 1831, Grobel, 'The Society for the Diffusion of Useful Knowledge', vol. 1, pp. 217–21.
32. See ibid., vol. 1, pp. 387–99; Charles Knight, *Passages of a Working Life during Half a Century*, 3 vols (London, 1864–5), vol. 2, pp. 132–5.
33. Dickens to Chapman and Hall, 27 September 1843, *The Letters of Charles Dickens*, ed. Madeline House, Graham Storey et al., 12 vols (Oxford, 1965–2002), vol. 3, p. 575; *The Speeches of Charles Dickens*, ed. K.J. Fielding (Hemel Hempstead, 1988), p. 48.
34. See *Punch*, vol. 2 (July–December 1842), p. 231; vol. 13 (July–December 1847), p. 30; vol. 19 (July–December 1850), p. 154.
35. Knight, *Passages of a Working Life*, vol. 2, pp. 186–8.
36. Ibid., vol. 2, p. 183.
37. For accounts of the *Penny Magazine*, the history of popular journalism, and printing innovations in the nineteenth century, see Gray, *Charles Knight*, pp. 62–4; R.D. Altick, *The English Common Reader* (Chicago, 1957); Scott Bennett, 'The Editorial Character and

Readership of the *Penny Magazine*, *Victorian Periodicals Review*, vol. 17 (1984), pp. 126–41; Patricia Anderson, *The Printed Image and the Transformation of Popular Culture 1790–1860* (Oxford, 1991); B.E. Maidment, *Reading Popular Prints 1790–1870* (Manchester, 1996).

38. Knight, *Passages of a Working Life*, vol. 2, pp. 223–4.
39. Ibid., vol. 2, pp. 222–4.
40. Sophia De Morgan, *Memoir of Augustus De Morgan*, p. 51.
41. See the British Library catalogue for all the penny magazines.
42. See Grobel, 'The Society for the Diffusion of Useful Knowledge', vol. 2, pp. 455–6.
43. John Passmore Edwards, *A Few Footprints*, p. 6.
44. Christopher Thomson, *The Autobiography of an Artisan* (London, 1847), p. 319; part quoted in Grobel, 'The Society for the Diffusion of Useful Knowledge', vol. 2, pp. 454–5.
45. *Penny Magazine*, vol. 1 (1832), Preface.
46. Ibid., vol. 1, no. 32 (29 September 1832).
47. See Grobel, 'The Society for the Diffusion of Useful Knowledge', vol. 1, p. 50.
48. *Poor Man's Guardian*, ed. Henry Hetherington (1831–5), reprinted with an introduction by Patricia Hollis, 4 vols (London, 1969), vol. 1, p. 353, quoted in Gray, *Charles Knight*, p. 8. See also George, *English Political Caricature 1793–1832*, pp. 248–50. Hetherington's biography was published by another courageous radical, George Jacob Holyoake, in 1849.
49. See Grobel, 'The Society for the Diffusion of Useful Knowledge', vol. 2, p. 461. For a helpful account of the history of taxes on newspapers and the case of the *Penny Magazine*, see Gray, *Charles Knight*, pp. 168–73.
50. See George, *Catalogue of Political and Personal Satires*, vol. 11, p. 684.
51. See *ODNB* entry on Seymour.
52. George, *Catalogue of Political and Personal Satires*, vol. 11, p. 687. The drawing is reproduced in Gray, *Charles Knight*, p. 92.
53. See Grobel, 'The Society for the Diffusion of Useful Knowledge', vol. 2, pp. 473–9.
54. Knight, *Passages of a Working Life*, vol. 2, pp. 229–34.
55. Ibid., vol. 2, p. 201.
56. *The Times*, 12 October 1854.
57. Knight, *Passages of a Working Life*, vol. 2, pp. 203–4; Gray, *Charles Knight*, pp. 54–5; Thomas Coates to Lord Brougham, 16 September 1858, Brougham Papers, UCL Special Collections.
58. Knight, *Passages of a Working Life*, vol. 2, pp. 165–6.
59. See the Introduction by Christopher Stray to the facsimile reprint of the *Quarterly Journal of Education*, 10 vols (London, 2008), vol. 1, p. x.
60. The contributors are identified by Christopher Stray in the Appendix to his Introduction, ibid., vol. 1, pp. xii–xvii.
61. De Morgan collected his own contributions to the *Journal* in a bound volume which is in the De Morgan Library, Senate House Library, University of London, [DeM] L° [De Morgan].
62. McCulloch's articles were both published in vol. 1 of the journal.
63. See Grobel, 'The Society for the Diffusion of Useful Knowledge', vol. 3, p. 664.
64. See Bellot, *University College London 1826–1926*, p. 107.
65. Lord Spencer to Thomas Coates, 6 February 1841, Grobel, 'The Society for the Diffusion of Useful Knowledge', vol. 2, p. 573.
66. George Long to Thomas Coates, 13 October 1843, ibid., vol. 2, p. 579.
67. Leonhard Schmitz to Edward Connolly, 24 November 1842, SDUK Papers, UCL Special Collections.
68. Schmitz to his editors, 4 July 1843, ibid.
69. See Bob Henderson, 'William Plate, an Unknown Acquaintance of Karl Marx at the British Museum: A Biographical Sketch', *British Library Journal*, 2005, Article 8.
70. See Grobel, 'The Society for the Diffusion of Useful Knowledge', vol. 2, pp. 597–612.
71. Henry Crabb Robinson to Thomas Coates, 11 April 1843, ibid., vol. 2, p. 594.
72. Grobel, 'The Society for the Diffusion of Useful Knowledge', vol. 3, pp. 702–3, 697.
73. Surprisingly little attention has been paid to the SDUK in studies of nineteenth-century reform movements. Even such wide-ranging studies as *Rethinking the Age of Reform: Britain 1780–1850*, ed. Arthur Burns and Joanna Innes (Cambridge, 2003), and *The Organisation*

of Knowledge in Victorian Britain, ed. Martin Daunton (Oxford, 2005), make no mention of the SDUK or its publications.

74. Knight, *Passages of a Working Life*, vol. 3, pp. 181–3.
75. Carlyle to Johann Peter Eckermann, 20 March 1830, *The Collected Letters of Thomas and Jane Welsh Carlyle*, vol. 5, pp. 84–5.
76. [William Makepeace Thackeray], 'Half-a-Crown's Worth of Cheap Knowledge', *Fraser's Magazine*, vol. 17 (March 1838), p. 279.
77. Dickens, 'Sunday Under Three Heads' (1836), in *Dickens' Journalism: Sketches by Boz and Other Early Papers 1833–39*, ed. Michael Slater (London, 1994), pp. 475–99. This is vol. 1 of 4 vols of Dickens's journalism edited by Slater.

Chapter 3 Gower Street Again: Scandals and Schools

1. Thomas Henry Huxley, memorial from 20 scientists to the Senate of the University of London, May 1858, quoted in Harte, *The University of London 1836–1986*, p. 109.
2. See *ODNB* on Charles Babbage; Lardner, 'Babbage's Calculating Engine', *Edinburgh Review*, vol. 59 (July 1834), pp. 263–327.
3. See Jack Morrell and Arnold Thackray, *Gentlemen of Science: The Early Years of the British Association for the Advancement of Science* (Oxford, 1981).
4. *Morning Chronicle*, 29 October 1828; *Examiner*, 2 November 1828.
5. See *ODNB* entry for McCulloch; Rosemary Ashton, *The Life of Samuel Taylor Coleridge: A Critical Biography* (Oxford, 1996), pp. 245–8.
6. See UCL Council Minutes, 6 July 1827, 11 October 1827, 5 and 17 November 1827, UCL Records Office.
7. Lardner's many hundreds of letters to Horner and Council members are in College Correspondence, UCL Special Collections.
8. Lardner to Brougham, 19 May 1827, MSS Applications: Maths 1827, UCL Special Collections. (Lardner applied for the maths chair in the first instance, before being offered the chair in natural philosophy and astronomy.)
9. Brougham to Lardner, 24 May 1827, MS College Correspondence 1827–8: Lardner, UCL Special Collections.
10. See Lardner to Leonard Horner, 4 November 1828, ibid.
11. Lardner to Maria Edgeworth, 7 June [1827], MS MISC 2L, UCL Special Collections.
12. *Second Statement by the Council of the University of London, explanatory of the Plan of Instruction*, published by John Taylor of 30 Upper Gower Street, November 1828, in UCL Special Collections.
13. Tom Moore's journal, 3 and 15 June 1829, *The Journals of Thomas Moore*, ed. Wilfred S. Dowden, 6 vols (Toronto and London, 1983–91), vol. 3, pp. 1219, 1229.
14. Lardner, 'Memorial of the Professors in the University of London to the Council', 14 August 1828, MS College Correspondence 1827–8: Lardner, UCL Special Collections.
15. The cartoon, by Robert Seymour, is reprinted in Harte, *The University of London 1836–1986*, p. 70.
16. See Council Minutes, 14 and 28 August 1828, UCL Records Office.
17. See Council Minutes, 8 May 1830, 3 December 1831, ibid.
18. See Council Minutes, 1 May 1830 (Malkin), 5 July 1830 (Hurwitz), 18 December 1830 (McCulloch), 5 March 1831 (Grant), ibid.
19. For an informative article on Lardner's life and work, see J.N. Hays, 'The Rise and Fall of Dionysius Lardner', *Annals of Science*, vol. 38 (1981), pp. 527–42.
20. See Lardner to Thomas Coates, 21 May 1834, MS College Correspondence 1834, UCL Special Collections. The Royal Institution had been set up by the Royal Academy in 1799 to offer public lectures. See Morris Berman, *Social Change and Scientific Organization: The Royal Institution 1799–1844* (London, 1978).
21. *The Times*, 25 May 1840.
22. Robert Southey to Henry Taylor, 29 October 1828, *New Letters of Robert Southey*, ed. Kenneth Curry, 2 vols (New York and London, 1965), vol. 2, p. 328; Southey to Grosvenor C. Bedford, 3 March 1830, *Selections from the Letters of Robert Southey*, ed. John Wood Warter, 4 vols (London, 1856), vol. 4, p. 170.
23. The advertisement is in College Correspondence 1827–8, UCL Special Collections.

24. 'The Yellowplush Correspondence: Mr Yellowplush's Ajew [adieu]', *Fraser's Magazine*, vol. 18 (August 1838), pp. 195–6. Thackeray's caricature to accompany the verbal sketch is reproduced by Gordon N. Ray, *Thackeray: The Uses of Adversity (1811–1846)* (London, 1955), between pp. 270 and 271.
25. See Hays, 'The Rise and Fall of Dionysius Lardner', pp. 528–9.
26. *The Times*, 30 October 1840.
27. *Era*, 12 April 1840.
28. Ibid., 2 August 1840; *The Times*, 19 March, 3, 14, 15, 16 April, 28 and 30 October 1840; *Annual Register for 1840*, pp. 289–304.
29. See Macready's diary entries, 12 January and 15 May 1833, 27 May and 27 October 1834, 1 May, 24 May, and 18 June 1835, and 8 June 1836, *The Diaries of William Charles Macready 1833–1851*, ed. William Toynbee, 2 vols (London, 1912), vol. 1, pp. 6, 32, 144, 194, 226, 229, 236, 326.
30. Macready Diary, 21 March and 14 April 1840, ibid., vol. 2, pp. 53, 57.
31. A copy of the marriage certificate is in the Calthrop Boucicault Collection, Templeman Library, University of Kent.
32. Macready Diary, 1 and 7 October 1843, *Diaries*, ed. Toynbee, vol. 2, pp. 225, 226.
33. See Richard Fawkes, *Dion Boucicault: A Biography* (London, 1979), pp. 8–17. For a history of marriage and divorce in England, see Lawrence Stone, *Road to Divorce: England 1530–1987* (Oxford, 1990).
34. See *London Dispatch and People's Political and Social Reformer*, 28 April 1839.
35. See Fawkes, *Dion Boucicault*, pp. 8–9, 11.
36. Boucicault's *London Assurance* was revived to ecstatic reviews at the National Theatre in London in 2010, starring Simon Russell Beale, Fiona Shaw, and Richard Briers.
37. *The Times*, 9 November 1848.
38. The *Annual Reports* show figures taken each February, in mid-session; in 1829, the first year, there were 557 students; in 1830, 596; in 1831, 516; in 1832, 400; in 1833, 432; in 1834, 469; in 1835, 489; UCL Records Office.
39. *The Greville Diary, including Passages hitherto withheld from Publication*, ed. Philip Whitwell Wilson, 2 vols (London, 1927), vol. 1, p. 480.
40. Leonard Horner to James Loch, 19 October 1828, Loch Papers, MS Add 131, UCL Special Collections.
41. Lardner to Horner, December 1827, MS College Correspondence 1827–8: Lardner, UCL Special Collections.
42. See R.A. Houston and W.W.J. Knox, *The New Penguin History of Scotland from the Earliest Times to the Present Day* (London, 2001), p. xlvi.
43. See W.P. Frith, *My Autobiography and Reminiscences*, 2 vols (London, 1887), vol. 1, pp. 20–54; John Callcott Horsley, *Recollections of a Royal Academician*, ed. Mrs Edmund Helps (London, 1903), pp. 23–4. See also *A Victorian Canvas: The Memoirs of W.P. Frith, RA*, ed. Nevile Wallis (London, 1957).
44. W.M. Thackeray, *The Newcomes* (1853–5), reprinted in 2 vols (London, 1952), vol. 1, p. 181. The chapter is entitled 'A School of Art'.
45. Henry Sass to the University of London Council, 21 June 1827, MS College Correspondence 1827, UCL Special Collections.
46. Ibid.
47. See Temple Orme, *University College School, London: Alphabetical and Topographical Register for 1831–1898* (London, 1898), p. 211.
48. Horner to Revd Thomas E. Peile, 30 January 1830, MS UCS Correspondence 1830, UCL Special Collections.
49. Council Minutes, 13 March 1830, UCL Records Office. There are several published accounts of the history of the school, later renamed University College School, including two by Temple Orme, in 1892 and 1898, Frederick William Felkin, *From Gower Street to Frognal: A Short History of University College School from 1830 to 1907* (London, 1909), and H.J.K. Usher and others, *An Angel without Wings: The History of University College School 1830–1980* (London, 1981). None of them gives the full history of the troubled early years of the school, which I have pieced together from a variety of documents in UCL Special Collections. Many papers in the University College School archives were destroyed in a fire

in 1978; the holdings which remain at the school relate mainly to the period after 1907, when the school moved to its present site in Hampstead.

50. Edward Maltby to Leonard Horner, 16 February 1830, MS UCS Correspondence, UCL Special Collections.
51. See correspondence between Horner and Browne, February–September 1830, ibid.; Council Minutes, 19 June 1830, UCL Records Office; notice of Browne's visit to Munich, *Freeman's Journal and Commercial Advertiser* (Dublin), 26 June 1830; advertisement for the new school, *Examiner*, 11 July 1830.
52. Draft report from the committee for the school, May 1830, MS UCS Correspondence, UCL Special Collections.
53. See Usher and others, *An Angel without Wings*, p. 10; Bellot, *University College London 1826–1926*, p. 170.
54. Horner to James Loch, 26 June 1830, Loch Papers, MS Add 131, UCL Special Collections.
55. See letters from Green Pemberton & Co. to Horner, 1 November 1830, 14 July and 13 September 1831, MSS UCS Correspondence, UCL Special Collections; and Christopher Haedy of the Bedford Estate Office to Thomas Coates, 4 and 27 January 1832, MSS College Correspondence 1832, ibid.
56. See Council Minutes, 18 December 1830, UCL Records Office.
57. See correspondence between Browne and Horner, July 1831, and Horner to Thomas Coates from Bonn, 10 January 1832, MSS UCS Correspondence, UCL Special Collections.
58. See Usher and others, *An Angel without Wings*, p. 15; the *ODNB* entry for Browne makes no mention of his year as the first headmaster of the University of London school.
59. *John Bull*, 11 April 1831.
60. See Browne to Walker, 29 July 1831, MS UCS Correspondence, UCL Special Collections.
61. For a record of his bankruptcy see *Ipswich Journal*, 17 December 1825.
62. Thomas Coates, 'Case for the opinion of Mr Jardine' (solicitor of the Temple), December 1831, with Jardine's reply, 15 February 1832, MSS UCS *Coates v. Walker* 1832, UCL Special Collections.
63. John Walker, printed letter to parents, 26 December 1831, MS UCS Correspondence, ibid.
64. Lardner to Coates, 30 November and 27 December 1831, 2 and 6 January 1832, and 27 September 1832, MSS College Correspondence, ibid.
65. See Thomas Coates's draft advertisement to be published in the *Athenaeum* on 31 December 1831, MS UCS Correspondence, ibid.
66. *The Times*, 12 March 1832.
67. See Michael Allen, *Charles Dickens' Childhood* (Basingstoke, 1988), pp. 78–84.
68. See *Morning Chronicle*, 14 May 1834.
69. Ibid., 10 June 1833.
70. *The Times*, 7 November 1835.
71. Council Minutes, 18 August 1831, UCL Records Office.
72. For Edward Fry's recollection of Malden's lectures, see Agnes Fry, *A Memoir of the Rt Hon Sir Edward Fry*, p. 44.
73. Thomas Hewitt Key to Isaac Lyon Goldsmid, 12 April 1833, MS Goldsmid Letterbook, Mocatta MSS, UCL Special Collections.
74. Usher and others, *An Angel without Wings*, pp. 18–19.
75. *Annual Report*, February 1835, UCL Records Office.
76. Scharf's print, which is in UCL Art Collections, is reproduced in Harte and North, *The World of UCL*, pp. 48–9.
77. See list of boys leaving the school, with their destinations, where known, MS UCS Papers, UCL Special Collections.
78. Ibid. Boucicault left in August 1835. Mr Haselwood advertised for pupil boarders in *The Times*, 18 January 1833.
79. See Fawkes, *Dion Boucicault*.
80. See Usher and others, *An Angel without Wings*, pp. 10–12, 19.

Chapter 4 Bloomsbury Medicine: Letting in the Light

1. For accounts of London's medical history and of the professionalisation of medicine in the nineteenth century, see Geoffrey Rivett, *The Development of the London Hospital System*

1823–1982 (London, 1986); Roy Porter, *Disease, Medicine and Society in England 1550–1860* (Basingstoke, 1987); *Living and Dying in London*, ed. W.F. Bynum and Roy Porter (London, 1991); Christopher Lawrence, *Medicine in the Making of Modern Britain 1700–1920* (London, 1994); *Medicine in Society*, ed. Andrew Wear (Cambridge, 1992); Nick Black, *Walking London's Medical History* (London, 2006).

2. For an account of the archival resources of the Foundling Hospital, held in the London Metropolitan Archives, see the UCL Leverhulme-funded Bloomsbury Project website, www.ucl.ac.uk/bloomsbury-project.

3. For an account of the Foundling Estate, see Olsen, *Town Planning in London*; for the history of the Foundling Hospital, see R.H. Nichols and F.A. Wray, *The History of the Foundling Hospital* (London, 1935); Gillian Pugh, *London's Forgotten Children: Thomas Coram and the Foundling Hospital* (Stroud, 2007).

4. For details of Queen Square's many small hospitals and charities in the nineteenth century, see the website of the UCL Leverhulme-funded Bloomsbury Project, www.ucl.ac.uk/bloomsbury-project. See also Walford, *Old and New London*, vol. 4, pp. 553–6.

5. Robert Louis Stevenson, draft prospectus for the College for Men and Women, 1874, quoted in Godfrey Heathcote Hamilton, *Queen Square: Its Neighbourhood & its Institutions* (London, 1926), p. 53. For the College for Men and Women, see Chapter 9.

6. Walford, *Old and New London*, vol. 4, pp. 554, 549.

7. Clarke, *Autobiographical Recollections*, p. 295.

8. Houston and Knox, *New Penguin History of Scotland*, p. xlvi.

9. Clarke, *Autobiographical Recollections*, pp. 299, 314–15.

10. See *Medical Gazette*, vol. 14 (1834), pp. 147–51; L.P. Le Quesne, 'Medicine', in *The University of London and the World of Learning 1836–1986*, pp. 128–9.

11. For accounts of the Burke and Hare murders and Robert Knox's career, see O.D. Edwards, *Burke and Hare* (Edinburgh, 1980); Ruth Richardson, *Death, Dissection, and the Destitute* (London, 1987); A.W. Bates, *The Anatomy of Robert Knox: Murder, Mad Science, and Medical Regulation* (Brighton, 2010).

12. *John Bull*, 22 September 1828.

13. Ibid., 5 January 1829.

14. See Stirling, *William De Morgan and his Wife*, p. 33.

15. See Martin Fido, *Bodysnatchers: A History of the Resurrectionists* (London, 1988), pp. 137, 169, 171.

16. Hospital Committee Minutes, 8 March 1828 and 17 January 1829, and Council Minutes, 30 March 1833, UCL Records Office.

17. This plan was announced in the *Second Statement by Council* (1828), p. 16, UCL Special Collections.

18. See Hospital Committee Minutes, 17 January 1829, UCL Records Office.

19. See Council Minutes, 16 January, 29 May, and 1 September 1830, ibid.

20. Charles Bell to George Joseph Bell, 18 February and 25 March 1831, *Letters of Sir Charles Bell selected from his Correspondence with his Brother George Joseph Bell* (London, 1870), pp. 316, 317.

21. For Pattison's career, see Frederick L.M. Pattison, *Granville Sharp Pattison: Anatomist and Antagonist 1791–1851* (Edinburgh, 1987); for the Pattison affair in the University of London, see Bellot, *University College London 1826–1926*, pp. 195–212.

22. Bellot, *University College London 1826–1926*, p. 197.

23. See *ODNB* entry for Pattison.

24. Pattison's reply to charges made by students, March 1831, MS College Correspondence: Pattison Case, UCL Special Collections.

25. See *Lancet*, 7 and 14 August and 18 September 1830, 27 August and 17 September 1831 (among many more articles and letters to the editor on the subject of Pattison); Bellot, *University College London 1826–1926*, p. 205.

26. See *The Times*, 24 September 1831; Council Minutes, 30 July 1831, UCL Records Office. For the correspondence between Pattison and his fellow professors and the Council, see MSS College Correspondence: Pattison Case, UCL Special Collections.

27. See Bellot, *University College London 1826–1926*, p. 149.

28. See Berman, *Social Change and Scientific Organization*.

29. Obituary of Elliotson, *Lancet*, vol. 92 (8 August 1868), p. 203.

30. See Harley Williams, *Doctors Differ: Five Studies in Contrast* (London, 1946), pp. 29–30.

31. See *Morning Chronicle*, 26 February 1825; Roger Jones, 'Thomas Wakley, Plagiarism, Libel, and the Founding of the *Lancet*', *Lancet*, vol. 371 (26 April 2008), pp. 1410–11.

32. Wakley, 'Preface, Advertisement, Address, and a Rare Whack at the Voracious Bats. Not forgetting a few useful hints to our beloved but cruelly-plundered friends, the British students in medicine', *Lancet*, vol. 17 (1 October 1831), pp. 1–16. For an account of Wakley's career, see John Hostettler, *Thomas Wakley: An Improbable Radical* (Chichester, 1993).

33. Wakley, 'Preface etc', p. 16.

34. *The Times*, 1 September 1841.

35. 1868 obituary of Elliotson, *Lancet*, vol. 92, p. 203.

36. John Elliotson, annual report to Council, May 1834, and letter to Council, 11 July 1834, MSS College Correspondence, UCL Special Collections.

37. Elliotson to Council, early 1837, ibid.

38. For the complicated history of UCL and the University of London, see Bellot, *University College London 1826–1836*, pp. 216–48.

39. Knight, *Knight's Cyclopædia of London* (London, 1851), p. 350.

40. See Roger Cooter, *The Cultural Meaning of Popular Science: Phrenology and the Organization of Consent in Nineteenth-Century Britain* (Cambridge, 1984).

41. *Lancet*, 26 May and 25 August 1838; *Athenaeum*, 21 July 1838; Winter, *Mesmerized*, pp. 46–50.

42. See Winter, *Mesmerized*, pp. 52–7.

43. See Rosemary Ashton, *142 Strand: A Radical Address in Victorian London* (London, 2006), pp. 22, 145–6, 266. For Harriet Martineau's career, see R.K. Webb, *Harriet Martineau: A Radical Victorian* (London, 1960).

44. For the experiment on Prince Albert, see *Illustrated London News* (1849), reproduced in Winter, *Mesmerized*, p. 150.

45. Dickens, *Oliver Twist; or, the Parish Boy's Progress*, by 'Boz' (1838), chapter 34.

46. Alison Winter points out the similarity to mesmeric trance in Cruikshank's illustration in *Mesmerized*, p. 58.

47. Elliotson to Council, 23 May 1838, MS College Correspondence, UCL Special Collections.

48. Council Minutes, 26 May 1838, UCL Records Office.

49. For a detailed discussion of Elliotson's work with the O'Key sisters, using Elliotson's case-books and Wakley's articles in the *Lancet*, see Winter, *Mesmerized*, pp. 67–78, 93–100.

50. Council Minutes, 6, 9, and 13 June 1838, UCL Records Office; see also Winter, *Mesmerized*, p. 95.

51. 'Animal Magnetism; or Mesmerism', *Lancet*, vol. 30 (1 September 1838), p. 811.

52. For a full account of the experiments which brought Elliotson down, see Clarke, *Autobiographical Recollections*, pp. 162–94.

53. Ibid., pp. 300–2.

54. Elliotson to C.C. Atkinson, secretary of University College, 27 December 1838, MS College Correspondence, UCL Special Collections.

55. Student memorandum to the Council, 5 January 1839, MS College Correspondence, UCL Special Collections; Council Minutes, 5 January 1839, UCL Records Office.

56. Isaac Lyon Goldsmid to William Tooke, 18 April 1839, MS College Correspondence, UCL Special Collections.

57. Braid published *Neurypnology, or, the Rationale of Nervous Sleep, considered in Relation with Animal Magnetism* in 1843.

58. See Dickens to George Cruikshank, 28 December 1838, to Dr R.H. Collyer, 27 January 1842, and to Daniel Maclise, 24 July 1842, *The Letters of Charles Dickens*, vol. 1, p. 480, vol. 3, pp. 22–3 and n, and p. 277.

59. Elliotson to Dickens, February 1841, quoted ibid., vol. 2, p. 210n.

60. William Makepeace Thackeray, Dedication to *The History of Pendennis* (London, 1850).

61. See Winter, *Mesmerized*, passim.

62. Henry Crabb Robinson Diary, 10 March 1842, MS Dr Williams's Library.

63. Henry Crabb Robinson Diary, 19 November 1844 and 15 April 1847, ibid.

64. The history of the Mesmeric Infirmary is complicated; historians have contradicted one another about its whereabouts and personnel. My information is gleaned from an online

search through digitised newspapers: *The Times* and Nineteenth-Century British Library Newspapers online. Useful articles include the following: *Morning Post*, 8 September 1846, 24 May 1850, 9 May 1851, 18 June and 15 September 1853, 8 June 1854; *The Times*, 17 February 1851, 2 May 1854, 6 June 1859, 2 June 1869. The 1851 Census shows 9 Bedford Street as the home of the 'Mesmeric Society'.

65. *Punch*, vol. 2 (January–June 1842), p. 182.

66. Henry Lonsdale, *A Sketch of the Life and Writings of Robert Knox the Anatomist* (London, 1870), p. 66. For more of Liston's exploits, see Fido, *Bodysnatchers*, pp. 89–96.

67. Council Minutes, 18 October 1834, UCL Records Office; Bellot, *University College London 1826–1926*, p. 164.

68. See Clarke, *Autobiographical Recollections*, p. 309.

69. Article on Carswell in the *University College Gazette*, vol. 1 (11 July 1887), p. 176. Carswell's drawings are in UCL Special Collections.

70. Robert Liston to Robert Carswell, 31 October 1835, MS College Correspondence, UCL Special Collections.

71. See William Squire, 'On the Introduction of Ether Inhalation as an Anaesthetic in London', *Lancet*, vol. 132 (22 December 1888), pp. 1220–1; F.W. Cock, 'The First Operation under Ether in Europe – The Story of Three Days', *University College Hospital Magazine*, vol. 1 (1911), pp. 127–44. See also Sir Henry Thompson, 'Robert Liston', *University College Gazette*, vol. 2 (June 1901), pp. 202–4, UCL Special Collections.

72. Squire, 'On the Introduction of Ether Inhalation', p. 1221; James Miller, 'Painless Operations in Surgery', *North British Review*, vol. 7 (1847), pp. 176–7. For the early uses of ether, see Winter, *Mesmerized*, pp. 177–83.

73. Squire, 'On the Introduction of Ether Inhalation', pp. 1220–1.

74. See the *ODNB* entry for Jenner.

75. Henry Crabb Robinson Reminiscence, 1851, in Henry Crabb Robinson, *Diary, Reminiscences and Correspondence*, ed. Thomas Sadler, 3 vols (London, 1869), vol. 2, p. 197.

76. Davis, *The University Site*, p. 94, identifies the spot as the west side of Gordon Square.

77. *The Speeches of Charles Dickens*, pp. 326–7, 329 and n.

78. See Jules Kosky, *Mutual Friends: Charles Dickens and Great Ormond Street Children's Hospital* (London, 1989), pp. 45–9.

79. Ibid., passim.

80. Dickens and Morley, 'Drooping Buds', *Household Words* (3 April 1852), in *The Uncollected Writings of Charles Dickens: Household Words 1850–1859*, ed. Harry Stone, 2 vols (London, 1969), vol. 2, pp. 404, 405.

81. Minutes of the Fourth Annual Meeting of Governors, 14 February 1856, MS GOS/1/2/5, Museum & Archives Service, Great Ormond Street Hospital for Children NHS Trust.

82. Minutes of the Committee of Management, 30 October 1857, MS GOS/1/2/6, ibid.

83. *The Speeches of Charles Dickens*, p. 251.

84. Dickens, *Our Mutual Friend* (1864–5), Book Two, chapter 9.

85. Quoted on the title page of Kosky, *Mutual Friends*.

86. See Dickens to Frederic Quin, 3 January 1839, *The Letters of Charles Dickens*, vol. 1, p. 490.

87. Thackeray to his mother, 16–20 December 1839, *The Letters and Private Papers of William Makepeace Thackeray*, ed. Gordon N. Ray, 4 vols (Cambridge, Massachusetts, 1945–6), vol. 1, p. 400.

88. St John Long was a well-known quack, called the 'King of Humbugs' by Wakley; see *Lancet*, vol. 13 (9 January 1830), p. 506.

89. Thackeray to Edward FitzGerald, October 1841, *The Letters and Private Papers of William Makepeace Thackeray*, vol. 2, pp. 36–7.

90. See Shirley Neale, 'Quackery at King's Cross: James Morison & the British College of Health', *Camden History Journal*, vol. 28 (2004), pp. 16–21.

91. Ibid., pp. 17–18.

92. See *Medical Fringe and Medical Orthodoxy 1750–1850*, ed. W.F. Bynum and Roy Porter (London, 1987); Phillip Nicholls, *Homœopathy and the Medical Profession* (London, 1988); Roy Porter, *Health for Sale: Quackery in England 1660–1850* (Manchester, 1989); Roberta Bivins, *Alternative Medicine? A History* (Oxford, 2007).

93. See Clarke, *Autobiographical Recollections*, pp. 312–13.

94. *Punch*, vol. 18 (January–June 1850), p. 153.
95. See Black, *Walking London's Medical History*, pp. 89–90.
96. See *History of the Italian Hospital in London, 1884–1906* (London, 1906), and David R. Green, 'Little Italy in Victorian London', *Camden History Review*, vol. 15 (1988), pp. 2–6.

Chapter 5 The British Museum, Panizzi, and the Whereabouts of Russell Square

1. *Fraser's Magazine*, vol. 17 (March 1838), p. 280.
2. See Ray, *Thackeray: The Uses of Adversity*, pp. 202, 255–60.
3. *Ambulator; or, A Pocket Companion for the Tour of London and its Environs* (London, 1811), p. 23.
4. *Cruchley's Picture of London*, second edition (London, 1835), p. 132.
5. Thackeray, *Vanity Fair* (London, 1848), chapter 56, 'Georgy is made a Gentleman', and chapter 42, 'Which treats of the Osborne Family'.
6. Walford, *Old and New London*, vol. 4, p. 484.
7. For a history of the so-called silver-fork school of fiction, see Alison Adburgham, *Silver Fork Society: Fashionable Life and Literature from 1814 to 1840* (London, 1983).
8. Theodore Hook, 'Merton', in *Sayings and Doings*, First Series (London, 1824, reprinted 1836), pp. 353–4.
9. See David M. Wilson, *The British Museum: A History* (London, 2002), p. 19. Of the many books on the history of the British Museum, Wilson's is the most comprehensive; unless otherwise stated, it is the chief source of information in my discussion.
10. See J. Mordaunt Crook, *The British Museum* (London, 1972), pp. 51–2.
11. Ibid., pp. 62–6; *Hansard*, 25 March 1833.
12. See, for example, Committee Minutes, vol. 10 (10 June 1826), vol. 12 (11 May 1833), vol. 13 (8 June 1833), British Museum Central Archive.
13. British Museum Accounts, 16 March 1847, in *Printed Papers etc. concerning the British Museum 1753–1851*, ibid.
14. *Hansard*, 1 July 1823.
15. Ibid., 29 March 1824.
16. *The Times*, 10 October 1823.
17. *Hansard*, 1 July 1823, 1 and 29 March 1824, 2 and 9 April 1824.
18. See Crook, *The British Museum*, p. 128; Robert Cowtan, *Memories of the British Museum* (London, 1872), p. 11.
19. *Hansard*, 28 March 1825.
20. Ibid., 16 May 1825.
21. *London Magazine*, new series 2 (1 June 1825), pp. 272, 273–4.
22. 'Increase of London, from the Rage for Building', *Morning Chronicle*, 25 October 1826. I am indebted to Matthew Ingleby for drawing my attention to this article, and to several other sources relating to Russell Square quoted here.
23. Disraeli, *Vivian Grey*, vol. 1, p. 71.
24. 'The Dandy School', *Examiner*, 18 November 1827.
25. '*The Young Duke*; by the Author of *Vivian Grey*', ibid., 11 September 1831.
26. Catherine Gore, 'The Special License', *The Fair of Mayfair*, 3 vols (London, 1832), vol. 3, p. 327. See also Edward Copeland, 'Crossing Oxford Street: Silverfork Geopolitics', *Eighteenth-Century Life*, vol. 25 (2001), pp. 116–34.
27. *Hansard*, 25 March 1833.
28. Ibid., 1 April 1833.
29. Select Committee Minutes, 1835, quoted in Edward Miller, *That Noble Cabinet: A History of the British Museum* (London, 1973), p. 139.
30. Select Committee Report, 14 July 1836, *Printed Papers etc. concerning the British Museum 1753–1851*, British Museum Central Archive.
31. See the annual *Statutes and Rules* of the British Museum, and the Indexes to the Standing Committees, General Meetings, and Sub-Committees, British Museum Central Archive.
32. *Punch*, vol. 2 (January–June 1842), p. 184.
33. *Hansard*, 20 March 1855.

34. *Punch*, vol. 29 (18 August 1855), p. 64.
35. Committee Minutes, vol. 29 (9 February and 9 March 1861); General Meeting Minutes, vol. 8 (13 July 1861), British Museum Central Archive.
36. Miller, *That Noble Cabinet*, p. 257.
37. Select Committee Minutes, 1836, quoted ibid., p. 145.
38. Miller, *Prince of Librarians*, pp. 329–30.
39. Anthony Panizzi to Revd Josiah Forshall (Secretary to the Museum), 25 July 1837, Original Letters and Papers, vol. 17, British Museum Central Archive.
40. Transcribed copy of Madden's MS diary, British Museum Central Archive.
41. Thomas Carlyle, 'Parliamentary History of the French Revolution', *London and Westminster Review* (1837), reprinted in *Critical and Miscellaneous Essays*, 5 vols (London, 1899), vol. 4, pp. 7–8.
42. Carlyle to Frederick Denison Maurice, 24 December 1838, *The Collected Letters of Thomas and Jane Welsh Carlyle*, vol. 10, p. 245.
43. Carlyle's speech, quoted ibid., vol. 12, p. 174 n.
44. See *The Times*, 24 June 1840 and 11 May 1844, *The Era*, 18 April 1841, and *The Standard*, 26 May 1845. For a history of the London Library, see John Wells, *Rude Words: A Discursive History of the London Library* (London, 1991).
45. Carlyle to Panizzi, 11 April 1853, *The Collected Letters of Thomas and Jane Welsh Carlyle*, vol. 28, pp. 105–6.
46. Carlyle's testimony to the commission of inquiry, 8 February 1849, quoted in David Alec Wilson, *Carlyle at his Zenith (1848–53)*, vol. 4 of a 6-volume biography of Carlyle (London, 1923–34), pp. 77–81.
47. Panizzi to Carlyle, 12 April 1853, MS Official Papers: Sir A. Panizzi, British Library; part published in *The Collected Letters of Thomas and Jane Welsh Carlyle*, vol. 28, p. 106 n.
48. Committee Minutes, vol. 26 (7 May 1853), British Museum Central Archive.
49. See Wilson, *The British Museum: A History*, pp. 118–19; Miller, *Prince of Librarians*, pp. 208–9; Crook, *The British Museum*, pp. 163–70.
50. *Publishers' Circular* and Madden's diary, 17 April 1857, quoted in Marjorie Caygill and Christopher Date, *Building the British Museum* (London, 1999), pp. 47–8.
51. Sir Henry Ellis to Panizzi, 21 April and 4 May 1857, quoted in Fagan, *Life of Sir Anthony Panizzi*, vol. 1, pp. 366–7.
52. Sir Henry Ellis to Panizzi, 14 February 1856, ibid., vol. 2, p. 5.
53. *Hansard*, 21 April 1856.
54. Committee Minutes, vol. 31 (24 June 1865), British Museum Central Archive.
55. Fagan, *Life of Sir Anthony Panizzi*, vol. 2, p. 269.
56. 'A Medal for the Museum', *Punch*, vol. 41 (17 August 1861), p. 69.
57. Quoted in Caygill and Date, *Building the British Museum*, p. 52. See also Crook, *The British Museum*, pp. 199–200.
58. Quoted in Edward Edwards, *Lives of the Founders of the British Museum*, 2 vols (London, 1870), vol. 1, pp. 593–4.
59. See Wilson, *The British Museum: A History*, Appendix 2, p. 379, for the developing departmental structure of the collections.
60. Ibid., pp. 74, 106–9; *The Times*, 23 July 1850; *Lloyd's Weekly Newspaper*, 6 October 1850; *Era*, 13 October 1850.
61. Thomas Donaldson to the trustees of the British Museum, 27 September 1853, Original Letters and Papers, vol. 49, British Museum Central Archive.
62. See Committee Minutes, vol. 28 (7 May 1859), British Museum Central Archive.
63. Terms of 'Dr George Swiney's Lecturer on Geology', April 1846, *Printed Papers etc. concerning the British Museum 1753–1851*, British Museum Central Archive.
64. The Grant Museum can still be visited at University College London.
65. See, for example, Original Letters and Papers, vols 15, 21, 24, and General Meetings Minutes, vols 6 and 7, British Museum Central Archive.
66. Crook, *The British Museum*, pp. 211–15.
67. *The Times*, 19 March 1894.
68. See John N. Henderson, 'The Museum Tavern in Bloomsbury', *Camden History Review*, vol. 16 (1989), p. 8.

69. George Arliss, *Up the Years from Bloomsbury: An Autobiography* (Boston, Massachusetts, 1927), pp. 19–20.
70. H.G. Wells, *Experiment in Autobiography: Discoveries and Conclusions of a Very Ordinary Brain (since 1866)*, 2 vols (London, 1934, reprinted 1966), vol. 1, p. 312. See also Christopher Rolfe, 'From Camden Town to Crest Hill: H.G. Wells's Local Connections', *Camden History Review*, vol. 10 (1982), p. 2.
71. *Tea and Anarchy! The Bloomsbury Diary of Olive Garnett*, ed. Barry C. Johnson, 2 vols (London, 1989), vol. 1, pp. 2–3. The diary covers the years 1890 to 1895.
72. Olive Garnett Diary, 13 January 1895, ibid., vol. 2, pp. 143–4.
73. Ibid., 24 February 1892 and 1 December 1891, vol. 1, pp. 62, 58.
74. See Robin Woolven, 'George Gissing's London Residences 1877–1891', *Camden History Review*, vol. 28 (2004), pp. 7, 9.
75. See Olive Garnett Diary, 15 November 1895, 4 May 1894, 30 March 1895, 23 February 1894, *Tea and Anarchy!*, vol. 2, pp. 216, 71, 164, 39.

Chapter 6 Towards the Millennium

1. See Francis Warre Cornish, *The English Church in the Nineteenth Century*, 2 vols (London, 1910); C.R. Sanders, *Coleridge and the Broad Church Movement* (New York, 1942, reprinted 1972); J. Hillis Miller, *The Disappearance of God* (Cambridge, Massachusetts, 1963); Owen Chadwick, *The Victorian Church*, 2 vols (London, 1970).
2. See Nigel Yates, *Anglican Ritualism in Victorian Britain 1830–1910* (Oxford, 1999).
3. For the influence of such works, culminating in David Friedrich Strauss's *Leben Jesu* (*Life of Jesus*, 1835), see E.S. Shaffer, *'Kubla Khan' and The Fall of Jerusalem* (Cambridge, 1975), and Rosemary Ashton, *The German Idea: Four English Writers and the Reception of German Thought 1800–1860* (Cambridge, 1980, reprinted London, 1994).
4. *John Bull*, 26 November 1827.
5. See *The Times*, 10 August 1861.
6. Dickens, 'The Bloomsbury Christening', *Monthly Magazine*, April 1834, reprinted in *Dickens' Journalism: Sketches by Boz and Other Early Papers*, ed. Slater, p. 452 (vol. 1 of 4 vols of Dickens's journalism). A blue plaque adorns the house, 14 Great Russell Street, where the Kitterbells are said to have lived.
7. Dickens, review of *The Drunkard's Children. A Sequel to the Bottle*, in Eight Plates, by George Cruikshank, in *Examiner*, 8 July 1848, reprinted in *Dickens' Journalism: 'The Amusements of the People' and Other Papers 1834–51*, ed. Michael Slater (London, 1996), p. 105 (vol. 2 of 4).
8. See Clinch, *Bloomsbury and St Giles's*, pp. 17, 73.
9. See White, *London in the Nineteenth Century*, p. 132.
10. See George, *Hogarth to Cruikshank*, p. 169. See also Pierce Egan's comic work, illustrated by George Cruikshank, *Life in London, or, the Day and Night Scenes of Jerry Hawthorne Esq and his elegant Friend Corinthian Tom, accompanied by Bob Logic the Oxonian in their Rambles and Sprees through the Metropolis* (London, 1821).
11. Quoted in the *Oxford English Dictionary*. See also John Gage, 'The Rise and Fall of the St Giles Rookery', *Camden History Review*, vol. 12 (1984), pp. 17–24.
12. Gage, 'Rise and Fall', pp. 21–2; see also Peter Woodford, 'Provident and Non-Provident Dispensaries in Camden', *Camden History Review*, vol. 25 (2001), p. 30.
13. Thomas Miller, 'Picturesque Sketches of London, Past and Present', *Illustrated London News*, vol. 15 (22 September 1849), p. 197. See also the excellent statistical study by Lynn Hollen Lees, *Exiles of Erin: Irish Migrants in Victorian London* (Manchester, 1979).
14. Beames, *The Rookeries of London*, pp. 41, 43.
15. Lehmann, *Holborn: An Historical Portrait of a London Borough*, pp. 132–8; Olsen, *Town Planning in London*, p. 191. See also Isobel Watson, 'Five Per Cent Philanthropy: Model Houses for the Working Classes in Victorian Camden', *Camden History Review*, vol. 9 (1981), pp. 4–9. For details of the inhabitants as described in the 1851 Census, compiled by Deborah Colville, see the UCL Leverhulme-funded Bloomsbury Project website, www.ucl.ac.uk/bloomsbury-project.
16. Lucas, *A Wanderer in London*, p. 188.
17. *Punch*, vol. 2 (January–June 1842), p. 184.

18. See Clinch, *Bloomsbury and St Giles's*, p. 6.
19. 'Census Returns on Religious Worship', *Manchester Times*, 11 January 1854.
20. 'The Census of Religious Bodies', *Newcastle Courant*, 3 February 1854.
21. See Arthur Sigismund Diamond, *The Building of a Synagogue: A Brief History*, a 12-page pamphlet published by the West London Synagogue (London, 1970).
22. St Pancras New Church was opened in 1822. It was called a 'Pagan temple' on account of its design, see Timbs, *Curiosities of London*, p. 195.
23. A.G. L'Estrange on William Harness in *Personal Reminiscences by Barham, Harness, and Hodder*, ed. Richard Henry Stoddard (New York, 1895), p. 233.
24. Thomas Carlyle, 'Death of Edward Irving', *Fraser's Magazine* (January 1835). For the relationship between Irving and Carlyle, see Ashton, *Thomas and Jane Carlyle*.
25. Edward Irving to Thomas Carlyle, 29 April 1822, quoted in Barbara Waddington, *The Rev. Edward Irving & the Catholic Apostolic Church in Camden and Beyond*, Occasional Paper No. 7 of the Camden History Society (London, 2007), pp. 13–14. Irving's letters to Carlyle are in the National Library of Scotland.
26. Ibid., p. 15. Everett Street was subsumed into Marchmont Street in 1877–8; see the UCL Leverhulme-funded Bloomsbury Project website: www.ucl.ac.uk/bloomsbury-project.
27. John Hair, *Regent Square: Eighty Years of a London Congregation* (London, 1899), pp. 39–40.
28. Thomas Carlyle, *Reminiscences* (1881), eds K.J. Fielding and Ian Campbell (Oxford, 1997), pp. 291–2.
29. Carlyle to Alexander Carlyle, 20 December 1822, *The Collected Letters of Thomas and Jane Welsh Carlyle*, vol. 2, p. 237.
30. Edward Irving to Grace Welsh (mother of Jane Welsh, later Jane Carlyle), 6 December 1822, quoted in Grass, *The Lord's Watchman*, p. 53.
31. See Columba Graham Flegg, *'Gathered Under Apostles': A Study of the Catholic Apostolic Church* (Oxford, 1992), p. 50.
32. Hair, *Regent Square*, pp. 47–8; Grass, *The Lord's Watchman*, p. 107.
33. Hair, *Regent Square*, p. 50.
34. For the most detailed account of Irving's career see Grass, *The Lord's Watchman*.
35. Ibid., p. 55.
36. See *Survey of London*, 42 vols so far (London, 1900—), vol. 24 (1952).
37. *The Times*, 2 July 1824.
38. Ibid., 12 May 1827.
39. Hair, *Regent Square*, p. 82.
40. Samuel Taylor Coleridge to Charlotte Brent, 7 July 1823, *Collected Letters of Samuel Taylor Coleridge*, ed. Earl Leslie Griggs, 6 vols (Oxford, 1956–71), vol. 5, p. 280.
41. Hair, *Regent Square*, p. 73.
42. Coleridge to Daniel Stuart, 8 July 1825, to Mrs Montagu, 1 May 1827, and to J.H. Green, 31 May 1830, *Collected Letters*, vol. 5, pp. 474–5, vol. 6, pp. 677, 840.
43. *John Bull*, 20 July 1823.
44. William Hazlitt, 'Rev. Mr Irving', *The Spirit of the Age* (London, 1825); the essay was first printed in the *New Monthly Magazine* in 1824.
45. For a full account of the 'speaking in tongues', see Grass, *The Lord's Watchman*, p. 205ff.
46. Cardale practised as a solicitor in Bedford Row, and his family appears to have lived there in the 1830s, see *The Times*, 22 October 1832.
47. *The Times*, 19 October 1831.
48. Ibid., 29 October 1831.
49. Quoted in David Tierney, 'The Catholic Apostolic Church: A Study in Tory Millenarianism', *Historical Research*, vol. 63 (October 1990), p. 294.
50. Henry Crabb Robinson Diary, 5 May 1825, MS Dr Williams's Library, London.
51. Grass, *The Lord's Watchman*, p. 260.
52. See Waddington, *The Rev. Edward Irving*, p. 34.
53. *The Times*, 5 May 1832.
54. Elmes, *Metropolitan Improvements*, pp. 142–3.
55. *The Times*, 1 March 1830; Robert Leon, 'The Man Who Made King's Cross: The Misfortunes of Stephen Geary', *Camden History Review*, vol. 17 (1992), pp. 13–16; David

Hayes, '"Without Parallel in the Known World": The Chequered Past of 277 Gray's Inn Road', ibid., vol. 25 (2001), pp. 5–9.

56. See Leon, 'The Man Who Made King's Cross', pp. 13–14.
57. *The Times*, 22 October 1832.
58. Grass, *The Lord's Watchman*, p. 276ff.
59. Ibid., p. 295.
60. Ibid., p. 196.
61. Ibid., p. 222.
62. Elizabeth Barrett to Hugh Stuart Boyd, 10 December 1831, *The Brownings' Correspondence*, eds Philip Kelley et al., 16 vols so far (Winfield, Kansas, 1984—), vol. 2, pp. 333–4.
63. For Carlyle's spiritual views, see *Sartor Resartus* (1833–4), which has a chapter entitled 'Natural Supernaturalism'.
64. Henry Drummond to James Loch, 22 October 1828, Loch Papers, MS Add 131, UCL Special Collections.
65. See printed document, published in 1830, about the founding of King's College London, in UCL Special Collections.
66. Flegg, '*Gathered Under Apostles*', pp. 34–9.
67. See Ashton, *Thomas and Jane Carlyle*, p. 118ff.
68. Carlyle to Jane Carlyle, 22 August 1831, *The Collected Letters of Thomas and Jane Welsh Carlyle*, vol. 5, p. 352.
69. Spencer Perceval to Isaac Lyon Goldsmid, 18 February 1831, MS Mocatta 22, UCL Special Collections.
70. See Grass, *The Lord's Watchman*, p. 245.
71. Flegg, '*Gathered Under Apostles*', p. 51.
72. Ibid., pp. 63–4.
73. Ibid., pp. 65–6.
74. Carlyle to Christian Bunsen, 7 July 1843, *The Collected Letters of Thomas and Jane Welsh Carlyle*, vol. 16, p. 238.
75. For Cardale's career, see Flegg, '*Gathered Under Apostles*', Tierney, 'The Catholic Apostolic Church', and John Lancaster, 'John Bate Cardale, Pillar of Apostles: A Quest for Catholicity', PhD thesis, St Andrews University, 1978.
76. There are many Cardale descendants, including Mark Cardale, who kindly allowed me access to his collection of family papers.
77. See Cardale's letters to Drummond, October 1846–November 1852, MSS in the Archives of the Duke of Northumberland at Alnwick Castle, DFP: C/11, with copies in the Bodleian Library, Oxford.
78. For Knight, see Seraphim Newman-Norton, *A Biographical Index of Those Associated with the Lord's Work* (London, 1972), p. 67.
79. [J.P. Knight], *On Building a Church for Divine Worship: A Discourse delivered by One of the Deacons of the Central Church, 3rd November 1850* (London, 1850), p. 3.
80. See Haedy's 1852 report, Annual Reports vol. 3 (1848–1852), BE RB6, Bedford Estate Office, Woburn Abbey; see also Hobhouse, *Thomas Cubitt*, pp. 76–8.
81. 'Particulars of Proposed Sale', December 1919, Bedford Estate Papers, NMR 19/6/1, Bedford Estate Office, Woburn Abbey.
82. [Knight], *On Building a Church*, p. 13.
83. Information from the minutes of the Councils and Conferences of Angels from 1850, MSS Archives of the New Apostolic Church of North Germany, Hamburg. I am indebted to the archivist, Manfred Henke, for copies of these minutes.
84. J. Malcolm Lickfold, *The Catholic Apostolic Church, Gordon Square, London: Notes on the Architectural Features and the Furniture, with a Glossary of Technical Terms* (London, 1935), p. 38.
85. Minutes of deacons' meetings, 3 October 1850, 3 and 11 June 1851, MSS Archives of the New Apostolic Church, Hamburg.
86. Minutes 13 May and 20 July 1853, ibid.
87. The architect John Belcher published a pamphlet, *Catholic Apostolic Church, Gordon Square London* (London, 1885), consisting of designs for completion which were never implemented.
88. I am indebted to Tim Grass for information about Isabella Irving.

89. Samuel Rawson Gardiner to Martin Irving, 25 April, 4, 13, and 16 May 1858; letters in private hands. I am grateful to Tim Grass for this information.
90. *Morning Chronicle*, 15 January 1853.
91. Thomas Carlyle to John Carlyle, 23 November 1850, *The Collected Letters of Thomas and Jane Welsh Carlyle*, vol. 25, p. 293.
92. [Francis Woodhouse], *The Census and the Catholic Apostolic Church* (London, 1854), p. 14.
93. Olsen, *Town Planning in London*, pp. 62–3.
94. [John Bate Cardale], *A Discourse delivered in the Catholic Apostolic Church, Gordon Square, on the Occasion of Consecrating the Altar, and Opening the Church for Public Worship, Christmas Eve, 1853* (London, 1854), pp. 3–5.
95. Ibid., pp. 6, 10, 12, 13.
96. *Morning Chronicle*, 2 and 23 January 1854.
97. Tierney, 'The Catholic Apostolic Church', pp. 303–4; see also Rowland A. Davenport, *Albury Apostles: The Story of the Body known as the Catholic Apostolic Church (sometimes called 'Irvingites')* (London, 1970), pp. 190–1.
98. 'When the Lamb opened the seventh seal, there was silence in heaven for about half an hour', before the seven angels blow their trumpets to signal the destruction of the earth, *Revelation*, 8:1 (Revised Standard Version of *The Bible*).
99. Flegg, '*Gathered Under Apostles*', pp. 88–9. The reason that a number of papers belonging to the Gordon Square church are available for consultation is that they were purchased by the Hamburg branch of the New Apostolic Church, which allows access to scholars. I am indebted to the archivist at Hamburg, Manfred Henke, for access to these papers. He has published a number of helpful articles on the Gordon Square church, in German, in his own church's journal, *Unsere Familie*.
100. Cardale to Drummond, 20 August 1853, MS Alnwick Castle, DFP: C/11/26.
101. Dickens to Henry Austin, 14 and 19 September 1851, and to Frank Stone, 19 and 21 September 1851, *The Letters of Charles Dickens*, vol. 6, pp. 482, 485–6, 487. See also Michael Slater, *Charles Dickens* (New Haven and London, 2009), p. 331ff.
102. Dickens to Cardale, 27 May 1852, *The Letters of Charles Dickens*, vol. 6, p. 684.
103. Dickens to W.H. Wills, 20 April 1854, ibid., vol. 7, p. 320.
104. [John Bate Cardale], *A Discourse upon the Obligation of Tithe, delivered in the Catholic Apostolic Church, Gordon Square, on Tuesday, October 5, 1858* (London, 1858).
105. Tierney, 'The Catholic Apostolic Church', pp. 309–10. The MS correspondence between Drummond and Cardale was inherited by the Duke of Northumberland and is in the archive at the family seat, Alnwick Castle.
106. Theodore Hook, *Peregrine Bunce; or, settled at last*, 3 vols (London, 1842), vol. 3, pp. 240–2.
107. *Morning Chronicle*, 10 May 1845.
108. *Examiner*, 16 August 1851; Besant, *London in the Nineteenth Century*, p. 397.
109. See Clement John Wilkinson, *James John Garth Wilkinson: A Memoir of his Life, with a Selection from his Letters* (London, 1911), pp. 17, 33, 43.
110. *Morning Chronicle*, 12 May 1852; *The Times*, 9 January 1854. The Swedenborg Society is now located on Bloomsbury Way in the south-east corner of Bloomsbury Square. It has its own bookshop and houses the archive of the Society, including MS letters of James John Garth Wilkinson. See the Society's website, www.swedenborg.org.uk. I am indebted to the Secretary of the Swedenborg Society, Richard Lines, for information on the Society and access to the archives. His *History of the Swedenborg Society 1810–2010* was published by the Society in 2011.

Chapter 7 A 'Quasi-Collegiate' Experiment in Gordon Square

1. Summary of the Albury conference, July 1830, in Grass, *The Lord's Watchman*, p. 216.
2. *Report of the Religious Liberty Memorial Committee*, p. 1, University Hall Minute Book 1844–8, MS 12.82, Dr Williams's Library.
3. Ibid.
4. Bellot, *University College London 1826–1926*, p. 300. The inscription was on the wall of the dining hall, but is now obscured by wallpaper (information from Dr David Wykes, Director of Dr Williams's Library).

5. See University Hall Minute Books and miscellaneous documents relating to the Hall, MSS 12.82 and 12.90, Dr Williams's Library.

6. See Marie Draper, 'Banking in Bloomsbury: A Savings Bank at No. 30 Montague Street', *Camden History Review*, vol. 14 (1986), pp. 8–9.

7. 'First Annual Report of the Council of University Hall', 20 July 1848, p. 5, MS 12.90, Dr Williams's Library; University Hall Council Minutes, 14 June 1855, MS 12.85, ibid.

8. Henry Crabb Robinson kept a diary for over 50 years; 33 volumes of the MS diaries, dating from 1811 to 1867, are in Dr Williams's Library, as are 29 volumes of travel journals and 32 volumes of letters. Selections have been published, including *Diary, Reminiscences and Correspondence*, ed. Sadler, and *Henry Crabb Robinson on Books and their Writers*, ed. Edith J. Morley, 3 vols (London, 1938). None of the published selections include Crabb Robinson's entries on the day-to-day business of University College and University Hall with which he was so closely involved.

9. Henry Crabb Robinson Diary, 12 October 1848, MS Dr Williams's Library.

10. Henry Crabb Robinson Diary, 10 November 1846, ibid.

11. For the history of Manchester New College, see Valentine David Davis, *A History of Manchester College* (London, 1932). The archives of Manchester New College are in Harris Manchester College, Oxford.

12. Henry Crabb Robinson to Thomas Robinson, 1 November 1851, and Diary, 30 October 1851, MSS Dr Williams's Library; Davis, *A History of Manchester College*, pp. 125–9.

13. Henry Crabb Robinson Diary, 12 October 1848, 29 January 1849, 1 June 1850, MSS Dr Williams's Library.

14. Henry Crabb Robinson Diary, 11 January 1852, ibid.

15. For Newman's career, see I. Giberne Sieveking, *Memoirs and Letters of Francis W. Newman* (London, 1909), and William Robbins, *The Newman Brothers: An Essay in Comparative Intellectual Biography* (London, 1966).

16. See Basil Willey, *More Nineteenth-Century Studies* (London, 1956), p. 50; Walter Bagehot to Edith Bagehot, December 1847, *The Collected Works of Walter Bagehot*, ed. Norman St John-Stevas, 15 vols (London, 1965–86), vol. 12, p. 265.

17. Agnes Fry, *A Memoir of the Rt Hon Sir Edward Fry*, p. 44.

18. F.W. Newman to Council, 23 December 1846, MS College Correspondence, UCL Special Collections.

19. Henry Crabb Robinson Diary, 20 July 1848, *Diary, Reminiscences and Correspondence*, vol. 3, pp. 321, 320.

20. Newman's speech, 'Addresses delivered on the Occasion of Laying the Foundation Stone, July 29th, 1848', MS 12.90, Dr Williams's Library.

21. Bagehot to W. C. Roscoe, 6 September 1848, *Collected Works*, vol. 12, pp. 279–80.

22. Bagehot to T. W. Bagehot, December 1848, ibid., vol. 12, p. 289; see also Henry Crabb Robinson Diary, 21 June 1852, MS Dr Williams's Library.

23. Newman to Crabb Robinson, 9 November 1848, MS Dr Williams's Library.

24. Henry Crabb Robinson to Thomas Robinson, 11 November 1848, ibid.

25. Henry Crabb Robinson Diary, 7 and 10 November 1848, ibid. Newman published three controversial books at this time: *History of the Hebrew Monarchy* (1847), *The Soul, her Sorrows and Aspirations* (1849), and *Phases of Faith* (1850).

26. Henry Crabb Robinson Diary, 13 November 1848, MS Dr Williams's Library.

27. Henry Crabb Robinson Diary, 1 January 1849, published in *Henry Crabb Robinson on Books and their Writers*, vol. 2, p. 684.

28. See *The Correspondence of Arthur Hugh Clough*, ed. Frederick L. Mulhauser, 2 vols (Oxford, 1957), vol. 1, pp. 220–7.

29. Clough to Le Breton, 4 January 1849, ibid., vol. 1, pp. 230–1.

30. University Hall Council Minutes, 11 and 18 January, MS 12.83, Dr Williams's Library. See also Katharine Chorley, *Arthur Hugh Clough, the Uncommitted Mind: A Study of his Life and Poetry* (Oxford, 1962), pp. 171–3.

31. Walter Bagehot to Richard Holt Hutton, 1 March 1849, *Collected Works*, vol. 12, p. 293.

32. Clough to Edwin Wilkins Field, [January 1849], MS Add 145, UCL Special Collections.

33. Clough to E. Hawkins, 21 January 1849, *Correspondence of Arthur Hugh Clough*, vol. 1, p. 233.

34. Clough to Tom Arnold, 15 February 1849, ibid., vol. 1, p. 242.

35. Clough to Tom Arnold, 29 October 1849, ibid., vol. 1, p. 273.
36. University Hall Council Minutes, 25 March 1847, MS 12.82, Dr Williams's Library.
37. Register of students, MS 12.93, and list of subscribers appended to the minutes of the Manchester meeting, 5 February 1847, MS 12.90, ibid.
38. Clough to Tom Arnold, 29 October 1849, *Correspondence of Arthur Hugh Clough*, vol. 1, pp. 273–4.
39. Bagehot, review of *Diary, Reminiscences and Correspondence of Henry Crabb Robinson* in the *Fortnightly Review*, August 1869, reprinted in Bagehot, *Collected Works*, vol. 4, pp. 480, 481–2.
40. See Bellot, *University College London 1826–1926*, pp. 258, 261.
41. Henry Crabb Robinson Diary, 25 September 1852, MS Dr Williams's Library.
42. Henry Crabb Robinson Diary, 3 March 1850, ibid.
43. Henry Crabb Robinson Diary, 10 October 1850, ibid.
44. Clough to University Hall Council, 30 October 1851, *Correspondence of Arthur Hugh Clough*, vol. 1, p. 294.
45. See Anthony Kenny, *Arthur Hugh Clough: A Poet's Life* (London, 2005), p. 192.
46. J. A. Froude, *Thomas Carlyle: A History of his Life in London 1834–1881*, 2 vols (London, 1885), vol. 1, p. 458.
47. See Kenny, *Arthur Hugh Clough*, p. 51ff.
48. Richard Holt Hutton, 'Walter Bagehot', *Fortnightly Review* (October 1877), reprinted in *Collected Works of Walter Bagehot*, vol. 15, p. 102.
49. Clough to Tom Arnold, 16 May 1851, 3 January 1850, *Correspondence of Arthur Hugh Clough*, vol. 1, pp. 290, 279.
50. Clough to Blanche Smith,.2 March 1852, ibid., vol. 1, p. 308.
51. Louise Creighton, *Life and Letters of Thomas Hodgkin* (London, 1917), pp. 19–20.
52. Agnes Fry, *Memoir of the Rt Hon Sir Edward Fry*, pp. 42, 45.
53. See Malcolm Woodfield, *R. H. Hutton: Critic and Theologian* (Oxford, 1986), pp. 5–6.
54. Council Minutes 23 November 1849 and 16 June 1852, University Hall Minute Book 1848–50, MS 12.83, and 1850–52, MS 12.84, Dr Williams's Library.
55. Henry Crabb Robinson Diary, 21 June 1852, MS Dr Williams's Library.
56. Richard Holt Hutton, 'Walter Bagehot', *Collected Works of Walter Bagehot*, vol. 15, pp. 85–6.
57. Disraeli, *Vivian Grey*, vol. 1, pp. 100–1.
58. University Hall Council Minutes, 10 January 1850, MS 12.83, Dr Williams's Library.
59. University Hall Council Minutes, 21 February 1850, ibid.
60. University Hall Council Minutes, 6 March 1851, ibid.
61. University Hall Council Minutes, 3 and 11 June 1852, ibid.
62. See Bellot, *University College London 1826–1926*, pp. 276–7.
63. University Hall Council Minutes, 26 November 1852, MS 12.85, and 9 February 1860, MS 12.86, Dr Williams's Library.
64. Report of annual meeting and dinner, 7 July 1853, MS 12.90, ibid.
65. University Hall Council Minutes, 16 June 1853, MS 12.85, ibid.
66. University Hall Council Minutes, 12 October 1854, ibid.
67. Report of University Hall Annual General Meeting, 7 July 1853, MS 12.90, p. 10; University Hall Council Minutes, 9 November 1854, MS 12.85, ibid.
68. University Hall Council Minutes, 25 March, 10, 19, 26 May, 13 December 1855, 10 January 1856, ibid.
69. University Hall Council Minutes, 12 and 26 June 1856, ibid.
70. University Hall Council Minutes, 13 November 1856, MS 12.86, ibid.
71. University Hall Council Minutes, 26 May 1859, ibid.
72. University Hall Council Minutes, 26 June 1862, ibid.
73. University Hall Council Minutes, 4 February and 9 July 1864, ibid.
74. University Hall Council Minutes, 2 October 1862, 4 June and 5 November 1863, 2 June and 1 December 1864, ibid.
75. University Hall Council Minutes, 5 December 1877, MS 12.87, ibid. The Shoolbred mattress factory is now Foster Court, part of University College London.
76. University Hall Council Minutes, 16 May 1868, MS 12.87, Dr Williams's Library.
77. See Annual Report, 23 June 1864, MS 12.86, ibid.

78. University Hall Council Minutes, 23 March 1867, ibid.
79. For the Ladies' College, see Chapter 8.
80. See Henry Crabb Robinson Diary, passim, MS Dr Williams's Library.
81. There are several folders of Flaxman Gallery material in UCL Special Collections.
82. The fresco, now covered by wallpaper, is reproduced in Edith J. Morley, *The Life and Times of Henry Crabb Robinson* (London, 1935), facing p.109.
83. Henry Crabb Robinson Diary, 15 October 1861, *Diary, Reminiscences and Correspondence*, vol. 3, p. 482.
84. University College Council Minutes, 23 July 1867, UCL Records Office.
85. University Hall Council Minutes, 9 December 1867, MS 12.86, Dr Williams's Library.
86. See Karl Marx to Friedrich Engels, 10 August 1868, *Marx–Engels Werke*, 39 vols (Berlin, 1956–68), vol. 32, p. 134; *Marx–Engels Collected Works*, 50 vols (London, 1975–2004), vol. 43, p. 81.
87. Edward Spencer Beesly to Karl Marx, 24 September 1867, MS Marx–Engels Collection, International Institute for Social History, Amsterdam; Beesly on Marx and the International, *Fortnightly Review*, vol. 8 (November 1870), pp. 529–30. For Beesly and Marx, see Henry Joseph Collins and Chimen Abramsky, *Karl Marx and the British Labour Movement* (London, 1965), p. 184; Royden Harrison, 'E.S. Beesly and Karl Marx', *International Review for Social History*, vol. 4 (1959), pp. 22–58; and Rosemary Ashton, *Little Germany: Exile and Asylum in Victorian England* (Oxford, 1986), pp. 128–33.
88. Marx to Ludwig Kugelmann, 13 December 1870, *Marx–Engels Collected Works*, vol. 44, p. 92.
89. See, for example, Beesly to Marx, 10 April 1874 and 14 April 1881, and to Engels, 15 July 1871, MSS Marx–Engels Collection, Amsterdam.
90. See Marx to Eleanor Marx, 26 April 1869, and Marx to Beesly, 19 October 1871, *Marx–Engels Collected Works*, vol. 43, p. 271, and vol. 44, p. 226.
91. University Hall Council Minutes, 20 October 1880, 12 January 1881, MS 12.87, and 14 December 1881, MS 12.88, Dr Williams's Library.
92. For the Working Men's College and Working Women's College, see Chapter 9.
93. Beesly to Marx, 13 June 1871, MS Marx–Engels Collection, Amsterdam.
94. See David Hayes, 'Holborn's Church of Humanity, its Roots and Offshoots', *Camden History Review*, vol. 24 (2000), p. 7. For the history of Comtism in England see Martha S. Vogeler, *Frederic Harrison: The Vocations of a Positivist* (Oxford, 1984) and Terence R. Wright, *The Religion of Humanity: The Impact of Comtean Positivism on Victorian Britain* (Cambridge, 1986).
95. Hayes, 'Holborn's Church of Humanity', p. 8.
96. Ibid., p. 10.
97. C.D. [Sophia De Morgan], *From Matter to Spirit. The Result of Ten Years' Experience in Spirit Manifestations. Intended as a Guide to Inquirers. By C.D. With a Preface by A.B. [Augustus De Morgan]* (London, 1863).
98. See Chapter 10.
99. See Henry Solly, *The Life of Henry Morley* (London, 1898), p. 29.
100. Ibid., pp. 41, 60, 216.
101. Ibid., p. 31.
102. Ibid., pp. 88, 101–23, 148–55, 187–9.
103. Ibid., p. 200.
104. Henry Morley, 'Infant Gardens', *Household Words*, 21 July 1855. The article has not been republished, but is accessible on the website of Roehampton University, which houses the Froebel Archive for Childhood Studies: http://core.roehampton.ac.uk/digital/froebe-lindex.htm. For a discussion of the kindergarten movement, see Chapter 10.
105. See Rita McWilliams-Tullberg, *Women at Cambridge: A Men's University, though of a Mixed Type* (London, 1975, revised Cambridge, 1998), and Judy Batson, *Her Oxford* (Nashville, Tennessee, 2008).
106. Solly, *Life of Henry Morley*, pp. 258–63.
107. Morley, 'The Pioneers of University Extension', July 1891, ibid., pp. 263–4.
108. Solly, *Life of Henry Morley*, pp. 340–1.
109. The building is now part of University College, and is called the Henry Morley Building.
110. Solly, *Life of Henry Morley*, p. 345.

111. 'Report as to University Hall' read out at University College Council, 4 May 1889, MS UCL Special Collections.
112. See Davis, *A History of Manchester College*, pp. 164–7. The College has been renamed Harris Manchester College, and is a constituent college of Oxford University.
113. 'Report as to University Hall', 4 May 1889, MS UCL Special Collections.
114. Solly, *Life of Henry Morley*, pp. 373–5.
115. Annual Report, 26 February 1890, UCL Records Office.
116. Solly, *Life of Henry Morley*, p. 375.
117. Council Minutes, 9 February 1889, UCL Records Office.
118. See Chapter 10.

Chapter 8 Educating Women

1. Elisabeth Jesser Reid to Sophia De Morgan, undated, but early 1849, MS PP40/5/4/4, Papers of Elisabeth Jesser Reid, Archives, Royal Holloway, University of London (RHUL).
2. For Maurice and the Working Men's College, see Chapter 9.
3. F. D. Maurice to A. J. Scott, 29 April [1849], *The Life of Frederick Denison Maurice chiefly told in his own Letters*, edited by his son Frederick Maurice, 2 vols (London, 1884), vol. 1, p. 470.
4. Ibid., vol. 1, p. 471.
5. Elisabeth Jesser Reid to Sophia De Morgan, undated but early 1849, MS PP40/5/4/2, Papers of Elisabeth Jesser Reid, RHUL Archives.
6. Elisabeth Jesser Reid to Jane Martineau and Eliza Bostock, undated but 1860, Margaret J. Tuke, *A History of Bedford College for Women 1849–1937* (Oxford, 1939), pp. 316, 317.
7. Elisabeth Jesser Reid to Sophia De Morgan, undated but early 1849, MS PP40/5/4/2, Papers of Elisabeth Jesser Reid, RHUL Archives.
8. See Louis and Rosamund Billington, 'A Burning Zeal for Righteousness: Women in the British Anti-Slavery Movement, 1820–1860', in *Equal or Different: Women's Politics 1800–1914*, ed. Jane Rendall (Oxford, 1987), p. 107.
9. Elisabeth Jesser Reid to Jane Martineau and Eliza Bostock, undated but 1860, Tuke, *A History of Bedford College*, pp. 316–17.
10. Tuke, *A History of Bedford College*, p. 129.
11. Post Office Directories show the Wedgwoods at 16 Gower Street until 1845, then at Chester Terrace, Regent's Park.
12. Elisabeth Jesser Reid to Sophia De Morgan, undated but early 1849, MS PP40/5/4/3, Papers of Elisabeth Jesser Reid, RHUL Archives.
13. Tuke, *A History of Bedford College*, p. 280; for Kinkel's career, see Ashton, *Little Germany*, pp. 150–67.
14. Anna Jameson to Sophia De Morgan, undated but 1849, MS PP40/5/4/11, Papers of Elisabeth Jesser Reid, RHUL Archives.
15. Lady Noel Byron to Sophia De Morgan, 5 April [1849], MS PP40/5/4/7, ibid.
16. Emily Taylor to Ann Scott, early 1849, MS PP40/5/4/12, ibid.
17. Emily Davies, *The Higher Education of Women* (London, 1866), p. 132.
18. In the Census of 1841 she is recorded in Tavistock Place, and in 1851 in Woburn Square. Post Office Directories place her at 7 Tavistock Place from 1840 to 1844, and at 27 Woburn Square from 1845.
19. *Anna Swanwick: A Memoir and Recollections 1813–1899*, compiled by her niece Mary L. Bruce (London, 1903), pp. 43–4.
20. Ibid., p. 45.
21. Mary Elizabeth Braddon, *Eleanor's Victory* (1863, reprinted 1996), pp. 81–2.
22. Frederick Miller, *Saint Pancras Past and Present: being Historical, Traditional and General Notes of the Parish, including Biographical Notices of Inhabitants associated with its Topographical and General History* (London, 1874), pp. 137–8.
23. See Olsen, *Town Planning in London*, pp. 205, 206.
24. Register of Students 1849–71, MS AR 201/1/1, Bedford College Papers, RHUL Archives.
25. *Anna Swanwick: A Memoir and Recollections*, p. 170.
26. Tuke, *A History of Bedford College*, pp. 47–51.

27. See *ODNB* entry for Shaen.
28. Ten points for consideration, probably for the prospectus, in Augustus De Morgan's hand, MS PP40/5/4/17, RHUL Archives.
29. Tuke, *A History of Bedford College*, pp. 63, 64.
30. Ibid., p. 65.
31. See *The Letters of Christina Rossetti*, ed. Antony H. Harrison, 4 vols (Charlottesville, Virginia, 1997–2004), passim.
32. See Tuke, *A History of Bedford College*, pp. 323–4.
33. Ibid., p. 62.
34. Ibid., p. 23.
35. Register of Students 1849–71, MS AR 201/1/1, Bedford College Papers, RHUL Archives.
36. Ibid.; Tuke, *A History of Bedford College*, pp. 342–4.
37. See Ashton, *142 Strand*, pp. 82–120.
38. Register of Students 1849–71, MS AR 201/1/1, Bedford College Papers, RHUL Archives.
39. See Gladys Storey, *Dickens and Daughter* (London, 1939); Lucinda Hawksley, *Katey: The Life and Loves of Dickens's Artist Daughter* (London, 2006).
40. For accounts of the career of Barbara Leigh Smith, later Bodichon, see Sheila R. Herstein, *A Mid-Victorian Feminist: Barbara Leigh Smith Bodichon* (New Haven, Connecticut, 1985); Pam Hirsch, *Barbara Leigh Smith Bodichon, 1827–1891: Feminist, Artist, and Rebel* (London, 1998). For the close relationship between George Eliot, Barbara Leigh Smith, and Bessie Rayner Parkes, see Rosemary Ashton, *George Eliot: A Life* (London, 1996).
41. Tuke, *A History of Bedford College*, pp. 56, 307.
42. Register of Students 1849–71, MS AR 201/1/1, Bedford College Papers, RHUL Archives.
43. *Daily News*, 7 December 1849.
44. *Standard*, 21 October 1850.
45. Thomas Wilson, *Catholicity, Spiritual and Intellectual: An Attempt at Vindicating the Harmony of Faith and Knowledge* (1850).
46. Thomas Carlyle to John Carlyle, 1 January and 20 February 1851, *The Collected Letters of Thomas and Jane Welsh Carlyle*, vol. 26, pp. 3, 35.
47. Tuke, *A History of Bedford College*, pp. 70–1.
48. Ibid., pp. 71–2.
49. George Eliot to Sara Hennell, 27 March 1874, *The George Eliot Letters*, ed. Gordon S. Haight, 9 vols (New Haven, Connecticut, 1954–5, 1978), vol. 6, p. 34.
50. Henry Crabb Robinson Diary, 22 June 1850 and 19 April 1852, MS Dr Williams's Library.
51. Tuke, *A History of Bedford College*, p. 325.
52. Ibid.
53. Henry Crabb Robinson to Elisabeth Jesser Reid, [1863], MS PP40/4/2/29, Papers of Elisabeth Jesser Reid, RHUL Archives.
54. Eliza Bostock to Elisabeth Jesser Reid, no date but probably 1850, MS PP40/4/1/32, ibid.
55. Eliza Bostock to Elisabeth Jesser Reid, [late summer 1851?], MS PP40/4/1/17, ibid.
56. Tuke, *A History of Bedford College*, p. 77. For the story of Bain's early life, see his *Autobiography* (London, 1904).
57. Henry Crabb Robinson Diary, 23 March 1856, MS Dr Williams's Library; Tuke, *A History of Bedford College*, p. 37n.
58. Henry Crabb Robinson to Elisabeth Jesser Reid, 6 November 1856, MS PP40/4/2/19, Papers of Elisabeth Jesser Reid, RHUL Archives.
59. Elisabeth Jesser Reid to Henry Crabb Robinson, 1856, TS PP40/5/3; Henry Crabb Robinson Diary, 13 December 1856, MS Dr Williams's Library.
60. Tuke, *A History of Bedford College*, pp. 144–5.
61. Ibid., pp. 147–8.
62. Virginia Woolf, *A Room of One's Own* (London, 1928), Chapter 1.
63. Tuke, *A History of Bedford College*, p. 93.
64. Henry Crabb Robinson to Elisabeth Jesser Reid, 19 December 1857, MS PP40/4/2/20, Papers of Elisabeth Jesser Reid, RHUL Archives.
65. Elisabeth Jesser Reid to Eliza Bostock and Jane Martineau, undated but 1860, Tuke, *A History of Bedford College*, p. 317.

66. Henry Crabb Robinson Diary, 6 April, 26 May, and 15 June 1866, MS Dr Williams's Library.
67. Jane Carlyle to Jeannie Welsh, *c.* 9 January 1844, *The Collected Letters of Thomas and Jane Welsh Carlyle*, vol. 17, p. 238.
68. There are letters of 1855 to Mrs Reid from her solicitor, James Sowton, of Great James Street, Bedford Row, discussing the lease and the restrictions on running a school on the premises, MSS PP40/3/1/3/21–31, Papers of Elisabeth Jesser Reid, RHUL Archives.
69. Tuke, *A History of Bedford College*, pp. 123, 188–95.
70. Ibid., p. 103. The numbering of the houses in Bedford Square changed about this time, so that No. 47 became 48 and No. 48 became 49.
71. See collection of cuttings entitled 'Students prior to 1903', BC15/6/5/1, Bedford College Papers, RHUL Archives. For the Passmore Edwards Settlement, see Chapter 10.
72. Tuke, *A History of Bedford College*, p. 53.
73. Ibid., p. 104.
74. Frances Martin to Alexander Macmillan, 11 May 1868, Add MS 54974, Macmillan MSS, British Library.
75. See Chapter 9.
76. Amy Greener, *A Lover of Books: The Life and Literary Papers of Lucy Harrison* (London, 1916), pp. 20–5.
77. Arthur Munby Diary, 9 March 1866, Derek Hudson, *Munby, Man of Two Worlds: The Life and Diaries of Arthur J. Munby 1828–1910* (London, 1972), p. 219.
78. See Gillian Sutherland, *Elementary Education in the Nineteenth Century* (London, 1971).
79. See Barbara Stephen, *Emily Davies and Girton College* (London, 1927); Daphne Bennett, *Emily Davies and the Liberation of Women 1830–1921* (London, 1990); Gillian Sutherland, *Faith, Duty, and the Power of Mind: The Cloughs and their Circle 1820–1960* (Cambridge, 2006).
80. See Jane Rendall, '"A Moral Engine?" Feminism, Liberalism and the *English Woman's Journal*', in *Equal or Different*, ed. Jane Rendall, pp. 112–38.
81. Emily Faithfull, 'Victoria Press', *The English Woman's Journal*, October 1860; reprinted in *Barbara Leigh Smith Bodichon and the Langham Place Group*, ed. Candida Ann Lacey (London, 1987), p. 283.
82. See Michelle Elizabeth Tusan, *Women Making News: Gender and Journalism in Modern Britain* (Urbana, Illinois, 2005).
83. Emily Faithfull, 'Victoria Press', in *Barbara Leigh Smith Bodichon and the Langham Place Group*, p. 279; see also Gerry Holloway, *Women and Work in Britain since 1840* (London, 2005); Elizabeth Crawford, *The Women's Suffrage Movement: A Reference Guide 1866–1928* (London, 1999), p. 213.
84. See Ellen Jordan, *The Women's Movement and Women's Employment in Nineteenth-century Britain* (London, 1999); Ellen Jordan and Anne Bridger, '"An Unexpected Recruit to Feminism": Jessie Boucherett's "Feminist Life" and the Importance of Being Wealthy', *Women's History Review*, vol. 15, no. 3 (July 2006), pp. 385–412.
85. See editors' introduction to *Rethinking the Age of Reform*, eds Burns and Innes, pp. 60–1.
86. Printed prospectus for the London Ladies' Educational Association, College Collection A3.3, UCL Special Collections.
87. Jessie Boucherett's essay was published in *Woman's Work and Woman's Culture: A Series of Essays*, ed. Josephine Butler (1869); see Kathrin Levitan, 'Redundancy, the "Surplus Woman" Problem, and the British Census 1851–1861', *Women's History Review*, vol. 17, no. 3 (July 2008), pp. 359–76.
88. See Jeffrey A. Auerbach, *The Great Exhibition of 1851: A Nation on Display* (New Haven, Connecticut, and London, 1999); Anthony Burton and Elizabeth Bonython, *The Great Exhibitor: The Life and Work of Henry Cole* (London, 2001).
89. Quoted in Pamela Gerrish Nunn, *Victorian Women Artists* (London, 1987), p. 48.
90. Ibid.
91. Richard Henry Horne, 'The Female School of Design in the Capital of the World', *Household Words*, 15 March 1851, pp. 579, 581. Horne's authorship is identified in Anne Lohrli, *Household Words. A Weekly Journal, 1850–1859, conducted by Charles Dickens. Table of Contents, List of Contributors and their Contributions based on the Household Words Office Book in the Morris L. Parrish Collection of Victorian Novelists, Princeton University Library* (Toronto, 1973).

92. F. Graeme Chalmers, 'Fanny McIan and London's Female School of Design, 1842–57', *Woman's Art Journal*, vol. 16 (Winter 1995–6), pp. 3–9. Information about student numbers is to be found in *Printed Papers etc. concerning the British Museum 1753–1851*, British Museum Central Archives.

93. Historians often state wrongly that the Female School of Art itself was located in South Kensington, because that was where the women were examined; see the UCL Leverhulme-funded Bloomsbury Project website, www.ucl.ac.uk/bloomsbury-project.

94. *Leader*, 29 January 1853.

95. Ibid., 17 March 1860.

96. *Builder*, 18 February, 14 and 28 April 1860.

97. *Leader*, 17 March 1860.

98. *Art Journal*, 1 February 1860; *Spectator*, 31 March 1860; *Macmillan's Magazine*, July 1860.

99. *Leader*, 17 March 1860.

100. Ibid.

101. *Journal of the Society of Arts*, 8 June 1860; see also ibid., 24 May and 7 June 1861 about an exhibition of watercolours by Female School of Art students at the Royal Society of Arts in John Adam Street, off the Strand.

102. *Builder*, 22 December 1860.

103. For the Working Women's College, see Chapter 9, and for the College of Preceptors, see Chapter 10.

104. Edward J. Poynter, *Ten Lectures on Art* (London, 1879), pp. 111–12.

105. Bellot, *University College London 1826–1926*, p. 347.

106. Nunn, *Victorian Women Artists*, p. 52. The De Morgans' diaries and correspondence, as well as a collection of their work, is in the De Morgan Centre in the West Hill Library, Wandsworth, south-west London.

107. Crawford, *Enterprising Women*, pp. 172–3.

108. Ibid., pp. 66, 185–7, 204–5.

109. Rhoda and Agnes Garrett, *Suggestions for House Decoration in Painting, Woodwork, and Furniture* (London, 1876). For an account, with illustrations, of their business, see Crawford, *Enterprising Women*, pp. 189–97.

110. Rhoda and Agnes Garrett, *Suggestions for House Decoration*, pp. 4–5.

111. For the Ladies' Residential Chambers company, see Jenifer Glynn, *The Pioneering Garretts: Breaking the Barriers for Women* (London, 2008), pp. 170–1; Crawford, *Enterprising Women*, pp. 206–14. For Fanny Wilkinson's career, see Crawford, pp. 218–39.

112. See Crawford, *Enterprising Women*, p. 162.

113. See Winifred Stephens, *The Life of Adeline Sergeant* (London, 1905), pp. 202–3, 207–9.

114. Adeline Sergeant, *Alison's Ordeal: A Story for Girls* (London, 1903), pp. 1–2.

115. Adeline Sergeant, *Anthea's Way* (London, 1903), p. 169.

116. Helen Black, *Notable Women Authors of the Day: Biographical Sketches* (Glasgow, 1893), pp. 158–60, 170.

117. For accounts of the medical profession and medical reforms in the nineteenth century, see M. Jeanne Peterson, *The Medical Profession in Mid-Victorian London* (Berkeley, California, and London, 1978); *Medical Fringe and Medical Orthodoxy 1750–1850*, eds Bynum and Porter; W.F. Bynum, *Science and the Practice of Medicine in the Nineteenth Century* (Cambridge, 1994).

118. For Elizabeth Garrett Anderson's career, see Jo Manton, *Elizabeth Garrett Anderson* (London, 1965); Crawford, *Enterprising Women*; Glynn, *The Pioneering Garretts*.

119. Margaret Todd, *The Life of Sophia Jex-Blake* (London, 1918), pp. 62–4, 67.

120. Census, 31 March 1861.

121. Todd, *The Life of Sophia Jex-Blake*, p. 421.

122. For Sophia Jex-Blake's career, see ibid., and Shirley Roberts, *Sophia Jex-Blake: A Woman Pioneer in Nineteenth-Century Medical Reform* (London, 1993); see also Manton, *Elizabeth Garrett Anderson*, pp. 240–60.

123. Francis Newman to James John Garth Wilkinson, 18 April 1870, MS Swedenborg Society Archives, London; Arthur Munby Diary, 3 January 1866, Hudson, *Munby, Man of Two Worlds*, p. 216.

124. See Crawford, *Enterprising Women*, p. 255.
125. Sophia Jex-Blake to Elizabeth Garrett, 21 August 1874, Todd, *The Life of Sophia Jex-Blake*, pp. 424–5.
126. Crawford, *Enterprising Women*, pp. 155–6.
127. Todd, *Life of Sophia Jex-Blake*, p. 448; Manton, *Elizabeth Garrett Anderson*, pp. 253–4.
128. Elizabeth Garrett Anderson, draft for a speech, quoted in Manton, *Elizabeth Garrett Anderson*, p. 285.
129. For a detailed account of the Euston Road building, see ibid., pp. 62–76. Part of the original 1890–1 building has been preserved and restored as a museum by Unison, the trade union which has built its own new headquarters next to and around the New Hospital building. The archives of the Elizabeth Garrett Anderson Hospital are in the London Metropolitan Archives.
130. Manton, *Elizabeth Garrett Anderson*, pp. 266–7, 297.

Chapter 9 Christian Brotherhood, Co-operation, and Working Men and Women

1. See, for example, the account of the day in the *Illustrated London News*, 15 April 1848.
2. Henry Crabb Robinson Diary, 10 April 1848, MS Dr Williams's Library.
3. Miller, *That Noble Cabinet*, p. 170, quoting from the diary of Frederic Madden. For a history of the Museum Tavern, see Henderson, 'The Museum Tavern in Bloomsbury', *Camden History Review*, vol. 16, pp. 5–9.
4. For a lucid account of Chartism and 10 April, see David Goodway, *London Chartism 1838–1848* (Cambridge, 1982).
5. The novel is told in the first person; its full title is *Alton Locke, Tailor and Poet: An Autobiography*. Chapter 34 is entitled 'The Tenth of April'.
6. For the birth of Christian Socialism, and the night school at Little Ormond Yard, see J.F.C. Harrison, *A History of the Working Men's College 1854–1954* (London, 1954), pp. 6–10, and Brenda Colloms, *Victorian Visionaries* (London, 1982), pp. 33–7, 45–6.
7. For Hughes, see Norman Vance, *The Sinews of the Spirit: The Idea of Christian Manliness in Victorian Literature and Religious Thought* (Cambridge, 1985); for Furnivall, see William Benzie, *Dr F.J. Furnivall: Victorian Scholar Adventurer* (Norman, Oklahoma, 1983).
8. *The Life of Frederick Denison Maurice*, vol. 1, p. 482.
9. Benzie, *Dr F.J. Furnivall*, pp. 41–2; Colloms, *Victorian Visionaries*, pp. 45–6.
10. Louisa Twining, *Recollections of Life and Work: Being the Autobiography of Louisa Twining* (London, 1893), pp. 214–15; for Little Ormond Yard and the street which replaced it in 1882, Orde Hall Street, see the UCL Leverhulme-funded Bloomsbury Project website, www.ucl.ac.uk/bloomsbury-project.
11. For a history of Bloomsbury's institutions, and its streets and squares, see the website of the UCL Leverhulme-funded Bloomsbury Project, www.ucl.ac.uk/bloomsbury-project.
12. Thackeray, *Vanity Fair* (1848), chapter 36; Dickens, 'Gone Astray', *Household Words*, 13 August 1853, in *Dickens' Journalism*, vol. 3, p. 160.
13. *The Times*, 22 and 23 January and 17 July 1824. For a full account of the Mendicity Society, see Deborah Colville's entry on the Society in the UCL Leverhulme-funded Bloomsbury Project website, www.ucl.ac.uk/bloomsbury-project.
14. Theodore Hook, 'Martha, the Gypsy', *Sayings and Doings* (1824, reprinted 1836), pp. 520, 523.
15. *Punch*, vol. 4 (January–June 1843), p. 52.
16. Letter of 14 June 1846, *The Life of Frederick Denison Maurice*, vol. 1, p. 427.
17. Tom Hughes, quoted in Harrison, *A History of the Working Men's College*, pp. 15–17.
18. *The Life of Frederick Denison Maurice*, vol. 2, pp. 215, 221–3.
19. Colloms, *Victorian Visionaries*, p. 174; Harrison, *A History of the Working Men's College*, p. 34.
20. Twining, *Recollections*, p. 14.
21. Matthew Arnold, *Literature and Dogma* (1873), in *The Complete Prose Works of Matthew Arnold*, ed. R.H. Super, 11 vols (Ann Arbor, Michigan, 1960–77), vol. 6, p. 383.

22. See Bernard M.G. Reardon, *From Coleridge to Gore: A Century of Religious Thought in Britain* (London, 1971).
23. Twining, *Recollections*, pp. 150–1.
24. *The Life of Frederick Denison Maurice*, vol. 2, pp. 65, 233.
25. Ibid., vol. 2, p. 232.
26. Harrison, *A History of the Working Men's College*, p. 21.
27. Ibid., pp. 91–2.
28. Ibid., p. 92.
29. Munby Diary, 3 March 1859, Hudson, *Munby, Man of Two Worlds*, p. 26.
30. Munby Diary, 28 May 1863, ibid., p. 163.
31. Benzie, *Dr F.J. Furnivall*, p. 48.
32. John Ruskin to F.J. Furnivall, 19 October 1854, *The Letters of John Ruskin 1827–1869*, vol. 36 of the 39-volume *Works of John Ruskin*, eds E.T. Cook and Alexander Wedderburn (London, 1903–12), p. 178.
33. Dante Gabriel Rossetti to William Allingham, 23 January 1855, *Letters of Dante Gabriel Rossetti*, eds Oswald Doughty and John Robert Wahl, 4 vols (Oxford, 1953, revised 1965–7), vol. 1, p. 239.
34. Rossetti to Charlotte Lydia Polidori, 3 May 1855, and to Ford Madox Brown, 6 June 1855, ibid., vol. 1, pp. 250, 255.
35. G[eorgiana] B[urne]-J[ones], *Memorials of Edward Burne-Jones*, 2 vols (London, 1912), vol. 1, p. 146. See also Fiona MacCarthy, *The Last Pre-Raphaelite: Edward Burne-Jones and the Victorian Imagination* (London, 2011).
36. Colloms, *Victorian Visionaries*, pp. 157, 165.
37. *Memorials of Edward Burne-Jones*, vol.1, p. 192.
38. Harrison, *A History of the Working Men's College*, p. 68.
39. *The Letters of Christina Rossetti*, vol. 1, pp. 155–6.
40. R.B. Litchfield, *The Beginnings of the Working Men's College*, a 12-page pamphlet dated 1 October 1902, in the collection of material relating to the Working Men's College in the London Metropolitan Archives, H09/GY/LIB/094.
41. Colloms, *Victorian Visionaries*, p. 262.
42. Harrison, *A History of the Working Men's College*, p. 4.
43. Litchfield, *The Beginnings of the Working Men's College*, p. 11.
44. Report of Maurice's inaugural lecture at the Working Men's College, *Journal of the Society of Arts*, vol. 2 (3 November 1854), p. 826.
45. Harrison, *A History of the Working Men's College*, pp. 75, 77.
46. *The Life of Frederick Denison Maurice*, vol. 2, pp. 319–20; Harrison, *A History of the Working Men's College*, pp. 76–7.
47. *The Life of Frederick Denison Maurice*, vol. 2, p. 260.
48. Ibid., vol. 2, p. 379. See also June Purvis, *Hard Lessons: The Lives and Education of Working-Class Women in Nineteenth-Century England* (Oxford, 1989), p. 175.
49. See Gillian Darley, *Octavia Hill* (London, 1990), pp. 56–7.
50. Purvis, *Hard Lessons*, pp. 179–80.
51. Emily Hill to Florence Hill, 12 December 1858, Darley, *Octavia Hill*, p. 55.
52. Ibid., p. 29.
53. 'The Ladies' Guild', *Daily News*, 18 February 1852.
54. Darley, *Octavia Hill*, p. 41. See also Janet Dunbar, *The Early Victorian Woman: Some Aspects of her Life (1837–57)* (London, 1953), pp. 148–9.
55. *Household Words*, 17 May 1856; see Darley, *Octavia Hill*, pp. 42–3.
56. 'The Cause of Labour: The City Working Tailors' Association', *Star of Freedom*, 26 June 1852.
57. Octavia Hill to Miranda Hill, 14 June 1852, *Life of Octavia Hill as Told in her Letters*, ed. C. Edmund Maurice (London, 1913), pp. 22–3.
58. Darley, *Octavia Hill*, pp. 51–3.
59. E. Moberly Bell, *Octavia Hill: A Biography* (London, 1942), pp. 37–8.
60. *Life of Octavia Hill*, ed. Maurice, pp. 78–9.
61. Ibid., p.80.
62. Darley, *Octavia Hill*, p. 64.
63. Ibid., p. 69.

64. *Life of Octavia Hill*, ed. Maurice, pp. 183, 186.
65. Herstein, *A Mid-Victorian Feminist*, pp. 63–4.
66. See Owen Stinchcombe, 'Elizabeth Malleson and the Working Women's College: An Experiment in Women's Education', *Camden History Review*, vol. 16 (1989), pp. 29, 31–2.
67. Hudson, *Munby: Man of Two Worlds*, pp. 13, 318.
68. Benzie, *Dr F.J. Furnivall*, p. 61.
69. Munby Diary, 25 January 1861, Hudson, *Munby, Man of Two Worlds*, p. 90.
70. *Elizabeth Malleson 1828–1916: Autobiographical Notes and Letters*, with a Memoir by Hope Malleson (privately printed, 1926), p. 58. For Elizabeth Malleson's friendship with George Eliot, see Ashton, *142 Strand*.
71. *Elizabeth Malleson 1828–1916*, p. 59.
72. Ibid., p. 63.
73. See Stinchcombe, 'Elizabeth Malleson and the Working Women's College', p. 31.
74. *Elizabeth Malleson 1828–1916*, pp. 62, 73.
75. Munby Diary, 22 November 1865, Hudson, *Munby Man of Two Worlds*, p. 215.
76. Stinchcombe, 'Elizabeth Malleson and the Working Women's College', p. 30.
77. Ibid., p. 29.
78. Munby Diary, 3 January 1866, Hudson, *Munby, Man of Two Worlds*, p. 216.
79. Munby Diary, 25 October 1865, ibid., p. 211.
80. Munby Diary, 9 January 1867, ibid., p. 236. James Powell & Sons, 'manufacturers of table & chemical glass, of finest coloured glass for artists, & makers of stained & painted windows for churches', was located in Temple Street, Whitefriars, according to the *Post Office London Directory 1863*.
81. Munby Diary, 9 March 1859, 16 January 1862, Hudson, *Munby Man of Two Worlds*, pp. 27, 113–14.
82. Munby Diary, 9 February 1867, ibid., p. 237.
83. Munby Diary, 11 February 1869 and 26 March 1870, ibid., pp. 265–6, 281–2.
84. Stinchcombe, 'Elizabeth Malleson and the Working Women's College', p. 32.
85. *Elizabeth Malleson 1828–1916*, p. 64.
86. Munby Diary, 10 December 1873, Hudson, *Munby, Man of Two Worlds*, pp. 353–4.
87. *Elizabeth Malleson 1828–1916*, pp. 64–5.
88. The papers of the College for Working Women are in the London Metropolitan Archives, as are those of the Working Men's College; those of the Working Women's College have not survived.
89. First Annual Report of the College for Working Women (1875), London Metropolitan Archives A/FMC/C/008.
90. Frances Martin, 'A College for Working Women', *Macmillan's Magazine*, vol. 40 (1879), p. 488.
91. *Report of the Council* (1874), quoted in Purvis, *Hard Lessons*, p. 189.
92. Robert Louis Stevenson, 'College for Men and Women', *The Academy*, vol. 127 (10 October 1874), p. 406.
93. Undated draft prospectus, quoted by Hamilton, *Queen Square: Its Neighbourhood & its Institutions*, p. 53.
94. See Robert Louis Stevenson to Frances Sitwell, 22 January and *c.* 9 July 1874, *The Letters of Robert Louis Stevenson*, ed. Bradford A. Booth and Ernest Mehew, 8 vols (New Haven and London, 1994–5), vol. 1, pp. 456–7; vol. 2, p. 29.
95. Robert Louis Stevenson and Fanny Van de Grift Stevenson, *The Dynamiter* (London, 1885), p. 138. For the hospitals see Hamilton, *Queen Square*, p. 79; Black, *Walking London's Medical History*, pp. 93–4.
96. Louisa Twining opened the Home for the Aged and Incurable at 22 New Ormond Street in 1862, having founded the Industrial Home for Workhouse Girls a year earlier in the next-door house, No. 23; for details see the UCL Leverhulme-funded Bloomsbury Project website, www.ucl.ac.uk/bloomsbury-project.
97. Twining, *Recollections*, p. 189.
98. For the Nursing Association see Florence Nightingale, letter to *The Times*, 14 April 1876; UCL Leverhulme-funded Bloomsbury Project website, www.ucl.ac.uk/bloomsbury-project.
99. Twining, *Recollections*, pp. 251–2; for illustrations of several buildings in the square see Hamilton, *Queen Square*.

100. See Hamilton, *Queen Square*, pp. 118–35.
101. *Elizabeth Malleson 1828–1916*, p. 72.
102. Froebel Society Minutes, 27 April 1875, 1 February, 10 June, and 3 October 1876, Froebel Archive for Childhood Studies, Roehampton University Archives and Special Collections.
103. Maria Grey speech, reported in the *Journal of the Women's Education Union*, 15 November 1875, in Purvis, *Hard Lessons*, p. 205.

Chapter 10 Work and Play in Tavistock Place

1. John Fretwell, *Johannes Ronge and the English Protestants*, a 16-page pamphlet reprinted from the *Unitarian Review* (January 1888), p. 3.
2. For an account of the German exiles in London and elsewhere, see Ashton, *Little Germany*.
3. See Ingrid Donner and Birgit Matthies, 'Jenny Marx über das Robert-Blum-Meeting am 9. November 1852 in London', *Beiträge zur Marx–Engels Forschung*, vol. 4 (1978); Marx to Engels, 19 October 1851, *Marx–Engels Collected Works*, vol. 38, p. 483; Johanna Kinkel to Kathinka Zitz, 18 March 1851, Rupprecht Leppla, 'Johanna und Gottfried Kinkels Briefe an Kathinka Zitz 1849–1861', *Bonner Geschichstsblätter*, vol. 12 (1958), p. 34.
4. See *Daily News*, 3 and 13 September 1851, and 17 April 1852.
5. See rossettiarchive.org for this unpublished poem.
6. Christina Rossetti to William Michael Rossetti, 30 July 1852, *The Letters of Christina Rossetti*, vol. 1, p. 57.
7. Fretwell, *Johannes Ronge*, pp. 7, 10.
8. Ibid., pp. 11, 13.
9. *Lloyd's Weekly Newspaper*, 31 July 1853.
10. Account by 'Christopher Crayon' (James Ewing Ritchie), quoted in Fretwell, *Johannes Ronge*, p. 12.
11. Ibid.
12. *Journal of the Society of Arts*, vol. 2 (8 September 1854), p. 711. Copies of the *Journal* and other papers relating to the Educational Exhibition are in the Royal Society of Arts, London.
13. Johannes Ronge, 'Reform in the Infant School', *Daily News*, 24 July 1854.
14. See, for example, *Newcastle Courant*, 23 and 30 January 1852; *Manchester Times*, 12 June 1852 and 26 March 1859; *Bristol Mercury*, 27 January 1855; *Leeds Mercury*, 31 March, 27 and 29 October 1859.
15. Dickens to Elizabeth Gaskell, 1 February 1855, *The Letters of Charles Dickens*, vol. 7, p. 520. Mrs Gaskell's letter has not survived; only a few letters from her to Dickens remain. See *The Letters of Mrs Gaskell*, eds J.A.V. Chapple and Arthur Pollard (Manchester, 1966).
16. See Peter Weston, *The Froebel Educational Institute: The Origins and History of the College* (Roehampton, 2002), p. 3.
17. Henry Morley, 'Infant Gardens', *Household Words*, 21 July 1855.
18. 'Infant Teaching', *Monthly Christian Spectator*, August 1855, p. 503.
19. Weston, *The Froebel Educational Institute*, pp. 4–5.
20. Froebel Society Minutes, 4 November 1874, Froebel Archive for Childhood Studies, Roehampton University Archives and Special Collections. See also P. Woodham-Smith, 'History of the Froebel Movement in England', in *Friedrich Froebel and English Education*, ed. Evelyn Lawrence (London, 1952).
21. See Kevin J. Brehony, 'English Revisionist Froebelians and the Schooling of the Urban Poor', in *Practical Visionaries: Women, Education and Social Progress 1790–1930*, eds Mary Hilton and Pam Hirsch (Harlow, 2000), p. 187.
22. See Edward W. Ellsworth, *Liberators of the Female Mind: The Shirreff Sisters, Educational Reform, and the Women's Movement* (Westport, Connecticut, 1979). Maria Grey relocated her college in 1883 to 5 Fitzroy Street, the address at which Frances Martin had started her College for Working Women in 1874, before it moved to 7 Fitzroy Street.
23. Weston, *The Froebel Educational Institute*, pp. 11, 21. See also Nanette Whitbread, *The Evolution of the Nursery–Infant School: A History of Infant and Nursery Education in Britain 1800–1970* (London, 1972).

24. See *Fifty Years of Progress in Education: A Review of the Work of the College of Preceptors from its Foundation in 1846 to its Jubilee in 1896* (London, 1896), pp. 4–6. This pamphlet, with other papers relating to the College, is in the records of the College of Preceptors, Institute of Education Archives, University of London.

25. *Fifty Years of Progress*, pp. 6, 15–16.

26. Minute Book 1848–57 of the College of Preceptors, 4 November 1848, 30 December 1854, Institute of Education Archives, COP/C/2/1.

27. Froebel Society Minutes, 10 June and 3 October 1876, and 21 July 1877, Froebel Archive for Childhood Studies, Roehampton.

28. Minute Book of the College of Preceptors, 18 January 1882, 16 June, 13 October, and 10 November 1883, and 16 February 1884, Institute of Education Archives, COP/C/2/1 and COP/C/2/2.

29. Minute Book, 13 December 1884, ibid., COP/C/2/2.

30. *Fifty Years of Progress*, pp. 31–2.

31. For a history of teacher training in Britain from the College of Preceptors to the present day, see Richard Willis, *The Struggle for the General Teaching Council* (London, 2005).

32. See his obituary in *The Times*, 25 March 1893.

33. See Olsen, *Town Planning in London*, p. 149.

34. See Marie Draper, 'Bloomsbury's Gates and Bars: The Maintenance of Tranquillity on the Bedford Estates', *Camden History Review*, vol. 12 (1984), pp. 2–5, and Mark Searle, *Turnpikes and Toll-Bars*, 2 vols (London, 1930).

35. See *The Times*, 15 and 21 January 1891. The coroner's inquest declared that the Duke shot himself in a fit of temporary insanity while suffering intense pain.

36. *Memorial to the Chairman and Members of the Metropolitan Board of Works*, 20 November 1879, in Box 19/7/1, Bedford Estate Office, Woburn Abbey.

37. Draper, 'Bloomsbury's Gates and Bars', pp. 4–5, and P.J. Atkins, 'University College London and the Gower Street Bar', *Camden History Review*, vol. 18 (1994), pp. 26–8.

38. See *The Times*, 19 March 1894; also Crook, *The British Museum*, pp. 211–15.

39. For Tom Arnold's career, see Bernard Bergonzi, *A Victorian Wanderer: The Life of Thomas Arnold the Younger* (Oxford, 2003).

40. Mrs Humphry Ward and C.E. Montague, *William Thomas Arnold, Journalist and Historian* (Manchester, 1907), p. 5.

41. See John Sutherland, *Mrs Humphry Ward: Eminent Victorian, Pre-eminent Edwardian* (Oxford, 1990).

42. Ibid., pp. 14–15.

43. Janet Penrose Trevelyan, *The Life of Mrs Humphry Ward* (London, 1923), pp. 35–6.

44. Mrs Humphry Ward, *Robert Elsmere* (1888), ed. Rosemary Ashton (Oxford, 1987).

45. Richard Holt Hutton in the *Spectator*; see Basil Willey, 'How "Robert Elsmere" Struck Some Contemporaries', *Essays and Studies*, New Series vol. 10 (1957), pp. 53–68.

46. Trevelyan, *The Life of Mrs Humphry Ward*, p. 33.

47. Mrs Humphry Ward, *A Writer's Recollections* (London, 1918), p. 252; for details of the number of copies sold and her earnings from them, see Sutherland, *Mrs Humphry Ward*, pp. 130–1.

48. Mrs Humphry Ward, *A Writer's Recollections*, p. 290.

49. Mary Ward to Joseph Estlin Carpenter, 2 November 1893, Trevelyan, *The Life of Mrs Humphry Ward*, p. 154. For Bedford Chapel, see the Leverhulme-funded UCL Bloomsbury Project website, www.ucl.ac.uk/bloomsbury-project.

50. Copeland Bowie, writing in the *Inquirer* in April 1920, quoted in Trevelyan, *The Life of Mrs Humphry Ward*, p. 82.

51. Trevelyan, *The Life of Mrs Humphry Ward*, pp. 82–3.

52. Ibid., pp. 83–4.

53. Ibid., p. 84.

54. Ibid., p. 88.

55. John Sutherland, *The Mary Ward Centre 1890–1990*, a 36-page pamphlet containing an edited extract from his biography of Mary Ward (London, 1990), p. 10.

56. Trevelyan, *The Life of Mrs Humphry Ward*, p. 87.

57. 'Mrs Humphry Ward on University Hall', *The Times*, 1 December 1890.

58. Report of University Hall, June 1895, in a scrapbook of papers relating to University Hall, Marchmont Hall, and the Passmore Edwards Settlement, London Metropolitan Archives, 4524/K/05/001.

59. 'University Hall', *Pall Mall Gazette*, 14 February 1891.

60. See Ricci de Freitas, *The Story of Marchmont Street* (London, 2008), and the website of the UCL Leverhulme-funded Bloomsbury Project, www.ucl.ac.uk/bloomsbury-project.

61. Printed sheets in University Hall Committee Papers 1890–5, London Metropolitan Archives, 4524/M/01/004.

62. Article in *The Associate*, no. 1 (October 1898), papers relating to University Hall, Marchmont Hall, and the Passmore Edwards Settlement, London Metropolitan Archives, 4524/K/02/001; and essay 'From a Settlement Worker' in the *In Memoriam* booklet prepared in June 1921 after Mary Ward's death, ibid., 4524/N/01/002.

63. Philip Wicksteed to Mary Ward, 1 March 1891, in 'Samples from the Mary Ward Archive', Mary Ward Centre website, www.marywardcentre.ac.uk/Exhibitions/Archive-Exhibition.asp.

64. *In Memoriam* booklet prepared in June 1921 after Mary Ward's death, London Metropolitan Archives, 4524/N/01/002.

65. Report, June 1895, London Metropolitan Archives, 4524/K/05/001.

66. Sutherland, *The Mary Ward Centre*, p. 15.

67. Mary Ward to John Passmore Edwards, 17 March 1894, MS correspondence in papers relating to University Hall and the Passmore Edwards Settlement, London Metropolitan Archives, 4524/M/02/001.

68. John Passmore Edwards to Mary Ward, 30 May 1894, Trevelyan, *The Life of Mrs Humphry Ward*, pp. 91–2.

69. See Dean Evans, *Funding the Ladder: The Passmore Edwards Legacy* (London, 2011), p. 225.

70. Ibid., pp. 28–45, 59–64, 262–4.

71. John Passmore Edwards, *A Few Footprints*, p. 40.

72. Herbrand Russell, eleventh Duke of Bedford, to Mary Ward, 27 July, 2, 9, 12, and 19 August 1894, MS correspondence in papers relating to University Hall, Marchmont Hall, and the Passmore Edwards Settlement, London Metropolitan Archives, 4524/M/02/001.

73. Alfred Stutfield report, 1 August 1894, Middlesex Report Book vol. 2 (1883–1895), BE RB69, Bedford Estate Office, Woburn Abbey.

74. Mary Ward to Herbrand Russell, eleventh Duke of Bedford, 11 August 1894, MS correspondence in papers relating to University Hall, Marchmont Hall, and the Passmore Edwards Settlement, London Metropolitan Archives, 4524/M/02/001.

75. Herbrand Russell, eleventh Duke of Bedford, to Mary Ward, 26 August 1894, ibid.

76. See Miller, *Saint Pancras Past and Present* (1870), p. 139; see also Olsen, *Town Planning in London*, p. 136, and the UCL Leverhulme-funded Bloomsbury Project website, www.ucl.ac.uk/bloomsbury-project.

77. Samuel Hadden Parkes, *Window Gardens for the People, and Clean and Tidy Rooms; Being an Experiment to Improve the Homes of the London Poor* (London, 1864), pp. 30, 43; see Kasia Boddy, 'Bloomsbury in Bloom', article on the UCL Leverhulme-funded Bloomsbury Project website, www.ucl.ac.uk/bloomsbury-project.

78. Mrs Humphry Ward, *Marcella*, 3 vols (London, 1894).

79. Herbrand Russell, eleventh Duke of Bedford, to Mary Ward, 1 November 1894, and Mary Ward to Herbrand Russell, 2 November 1894, MS correspondence in papers relating to University Hall, Marchmont Hall, and the Passmore Edwards Settlement, London Metropolitan Archives, 4524/M/02/001.

80. Mary Ward to John Passmore Edwards, 2 November 1894, ibid.

81. John Passmore Edwards to Mary Ward, 2 November 1894, MS in the Mary Ward Centre and Settlement, London; part quoted in Peter Baynes, *John Passmore Edwards & Mary Ward: A Beneficial Relationship*, a 24-page pamphlet published by the Mary Ward Centre (London, 1991), p. 14.

82. Mary Ward to John Passmore Edwards, 2 November 1894, MS correspondence in papers relating to University Hall, Marchmont Hall, and the Passmore Edwards Settlement, London Metropolitan Archives, 4524/M/02/001.

83. John Passmore Edwards to Mary Ward, 3 November 1894, MS in the Mary Ward Centre, London.

84. Alfred Robinson to Alfred Stutfield, 7 March 1895, MS correspondence and plans for the Passmore Edwards Settlement in the Bedford Estate Office, Woburn Abbey, NMR/11/14/2.
85. See [Richard] Norman Shaw to G.F. Watts, 19 January 1895, MS correspondence in papers relating to University Hall, Marchmont Hall, and the Passmore Edwards Settlement, London Metropolitan Archives, 4524/M/02/003.
86. Typed extract of John Passmore Edwards to Mary Ward, 23 March 1895, MS correspondence in papers relating to University Hall, Marchmont Hall, and the Passmore Edwards Settlement, London Metropolitan Archives, 4524/M/02/003; part quoted in Baynes, *John Passmore Edwards & Mary Ward*, p. 16.
87. See *The Times*, 11 October 1897; Sutherland, *Mrs Humphry Ward*, p. 223.
88. See Alfred Robinson to Alfred Stutfield, 8 August 1895, MS correspondence and plans for the Passmore Edwards Settlement in the Bedford Estate Office, Woburn Abbey, NMR/11/14/2.
89. For an account of the demolition *c.*1900 of Tavistock, Bedford, and Russell Houses, and the building of the British Medical Association building on the site, see E. Muirhead Little, 'Historical Notes on the Site of the Association's New House', *British Medical Journal*, no. 3368 (18 July 1925), pp. 111–14.
90. Herbrand Russell, eleventh Duke of Bedford, to Mary Ward, 10 January 1899 and 15 May 1902, MS correspondence in papers relating to University Hall, Marchmont Hall, and the Passmore Edwards Settlement, London Metropolitan Archives, 4524/M/02/001.
91. See John Rodgers, *Mary Ward Settlement: A History 1891–1931*, a pamphlet published by the Settlement (London, 1931), p. 7.
92. See Smith and Brewer's plan, 'New Settlement Buildings, Proposed New Site. Block Plan', 9 August 1895, MS correspondence and plans for the Passmore Edwards Settlement in the Bedford Estate Office, Woburn Abbey, NMR/11/14/2.
93. *The Times*, 16 June 1896.
94. See Nikolaus Pevsner, *London except the Cities of London and Westminster* (London, 1952), p. 212; Adrian Forty, 'The Mary Ward Settlement', *Architects' Journal* (2 August 1989) pp. 28–49; Jones and Woodward, *A Guide to the Architecture of London*, p. 121.
95. See the Mary Ward Centre website, www.marywardcentre.ac.uk/Exhibitions/Archive-Exhibition.asp, and Karen Butti's 2004 PhD thesis, 'The Mary Ward Settlement', lodged with the Architectural Association, London.
96. Printed programme for the 'First Social Evening of the Associates of the Passmore Edwards Settlement, Oct 9, 1897', papers relating to University Hall, Marchmont Hall, and the Passmore Edwards Settlement, London Metropolitan Archives, 4524/M/02/004.
97. Printed prospectus for Spring Term 1898, ibid.
98. Trevelyan, *The Life of Mrs Humphry Ward*, p. 123.
99. Ibid., pp. 125–6. See also Janet Penrose Trevelyan, *Evening Play Centres for Children: The Story of their Origin and Growth* (London, 1920).
100. Sutherland, *Mrs Humphry Ward*, p. 225; *The Mary Ward Centre*, p. 25.
101. 'Particulars of the Proposed Purchase', 25 January 1940, MS correspondence and plans for the Passmore Edwards Settlement in the Bedford Estate Office, Woburn Abbey, NMR/11/14/2.
102. See Baynes, *John Passmore Edwards & Mary Ward*, pp. 19–21.
103. *The Times*, 11 and 14 February 1898.
104. Speech given by one of Mary Ward's daughters (it is not clear which), 1907, in collection of speeches given at or regarding the Passmore Edwards Settlement, London Metropolitan Archives, 4524/M/02/010.
105. *Report and Calendar for the Year 1885 of the Froebel Society for the Promotion of the Kindergarten System* (London, 1885).
106. 'The Vacation School at Tavistock Place', *Child Life*, vol. 4 (October 1902), p. 218. See also Kevin J. Brehony, 'A "Socially Civilising Influence"? Play and the Urban "Degenerate"', *Paedagogica Historica*, vol. 39 (2003), pp. 87–106.
107. Mary Ward to Herbrand Russell, eleventh Duke of Bedford, 5 February 1899, MS correspondence in papers relating to University Hall, Marchmont Hall, and the Passmore Edwards Settlement, London Metropolitan Archives, 4524/M/02/001.
108. Trevelyan, *The Life of Mrs Humphry Ward*, pp. 131–2.

109. Ibid., pp. 132–5.

110. Ibid., p. 309.

111. See the Mary Ward Centre website, www.marywardcentre.ac.uk, and the UCL Leverhulme-funded Bloomsbury Project website, www.ucl.ac.uk/bloomsbury-project.

112. M. Milligan, 'The Invalid or "Physically Defective" School, by Miss Milligan, First Head Teacher', *In Memoriam* booklet prepared in June 1921 after Mary Ward's death, London Metropolitan Archives, 4524/N/01/002.

113. See Sutherland, *Mrs Humphry Ward*, p. 299ff.

114. W.H. Mallock, *The Individualist* (London, 1899), p. 16.

115. Ibid., p. 21.

Epilogue

1. See [William Heath?], *The Blunders of a Big-Wig; or Paul Pry's Peeps into the Sixpenny Sciences* (1827); Henry Irving's speech at the ceremony for the Dulwich Free Library in 1896, quoted in R.S. Best, *The Life and Good Works of John Passmore Edwards* (Redruth, Cornwall, 1981), p. 36.

2. According to Olsen, *Town Planning in London*, p. 222, the Bedford Estate raised over £65,000 in rents in 1880.

3. See Rosemary Ashton, 'Oh So Quietly: The Death of John Dickens', *Times Literary Supplement*, no. 5635 (1 April 2011), p. 14.

Bibliography

1. Manuscript Sources

Archives of the Duke of Northumberland at Alnwick Castle (Cardale–Drummond Correspondence).

Bedford Estate Office, Woburn Abbey (Annual Reports; Correspondence and Plans for the Passmore Edwards Settlement; Middlesex Report Books).

British Library (Macmillan MSS; Official Papers: Sir A. Panizzi).

British Library of Political and Economic Science, London School of Economics (Booth Notebooks; see also Charles Booth Online Archive, http://booth.lse.ac.uk).

British Museum Central Archive (Accounts and Select Committee Reports, in *Printed Papers etc. concerning the British Museum 1753–1851*; Book of Admissions to Reading Room; Committee Minutes; *Statutes and Rules* of the British Museum, and Indexes to the Standing Committees, General Meetings, and Sub-Committees; transcribed copy of Sir Frederic Madden's MS Diary).

Dr Williams's Library, London (Henry Crabb Robinson Diary and Correspondence; University Hall Minute Books).

Institute of Education Archives, University of London (Archive of the College of Preceptors).

International Institute for Social History, Amsterdam (Marx-Engels Collection).

London Metropolitan Archives (Papers of the College for Working Women; Papers of the Working Men's College; Papers relating to University Hall, Marchmont Hall, and the Passmore Edwards Settlement; Records of the Elizabeth Garrett Anderson Hospital).

Mary Ward Centre and Settlement, London (Mary Ward Archive, see also 'Samples from the Mary Ward Archive', www.marywardcentre.ac.uk/Exhibitions/Archive-Exhibition.asp).

Museum & Archives Service, Great Ormond Street Hospital for Children NHS Trust (Archives of the Hospital for Sick Children).

New Apostolic Church of North Germany, Hamburg (Minutes of the Catholic Apostolic Church Building Committee, Deacons' and Deaconesses' Committees, Councils and Conferences of Angels).

Roehampton University Archives and Special Collections (Froebel Archive for Childhood Studies).

Royal Holloway, University of London Archives (Papers of Elisabeth Jesser Reid; Bedford College Papers).

Senate House Library, University of London (De Morgan Library; SDUK Papers).

Swedenborg Society Archives, London (Correspondence of Francis Newman and James John Garth Wilkinson).

UCL Records Office (*Annual Reports*, 1829ff.; UCL Council Minutes; Education Committee Minutes).

UCL Special Collections (Brougham Papers; Clough Correspondence; College Collection; College Correspondence; De Morgan Collection; Goldsmid Letterbook, Mocatta MSS;

Loch Papers; London Mathematical Society Papers; MSS Applications; SDUK Papers; UCL Memoranda: Bellot; UCS Correspondence and Papers).

2. Books, Articles, and Online Sources

The A to Z of Georgian London, with Introductory Notes by Ralph Hyde, London Topographical Society, London, 1982.

Adburgham, Alison, *Silver Fork Society: Fashionable Life and Literature from 1814 to 1840*, London, 1983.

Allen, Michael, *Charles Dickens' Childhood*, Basingstoke, 1988.

Altick, R.D., *The English Common Reader*, Chicago, 1957.

Ambulator; or, A Pocket Companion for the Tour of London and its Environs, London, 1811.

Anderson, Patricia, *The Printed Image and the Transformation of Popular Culture 1790–1860*, Oxford, 1991.

Annan, Noel, *Leslie Stephen: The Godless Victorian*, London, 1984.

Arliss, George, *Up the Years from Bloomsbury: An Autobiography*, Boston, Massachusetts, 1927.

Arnold, Dana, *Rural Urbanism: London Landscapes in the Early Nineteenth Century*, Manchester, 2005.

Arnold, Matthew, *Literature and Dogma* (1873), in *The Complete Prose Works of Matthew Arnold*, ed. R.H. Super, 11 vols, Ann Arbor, Michigan, 1960–77, vol. 6.

Ashton, Rosemary, *142 Strand: A Radical Address in Victorian London*, London, 2006.

—— 'Barrie and Bloomsbury', in *Gateway to the Modern: Resituating J.M. Barrie*, eds Andrew Nash and Valentine Bold, forthcoming.

—— *George Eliot: A Life*, London, 1996.

—— *The German Idea: Four English Writers and the Reception of German Thought 1800–1860*, Cambridge, 1980, reprinted London, 1994.

—— *The Life of Samuel Taylor Coleridge: A Critical Biography*, Oxford, 1996.

—— *Little Germany: Exile and Asylum in Victorian England*, Oxford, 1986.

—— 'Oh So Quietly: The Death of John Dickens', *Times Literary Supplement*, no. 5635 (1 April 2011), p.14.

—— 'Peter Pan and Bloomsbury', *Times Literary Supplement*, no. 5619 (10 December 2010), p. 15.

—— *Thomas and Jane Carlyle: Portrait of a Marriage*, London, 2002.

Atkins, P.J., 'University College London and the Gower Street Bar', *Camden History Review*, vol. 18 (1994), pp. 26–8.

Auerbach, Jeffrey A., *The Great Exhibition of 1851: A Nation on Display*, New Haven, Connecticut, and London, 1999.

Bagehot, Walter, *The Collected Works*, ed. Norman St John-Stevas, 15 vols, London, 1965–86.

Bain, Alexander, *Autobiography*, London, 1904.

Barham, R.H. Dalton, *The Life and Remains of Theodore Edward Hook*, 2 vols, London, 1849.

Barrie, J.M., *The Greenwood Hat, being a Memoir of James Anon 1885–1887*, London, 1937.

Bates, A.W., *The Anatomy of Robert Knox: Murder, Mad Science, and Medical Regulation*, Brighton, 2010.

Batson, Judy, *Her Oxford*, Nashville, Tennessee, 2008.

Baynes, Peter, *John Passmore Edwards & Mary Ward: A Beneficial Relationship*, London, 1991.

Beames, Thomas, *The Rookeries of London*, London, 1852.

Belcher, John, *Catholic Apostolic Church, Gordon Square London*, London, 1885.

Bell, Sir Charles, *Letters of Sir Charles Bell selected from his Correspondence with his Brother George Joseph Bell*, London, 1870.

Bell, E. Moberly, *Octavia Hill: A Biography*, London, 1942.

Bell, Vanessa, 'Notes on Bloomsbury' (1951), in *Sketches in Pen and Ink*, ed. Lia Giachero, London, 1997.

Bellot, H. Hale, *University College London 1826–1926*, London, 1929.

Bennett, Daphne, *Emily Davies and the Liberation of Women 1830–1921*, London, 1990.

Bennett, Scott, 'The Editorial Character and Readership of the *Penny Magazine*', *Victorian Periodicals Review*, vol. 17 (1984), pp. 126–41.

Benzie, William, *Dr F.J. Furnivall: Victorian Scholar Adventurer*, Norman, Oklahoma, 1983.

Bergonzi, Bernard, *A Victorian Wanderer: The Life of Thomas Arnold the Younger*, Oxford, 2003.

Berman, Morris, *Social Change and Scientific Organization: The Royal Institution 1799–1844*, London, 1978.

Besant, Walter, *London in the Nineteenth Century*, London, 1909.

Best, R.S., *The Life and Good Works of John Passmore Edwards*, Redruth, Cornwall, 1981.

Billington, Louis and Rosamund, 'A Burning Zeal for Righteousness: Women in the British Anti-Slavery Movement, 1820–1860', in *Equal or Different: Women's Politics 1800–1914*, ed. Jane Rendall, Oxford, 1987.

Bivins, Roberta, *Alternative Medicine? A History*, Oxford, 2007.

Black, Helen, *Notable Women Authors of the Day: Biographical Sketches*, Glasgow, 1893.

Black, Nick, *Walking London's Medical History*, London, 2006.

The Blackmailing of the Chancellor: Some Intimate and Hitherto Unpublished Letters from Harriette Wilson to her friend Henry Brougham, Lord Chancellor of England, ed. Kenneth Bourne, London, 1975.

Blakey, Robert, *Memoirs of Dr Robert Blakey*, ed. Revd Henry Miller, London, 1879.

Boddy, Kasia, 'Bloomsbury in Bloom', article on the UCL Leverhulme-funded Bloomsbury Project website, www.ucl.ac.uk/bloomsbury-project.

Bodichon, Barbara, *Barbara Leigh Smith Bodichon and the Langham Place Group*, ed. Candida Ann Lacey, London, 1987.

Braddon, Mary Elizabeth, *Eleanor's Victory*, London, 1863, reprinted 1996.

Braid, James, *Neurypnology, or, the Rationale of Nervous Sleep, considered in Relation with Animal Magnetism*, London and Edinburgh, 1843.

Brehony, Kevin J., 'English Revisionist Froebelians and the Schooling of the Urban Poor', in *Practical Visionaries: Women, Education and Social Progress 1790–1930*, ed. Mary Hilton and Pam Hirsch, Harlow, 2000.

—— 'A "Socially Civilising Influence"? Play and the Urban "Degenerate"', *Paedagogica Historica*, vol. 39 (2003), pp. 87–106.

British Postal Museum and Archive, www.postalheritage.org.uk.

Brooks, Constance, *Antonio Panizzi: Scholar and Patriot*, London, 1931.

Brougham, Henry, *A Discourse of the Objects, Advantages, and Pleasures of Science*, London, 1827.

—— *Practical Observations upon the Education of the People, addressed to the Working Classes and their Employers*, 13th edition, London, 1825.

Browne, Janet, *Charles Darwin*, 2 vols, London, 1995–2002.

Browning, Robert and Elizabeth Barrett, *The Brownings' Correspondence*, ed. Philip Kelley et al., 16 vols so far, Winfield, Kansas, 1984—.

B[urne]-J[ones], G[eorgiana], *Memorials of Edward Burne-Jones*, 2 vols, London, 1912.

Burton, Anthony and Bonython, Elizabeth, *The Great Exhibitor: The Life and Work of Henry Cole*, London, 2001.

Butti, Karen, 'The Mary Ward Settlement', PhD, Architectural Association, London, 2004.

Bynum, W. F., *Science and the Practice of Medicine in the Nineteenth Century*, Cambridge, 1994.

Campbell, Thomas, *Life and Letters of Thomas Campbell*, ed. William Beattie, 3 vols, London, 1849.

—— *The Pleasures of Hope*, Edinburgh, 1799.

[Cardale, John Bate], *A Discourse delivered in the Catholic Apostolic Church, Gordon Square, on the Occasion of Consecrating the Altar, and Opening the Church for Public Worship, Christmas Eve, 1853*, London, 1854.

—— *A Discourse upon the Obligation of Tithe, delivered in the Catholic Apostolic Church, Gordon Square, on Tuesday, October 5, 1858*, London, 1858.

Carlyle, Thomas, *The Collected Letters of Thomas and Jane Welsh Carlyle*, eds C.R. Sanders, K.J. Fielding et al., 37 vols so far, Durham, North Carolina, 1970—.

—— *Critical and Miscellaneous Essays*, 5 vols, London, 1899.

—— *Reminiscences* (1881), eds K.J. Fielding and Ian Campbell, Oxford, 1997.

Caygill, Marjorie and Date, Christopher, *Building the British Museum*, London, 1999.

Chadwick, Owen, *The Victorian Church*, 2 vols, London, 1970.

Chalmers, F. Graeme, 'Fanny McIan and London's Female School of Design, 1842–57', *Woman's Art Journal*, vol. 16 (Winter 1995–6), pp. 3–9.

Chancellor, E. Beresford, *London's Old Latin Quarter, being an Account of Tottenham Court Road and its Immediate Surroundings*, London, 1930.

Cherry, Bridget and Pevsner, Nikolaus, *The Buildings of England: London 4: North*, London, 1998.

Chorley, Katharine, *Arthur Hugh Clough, the Uncommitted Mind: A Study of his Life and Poetry*, Oxford, 1962.

Clarke, James Fernandez, *Autobiographical Recollections of the Medical Profession*, London, 1874.

Clarke, Richard, McKellar, Elizabeth, and Symes, Michael, *Russell Square: A Lifelong Resource for Teaching and Learning*, Birkbeck Faculty of Continuing Education Occasional Paper, London, 2004.

Clinch, George, *Bloomsbury and St Giles's: Past and Present*, London, 1890.

Clough, Arthur Hugh, *The Correspondence of Arthur Hugh Clough*, ed. Frederick L. Mulhauser, 2 vols, Oxford, 1957.

Clowes, W.B., *Family Business 1803–1953*, London, 1953.

Cock, F.W., 'The First Operation under Ether in Europe – The Story of Three Days', *University College Hospital Magazine*, vol. 1 (1911), pp. 127–44.

Coleridge, Samuel Taylor, *Collected Letters of Samuel Taylor Coleridge*, ed. Earl Leslie Griggs, 6 vols, Oxford, 1956–71.

Collins, Henry Joseph and Abramsky, Chimen, *Karl Marx and the British Labour Movement*, London, 1965.

Collins, Wilkie, *Heart and Science: A Story of the Present Time*, 3 vols, London, 1883.

Colloms, Brenda, *Victorian Visionaries*, London, 1982.

Cooter, Roger, *The Cultural Meaning of Popular Science: Phrenology and the Organization of Consent in Nineteenth-Century Britain*, Cambridge, 1984.

Copeland, Edward, 'Crossing Oxford Street: Silverfork Geopolitics', *Eighteenth-Century Life*, vol. 25 (2001), pp. 116–34.

Cornish, Francis Warre, *The English Church in the Nineteenth Century*, 2 vols, London, 1910.

Cowtan, Robert, *Memories of the British Museum*, London, 1872.

Crawford, Elizabeth, *Enterprising Women: The Garretts and their Circle*, London, 2002.

—— *The Women's Suffrage Movement: A Reference Guide 1866–1928*, London, 1999.

Creevey, Thomas, *The Creevey Papers: A Selection from the Correspondence and Diaries of the Late Thomas Creevey, MP*, ed. Sir Herbert Maxwell, London, 1903, reprinted 1933.

Creighton, Louise, *Life and Letters of Thomas Hodgkin*, London, 1917.

Crook, J. Mordaunt, 'The Architectural Image', in *The University of London and the World of Learning 1836–1986*, ed. F.M.L. Thompson, London, 1990.

—— *The British Museum*, London, 1972.

Cruchley's Picture of London, second edition, London, 1835.

Darley, Gillian, *Octavia Hill*, London, 1990.

Darwin, Charles, *The Autobiography of Charles Darwin 1809–1882*, ed. Nora Barlow, London, 1958.

—— *The Correspondence of Charles Darwin*, eds Frederick Burkhardt et al., 18 vols so far, Cambridge, 1985—.

Davenport, Rowland A., *Albury Apostles: The Story of the Body known as the Catholic Apostolic Church (sometimes called 'Irvingites')*, London, 1970.

Davies, Emily, *The Higher Education of Women*, London, 1866.

Davis, Eliza Jeffries, *The University Site, Bloomsbury*, London, 1936.

Davis, Valentine David, *A History of Manchester College*, London, 1932.

Dennis, Richard, 'George Gissing (1857–1903): London's Restless Analyst', *The Gissing Journal*, vol. 40, no. 3 (2004), pp. 1–15.

Diamond, Arthur Sigismund, *The Building of a Synagogue: A Brief History*, London, 1970.

Dickens, Charles, *Dickens' Journalism*, ed. Michael Slater, 4 vols, London, 1994–2000.

—— *The Letters of Charles Dickens*, ed. Madeline House, Graham Storey et al., 12 vols, Oxford, 1965–2002.

—— *Oliver Twist; or, the Parish Boy's Progress*, by 'Boz', London, 1838.

—— *Our Mutual Friend*, London, 1864–5.

—— *The Speeches of Charles Dickens*, ed. K.J. Fielding, Hemel Hempstead, 1988.

—— *The Uncollected Writings of Charles Dickens: Household Words 1850–1859*, ed. Harry Stone, 2 vols, London, 1969.

Disraeli, Benjamin, *Vivian Grey* (1826–7), ed. Lucien Wolf, 2 vols, London, 1904.

Dobie, Rowland, *The History of the United Parishes of St Giles in the Fields and St George Bloomsbury*, London, 1829.

Donner, Ingrid and Matthies, Birgit, 'Jenny Marx über das Robert-Blum-Meeting am 9. November 1852 in London', *Beiträge zur Marx–Engels Forschung*, vol. 4 (1978), pp. 69–77.

Draper, Marie, 'Banking in Bloomsbury: A Savings Bank at No. 30 Montague Street', *Camden History Review*, vol. 14 (1986), pp. 8–9.

—— 'Bloomsbury's Gates and Bars: The Maintenance of Tranquillity on the Bedford Estates', *Camden History Review*, vol. 12 (1984), pp. 2–5.

Dunbar, Janet, *The Early Victorian Woman: Some Aspects of her Life (1837–57)*, London, 1953.

Dunn, Bill Newton, *The Man Who Was John Bull: The Biography of Theodore Edward Hook 1778–1841*, London, 1996.

Durant, Catherine, 'London's First Northern By-pass: Urban Development and the New Road from Paddington to Islington', *Camden History Review*, vol. 15 (1988), pp. 15–19.

Edwards, Edward, *Lives of the Founders of the British Museum*, 2 vols, London, 1870.

Edwards, John Passmore, *A Few Footprints*, London, 1905.

Edwards, O.D., *Burke and Hare*, Edinburgh, 1980.

Egan, Pierce, *Life in London, or, the Day and Night Scenes of Jerry Hawthorne Esq and his elegant Friend Corinthian Tom, accompanied by Bob Logic the Oxonian in their Rambles and Sprees through the Metropolis*, London, 1821.

Eliot, George, *The George Eliot Letters*, ed. Gordon S. Haight, 9 vols, New Haven, Connecticut, 1954–5, 1978.

Ellsworth, Edward W., *Liberators of the Female Mind: The Shirreff Sisters, Educational Reform, and the Women's Movement*, Westport, Connecticut, 1979.

Elmes, James, *Metropolitan Improvements; or London in the Nineteenth Century: being a Series of Views, of the New and Most Interesting Objects, in the British Metropolis & its Vicinity: from Original Drawings by Mr Thos. H. Shepherd. With Historical, Topographical & Critical Illustrations*, London, 1827, reprinted 1978.

Emblen, D.L., *Peter Mark Roget: The Word and the Man*, London, 1970.

Evans, Dean, *Funding the Ladder: The Passmore Edwards Legacy*, London, 2011.

Fagan, Louis, *The Life of Sir Anthony Panizzi, KCB, Late Principal Librarian of the British Museum, Senator of Italy &c., &c.*, 2 vols, London, 1880.

Fawkes, Richard, *Dion Boucicault: A Biography*, London, 1979.

Felkin, Frederick William, *From Gower Street to Frognal: A Short History of University College School from 1830 to 1907*, London, 1909.

Fido, Martin, *Bodysnatchers: A History of the Resurrectionists*, London, 1988.

Fifty Years of Progress in Education: A Review of the Work of the College of Preceptors from its Foundation in 1846 to its Jubilee in 1896, London, 1896.

Flegg, Columba Graham, *'Gathered Under Apostles': A Study of the Catholic Apostolic Church*, Oxford, 1992.

Forty, Adrian, 'The Mary Ward Settlement', *Architects' Journal*, 2 August 1989, pp. 28–49.

Freitas, Ricci de, *The Story of Marchmont Street*, London, 2008.

Fretwell, John, *Johannes Ronge and the English Protestants*, reprinted from the *Unitarian Review*, January 1888.

Frith, W.P., *My Autobiography and Reminiscences*, 2 vols, London, 1887.

—— *A Victorian Canvas: The Memoirs of W.P. Frith, RA*, ed. Nevile Wallis, London, 1957.

Froude, James Anthony, *Thomas Carlyle: A History of his Life in London 1834–1881*, 2 vols, London, 1885.

Fry, Agnes, *A Memoir of the Rt Hon Sir Edward Fry, GCB, 1827–1918*, London, 1921.

Gage, John, 'The Rise and Fall of the St Giles Rookery', *Camden History Review*, vol. 12 (1984), pp. 17–24.

Garnett, Olive, *Tea and Anarchy! The Bloomsbury Diary of Olive Garnett*, ed. Barry C. Johnson, 2 vols, London, 1989.

Garrett, Rhoda and Agnes, *Suggestions for House Decoration in Painting, Woodwork, and Furniture*, London, 1876.

Gaskell, Elizabeth, *The Letters of Mrs Gaskell*, ed. J.A.V. Chapple and Arthur Pollard, Manchester, 1966.

Gatrell, V.A.C., *City of Laughter: Sex and Satire in Eighteenth-Century London*, London, 2006.

George, M. Dorothy, *Catalogue of Political and Personal Satires preserved in the Department of Prints and Drawings in the British Museum*, especially vols 10 and 11, London, 1952, 1954.
—— *English Political Caricature 1793–1832: A Study of Opinion and Propaganda*, Oxford, 1959.
—— *Hogarth to Cruikshank: Social Change in Graphic Satire*, London, 1967.
Gissing, George, *The Collected Letters of George Gissing*, eds Paul F. Mattheisen, Arthur C. Young, and Pierre Coustillas, 9 vols, Athens, Ohio, 1990–7.
—— *Workers in the Dawn*, 3 vols, London, 1880.
Glynn, Jenifer, *The Pioneering Garretts: Breaking the Barriers for Women*, London, 2008.
Goldgar, Anne, 'The British Museum and the Virtual Representation of Culture in the Eighteenth Century', *Albion: A Quarterly Journal concerned with British Studies*, vol. 32, no. 2 (2000), pp. 195–231.
Goodway, David, *London Chartism 1838–1848*, Cambridge, 1982.
Gore, Catherine, 'The Special License', *The Fair of Mayfair*, 3 vols, London, 1832.
Grass, Timothy, *The Lord's Watchman: Edward Irving*, Milton Keynes, 2011.
Gray, Valerie, *Charles Knight: Educator, Publisher, Writer*, Aldershot, 2006.
Green, David R., 'Little Italy in Victorian London', *Camden History Review*, vol. 15 (1988), pp. 2–6.
Greener, Amy, *A Lover of Books: The Life and Literary Papers of Lucy Harrison*, London, 1916.
Greville, Charles, *The Diaries of Charles Greville*, ed. Edward Pearce with Deanna Pearce, London, 2005.
—— *The Greville Diary, including Passages hitherto withheld from Publication*, ed. Philip Whitwell Wilson, 2 vols, London, 1927.
—— *The Greville Memoirs 1814–1860*, eds Lytton Strachey and Roger Fulford, 7 vols, London, 1938.
Grobel, Monica C., 'The Society for the Diffusion of Useful Knowledge 1826–1846 and its Relation to Adult Education in the First Half of the Nineteenth Century, alias "The Sixpenny Science Company" alias "The Steam Intellect Society"', MA thesis, University of London, 1933.
Hair, John, *Regent Square: Eighty Years of a London Congregation*, London, 1899.
Hamilton, Godfrey Heathcote, *Queen Square: Its Neighbourhood & its Institutions*, London, 1926.
Harrison, J.F.C., *A History of the Working Men's College 1854–1954*, London, 1954.
—— *Learning and Living 1790–1960: A Study in the History of the English Adult Education Movement*, London, 1961.
Harrison, Royden, 'E.S. Beesly and Karl Marx', *International Review for Social History*, vol. 4 (1959), pp. 22–58.
Harte, Negley, *The University of London 1836–1986*, London, 1986.
Harte, Negley and North, John, *The World of UCL 1828–1990*, revised edition, London, 1991.
Hawksley, Lucinda, *Katey: The Life and Loves of Dickens's Artist Daughter*, London, 2006.
Hayes, David, 'Holborn's Church of Humanity, its Roots and Offshoots', *Camden History Review*, vol. 24 (2000), pp. 6–11.
—— '"Without Parallel in the Known World": The Chequered Past of 277 Gray's Inn Road', *Camden History Review*, vol. 25 (2001), pp. 5–9.
Hays, J.N., 'The Rise and Fall of Dionysius Lardner', *Annals of Science*, vol. 38 (1981), pp. 527–42.
Hazlitt, William, 'Rev. Mr Irving', *The Spirit of the Age*, London, 1825.
[Heath, William?],*The Blunders of a Big-Wig; or Paul Pry's Peeps into the Sixpenny Sciences*, London, 1827.
Henderson, Bob, 'William Plate, an Unknown Acquaintance of Karl Marx at the British Museum: A Biographical Sketch', *British Library Journal*, 2005, Article 8.
Henderson, John N., 'The Museum Tavern in Bloomsbury: The History of a Famous Public House', *Camden History Review*, vol. 16 (1989), pp. 5–9.
Henke, Manfred, 'Diakonissen in der Katholisch-apostolischen Kirche', *Unsere Zeit*, August 2006, pp. 31–7.
Herstein, Sheila R., *A Mid-Victorian Feminist: Barbara Leigh Smith Bodichon*, New Haven, Connecticut, 1985.
Hill, Octavia, *Life of Octavia Hill as Told in her Letters*, ed. C. Edmund Maurice, London, 1913.

Hirsch, Pam, *Barbara Leigh Smith Bodichon, 1827–1891: Feminist, Artist, and Rebel*, London, 1998.

History of the Italian Hospital in London, 1884–1906, London, 1906.

Hobhouse, Emily, 'Women Workers: How They Live, How They Wish to Live', *Nineteenth Century*, vol. 27 (March 1900), pp. 471–84.

Hobhouse, Hermione, *Thomas Cubitt: Master Builder*, London, 1971.

Holloway, Gerry, *Women and Work in Britain since 1840*, London, 2005.

Hook, Theodore, *Peregrine Bunce; or, settled at last*, 3 vols, London, 1842.

—— *Sayings and Doings*, First Series, London, 1824, reprinted 1836.

Horne, Richard Henry, 'The Female School of Design in the Capital of the World', *Household Words*, 15 March 1851.

Horsley, John Callcott, *Recollections of a Royal Academician*, ed. Mrs Edmund Helps, London, 1903.

Hostettler, John, *Thomas Wakley: An Improbable Radical*, Chichester, 1993.

Houston, R.A. and Knox, W.W.J., *The New Penguin History of Scotland from the Earliest Times to the Present Day*, London, 2001.

Hudson, Derek, *Munby, Man of Two Worlds: The Life and Diaries of Arthur J. Munby 1828–1910*, London, 1972.

Hudson, Roger, *Bloomsbury, Fitzrovia & Soho*, London, 1996.

Jones, Edward and Woodward, Christopher, *A Guide to the Architecture of London*, London, 1983, reprinted 1992.

Jones, Roger, 'Thomas Wakley, Plagiarism, Libel, and the Founding of the *Lancet*', *Lancet*, vol. 371 (26 April 2008), pp. 1410–11.

Jordan, Ellen, *The Women's Movement and Women's Employment in Nineteenth-century Britain*, London, 1999.

Jordan, Ellen and Bridger, Anne, '"An Unexpected Recruit to Feminism": Jessie Boucherett's "Feminist Life" and the Importance of Being Wealthy', *Women's History Review*, vol. 15, no. 3 (July 2006), pp. 385–412.

Kelly, Thomas, *George Birkbeck: Pioneer of Adult Education*, Liverpool, 1957.

Kenny, Anthony, *Arthur Hugh Clough: A Poet's Life*, London, 2005.

Kingsley, Charles, *Alton Locke, Tailor and Poet: An Autobiography*, 1850.

Knight, Charles, *Knight's Cyclopædia of London*, London, 1851.

—— *Knight's Pictorial London*, London, 1851.

—— *Passages of a Working Life during Half a Century*, 3 vols, London, 1864–5.

[Knight, J.P.], *On Building a Church for Divine Worship: A Discourse delivered by One of the Deacons of the Central Church, 3rd November 1850*, London, 1850.

Kosky, Jules, *Mutual Friends: Charles Dickens and Great Ormond Street Children's Hospital*, London, 1989.

Lancaster, John, 'John Bate Cardale, Pillar of Apostles: A Quest for Catholicity', PhD thesis, St Andrews University, 1978.

Lawrence, Christopher, *Medicine in the Making of Modern Britain 1700–1920*, London, 1994.

Lees, Lynn Hollen, *Exiles of Erin: Irish Migrants in Victorian London*, Manchester, 1979.

Lehmann, John, *Holborn: An Historical Portrait of a London Borough*, London, 1970.

Leon, Robert, 'The Man Who Made King's Cross: The Misfortunes of Stephen Geary', *Camden History Review*, vol. 17 (1992), pp. 13–16.

Leppla, Rupprecht, 'Johanna und Gottfried Kinkels Briefe an Kathinka Zitz 1849–1861', *Bonner Geschichstsblätter*, vol. 12 (1958), pp. 7–82.

Le Quesne, L. P., 'Medicine', in *The University of London and the World of Learning 1836–1986*, ed. F.M.L. Thompson, London, 1990.

L'Estrange, A.G., 'William Harness', in *Personal Reminiscences by Barham, Harness, and Hodder*, ed. Richard Henry Stoddard, New York, 1895.

Levitan, Kathrin, 'Redundancy, the "Surplus Woman" Problem, and the British Census 1851–1861', *Women's History Review*, vol. 17, no. 3 (July 2008), pp. 359–76.

Lickfold, J. Malcolm, *The Catholic Apostolic Church, Gordon Square, London: Notes on the Architectural Features and the Furniture, with a Glossary of Technical Terms*, London, 1935.

Lines, Richard, *History of the Swedenborg Society 1810–2010*, London, 2011.

Liscombe, R.W., *William Wilkins 1778–1839*, Cambridge, 1980.

Litchfield, R.B., *The Beginnings of the Working Men's College*, London, 1902.

Little, E. Muirhead, 'Historical Notes on the Site of the Association's New House', *British Medical Journal*, no. 3368 (18 July 1925), pp. 111–14.

Living and Dying in London, eds W.F. Bynum and Roy Porter, London, 1991.

Lohrli, Anne, *Household Words. A Weekly Journal, 1850–1859, conducted by Charles Dickens. Table of Contents, List of Contributors and their Contributions based on the Household Words Office Book in the Morris L. Parrish Collection of Victorian Novelists, Princeton University Library*, Toronto, 1973.

The London Encyclopædia, third edition revised, eds Ben Weinreb, Christopher Hibbert, Julia Keay, and John Keay, London, 2008.

Lonsdale, Henry, *A Sketch of the Life and Writings of Robert Knox the Anatomist*, London, 1870.

Lucas, E.V., *A Wanderer in London*, London, 1906, revised 1913.

Lutyens, Edwin, *The Letters of Edwin Lutyens to his Wife Lady Emily*, eds Clayre Percy and Jane Ridley, London, 1985.

MacCarthy, Fiona, *The Last Pre-Raphaelite: Edward Burne-Jones and the Victorian Imagination*, London, 2011.

Macready, William Charles, *The Diaries of William Charles Macready 1833–1851*, ed. William Toynbee, 2 vols, London, 1912.

McWilliams-Tullberg, Rita, *Women at Cambridge: A Men's University, though of a Mixed Type*, London, 1975, revised Cambridge, 1998.

Maidment, B.E., *Reading Popular Prints 1790–1870*, Manchester, 1996.

Malleson, Elizabeth, *Elizabeth Malleson 1828–1916: Autobiographical Notes and Letters*, with a Memoir by Hope Malleson, privately printed, 1926.

Mallock, W.H., *The Individualist*, London, 1899.

Manton, Jo, *Elizabeth Garrett Anderson*, London, 1965.

Martin, Frances, 'A College for Working Women', *Macmillan's Magazine*, vol. 40 (1879), pp. 483–8.

Maurice, Frederick Denison, *The Life of Frederick Denison Maurice chiefly told in his own Letters*, edited by his son Frederick Maurice, 2 vols, London, 1884.

Marx, Karl (with Friedrich Engels), *The Communist Manifesto*, 1848; reprinted with an introduction by David McLellan, Oxford, 1998.

Marx–Engels Collected Works, 50 vols, London, 1975–2004.

Marx–Engels Werke, 39 vols, Berlin, 1956–68.

Medical Fringe and Medical Orthodoxy 1750–1850, eds W.F. Bynum and Roy Porter, London, 1987.

Medicine in Society, ed. Andrew Wear, Cambridge, 1992.

Miller, Edward, *Prince of Librarians: The Life and Times of Antonio Panizzi of the British Museum*, London, 1988.

—— *That Noble Cabinet: A History of the British Museum*, London, 1973.

Miller, Frederick, *Saint Pancras Past and Present: being Historical, Traditional and General Notes of the Parish, including Biographical Notices of Inhabitants associated with its Topographical and General History*, London, 1874.

Miller, J. Hillis, *The Disappearance of God*, Cambridge, Massachusetts, 1963.

Moncrieff, William Thomas, *An Original Collection of Songs*, London, 1850.

Moore, Thomas, *The Journals of Thomas Moore*, ed. Wilfred S. Dowden, 6 vols, Toronto and London, 1983–91.

Moretti, Franco, *Atlas of the European Novel 1800–1900*, London, 1998.

[Morgan, Sophia De], *From Matter to Spirit. The Result of Ten Years' Experience in Spirit Manifestations. Intended as a Guide to Inquirers. By C.D. With a Preface by A.B. [Augustus De Morgan]*, London, 1863.

—— *Memoir of Augustus De Morgan*, London, 1882.

Morley, Edith J., *The Life and Times of Henry Crabb Robinson*, London, 1935.

Morley, Henry, 'Infant Gardens', *Household Words*, 21 July 1855; republished on the website of Roehampton University, which houses the Froebel Archive for Childhood Studies: http://core.roehampton.ac.uk/digital/froebelindex.htm.

[Morley, Henry], 'A Short History of the College: II', *University College Gazette*, vol. 1 (22 October 1886).

Morrell, Jack and Thackray, Arnold, *Gentlemen of Science: The Early Years of the British Association for the Advancement of Science*, Oxford, 1981.

Nead, Lynda, *Victorian Babylon: People, Streets, and Images in Nineteenth-Century London*, London, 2000.

Neale, Shirley, 'Quackery at King's Cross: James Morison & the British College of Health', *Camden History Journal*, vol. 28 (2004), pp. 16–21.

New, Chester William, *The Life of Henry Brougham to 1830*, Oxford, 1961.

Newman, F.W., *On the Relations of Free Knowledge to Moral Sentiments. A Lecture delivered in University College, London, on the 13th of October, 1847, as introductory to the session of 1847–8*, printed for Taylor and Walton, booksellers and publishers to University College, 28, Upper Gower Street, London, 1847.

Newman-Norton, Seraphim, *A Biographical Index of Those Associated with the Lord's Work*, London, 1972.

Nicholls, Phillip, *Homœopathy and the Medical Profession*, London, 1988.

Nichols, R.H. and Wray, F.A., *The History of the Foundling Hospital*, London, 1935.

Nineteenth-Century British Library Newspapers Database

Nunn, Pamela Gerrish, *Victorian Women Artists*, London, 1987.

Olsen, Donald J., *The Growth of Victorian London*, London, 1976.

—— *Town Planning in London: The Eighteenth and Nineteenth Centuries*, New Haven, Connecticut, and London, 1964, revised 1982.

The Organisation of Knowledge in Victorian Britain, ed. Martin Daunton, Oxford, 2005.

Orme, Temple, *University College School, London: Alphabetical and Topographical Register for 1831–1898*, London, 1898.

Parkes, Samuel Hadden, *Window Gardens for the People, and Clean and Tidy Rooms; Being an Experiment to Improve the Homes of the London Poor*, London, 1864.

Pattison, Frederick L.M., *Granville Sharp Pattison: Anatomist and Antagonist 1791–1851*, Edinburgh, 1987.

Peacock, Thomas Love, *Crotchet Castle*, London, 1831.

Personal Reminiscences by Barham, Harness, and Hodder, ed. Richard Henry Stoddard, New York, 1895.

Peterson, M. Jeanne, *The Medical Profession in Mid-Victorian London*, Berkeley, California, and London, 1978.

Pevsner, Nikolaus, *London except the Cities of London and Westminster*, London, 1952.

Picard, Liza, *Victorian London: The Life of a City 1840–1870*, London, 2005.

Porter, Roy, *Disease, Medicine and Society in England 1550–1860*, Basingstoke, 1987.

—— *Health for Sale: Quackery in England 1660–1850*, Manchester, 1989.

Poynter, Edward J., *Ten Lectures on Art*, London, 1879.

Praed, Winthrop Mackworth, *Selected Poems*, ed. Kenneth Allott, London, 1953.

Pugh, Gillian, *London's Forgotten Children: Thomas Coram and the Foundling Hospital*, Stroud, 2007.

Purvis, June, *Hard Lessons: The Lives and Education of Working-Class Women in Nineteenth-Century England*, Oxford, 1989.

Quarterly Journal of Education, 10 vols, 1831–5, reprinted with an introduction by Christopher Stray, 10 vols, London, 2008.

Ray, Gordon N., *Thackeray: The Uses of Adversity (1811–1846)*, London, 1955.

Reardon, Bernard M.G., *From Coleridge to Gore: A Century of Religious Thought in Britain*, London, 1971.

Redding, Cyrus, *Literary Reminiscences and Memoirs of Thomas Campbell*, 2 vols, London, 1860.

Rendall, Jane, '"A Moral Engine?" Feminism, Liberalism and the *English Woman's Journal*', in *Equal or Different: Women's Politics 1800–1914*, ed. Jane Rendall, Oxford, 1987.

Rennie, Neil, 'Imaginary Bloomsbury: Dynamite and Peter Pan', conference paper, April 2011, published on the website of the UCL Leverhulme-funded Bloomsbury Project, www.ucl.ac.uk/bloomsbury-project.

Report and Calendar for the Year 1885 of the Froebel Society for the Promotion of the Kindergarten System, London, 1885.

Rethinking the Age of Reform: Britain 1780–1850, eds Arthur Burns and Joanna Innes, Cambridge, 2003.

Richardson, Ruth, *Death, Dissection, and the Destitute*, London, 1987.

Rivett, Geoffrey, *The Development of the London Hospital System 1823–1982*, London, 1986.

Robbins, William, *The Newman Brothers: An Essay in Comparative Intellectual Biography*, London, 1966.

Roberts, Shirley, *Sophia Jex-Blake: A Woman Pioneer in Nineteenth-Century Medical Reform*, London, 1993.

Robinson, Henry Crabb, *Diary, Reminiscences and Correspondence*, ed. Thomas Sadler, 3 vols, London, 1869.

—— *Henry Crabb Robinson on Books and their Writers*, ed. Edith J. Morley, 3 vols, London, 1938.

Rodgers, John, *Mary Ward Settlement: A History 1891–1931*, London, 1931.

Rolfe, Christopher, 'From Camden Town to Crest Hill: H.G. Wells's Local Connections', *Camden History Review*, vol. 10, (1982), pp. 2–4.

Romilly, Mimi, 'Sir Samuel Romilly of Russell Square and his Descendants', *Camden History Review*, vol. 20 (1996), pp. 5–8.

Rossetti Archive, www.rossettiarchive.org.

Rossetti, Christina, *The Letters of Christina Rossetti*, ed. Antony H. Harrison, 4 vols, Charlottesville, Virginia, 1997–2004.

Rossetti, Dante Gabriel, *Letters of Dante Gabriel Rossetti*, eds Oswald Doughty and John Robert Wahl, 4 vols, Oxford, 1953, revised 1965–7.

Ruskin, John, *The Letters of John Ruskin 1827–1869*, vol. 36 of *The Works of John Ruskin*, eds E.T. Cook and Alexander Wedderburn, 39 vols, London, 1903–12.

Sanders, C.R., *Coleridge and the Broad Church Movement*, New York, 1942, reprinted 1972.

Searle, Mark, *Turnpikes and Toll-Bars*, 2 vols, London, 1930.

Sergeant, Adeline, *Alison's Ordeal: A Story for Girls*, London, 1903.

—— *Anthea's Way*, London, 1903.

Shaffer, E.S., *'Kubla Khan' and The Fall of Jerusalem*, Cambridge, 1975.

Shepherd, Thomas H., *London and its Environs in the Nineteenth Century, illustrated by a Series of Views from Original Drawings*, London, 1829, reprinted 1970.

Sieveking, I. Giberne, *Memoirs and Letters of Francis W. Newman*, London, 1909.

Slater, Michael, *Charles Dickens*, New Haven, Connecticut and London, 2009.

Smith, Sydney, *The Letters of Sydney Smith*, ed. Nowell C. Smith, 2 vols, Oxford, 1953.

Solly, Henry, *The Life of Henry Morley*, London, 1898.

Southey, Robert, *New Letters of Robert Southey*, ed. Kenneth Curry, 2 vols, New York and London, 1965.

—— *Selections from the Letters of Robert Southey*, ed. John Wood Warter, 4 vols, London, 1856.

Spring, David, *The English Landed Estate in the Nineteenth Century: Its Administration*, Baltimore, Maryland, 1963.

Squire, William, 'On the Introduction of Ether Inhalation as an Anaesthetic in London', *Lancet*, vol. 132 (22 December 1888), pp. 1220–1.

Stephen, Barbara, *Emily Davies and Girton College*, London, 1927.

Stephens, Winifred, *The Life of Adeline Sergeant*, London, 1905.

Stevenson, Robert Louis, 'College for Men and Women', *The Academy*, vol. 127 (10 October 1874), p. 406.

—— *The Letters of Robert Louis Stevenson*, eds Bradford A. Booth and Ernest Mehew, 8 vols, New Haven and London, 1994–5.

Stevenson, Robert Louis and Stevenson, Fanny Van de Grift, *The Dynamiter*, London, 1885.

Stewart, W.A.C. and McCann, W.P., *The Educational Innovators*, 2 vols, London, 1968–9.

Stinchcombe, Owen, 'Elizabeth Malleson and the Working Women's College: An Experiment in Women's Education', *Camden History Review*, vol. 16 (1989), pp. 29–33.

Stirling, A.M.W., *William De Morgan and his Wife*, London, 1922.

Stone, Lawrence, *Road to Divorce: England 1530–1987*, Oxford, 1990.

Storey, Gladys, *Dickens and Daughter*, London, 1939.

Surtees, R.S., *Handley Cross; or, Mr Jorrocks's Hunt*, London 1854, reprinted 1903.

Survey of London, 42 vols so far, London, 1900—.

Sutherland, Gillian, *Elementary Education in the Nineteenth Century*, London, 1971.

—— *Faith, Duty, and the Power of Mind: The Cloughs and their Circle 1820–1960*, Cambridge, 2006.

Sutherland, John, *Mrs Humphry Ward: Eminent Victorian, Pre-eminent Edwardian*, Oxford, 1990.

—— *The Mary Ward Centre 1890–1990*, London, 1990.

Swanwick, Anna, *Anna Swanwick: A Memoir and Recollections 1813–1899*, compiled by her niece Mary L. Bruce, London, 1903.

Tames, Richard, *Bloomsbury Past: A Visual History*, London, 1993.

Thackeray, William Makepeace, 'The History of Dionysius Diddler', *Autobiographic Mirror* (1864), reprinted in *The Works of William Makepeace Thackeray*, with biographical introductions by his daughter Anne Ritchie, 13 vols, London, 1898–9, vol. 13.

—— *The History of Pendennis*, London, 1850.

—— *The Letters and Private Papers of William Makepeace Thackeray*, ed. Gordon N. Ray, 4 vols, Cambridge, Massachusetts, 1945–6.

—— *The Newcomes* (1853–5), reprinted in 2 vols, London, 1952.

—— *Vanity Fair*, London, 1848.

Thompson, Sir Henry, 'Robert Liston', *University College Gazette*, vol. 2 (June 1901), pp. 202–4.

Thomson, Christopher, *The Autobiography of an Artisan*, London, 1847.

Thomson, Gladys Scott, *The Russells in Bloomsbury 1669–1771*, London, 1940.

Tierney, David, 'The Catholic Apostolic Church: A Study in Tory Millenarianism', *Historical Research*, vol. 63 (October 1990), pp. 289–315.

Timbs, John, *Curiosities of London*, London, 1855.

Times Digital Archive.

Todd, Margaret, *The Life of Sophia Jex-Blake*, London, 1918.

Trevelyan, Janet Penrose, *Evening Play Centres for Children: The Story of their Origin and Growth*, London, 1920.

—— *The Life of Mrs Humphry Ward*, London, 1923.

Tuke, Margaret J., *A History of Bedford College for Women 1849–1937*, Oxford, 1939.

Tusan, Michelle Elizabeth, *Women Making News: Gender and Journalism in Modern Britain*, Urbana, Illinois, 2005.

Twining, Louisa, *Recollections of Life and Work: Being the Autobiography of Louisa Twining*, London, 1893.

UCL Leverhulme-funded Bloomsbury Project website, www.ucl.ac.uk/bloomsbury-project.

Usher, H.J.K., Black-Hawkins, C.D., and Carrick, G.J., *An Angel without Wings: The History of University College School 1830–1980*, London, 1981.

'The Vacation School at Tavistock Place', *Child Life*, vol. 4 (October 1902), pp. 218–20.

Vance, Norman, *The Sinews of the Spirit: The Idea of Christian Manliness in Victorian Literature and Religious Thought*, Cambridge, 1985.

Vogeler, Martha S., *Frederic Harrison: The Vocations of a Positivist*, Oxford, 1984.

Waddington, Barbara, *The Rev. Edward Irving & the Catholic Apostolic Church in Camden and Beyond*, Occasional Paper No. 7 of the Camden History Society, London, 2007.

Walford, Edward, *Old and New London: A Narrative of its History, its People, and its Places*, 6 vols, London, 1873–8, of which vol. 4 deals with Bloomsbury.

Ward, Mrs Humphry, *Marcella*, 3 vols, London, 1894.

—— *Robert Elsmere* (1888), ed. Rosemary Ashton, Oxford, 1987.

—— *A Writer's Recollections*, London, 1918.

Ward, Mrs Humphry and Montague, C.E., *William Thomas Arnold, Journalist and Historian*, Manchester, 1907.

Watson, Isobel, 'Five Per Cent Philanthropy: Model Houses for the Working Classes in Victorian Camden', *Camden History Review*, vol. 9 (1981), pp. 4–9.

Webb, R.K., *The British Working Class Reader 1790–1848*, London, 1935.

—— *Harriet Martineau: A Radical Victorian*, London, 1960.

The Wellesley Index to Victorian Periodicals 1824–1900, eds Walter E. Houghton et al., 5 vols, Toronto, 1966–89.

Wells, H.G., *Experiment in Autobiography: Discoveries and Conclusions of a Very Ordinary Brain (since 1866)*, 2 vols, London, 1934, reprinted 1966.

Wells, John, *Rude Words: A Discursive History of the London Library*, London, 1991.

Weston, Peter, *The Froebel Educational Institute: The Origins and History of the College*, Roehampton, 2002.

Whitbread, Nanette, *The Evolution of the Nursery–Infant School: A History of Infant and Nursery Education in Britain 1800–1970*, London, 1972.

White, Jerry, *London in the Nineteenth Century*, London, 2007.

Wicks, Margaret C.W., *The Italian Exiles in London 1816–1848* (Manchester, 1937).

Wilkinson, Clement John, *James John Garth Wilkinson: A Memoir of his Life, with a Selection from his Letters*, London, 1911.

Willey, Basil, 'How "Robert Elsmere" Struck Some Contemporaries', *Essays and Studies*, new series vol. 10 (1957), pp. 53–68.

—— *More Nineteenth-Century Studies*, London, 1956.

Williams, Harley, *Doctors Differ: Five Studies in Contrast*, London, 1946.

Willis, Richard, *The Struggle for the General Teaching Council*, London, 2005.

Wilson, David Alec, *Carlyle at his Zenith (1848–53)*, vol. 4 of a six-volume biography of Carlyle, London, 1923–34.

Wilson, David M., *The British Museum: A History*, London, 2002.

Wilson, Thomas, *Catholicity, Spiritual and Intellectual: An Attempt at Vindicating the Harmony of Faith and Knowledge*, 1850.

Winter, Alison, *Mesmerized: Powers of Mind in Victorian Britain*, Chicago and London, 1998.

Woodfield, Malcolm, *R. H. Hutton: Critic and Theologian*, Oxford, 1986.

Woodford, Peter, 'Provident and Non-Provident Dispensaries in Camden', *Camden History Review*, vol. 25 (2001), pp. 28–31.

Woodham-Smith, P., 'History of the Froebel Movement in England', in *Friedrich Froebel and English Education*, ed. Evelyn Lawrence, London, 1952.

[Woodhouse, Francis], *The Census and the Catholic Apostolic Church*, London, 1854.

Woodward, Frances J., *Portrait of Jane: A Life of Lady Franklin*, London, 1951.

Woolf, Virginia, *The Letters of Virginia Woolf*, ed. Nigel Nicholson, 6 vols, London, 1975–80.

—— *A Passionate Apprentice: The Early Journals 1897–1909*, ed. Mitchell A. Leaska, London, 1990.

—— 'Phyllis and Rosamond' (1906), in *The Complete Shorter Fiction of Virginia Woolf*, ed. Susan Dick, London, 1958.

—— *A Room of One's Own*, London, 1928.

Woolven, Robin, 'George Gissing's London Residences 1877–1891', *Camden History Review*, vol. 28 (2004), pp. 7–11.

Wright, Terence R., *The Religion of Humanity: The Impact of Comtean Positivism on Victorian Britain*, Cambridge, 1986.

Yates, Nigel, *Anglican Ritualism in Victorian Britain 1830–1910*, Oxford, 1999.

3. Nineteenth-Century Newspapers and Journals

Age
Annual Register for 1840
Art Journal
Athenaeum
Biographical Magazine
Bristol Mercury
Builder
Daily News
Edinburgh Review
Era
Examiner
Fortnightly Review
Fraser's Magazine
Freeman's Journal and Commercial Advertiser
Hansard
Illustrated London News
Ipswich Journal
John Bull
Journal of the Society of Arts
Lancet
Leader
Leeds Mercury

Liverpool Mercury
Lloyd's Weekly Newspaper
London Dispatch and People's Political and Social Reformer
Macmillan's Magazine
Manchester Times
Medical Gazette
Monthly Christian Spectator
Morning Chronicle
Morning Post
Newcastle Courant
North British Review
Pall Mall Gazette
Penny Magazine
Poor Man's Guardian
Publishers' Circular
Punch
Spectator
Standard
Star of Freedom
The Times
Times Literary Supplement
University College Gazette
University College Hospital Magazine
University College School Miscellany
Unsere Familie

Index